THE COMPLETE GUIDE TO BOWLING SPARES

(The Encyclopedia of Spares)

Dick Ritger, Professional Bowler

President, Professional Bowlers Association, 1977 and 1978
Member, P.B.A. Hall of Fame
Winner of 20 P.B.A. Titles

George Allen, Doctor of Business Administration

The American University, Washington, D.C.

Ritger Sports Company
Tempe, Arizona • River Falls, Wisconsin

ACKNOWLEDGEMENTS: OUR SPECIAL THANKS . . .

to the American Bowling Congress (ABC), especially Steve James, for permission to use several Statistics and Oddities in Appendix B.

to the AMF Bowling Products Group, especially Al Spanjer, for financial assistance in preparing the 1,400 photographs required for this book.

to the Brunswick Corporation, especially Art Serbo, for financial assistance in preparing the 1,400 photographs required for this book.

to Bob Lubin, proprietor of Strike and Spare West, in Springfield, Illinois, for the generous use of his bowling establishment over the two week period needed to complete the photographing sessions and test some of the spare principles.

to Eddie Lubin and Steve Myers for taking every photograph.

to Elsa Brett for developing every photograph.

to Carroll J. Sutton of WICS-TV in Springfield, Illinois, for assistance in the photographing sessions.

to Wayne Zahn, and his father, Earl Zahn, for the use of the Tempe Bowl facilities for taking the cover photos; and to Bill Heady for helping us take these photographs.

to Judy, Scott, Danny, Shari and Cindy.

to Joanne, Richard, Karen, and Barbara.

to Simon and Schuster Inc., for providing Appendix A, The Bowlers Dictionary. Reproduced by permission.

to my Rags For Men team in Kitchner/Waterloo, Ontario, Canada

First Edition, 1979   Second Printing, September 1979.

Published in the United States of America by RITGER SPORTS COMPANY

Library of Congress Catalog Card Number: 78-68659

ISBN: Hard Cover: 0-933554-04-4   Soft Cover: 0-933554-05-2

Cover Design by Julia Shea

Cover Photographs by Paul Yandre, Cholula, Puebla, Mexico.

Printed in the United States of America
by Imperial Litho/Graphics, Phoenix, AZ

CONTENTS

LIST OF EXHIBITS AND ILLUSTRATIONS

PURPOSE OF THE BOOK

"There are 1,023 possible spare leaves in 10-pin bowling. Every one of these leaves is pictured in this book."

The purpose of this book is to present a complete guide to the conversion of every spare that any bowler could expect to leave during his or her entire bowling career! This goal required the most extensive, scientific, computer-based analysis ever made on all 1,023 *possible* spare leaves. This analysis included: assigning a unique Spare Number to each possible leave; determining which possible leaves might reasonably be expected to be faced by either a Left Handed Bowler (LHB) or a Right Handed Bowler (RHB); summarizing the basic principles of spare shooting and applying these principles to all spare leaves which have a reasonable chance of occurring. All of these factors had to be addressed from both the RHB and LHB points of view. *The result is a presentation of the best way to make every spare which any bowler is ever likely to face on the lanes!* In short, we have tried to develop *an encyclopedia of spares,* so that any serious bowler could greatly improve his or her percentage of successfully completed spares. We believe that this is the first time all 1,023 possible spares have ever been analyzed or have ever been seen!

SECTION I (PRINCIPLES OF SPARE SHOOTING) discusses the major principles and concepts of spare bowling. This section includes a great deal of original material, appearing in print for the first time, and also summarizes the available knowledge on shooting for spares. The pictures of a pin setup in the upper left or right corner of each page in this section is provided to assist you in visualizing the spares which we refer to when illustrating all of the spare principles.

SECTION II (HOW TO CONVERT THE 249 PROBABLE SPARES) contains pictures of the 249 spare leaves which have been classified as "Probable." *The analysis indicated that these are (with few exceptions) the only spares which a bowler will leave at any time in his or her bowling career!* Information is provided for each spare in sufficient detail to enable any bowler to prepare for any spare that he or she will likely ever face on the lanes. Rather than simply give a few examples of the various kinds of spares, *we have tried to present pictures and explanations for all spares that you may ever have to convert.*

For each spare these items of information are given: the Numbers of the Pins in the spare (such as the 1-2-10 spare, the 5-7 spare, etc.); the Key Pin in the spare leave; the Spare Number, followed by a letter "S" for the 98 probable *splits;* the Opposite Spare number (for example, the opposite of the 2-7 split is the 3-10 split; the opposite of the 6-10 spare is the 4-7 spare, etc.); the Spare Zone in which the spare falls; the Contact Area on the Key Pin which gives the best chance for making the spare; and the Approach Position and Target which gives the best angle to make the spare (using the two most widely used Spare Systems—the 3-6-9 Spare System and the 2-4-6 Spare System).

If the Contact Area is different for the LHB versus the RHB, then two pictures are presented, illustrating each hit. If special problems exist on a spare (concerning chop possibilities, pin or ball deflection, etc.) then the situation is highlighted and suggestions are given to reduce the potential problem. All of these items are explained for both the Right Handed Bowler and the Left Handed Bowler. This explanation is given in a Special Note to each one at the beginning of Section II.

SECTION III (PICTURES OF THE 774 RARE SPARES) contains pictures of the 774 spare leaves which have been classified as "Rare." *Few of these spares will ever be left for conversion.* For each Rare Spare we have given the unique Spare Number, followed by the letter "S" if the leave is a split, as in Section II. Therefore, all 459 possible splits have been identified for the first time. (There are 98 Probable Splits and 361 Rare Splits!)

No spare leave has been classified as "Impossible," although many might never occur. This section illustrates some of the rarest spare leaves which have actually been left standing after the first ball was rolled. (Please see Exhibit 20, page 175.)

The 774 Rare Spares in this section, combined with the 249 Probable Spares in Section II, illustrate all 1,023 possible spare leaves which could happen with ten pins. *There is no other possible combination of pins!*

Appendix A contains a very complete Dictionary of Bowling Terms. It can assist you in learning many bowling terms in a short period of time.

Appendix B gives many very interesting statistics and facts about the 1,023 possible spares, and about splits which have been left and converted. You might find this appendix very enjoyable reading.

Appendix C lists additional sources of information about spares, and describes several books which the authors think you might find useful.

Exhibit 1 on the following page gives a breakdown of the 1,023 Possible Spares into the Probable and Rare categories. *This classification serves as the basis for the book.*

EXHIBIT 1
Classification of the 1,023 *Possible* Spares into *Probable* and *Rare* Categories.

Number of Pins in The Spare Leave	Possible Spare Leaves	Probable Spares: Section II	Rare Spares: Section III
Spares With 1 Pin	10	10	0
Spares With 2 Pins	45	45	0
Spares With 3 Pins	120	64	56
Spares With 4 Pins	210	77	133
Spares With 5 Pins	252	36	216
Spares With 6 Pins	210	8	202
Spares With 7 Pins	120	4	116
Spares With 8 Pins	45	2	43
Spares With 9 Pins	10	2	8
Spares With 10 Pins	1	1	0
Totals	1,023	249	774

For the first time all 1,023 possible spare leaves have been analyzed and appear in one book. The 249 Probable Spares are in Section II and the 774 Rare Spares are pictured in Section III. Notice that only about 24% of the possible spare leaves will ever be left for conversion.

The one spare with 10 pins results from a gutter ball or foul on the first ball. The ten spares with 1 pin in them are, of course, the 1-Pin, 2-Pin, etc. Also, notice that only 36 of the 252 possible spares having five pins in them will likely be left for conversion. You might scan sections II and III briefly to review all 1,023 possible spares.

Dick Ritger, Professional Bowler

President, Professional Bowlers Association, 1977 and 1978.
Member, P.B.A. Hall of Fame.
Winner of 20 P.B.A. Titles.
Highest Average, 10 years (1970–1979), ABC Tournament.
Steve Nagy Sportsmanship Award, 1970 and 1973.

SECTION I
PRINCIPLES OF SPARE SHOOTING

"There are certain principles of bowling that you must understand and then master before you can become a successful spare shooter."

Many spares are needlessly missed, simply because the bowler was not aware of certain principles of bowling that come into play on various spares. There are no secrets to successful spare shooting. Anyone can become extremely effective and consistent at converting spares. This section presents a summary of the basic principles underlying all of the spares which you may ever leave. They are only briefly defined here, and on the following pages more detail is given for each one.

THE KEY PIN–IMPACT POINT: There is a specific *impact point* to contact each spare setup. There is also a *key pin* in each spare. The point of contact—impact point—may be the same for both LHB and RHB or it may be different. It represents the best place to hit the Leave to make a spare. In some cases there are two or more ways to make a given spare. But there is generally one best impact point, and it is given for all 249 Probable Spares in Section II.

CROSS-LANE ANGLES: There is one best angle to make each spare. If you can hit the key pin at the proper point of contact, and with the ball coming at the best angle, then you will make the spare. Spare Leaves on the left side of the Pin Deck are normally played from the right side of the approach. Spares on the right side of the Pin Deck are normally played from the left side of the approach. Spares in the center of the Pin Deck are normally played from the center of the approach. These angles are the same for both the RHB and the LHB. Adjustments to these general rules will be discussed later.

PIN AND BALL DEFLECTION: Deflection is the path taken by the ball and the pins after they make contact with each other. Both ball and pin deflection must be understood and taken into consideration on all Spare Leaves having two or more pins. On some spares, deflection works for or against you depending upon whether you bowl left or right

handed. You must know when deflection is a factor and how you can adjust to make it work for you.

CHOPS AND SPARES: A chop is a special kind of problem you face on certain spares. (See Appendix A for a definition of Chops.) Some spares present more of a chop possibility than others. You should know when a chop problem exists and what adjustments you can make to minimize the problem.

SPEED AND SPARES: Speed can work for or against you, since it has an effect upon pin and ball deflection and the working action of the pins. Too much speed can be just as bad as too little speed. The speed of the ball should be consistent, but on some spares you may wish to increase or reduce speed to improve your chances for making the spare.

SPLITS AND SPARES: Splits are special kinds of Spare Leaves, and are usually more difficult than Non-Split Spares. There are 98 Probable Splits that you might face at one time or another. You should attempt to convert some splits, but not all of them. Pin count is very important on splits, and must be understood if you are to handle splits properly.

AIMING: SPOT AND LINE BOWLING: The two most widely used methods of aiming or targeting for spares are Spot and Line bowling. Each method has advantages and disadvantages. Only you can determine which one is best for you. We will discuss both methods.

APPROACH POSITIONS: Your Approach Position determines the angle at which the ball will contact the key pin in the Spare Leave. Several methods have been developed for locating the proper approach position. We will discuss the two most popular ones. Then we will suggest Seven Basic Approach Positions for covering all of the Probable Spares, and how you can select the best position for you on any spare.

ADJUSTING FOR LANE CONDITIONS: Lane conditions affect what your ball does and must be considered each time you bowl. You should know what kind of lane conditions could exist and how you can adjust to take advantage of these conditions. Don't fight the lanes.

FAMILIES OF SPARES: Almost all of the 249 Probable Spares can be grouped into families. All members of the family can be converted by hitting the same key pin at a certain impact point and from the same Approach Position. If you learn the most common families of spares you can practice several spares at the same time.

THE TEN PIN SPARE—The Strike Ball: When the first ball goes into the Channel or a foul is committed, then the Ten Pin Spare arises. All ten pins are standing and a "Strike Ball" is needed. You should know what ball and pin deflection occur on a perfect strike hit, since 20% of the Probable Spares can be converted by a strike hit. Almost all spares with 5 or more pins in them are made by a strike ball.

COUNTDOWN ON ALL SPARES: There are 10 items you should consider on every Spare Leave. Four of these factors should be determined before you step on the approach. All 10 points should be practiced until they become automatic on every spare. (These are on page 31.)

Now we will discuss each of these principles in more detail. It might be helpful for you to scan Appendix A before reading this section, although you could refer to it as needed. You should re-read this Section I from time to time so that these principles of spare shooting come into mind each time you bowl. You will then become a very successful spare shooter.

THE KEY PIN—
IMPACT POINT

"There is a key pin in every spare, and an impact point that gives you the best chance to make the spare."

In every Spare Leave there is a specific point where the ball should contact the pin setup. It is called the point of contact or impact point. This contact point is very obvious on some spares (especially on the ten spares having only one pin in them) but on the more difficult Spare Leaves some thought is required.

There is one best way to make any given spare, but there may be more than one point of contact that might enable you to make a spare. You must decide which point of contact is best for you, considering the way you roll the ball and other factors such as pin or ball deflection, chop possibilities, etc. On most Spare Leaves there is complete agreement on the ideal point of contact. On others there may be more than one method to make the spare.

For example, on the 3-10 Baby Split there is agreement that the ball should hit the 3-pin on the far right side and then deflect slightly to the right and into the 10-pin. This spare could be made by hitting the 3-pin on the left side and having *it* deflect into the 10-pin. Trying to cover both pins with the ball is a better method since ball deflection gives you more chance for the spare and you will probably get at least one pin on this try and could get both. Since "pin count" is a very important part of shooting for

spares, you should normally choose the spare conversion method which gives you the best chance to make the spare or to get the highest possible pin count if you should miss it.

Every spare setup has a key pin. This key pin will generally be the pin closest to you. This is the pin which you should hit in order to make the spare. Sometimes the key pin is an "imaginary pin." On the 4-5 Split Leave, the key pin is an imaginary 2-pin. On the 3-10 Split the key pin is an imaginary 6-pin. In other words, your point of aim might be a pin that is missing and if you aim for it you will have a good chance for converting the spare. Yet on most spares the key pin is part of the setup. On the 5-8 and 5-9 Spare Leaves, the 5-pin is the key pin. If the ball does not hit the 5-pin then the spare will probably not be made.

With each Spare Leave the first thing you should do is determine the key pin that must be hit. Then decide upon the required impact point on that pin. The third item is to select the Approach Position and target that give you the correct angle to hit the key pin, and deliver your ball in your normal manner.

You should study the point of contact for all the Probable Spares before you are confronted with them, especially those spares which you normally leave. Then, when you are faced with the spare you will already know the key pin and point of contact needed to make the spare. You will now be prepared to make all of your "Makable" Spares.

CROSS-LANE ANGLES

"There is a best angle to shoot each spare."

If there is any aspect of bowling upon which there appears to be almost complete agreement it is upon the proper use of angles. Successful spare bowling requires the correct use of angles. On a full pin setup the greater the angle at which the ball comes into the pocket, the greater the power on the ball. For any given Spare Leave, there is one best angle to hit the Leave which will maximize your chances for converting the spare. To be able to hit the key pin, at the proper point of contact, with the ball coming at the best angle, is the ideal way to convert any spare. At times you will want to use a wide angle. At other times you will want to cut down the angle.

There are only three basic angles for spare bowling:

1. *The CENTER angle:* From the center of the approach. This angle is used for the strike ball and for Spare Leaves in which the 1-pin or the 5-pin is the key pin.
2. *The RIGHT SIDE angle:* From the far left side of the approach. This angle is used for Spare Leaves which are on the opposite (right) side of the lane.

3. *The LEFT SIDE angle:* From the far right side of the approach. This angle is used for Spare Leaves which are on the opposite (left) side of the lane.

This Cross-Lane Approach to developing the proper angle for spares is generally accepted as the best method for converting spares. It is often referred to as "using the full width of the lane." Both the RHB and LHB should use this method for converting spares and modify it to meet individual needs.

These three basic spare angles are illustrated in Exhibits 2 and 3. Later we will refine these into the Seven Basic Approach Positions used throughout the book. In each case, the angle is either being increased or reduced to improve chances for a successful spare conversion.

NOTE: Increasing the angle of a shot generally means increasing the number of boards the ball crosses on the lane. Reducing the angle generally means reducing the number of boards the ball crosses. For example, if you roll the ball down the 10th Board and it hits the pocket at the 17th Board the ball has crossed 7 boards. To increase the angle you might roll the ball down the 8th Board so that it has to cross 9 boards to hit the pocket.

4

EXHIBIT 2
The Three Basic Spare Angles
For the *Right* Handed Bowler

The *Left Angle* is played from the right side of the approach. The *Right Angle* is played from the left side of the approach. And the *Center Angle* is played from the center of the approach. These three angles illustrate the correct use of the "cross lane" principle. Point your feet and body at the target on the lanes and walk towards the target.

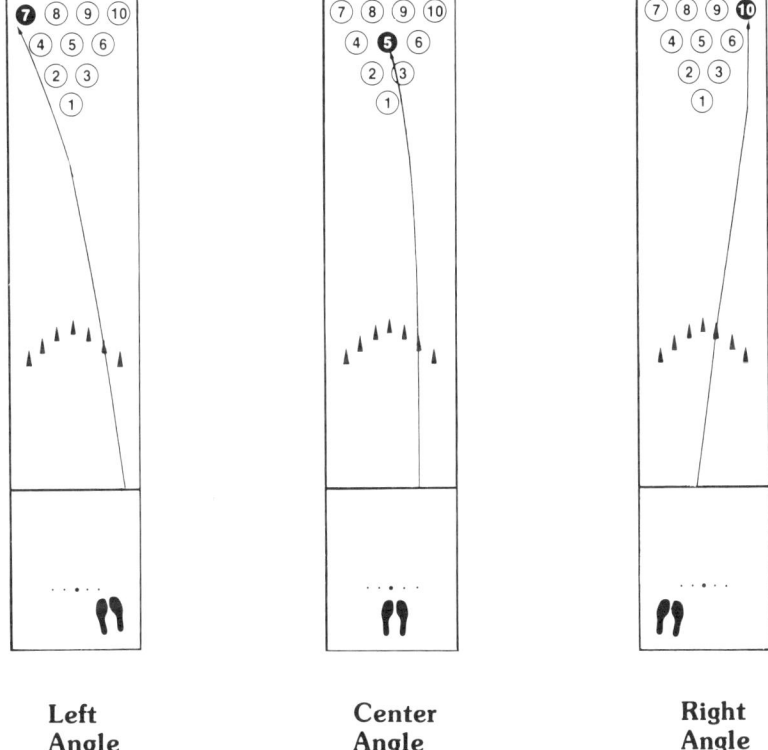

Left Angle   **Center Angle**   **Right Angle**

Notice that the 2nd Arrow from the right side is used as the target for the Center Angle and the Left Angle. The 3rd Arrow is used as the target for the Right Angle. These targets are guidelines only. You may have to adjust them somewhat, depending upon lane conditions and how you roll your ball.

EXHIBIT 3
The Three Basic Spare Angles
For the *Left* Handed Bowler

The *Left Angle* is played from the right side of the approach. The *Right Angle* is played from the left side of the approach. And the *Center Angle* is played from the center of the approach. These three angles illustrate the correct use of the "cross lane" principle. Point your feet and body at the target on the lanes and walk towards the target.

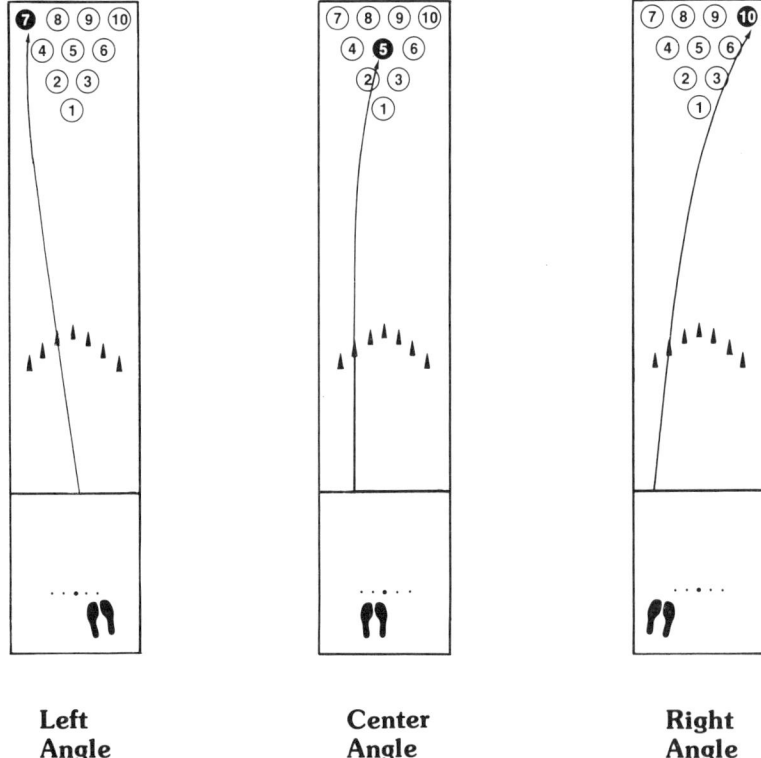

| Left
Angle | Center
Angle | Right
Angle |

Notice that the 2nd Arrow for the left side is used as the target for the Center Angle and the Right Angle. The 3rd Arrow is used as the target for the Left Angle. These targets are guidelines only. You may have to adjust them somewhat, depending upon lane conditions and how you roll your ball. (Many LHB use the 1st Arrow for the Center Angle, and Strike Ball.)

PIN AND BALL DEFLECTION

"Deflection is neither good nor bad, but should be considered on all Spare Leaves of two or more pins."

Deflection refers to what happens to the ball and pins when they come into contact with each other. The two kinds of deflection are Ball Deflection and Pin Deflection.

Ball Deflection: The movement or *path of the ball* after it comes into contact with the pin or pins.

Pin Deflection: The *path of the pin or pins* after being hit by the ball.

Deflection is something that has to be considered on all Spare Leaves of two or more pins. Deflection may present a potential problem or may be working in your favor and make a Spare Leave somewhat easier. First, let's consider what happens when the ball hits a pin.

Full Hit: If a pin is hit fully (in the center of the pin) then the pin will be driven straight back into the pit and the ball will not be deflected to either side. The ball will continue in the path that it had before contact.

Left Side Hit: If a pin is hit on the left side, the pin will deflect to the right and the ball will be deflected to the left, or opposite direction.

Right Side Hit: If a pin is hit on the right side, the pin will deflect to the left and the ball will be deflected to the right, or opposite direction.

The amount of deflection will depend upon many factors, including: (1) the weight of the ball, (2) the weight of the pin, (3) the speed of the ball, (4) the angle at which the ball hits the pin, and (5) the lift or spin put on the ball. The following statements should give you a better understanding of both ball and pin deflection.

1. If a pin is hit in the center, little or no deflection of the ball will take place.

2. If a pin is hit on the left side, the ball and pin will deflect in opposite directions. This is also true when the ball hits the right side of the pin.
3. A light ball will deflect more than a heavier ball.
4. A light pin will deflect the ball less than a heavy pin.
5. A light pin will be deflected more than a heavier pin.
6. A fast ball will deflect less than a slow ball.
7. If a RHB hits a pin on the left side, the ball will deflect more than when a LHB hits a pin on the left side.
8. If a LHB hits a pin on the right side, the ball will deflect more than when a RHB hits a pin on the right side.
9. A pin will tend to fall in a horizontal position when hit by a slow ball, but will tend to remain in an upright position when hit by a fast ball. (This explains why a bowler who rolls the ball very fast and hard will often fail to knock down as many pins as someone who rolls the ball at medium speed.)

NOTE: The weight of the ball may range from 8 or less pounds up to a maximum of 16 pounds. Pins may be as light as 2 pounds and 14 ounces or as heavy as 3 pounds and 10 ounces. A set of 10 pins can not vary by more than 4 ounces; that is, the difference between any two pins in the set cannot exceed 4 ounces.

Ball deflection can be used to cover all the pins on many spares. "Hit them all, with the ball" (Harry Smith) is a useful phrase to remember, since it is desirable to try to hit all pins with the ball on many spares. When you rely upon pin deflection and you don't need to do so, then you are taking an unnecessary chance of missing the Spare Leave. (See the 3-10 or 2-7 Split.)

However, on some Spare Leaves you must use pin deflection. The 5-7 Split is such a Leave. You should deflect the 5-pin into the 7-pin. Ball deflection would not be able to make this split. On other Leaves either ball or pin deflection could be used, but generally one method is better than the other. For example, on the 3-10 Split either one could be used, but ball deflection is better. The ball should hit the 3-pin on the far right and deflect to the right into the 10-pin. You should not hit the 3-pin on the left to deflect it into the 10-pin. On other spares, deflection is a problem that might result in a chop or miss. The 2-8 and 3-9 Tandem Leaves are often missed because the ball hits the front pin too much on either side. Once you understand how pin and ball deflection operate, you should be able to make either one or both of them work for you.

On a perfect "pocket hit" for a strike, the ball will only hit four pins. These are the 1-3-5-9-pins for the RHB and the 1-2-5-8-pins for the LHB. In fact, a ball will rarely (if ever) hit more than four pins on any Spare Leave. Thus, deflection needs to be kept in mind on the strike ball for two reasons: (1) the ball must hit the pocket in such a manner that it is not deflected out of its path through the four pins it should hit, and (2) pin deflection is required to knock down the other six pins. (We will discuss the Ten Pin Spare—The Strike Ball—in this section).

In the section on CHOPS AND SPARES, deflection is discussed as a major area of concern and several suggestions are offered to reduce the deflection problem on possible Chop Leaves. However, on all Spare Leaves with more than one pin, ask

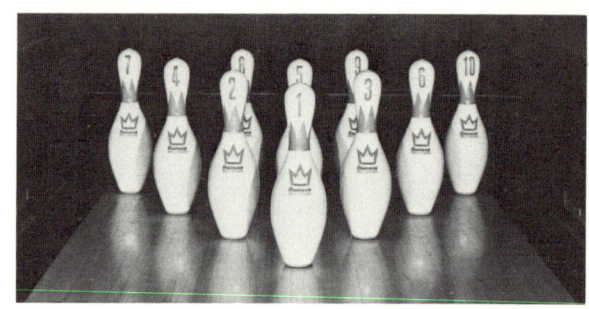

yourself if either ball or pin deflection is working for or against you. On the 4-7 Spare, for example, both ball and pin deflection work for the RHB and against the LHB. But on the 6-10 Spare both ball and pin deflection favor the LHB and work against the RHB. As you will see in the Section II discussion of the 249 Probable Spares, there are many instances when deflection works for or against you depending upon whether you bowl right handed or left handed.

If you determine that deflection is a problem on a given spare, make some adjustment in your approach, delivery, target, speed, etc. to reduce the problem. Often it is simply a case of reducing or widening the angle of the shot by moving to the left or right on the approach. Deflection will not remain a problem if you are aware of it and make some adjustment to minimize it.

CHOPS AND SPARES

"Learn to recognize the most common chop possibilities, and what adjustment you can make to increase your chances for making the spare."

A Chop is defined as "Knocking down the front pin of a Spare Leave while a pin behind or to the left or right remains standing." (Appendix A, Dictionary of Bowling Terms).

Several spares present the potential of chopping and missing. It is possible to reduce this problem if you will learn to recognize these spares and take some action to give you a better chance to convert the spare. Such corrective action will usually mean an adjustment of your position on the approach to change the angle at which you hit the pins.

Specific chop possibilities depend upon whether you bowl Right or Left Handed. For the *Right* Hander these are some of the spares which might be chopped:

1-3; 1-3-6; 2-5; 2-4-5; 3-6; 5-9; 6-10; 3-6-10; etc.

For the *Left* Hander these spares are likely to be chopped:

1-2; 1-2-4; 3-5; 3-5-6; 2-4; 5-8; 4-7; 2-4-7; etc.

Many other Spare Leaves might be chopped and need special attention if they are to be converted. Whenever a chop possibility exists on any of the Probable Spares, suggestions are made to improve your chances for covering the spare. Thus, only general comments will be made at this time.

The most common method for avoiding a chop is to "straighten out the shot," that is, to change the angle at which the ball hits the pin setup. This adjustment will have the ball coming into the spare at an angle which will have pin and ball deflection working for you. For example, on the 2-4-5-8, a chop might happen if the ball should hit the 2-pin "dead center" so that the 2-pin and ball drive straight back into the 8-pin. If the 2-pin is hit on the far left or far right, the ball and pins may deflect to either side of the 8-pin

and a miss would occur. An accurate angle on the 2-pin is needed to make this spare.

Changing the angle of the shot usually means a left or right adjustment on the approach, depending upon the particular Spare Leave and chop possibility. The left handed bowler might move slightly to the right when facing the 5-8 chop possibility, whereas, the right handed bowler might move to the left when facing the 5-9 chop possibility. Another way to adjust would be to change the point of aim (target) to the left or right. Either of these two types of adjustments should reduce the possibility of a chop and increase the chances for making the spare.

The 2-4-5 chop possibility for the Right Handed Bowler and the 3-5-6 Spare Leave for the Left Handed Bowler are two Leaves which present some difference of opinion on how the chop possibility can be reduced.

The RHB can shoot the 2-4-5 from the left or right side of the approach. The ball should hit the 2-pin on the right side so that the ball takes out the 5-pin while the 4-pin is taken out by the 2-pin. If the 2-pin is hit too full the possibility of a chop exists. Depending upon how you roll the ball, lane conditions, etc., you might choose to shift either left or right on the approach. As long as you keep the chop possibility firmly in mind and make the adjustment which appears correct for you, you should be able to convert this spare with a minimum of difficulty.

The LHB faces the same situation with the 3-5-6 Spare that the RHB faces with the 2-4-5 Leave. Thus, the LHB could shoot this spare from either the right or left side of the approach, whichever Approach Position seems most likely to reduce the possibility of chopping the Leave. Even the center of the approach could be used, with some change in the target or point of aim.

Learn to recognize the most common chop possibilities and what adjustment you need to make to increase your chances for making the spare. Study the few spares mentioned above, since these are common Chop Leaves. Never shoot for a spare until you have determined whether a chop possibility exists and have made the necessary adjustment—for you!

SPEED AND SPARES

"Too much speed is just as bad as not enough speed."

It is impressive to hear the sound of a fast ball crashing into the pins, but generally not very effective in terms of knocking the pins down. There is an ideal speed for you, depending upon your personal strength and the way you deliver and release the ball. Find your ideal speed and develop a consistent release and delivery.

A ball is supposed to skid, roll, and then hook as it heads towards the pins. Too much speed increases the amount of skid and prevents the ball from getting a greater number of turns on it before it hits the pin setup. The result is a very "ineffective ball." The ball does not "work"; that is, there is very little mixing of the pins after contact. Pins fly almost upright back into the pit and do not take out as many pins as they would if they were heading for the pit in a horizontal position.

A ball that is rolled too fast will often leave one of the corner pins (7 or 10) and will often result in splits such as the 5-7, 5-10, 7-9, or 8-10. With increased speed the impact point on your strike ball has to be almost perfect.

Excessive speed increases the danger of chopping off pins on multiple Pin Leaves. On the other hand, increased speed prevents ball deflection and miss possibilities might be reduced! For example, on the 2-8 or 3-9 Tandem Leaves a fast ball might drive straight through the front pin and take out the back one, whereas, a slower ball might be deflected to either side and the back pin could be left standing.

Just as too much speed is not desirable, too little speed may create unique problems. A slow ball may hit the 1-3 or 1-2 pocket with little action on it and be deflected out of the pocket, leaving the 5-pin or the 5-7 or 5-10 Split. The ball may literally bounce off the pins if it does not have sufficient speed on it.

Ball deflection is much greater with a slow ball than with a fast one. This additional deflection may be used to advantage on some spares, even enabling you to cover all the pins on some situations. (See the 1-2-4-7 for the RHB or 1-3-6-10 for the LHB.) The 2-4-7 Spare is easier if the ball is thrown slightly slower than normal by the RHB. The LHB might reduce speed on the 3-6-10 Spare for the same reason.

What is considered fast for one bowler might not be considered the same for another. A difference in body build, height of backswing, etc. might create a "natural" fast delivery for one person. But, there is an ideal speed for you and you should try to develop it.

Whether you normally roll the ball fast or slow is neither an advantage nor a disadvantage. You must become familiar with the result that speed has upon your chances for covering spares (and for striking) and learn to adjust accordingly. It is difficult to change your natural speed. This ability will require long hours of practice. You would, of course, want to develop this ability should you desire to one day become a professional. But, until that time a consistent, natural speed is a very desirable goal. Consistency in speed is far more important than the rate of speed. Develop a speed appropriate for your strength and the way you deliver and release the ball. If your ball is always rolled the same way, with the same amount of speed, then you are in a better position to control its path to the pins and to predict the amount of ball deflection you will have. Once you know what your ball will do, then you can adjust to lane conditions to raise your percentage of successful spare conversions.

"Keep pin count in mind on all splits."

A Split is defined as "A Spare Leave in which the headpin is down and the remaining combination of pins have an intermediate pin down immediately ahead of or between them." (See Appendix A, Dictionary of Bowling Terms.)

There are 459 possible splits that could be left, out of the 1,023 possible Spare Leaves! Many of these splits will never occur, but some strange Leaves have already been left. For example, the most unusual splits which have been reliably reported are the: 4-5-6 Split! 7-8-9-10 Split; and the Leave of six pins in one split—the 3-4-6-7-8-10 and 4-6-7-8-9-10 Splits! (For details on these and other splits, see BOWLING, January, 1976, pages 44–45, and Appendix B of this book.)

On some nights it seems like every split that can happen does happen. There have been instances of individual teams leaving as high as 50 splits in one session of bowling. And, two teams once left a total of 76 splits in one session. Also, on at least one instance all five members of a bowling team left AND CONVERTED a split in the same frame!

Despite these rare occurrences with splits, there are *only* 98 splits which have been classified as PROBABLE; that is, which are likely to be left by the majority of bowlers. Each split is identified by the letter "S" which follows the Spare Number. This occurs both in the Probable and Rare Sections. Thus, all 459 possible splits are identified.

Splits can be classified in several ways (Fit-In-Between, Slide-Over, etc.). For this book they have been classified into four categories: MAKABLE, DIFFICULT, VERY DIFFICULT, and EXTREMELY DIFFICULT! No split is considered as impossible, although several could easily qualify for that title. But two such splits that are frequently left—the 7-10 and the 4-6-7-10—are converted almost 3,000 times each bowling season!

If the split is MAKABLE (the 3-10, 2-7, 4-5, 5-6, etc.) then try to convert it. Trying to convert these splits will not normally cause you to lose any pin count, since the recommended method for converting these splits will normally allow you to get one or more of the pins anyway.

If the split is DIFFICULT (the 5-7, 5-10, 4-9, 6-8, etc.) you should still try to make it, but be sure that you get as many pins as possible should you miss the split. If there are several pins in the split (the 5-8-10, 5-7-9, 4-7-9, or 6-8-10, etc.) try to get the most pins that you can while still trying for the conversion.

If the split is VERY DIFFICULT (the 4-10, 6-7, 4-7-10, 6-7-10, etc.) it is still a good idea to try for the conversion—especially if you are in a situation when a spare is required. But, still keep pin count in mind and try to get as many pins as possible should you fail to make the spare.

If the split is EXTREMELY DIFFICULT (the 4-6, 4-6-7-10, 7-9, 8-10, 7-10, etc.) you should try for maximum pin count *without seriously trying to convert the split.* An attempt will often cause you to lose valuable pin count when there is only a very remote possibility of getting a spare! Of course, should the situation be such that a spare is essential and you must gamble, by all means try to make the split. If you do try for the conversion, use the method which will give you the best chance to convert the split with the minimum risk of losing pin count.

The most important thing to keep in mind when you leave a split (besides how to avoid leaving another split on your next frame) is the pin count, or simply the count! Many games and matches are lost by a single pin, so it is important to get as many of the pins in the split as possible. If you had a strike in the previous frame, then each pin counts TWICE—once in the strike frame and again in the split frame. Trying for an almost impossible split may cause you to lose valuable pin count when the odds in favor of making the conversion are very much against you.

Exhibit 4 lists all of the 98 Probable Splits according to the four categories mentioned above. Learn which splits you should try to convert and the methods which give you the best chance to convert them. The next time you leave a split just consider that you have made one mistake (on your first ball) and try to correct that mistake in the next frame.

EXHIBIT 4
The 98 Probable Splits, Grouped by Degree of Difficulty.

The 98 probable splits have been grouped into four categories, as indicated below. The 5-7-10 split should probably be in a category of its own, since there is only 1 authenticated conversion of it! However, the 5-7-10 split has been knocked down on the *first* ball!

The 18 Makable Splits:

2-3;   2-7;   2-9;   3-8;   3-10;   4-5;   5-6;   7-8;   8-9;   9-10;
2-5-7;   3-5-10;   4-5-7;   4-5-8;   5-6-9;   5-6-10;
4-5-7-8;   5-6-9-10;

The 32 Difficult Splits:

2-6;   3-4;   4-9;   5-7;   5-10;   6-8;
2-7-8;   2-7-9;   3-8-10;   3-9-10;   4-5-10;   4-7-9;   5-6-7;   5-7-9;   5-8-10;   6-8-10;
2-4-5-10;   2-4-6-7;   2-4-6-10;   2-5-7-8;   2-6-7-10;   3-4-6-7;   3-4-6-10;   3-4-7-10;
3-5-6-7;   3-5-9-10;   4-5-7-10;   5-6-7-10;
2-4-5-8-10;   2-4-6-7-10;   3-4-6-7-10;   3-5-6-7-9;

The 24 Very Difficult Splits:

2-10;   3-7;   4-10;   6-7;
2-4-10;   2-7-10;   3-6-7;   3-7-10;   4-7-10;   4-8-10;   4-9-10;   6-7-8;   6-7-9;   6-7-10;
2-4-7-10;   2-7-9-10;   3-6-7-10;   3-7-8-10;   4-7-8-10;   4-7-9-10;   6-7-8-10;   6-7-9-10;
2-4-7-9-10;   3-6-7-8-10;

The 24 Extremely Difficult Splits:

4-6;   7-9;   7-10;   8-10;
2-8-10;   3-7-9;   4-6-7;   4-6-10;   5-7-10;   7-8-10;   7-9-10;
2-4-8-10;   2-7-8-10;   3-6-7-9;   3-7-9-10;   4-6-7-8;   4-6-7-9;   4-6-7-10;   4-6-8-10;
4-6-9-10;
2-4-7-8-10;   3-6-7-9-10;   4-6-7-8-10;   4-6-7-9-10;

All of these splits appear in Section II. They are identified by the letter "S" appearing after the Spare Number. To review or study all Probable Splits, scan the Probable Spares, stopping at each one identified as a split.

AIMING: SPOT AND LINE BOWLING

"Accuracy requires aiming. Select your target and hit it consistently."

Bowling for spares (or strikes) requires a high degree of accuracy. On the strike ball your goal is to hit the 1-3 pocket if you bowl Right Handed, and the 1-2 pocket for Left Handed Bowlers. On any given Spare Leave you want to hit the key pin at the suggested point of contact.

Two techniques for aiming are used by almost all high average bowlers.

SPOT BOWLING: Aim at a "spot" or target out on the lanes, without looking at the pins. Your spot or target might be the Dots imbedded in the lane about 6 feet beyond the foul line; or the Arrows (range-finders) imbedded in the lanes about 15 feet from the foul line; or some other spot such as a light or dark board on the lane.

LINE BOWLING: Imagine a line drawn from the point on the lane where the ball is released to the spot in the pin setup that you wish to hit—the point of contact. Then roll your ball so that it will follow this imaginary line. (*This method is sometimes called Line/Area Bowling.*)

SPOT Bowling is an accurate method of aiming or targeting, and is used by many of the top bowlers. The principle of spot bowling is that it is easier to hit a target that is 3 feet, 6 feet, or 15 feet out on the lane rather than the pin target which is over 60 feet from the foul line. And, if you hit your target (or spot) then you should hit the pin setup at the point of contact you are aiming for. However, it is absolutely essential that you do not vary any other part of your delivery, such as speed, lift, extension, angle, etc. Spot bowling will only work when you have developed a consistent delivery.

Since many great bowlers use Spot Bowling, you should start with this method right away. Rather than selecting a specific spot, or board, you might select an area on the lanes such as between the 2nd

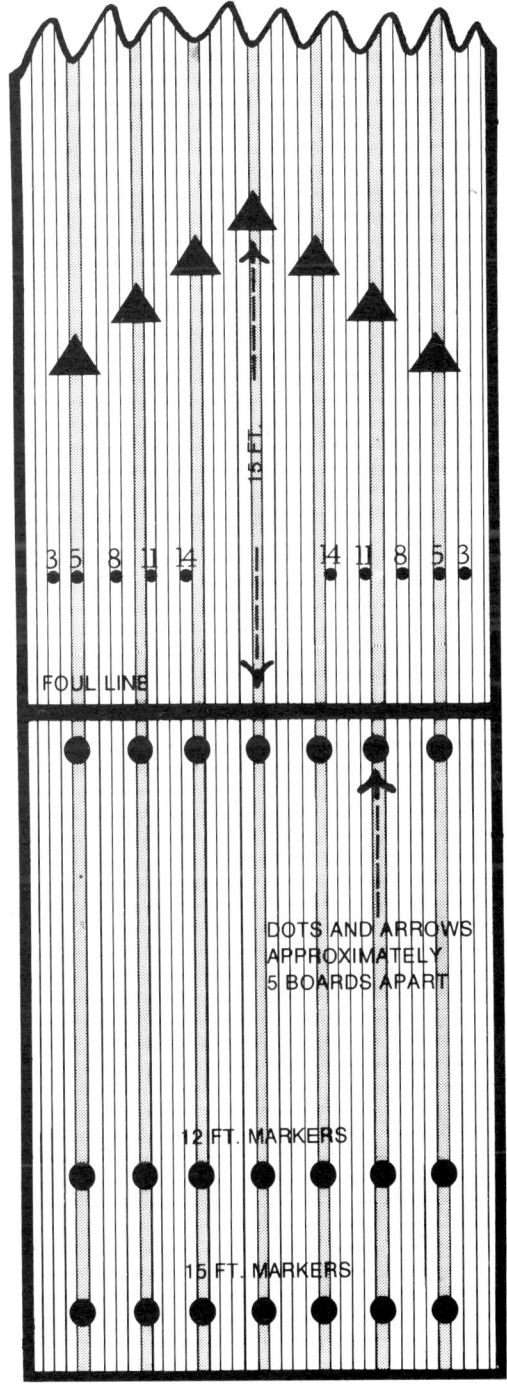

Illustration 1. Approach markers and targeting arrows.

13

and 3rd Arrows for RHB and 1st and 2nd Arrows on the left for LHB. This would make it easier for you to learn Spot Bowling.

The next time you go to a bowling establishment, notice the various "spots" on the lanes which are there to help you in your aiming (see Illustration 1). There are Dots imbedded about 6 feet out on the lanes on the 3rd, 5th, 8th, 11th, and 14th Boards—both on the right and left side of the lane. Arrows are imbedded in the lanes about 15 feet beyond the foul line. There are 7 arrows spaced 5 boards apart. The Center Arrow is in the 20th Board. Most RHB use the 2nd and 3rd Arrows for spotting. The 2nd Arrow is used for their strike ball and Left Side Spares, and the 3rd Arrow for Right Side Spares. Most LHB use the 1st Arrow from the left side of the lane for their strike ball and Right Side Spares. The 3rd Arrow is often used for Left Side Spares. Dots are imbedded in the lanes at the foul line that could be used for aiming, but these are not used by many of the best bowlers. It is too difficult to watch these spots and to maintain the proper stance at the time of delivery and release of the ball. (These Dots at the foul line are, however, useful for seeing if you are "drifting" left or right on your approach!) Notice also that there are Dots im-

bedded on the approach, sometimes two sets of them. These are used to help you select the proper starting position on the approach, which is essential to proper aiming.

While you are looking at the various items on the lane which are there to help you in your targeting and aiming, you might also take a close look at the Pin Deck (see Illustration 2). You should know that the headpin is centered on the 20th Board. The 1-3 pocket is the 17th Board from the right side of the lane, and the 1-2 pocket is 17 boards from the left side of the lane. These locations are vital in adjusting to lane conditions, and in knowing what your ball is doing. (Adjusting to Lane Conditions is discussed later.)

The second method of aiming or targeting is *LINE Bowling*. An imaginary line is drawn from the point that the ball is released on the lane to the point of contact on the key pin in the spare. *Then two or more checkpoints are located on the path or line that the ball is supposed to travel.* These checkpoints might be the Dots or Arrows in the lanes, or could be light or dark boards along the line. The principle of the use of a line with more than one checkpoint is that this will be more accurate than just hitting one spot. For example, you may hit your spot exactly, but at a different angle than normal and the ball will not hit the pins as you had planned. With two checkpoints along the line it would become obvious that you had done something different, such as more or less speed, a different angle, more reach out on the lanes, etc.

To improve your accuracy in converting spares you must develop an accurate method for aiming at your target. Choose the system of aiming that is best for you; one in which you can develop confidence in yourself. But, keep in mind that the best bowlers have adopted some variation of Spot or Line Bowling.

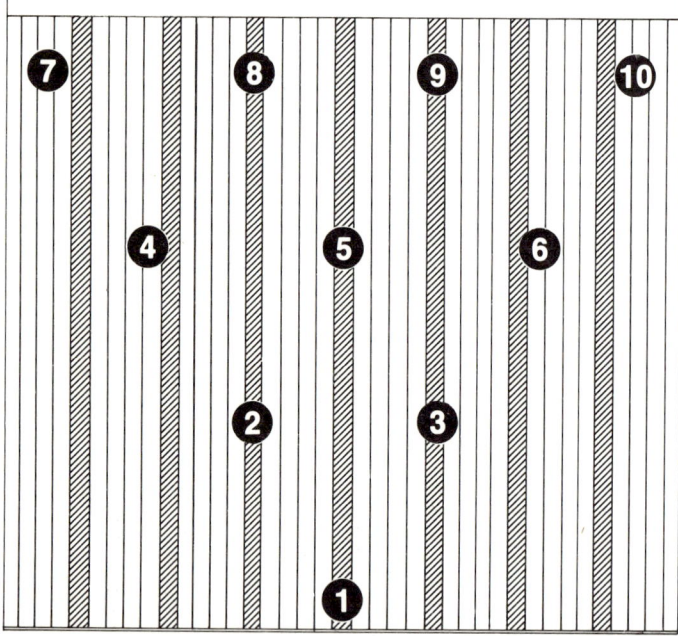

Illustration 2. The pindeck from overhead, with every 5th board shaded.

APPROACH POSITIONS—*RIGHT* HANDED BOWLERS

"Selecting the correct approach position is an important step towards improving your performance as a spare shooter."

IMPORTANT: *This part is written for Right Handed Bowlers only. Left Handed Bowlers should skip ahead to the next part, written especially for them.*

A bowling lane is composed of 39 to 42 boards, each one slightly more than one inch wide. In addition, the approach is 10 or more boards wider than the lane. Thus, there are over 50 different approach positions, and more if you "split a board" in selecting one. In reality, there are a few basic approach positions, and variations of these to take into consideration personal bowling differences and lane conditions.

The two most widely used methods for shooting at spares are: The 3-6-9 Spare System, and the 2-4-6 Spare System. These two systems have been developed in a very scientific manner and have proven to be very effective. Both will be discussed in some detail, and both will be used to illustrate the suggested approach position for all the Probable Spares in Section II.

THE 3-6-9 SPARE SYSTEM: This system for determining the starting position on the approach is relatively easy to understand. The numbers 3, 6, and 9 refer to the number of boards you *shift to the right* on the approach to locate the Seven Basic Approach Positions. Exhibit 5 illustrates these seven approach positions, although it does not give the precise location of the approach for any of the positions. This will vary with the individual bowler and lane conditions. We will, however, suggest ways to locate all seven positions.

To use the 3-6-9 System you must determine two of the seven basic approach positions. The other five are located by shifting 3, 6, or 9 boards *to the right* of these two: From the Strike Position you *shift to the right* to cover all left side spares; From the 10-Pin Position you *shift to the right* for all right side spares. Now let's see how you can locate the Strike Position and the 10-Pin Approach Position.

Locating the Strike Ball Position: Many of the

best RHB use the 2nd Arrow from the right side of the lane as the point of aim for their strike ball—under "normal" lane conditions. (Adjusting for Lane Conditions will be presented later.) Thus, the starting position on the approach should be slightly to the right of center. Begin with this approach position and target, and adjust to the left or right on the approach until you have determined your Strike Position. After that has been located you are ready to determine the approach position for all *left side spares*. Move 3 Boards to the right of your strike position on the approach when the 2-pin or 8-pin is the point of contact in the spare leave; 6 Boards to the right of the strike position when the 4-pin is the key pin; and 9 Boards to the right when the 7-pin is the point of contact in the spare. Keep using the same target on the lanes (perhaps around the 2nd Arrow) so that you are hitting the same target but at a different angle for the *left side spares*. On some spares you may have to shift right more or less than the "3 Board Increment," depending upon the point of contact. (This adjustment will be discussed later.) Now, how about the right side spares. For those we need to locate the 10-Pin Approach Position.

Locating the 10-Pin Approach Position: Many of the best bowlers use the 3rd Arrow from the right side of the lane as the point of aim for all *right side spares* —under "normal" lane conditions. (See "Adjusting for Lane Conditions"). Picture an imaginary "sight line" through your right shoulder, across the 3rd Arrow from the right side of the lane, and into the center or right side of the 10-pin. This should create the best cross-lane angle for covering the 10-pin. Experiment to the left or right until you have located your approach position for covering the 10-pin. After that is located you are ready to determine the approach position for all *right side spares*. Move 3 Boards to the right of your 10-Pin Position when the 6-pin is the key pin in the spare; and 6 Boards to the right of the 10-Pin Position when the 3-pin or 9-pin is the key one in the spare. Keep your same target on the lanes (near the 3rd Arrow) so that you are hitting the same target but at a different angle for the various *right side spares*. On some spares, depending

EXHIBIT 5
The Seven Basic Approach Positions
For the *Right* Handed Bowler

Using the 3-6-9 Spare System for locating starting positions on the approach results in Seven Basic Approach Positions. The numbers 3, 6, and 9 refer to a 3, 6, or 9 Board *Shift to the Right* from either the Strike Position or the 10-Pin Position as the key pin in the spare setup changes.

APPROACH POSITIONS	KEY PIN IN THE SPARE	*APPROXIMATE LOCATION ON THE APPROACH
10-Pin Position	The 10-Pin	*Determined by Trial and Error.* Used as the base to locate the 3-pin and 6-pin Positions.
6-Pin Position	The 6-Pin	Located 3 Boards to the Right of the 10-Pin Approach Position. (Use 10-Pin Target).
3-Pin Position	The 3-Pin & The 9-Pin	Located 6 Boards to the Right of the 10-Pin Approach Position. (Use 10-Pin Target).
STRIKE POSITION	The 1-Pin & The 5-Pin	*Determined by Trial and Error.* Used as the base to locate the 2-pin, 4-pin, and 7-pin Approach Position.
2-Pin Position	The 2-Pin & The 8-Pin	Located 3 Boards to the Right of the Strike Position. (Use Strike Target).
4-Pin Position	The 4-Pin	Located 6 Boards to the Right of the Strike Position. (Use Strike Target).
7-Pin Position	The 7-Pin	Located 9 Boards to the Right of the Strike Position. (Use Strike Target).

*It is not possible to give the precise location on the approach, since that will depend upon lane conditions. The 3, 6 and 10-pin positions are to the left of the Strike Position, and the 2, 4 and 7-pin positions are to the right of the Strike Positions. These approach positions are consistent with the cross-lane technique. When the spare is on the left, start your approach from the right. When the spare is on the right, start your approach from the left.

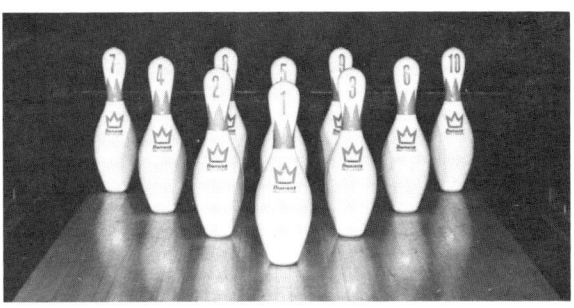

for right handed bowlers only (cont'd)

upon the specific point of contact needed, you may have to shift right more or less than the "3 Board Increment." (We will discuss this later.)

These Seven Basic Approach Positions should enable you to take the proper position on all spares. However, there is another system that you may want to use, or have to use. This is called the 2-4-6 Spare System.

THE 2-4-6 SPARE SYSTEM: *This spare system is often used for left side spares if you bowl right handed.* The system is necessary, or desirable, when you are using a strike target on the lanes around the 1st Arrow from the right. It would be impractical to use the 3-6-9 system and shift as much as nine boards to the right for the left side spares. You would have to loft the ball out over the Channel to keep it near the same target. It is much easier to *shift the target* for those *left side spares.* So, unlike the 3-6-9 system where the target remains the same and the approach position changes, *the target shifts* and the approach position remains the same under the 2-4-6 system. The numbers 2, 4, and 6 refer to the number of boards you *shift your target* to cover the various left side spares. Move your target 2 Boards *to the left* of your strike target when the 2-pin is the key pin in the setup; 4 Boards *to the left* of your strike target when the 4-pin is the key pin; and 6 Boards *to the left* of your strike target when the 7-pin is the key pin or point of contact. On some spares you may want to move the target slightly more or less than the "2 Board Increment," but that is still consistent with the 2-4-6 concept. (This adjustment will be discussed later.)

Why the 2 Board adjustment of the target for left side spares? The reason is that for each 1-Board shift of the target to the left there is a 3-Board shift to the left in the point of contact on the pin deck. The 1-3

pocket is the 17th board from the right side of the lane. The 1-pin is centered on the 20th board. The 1-2 pocket is the 23rd board from the right side of the lane. Thus, if you are using the 1st Arrow from the right as your strike target and you are hitting the pins on the 17th board from the right, you would have to move your target 2 Boards to the left to hit the pin setup at the 23rd board from the right. Remember that each 1 board target shift results in a 3 board shift on the pin deck. So, a 2 Board shift of the target would change the contact point by 6 Boards; a 4 Board target shift to the left would mean a 12 Board change in the point of contact, etc. Thus the 2 Board shift covers the 2-pin; 4 boards covers the 4-pin; and 6 boards covers the 7-pin.

But, what about the right side spares when you are using the 1st Arrow from the right for strikes, and the 2-4-6 system for the left side spares? You simply use the 3-6-9 Spare Shooting System for the right side spares. First determine the 10-Pin Approach Position as discussed before. Then shift the approach position 3, 6, 9 boards to the right as the spare dictates, exactly as described under the 3-6-9 System. As before, try using the 3rd Arrow from the right as your target for all right side spares.

The 3-6-9 system and the 2-4-6 system should help you determine an approach position for the various spares. The Seven Basic Approach Positions (and variations of them) can be used for all of the probable spares in this book—all that you will perhaps ever face on the lanes. However, you must adjust to suit your method of rolling the ball, lane conditions, and the particular spare leave.

The suggested methods for determining the target and approximate starting position on the approach are *only guidelines* to assist you in determining what is best for you. *No approach position or point of aim (target) is best for every bowler.*

You must be able to modify your approach to lane conditions found in different bowling houses and to different lanes in the same house. As a general rule, "follow the ball." If you are missing your spares to the left, then move left on the approach. If you are missing to the right, then move right. This is also called "straightening out the shot." To make these adjustments it is necessary to "read the lanes."

Please skip the following section (for LHB only) and continue to "ADJUSTING FOR LANE CONDITIONS."

APPROACH POSITIONS—*LEFT* HANDED BOWLERS

"**The proper approach position is essential to converting spares. It determines the angle at which the ball will contact the pin setup.**"

IMPORTANT: *This part is written for Left Handed Bowlers only. Right Handed Bowlers should skip to the next part, "ADJUSTING FOR LANE CONDITIONS."*

A bowling lane is composed of 39 to 42 boards, each one slightly more than one inch wide. In addition, the approach is 10 or more boards wider than the lane. Thus, there are over 50 different approach positions and more if you "split a board" in selecting one. In reality, there are a few basic approach positions and variations of these to take into consideration personal bowling differences and lane conditions.

The two most widely used methods for shooting at spares are: The 3-6-9 Spare System and the 2-4-6 Spare System. These two systems have been developed in a very scientific manner and have proven to be very effective. Both will be discussed in some detail and will be used to illustrate the suggested approach position for all 249 Probable Spares in Section II. We will suggest the approach position for both systems on every probable spare.

THE 3-6-9 SPARE SYSTEM: This system for determining the starting position on the approach is relatively easy to understand. The numbers 3, 6, and 9 refer to the number of boards you *shift to the left* on the approach to locate the Seven Basic Approach Positions. Exhibit 6 illustrates these seven approach positions, although it does not give the precise location on the approach for any of the positions. This will vary with the individual bowler and lane conditions. We will, however, suggest ways to locate all seven positions.

To use the 3-6-9 system you must determine two of the Seven Basic Approach Positions. The other five are located by shifting 3, 6, or 9 boards *to the left* of these two: The Strike Position and the 7-Pin Approach Position. From the Strike Position you *shift to the left* to cover all right side spares. You *shift to the left* of the 7-Pin Approach Position for all left side

spares. Now let's see how you can locate the Strike Position and the 7-Pin Approach Positions.

Locating the Strike Ball Position: Many LHB use the 2nd Arrow from the left side of the lane as the point of aim for their strike ball—under "normal" lane conditions. (Adjusting for Lane Conditions is presented next.) Thus, the starting position on the approach should be slightly to the left of the center of the approach. Begin with this approach position and target, and adjust to the left or right on the approach until you have determined your Strike Position. After that has been located, you are ready to determine the approach positions for all *right side spares*. Move 3 Boards to the left of your Strike Position on the approach when the 3-pin or 9-pin is the point of contact in the spare leave; 6 Boards to the left of the Strike Position when the 6-pin is the key pin in the setup; and 9 Boards to the left of the Strike Position when the 10-pin is the key pin. Keep your same target on the lanes (perhaps near the 2nd Arrow) so that you are hitting the same target but at a different angle for the various *right side spares*. On some spares you may have to shift left more or less than the "3 Board Increment," depending upon the specific point of contact or other problems. Now, how about the left side spares? For those we need to locate a 7-Pin Approach Position.

Locating the 7-Pin Approach Position: Many of the best LHB use the 3rd Arrow from the left side of the lane as the point of aim for all *left side spares*—under "normal" lane conditions. (See "Adjusting for Lane Conditions"). Picture an imaginary "sight line" through your left shoulder, across the 3rd Arrow from the left side of the lane, and into the center of the 7-pin. This should create the best cross-lane angle for covering the 7-pin. Experiment to the left or right until you have located your approach position for covering the 7-pin. After that is located you are ready to determine the approach position for all *left side spares*. Move 3 Boards to the left of your 7-Pin Approach Position when the 4-pin is the key pin in the spare; and 6 Boards to the left of your 7-Pin Approach Position when the 2-pin or 8-pin is the key one in the spare. Keep your same target on the lanes (near the 3rd Arrow) so that you are hitting the same target

EXHIBIT 6
The Seven Basic Approach Positions
For the *Left* Handed Bowler.

Using the 3-6-9 Spare System for locating starting positions on the approach results in Seven Basic Approach Positions. The numbers 3, 6, and 9 refer to a 3, 6, or 9 Board *Shift to the left* from either the Strike Position or the 7-Pin Position as the key pin in the spare setup changes.

APPROACH POSITIONS	KEY PIN IN THE SPARE	*APPROXIMATE LOCATION ON THE APPROACH
7-Pin Position	The 7-Pin	*Determined by Trial and Error.* Used as the base to locate the 2-pin and 4-pin Positions.
4-Pin Position	The 4-Pin	Located 3 Boards to the Left of the 7-Pin Approach Position (Use 7-Pin Target).
2-Pin Position	The 2-Pin & The 8-Pin	Located 6 Boards to the Left of the 7-Pin Approach Position. (Use 7-Pin Target).
STRIKE POSITION	The 1-Pin & The 5-Pin	*Determined by Trial and Error.* Used as the base to locate the 3-pin, 6-pin and 10-pin Approach Positions.
3-Pin Position	The 3-Pin & The 9-Pin	Located 3 Boards to the Left of the Strike Position. (Use Strike Target).
6-Pin Position	The 6-Pin	Located 6 Boards to the Left of the Strike Position. (Use Strike Target).
10-Pin Position	The 10-Pin	Located 9 Boards to the Left of the Strike Position. (Use Strike Target).

*It is not possible to give the precise location, since that will depend upon lane conditions. The 2, 4 and 7-pin positions are to the right of the Strike Position. The 3, 6 and 10-pin positions are to the left of the Strike Position. These approach positions are consistent with the cross-lane technique. When the spare is on the left side of the pin deck, start the approach from the right side. When the spare is on the right side, start the approach from the left.

but at a different angle for the various left side spares. On some spares, depending upon the specific point of contact needed, you may have to shift left more or less than the "3 Board Increment." (This will be discussed later.)

These Seven Basic Approach Positions should enable you to take the proper position on all spares. However, there is another system Left Handed Bowlers frequently use. It is called the 2-4-6 Spare System.

THE 2-4-6 SPARE SHOOTING SYSTEM:
This spare shooting system is often used for right side spares if you bowl left handed. The system is necessary when you are using a strike target on the lanes around the first arrow from the left, which many of the top LHB frequently do use.

It would not be practical to use the 3-6-9 system and shift as much as nine boards to the left for some of the right side spares. You would have to loft the ball out over the Channel to keep it near the same target. It is much easier to *shift the target* for those *right side spares*. So, unlike the 3-6-9 system where the target remains the same and the approach position changes, *the target shifts* and the approach position remains the same under the 2-4-6 system. The numbers 2, 4, and 6 refer to the number of boards you *shift your target* to cover the various right side spares. Move your target 2 Boards *to the right* of your strike target when the 3-pin is the key pin in the setup; 4 Boards *to the right* of your strike target when the 6-pin is the key pin; and 6 Boards *to the right* of your strike target when the 10-pin is the key pin or point of contact. On some spares you may want to move the target slightly more or less than the "2 Board Increment" but that is still consistent with the 2-4-6 concept. (This adjustment will be discussed later.)

Why the 2-Board adjustment of the target for right side spares? The reason is that for each 1-Board shift to the right of the target there is a 3-Board shift to the right in the point of contact on the pin deck. The 1-2 pocket is the 17th board from the left side of the lane. The 1-pin is centered on the 20th board. The 1-3 pocket is the 23rd board from the left side of the lane. Thus, if you are using the 1st Arrow from the left as your strike target, and you are hitting the pins on the 17th board from the left, you would have to move your target 2 boards to the right to hit the pin setup at the 23rd board from the left. Remember that each 1 board target shift results in a 3 board shift on the pin deck.

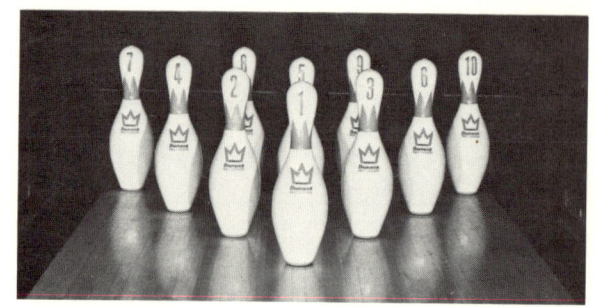

So, a 2 board shift of the target would change the contact point by 6 boards; a 4 board target shift to the right would mean a 12 board change in the point of contact, etc. Thus, the 2 board shift covers the 3-pin; 4 boards covers the 6-pin; and 6 boards covers the 10-pin.

But, what about the left side spares when you are using the 1st Arrow from the left for the strikes and the 2-4-6 system for the right side spares? You simply use the 3-6-9 Spare System for the left side spares. First determine the 7-Pin Approach Position as discussed before. Then shift the approach position 3, 6, or 9 boards to the left as the spare dictates, exactly as described under the 3-6-9 system. As before, try using the 3rd Arrow from the left as your target for all left side spares.

The 3-6-9 system and the 2-4-6 system should help you determine an approach position for the various spares. The Seven Basic Approach Positions (and variations of them) can be used for all of the probable spares in this book—all that you will perhaps ever face on the lanes. However, you must adjust to suit your method of rolling the ball, lane conditions, and the particular spare leave.

The suggested methods for determining a target and approximate starting position on the approach are *only guidelines* to assist you in determining what is best for you. No approach position or point of aim (target) is best for every bowler.

You must be able to modify your approach to lane conditions found in different bowling lanes within the same establishment. As a general rule, "follow the ball." If you are missing your spares to the left, then move left on the approach. If you are missing your spares to the right, then move right. This is also called "straightening out the shot."

To make these adjustments it is necessary to "read the lanes!" The part which follows will discuss "ADJUSTING FOR LANE CONDITIONS."

"You must learn how to read the lanes quickly and adjust accordingly. Don't fight the lanes."

All lanes must undergo a lane certification test each year in order to get an ABC Certification sticker. These certification tests are designed to insure uniformity within acceptable tolerances. These are some of the conditions which are tested: the width of the lane; the depth of the pit; the width of the pit; the crosswise tilt of the pin deck; the lengthwise tilt of the pin deck; the size of the pin spots; the thickness of the kickback; the location of the targeting arrows; and many other measurements. Despite these tests to insure uniformity and consistency between lanes, lane conditions vary from bowling center to bowling center, and even within the same house. In fact, the same lane may change during a given match or game. The amount of dressing put on the lane, when it was conditioned, and the amount of play the lane has received all affect the condition of the lane.

The low average or beginning bowler is generally unconcerned about the condition of the lanes. He or she has too many other things to think about. However, to become a high average bowler and to increase the percentage of successfully converted spares one needs a knowledge of the lanes. The better bowlers know how to read the lanes and adjust accordingly. No two lanes are exactly alike. Some lanes hook sharply during the end of the evening. Yet, in the earlier part of the evening they would take no hook at all. Noticing what your ball is doing, and what other bowlers are doing will give you some indication of the condition of the lanes and tell you whether the lanes are changing.

What are the various kinds of lane conditions, and how can you tell which conditions exist? Basically there are three lane conditions, with variations: "normal," "non-hooking," or "hooking."

1. *Normal Lanes:* There is no such thing as a "normal" lane! This is an individual description which a bowler gives to a lane that appears to be suited to the way he or she "normally" plays a lane. Another bowler, on the same lane at the same time might think that the lane is either hooking or non-hooking.

2. *Hooking Lanes:* These are lanes which will hook, perhaps too much. They are lanes which have not been conditioned recently or which have been heavily used. The ball is able to grip the lane. For the RHB, missing spares (or strikes) to the left is an indication of hooking lanes. For the LHB, missing spares (or strikes) to the right is an indication of hooking lanes. (This assumes that both bowlers are hitting their respective targets and no other change has been made in speed, delivery, etc.)

3. *Non-hooking Lanes:* These are lanes which will not hook very much. They have probably just been conditioned and are wet and oily. The ball cannot grip the surface of the lane well enough to drive or hook into the pin setups consistently. For the RHB, missing spares or strikes to the right is an indication of non-hooking lanes. For the LHB, missing to the left is usually an indication of non-hooking lanes. (Again, this assumes hitting the target and no other adjustments on the approach, release, and delivery).

NOTE: Please see the definitions of Slow and Fast Lanes in Appendix A.

Several methods for adjusting to lane conditions are fairly standard for both the RHB and LHB. Six methods will be discussed at this time. Although there are degrees of hooking and non-hooking (a little, a lot, etc.) we will only make reference to the extremes: hooking or non-hooking. The six most commonly used methods for adjusting deal with: approach positions; targets on the lane; lift on the ball; ball surfaces; speed of the ball; and placement of the ball on the lane (sometimes called arm extension, reach, loft, etc.).

1. *Approach Position Changes:* Moving inside on the approach is a normal adjustment for hooking lanes. Moving outside on the approach is the common adjustment for non-hooking lanes.

2. *Target Changes:* The target or point of aim is normally moved left or right. For hooking lanes the target is moved more towards the outside of the lane, and towards the center for non-hooking lanes. (A change in target is usually combined with a change in the approach position in the opposite direction.)

3. *Placement of the Ball on the Lane (Reach):* The ball may be set down just over the foul line or further out on the lanes. More distance is used to adjust to hooking lanes, and less distance is an adjustment for non-hooking lanes. This gives the ball more or less skid and roll. More skid (less roll) is needed for hooking lanes; less skid (more roll) for non-hooking lanes.

4. *Speed of the Ball:* A slow ball will grip the lanes better than a fast ball. Thus, more speed is used as an adjustment to hooking lanes to give less time and opportunity for the ball to grip the lane. Less speed allows the ball to grip the lane (to hook more) and is an adjustment for non-hooking lanes. This is one of the most difficult adjustments to make. Holding the ball slightly higher in your stance increases ball speed; lower reduces ball speed. A higher backswing is used to increase ball speed; lower to reduce speed. (Be careful of timing!)

5. *Ball Surface:* Bowling balls differ in their degree of hardness or softness. A ball with a soft surface will grip the lanes better than one with a hard surface. So, hooking lanes suggest a harder surface on the ball, while a softer surface on the ball is an adjustment for non-hooking lanes. This adjustment is one that is not normally made by the "once a week bowler" who probably only owns one ball. But for the better bowlers it is one of the most frequently made adjustments. The best bowlers own many bowling balls and change them to suit the lanes.

6. *Lift on the Ball:* This is called action, fingers, lift, turn, etc. It refers to the tendency of the ball to hook. Lots of lift or turn means a hooking ball. Therefore, lift

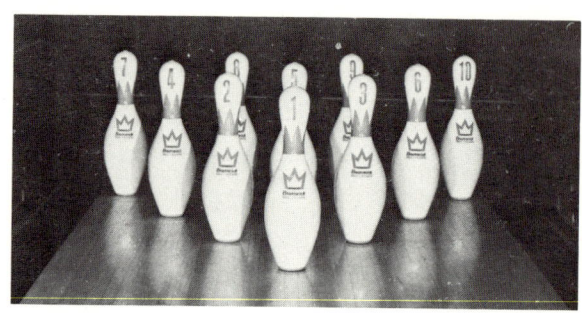

would be increased as an adjustment for non-hooking lanes, and reduced when the lanes are hooking already. Like ball speed, this is a difficult adjustment to make.

These six methods of adjusting to hooking and non-hooking lanes are summarized in Exhibit 7 for both the RHB and LHB. Keep in mind that more than one of these methods could be used in combination to adjust to a particular lane.

You must decide which adjustments are easiest for you to make; which ones work for you. The easiest single adjustment is to change your approach position, and by far the two most difficult ones are to alter the speed or lift on the ball.

Since changing the approach position is the most widely used way to adjust to hooking or non-hooking lanes, one simple rule for adjusting might make it easier for you to decide what to do. *"Follow the ball."* If your ball is going too much to the left, then move left on the approach. If your ball is going too much to the right, then move right on the approach. The rule applies to both the RHB and LHB.

It is essential that you determine the condition of the lanes as quickly as possible so that you are able to make some adjustment to take advantage of the lanes. *Don't fight the lanes.* Once you have developed a consistent approach, release, and delivery of your ball, it is relatively easy to determine the condition of the lanes. Watch what your ball is doing. Watch what other bowlers are doing. Be sure that you are not doing anything differently in your approach, timing, release, delivery or speed, etc. Any change in the path of your ball can then be attributed to the lanes, and an adjustment can be made.

In summary, once you have determined that the lanes are either hooking or non-hooking, make an immediate adjustment. Find the adjustment method that works well for you. As your average increases you will probably want to get additional information on lane conditions in order to study the subject. The sources of such information are listed in Appendix C.

EXHIBIT 7
Summary of Usual Adjustment for Hooking and Non-Hooking Lanes.

Usual Adjustments for the Right Handed Bowler:

ADJUSTMENT METHOD	HOOKING LANES	NON-HOOKING LANES
Approach Position	Move to Left	Move to Right
Target on the Lanes	Move Target Right	Move Target Left
Reach over Foul Line	Use More Reach	Use Less Reach
Speed of the Ball	Use More Speed	Use Less Speed
Lift on the Ball	Use Less Lift	Use More Lift
Ball Surface	Use Harder Ball	Use Softer Ball

Usual Adjustments for the Left Handed Bowler:

ADJUSTMENT METHOD	HOOKING LANES	NON-HOOKING LANES
Approach Position	Move to Right	Move to Left
Target on the Lanes	Move Target Left	Move Target Right
Reach Over Foul Line	Use More Reach	Use Less Reach
Speed of the Ball	Use More Speed	Use Less Speed
Lift on the Ball	Use Less Lift	Use More Lift
Ball Surface	Use Harder Ball	Use Softer Ball

Note: Combinations of these adjustments (or others) might be necessary to properly play either hooking or non-hooking lanes. For example, a change in the target on the lanes is almost always accompanied by a change in the approach position.

FAMILIES OF SPARES

"Spare leaves can be grouped into 'families.' If you can convert one 'member' of the family, you should be able to convert them all."

Although there are 249 probable spare leaves that you might face at one time or another, there are not 249 different spare shots that you have to develop. Many of the spares can be grouped into families, and if you are able to develop the proper way to convert one member of the family you should be well on your way to converting them all.

One of these families of *left side* spares includes these members:

1-2; 1-2-4; 1-2-4-7; 1-2-8;
1-2-4-7-8; etc.

If you can cover the 1-2 pin spare with little difficulty then you should be able to cover all of the spares in this family. The same approach position and point of contact may be used on all of them. You may have to make a slight adjustment in the starting position on the approach, but the principle of converting all spares in a given family with one basic point of contact is still true.

A similar family of *right side* spares includes these leaves:

1-3; 1-3-6; 1-3-6-10; 1-3-9;
1-3-6-9-10; etc.

For this family a 1-3 pocket hit will cover most of them, with possibly a minor adjustment on the starting position.

To illustrate the point a little further, two other families would include these spares:

Left Side: 2-5; 2-4-5; 2-4-5-8;
2-5-8; etc.
Right Side: 3-5; 3-5-6; 3-5-6-9;
3-6-9; etc.

Although these spares might be converted slightly differently by a RHB or a LHB, they still follow the concept of family groups. Look for other spares having the same key pin and approach positions and you should be able to spot several other families of spares.

Knowing that families of spares exist will allow you to focus your attention on the key pin of the group and will reduce the time required to learn how to convert many different spares. Keep in mind that you may have to make some small adjustment from one spare to another.

THE TEN PIN SPARE —The Strike Ball

"The more strikes you get, the less spares you will have to shoot at."

Although this is a book about spares, it would be incomplete without a full discussion about The Strike Ball for several reasons: (1) The best way to avoid a missed spare is to get a strike and have no spare to shoot at; (2) About 20% of the 249 probable spares can be converted by a strike ball (this applies to both Left Handed and Right Handed Bowlers); (3) Almost all 6, 7, 8, and 9 pin spares are converted by a Strike Ball; (4) The more times you are able to hit the strike pocket, the greater will be your first ball count (number of pins on the first ball) and the fewer number of pins you will leave standing. The fewer the pins in the spare the easier the spare (in most cases); and (5) To really improve your average beyond 180-190 you will have to increase the percentage of strikes you are getting, so why not start thinking about the strike ball now as you are working on your "spare game"? After all, the strike ball delivery occurs in every frame you bowl, but the spare ball delivery only occurs when you have failed to carry a strike.

Study Exhibit 8 very carefully. Become familiar with both ball and pin deflection needed for a perfect strike hit. The same deflection is needed on many spares. Also, you should understand why seemingly perfect pocket hits do not result in strikes.

On a perfect Right Handed 1-3 pocket strike the ball only contacts four pins: the 1-3-5-9 pins. The 1-pin takes out the 2-pin and a chain reaction causes the 2-pin to take out the 4-pin which takes out the 7-pin. The 3-pin takes out the 6-pin which takes out the 10-pin. The ball drives through and sends the 5-pin into the 8-pin and continues to take out the 9-pin. (On occasion, the 3-pin will take out the 9-pin.)

On a perfect Left Handed 1-2 pocket strike the chain reaction is similar, and the ball only hits four pins: the 1-2-5 and 8-pins. The 2-pin sends the 4-pin into the 7-pin. The 3-pin takes out the 6-pin which takes out the 10-pin. The ball continues through the pocket and sends the 5-pin into the 9-pin as the ball

takes out the 8-pin. (On occasion, the 2-pin will take out the 8-pin.)

Hitting the pocket perfectly does not, of course, guarantee that you will get a strike. Faulty pin action, hitting the pocket at the wrong angle, a late-breaking hook, not enough roll on the ball, and other reasons may account for less than a strike on what looks like a perfect hit. On some hits, pins will fly over pins they are supposed to take out, or will appear to "wrap around" the pin without knocking it over. Such pin action often is a result of excessive speed, but might not be caused by speed. There are, however, two rather common occurrences or leaves resulting from pocket hits: the "tap" and the "pocket split."

When the ball enters the pocket at the correct angle and everything appears to be perfect (speed, hook, angle, etc.) and a pin is still left standing then a *tap* has occurred. For the Right Handed Bowler a common tap is the 10-pin, whereas, for the Left Handed Bowler it is the 7-pin. Taps may be caused by excessive speed, faulty pin action, or any of a number of reasons. The solid 8-pin tap for RHB and 9-pin for LHB are generally conceded to be the only true taps, and are caused by the 5-pin being driven straight back into the pit right beside the 8-pin (or 9-pin for LHB). In effect, the 5-pin is "chopped" off the 8-pin or 9-pin, resulting in the tap. There appears to be no way to insure against taps—they are here to stay as a part of the game of bowling. Changing the angle might reduce the chances for tapping one pin but it will probably increase the chances of tapping another one. So, concentrate on hitting the pocket solidly and forget about the tap that you might get.

Pocket splits are another matter, and the causes for these leaves on pocket hits can generally be attributed to faulty ball roll, incorrect angle, or too much ball deflection. The most common of the pocket splits are: the 5-7; 6-8; 5-10; 8-10; 7-9; and 4-9. If the ball is deflected out of the pocket and does not "drive through" to take out the 5-pin, a pocket split is a real possibility. Or, if the ball barely gets a piece of

EXHIBIT 8
Ball and Pin Deflection
on a Perfect Strike

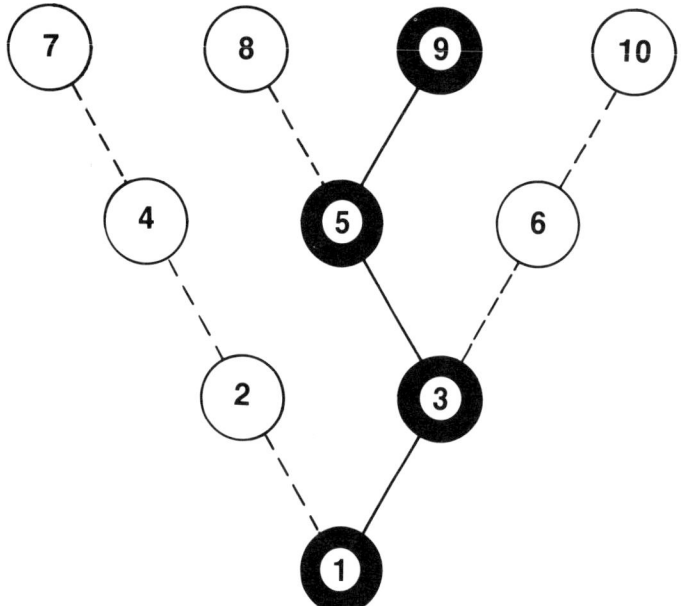

The *Right* Handed Bowler Covers the 1-3-5 and 9-pins with the Ball. The other six pins must be taken out by pin deflection. The 1-pin sends the 2 into the 4 and into the 7-pin. The 5-pin takes out the 8-pin. The 3-pin sends the 6-pin into the 10-pin.

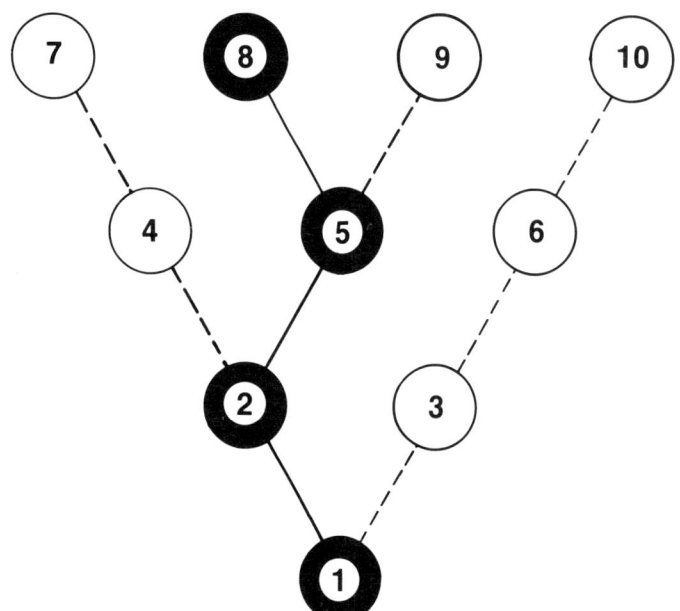

The *Left* Handed Bowler Covers the 1-2-5 and 8-pins with the Ball. The other six pins must be taken out by pin deflection. The 1-pin sends the 3 into the 6 and into the 10-pin. The 5-pin takes out the 9-pin. The 2-pin sends the 4-pin into the 7-pin.

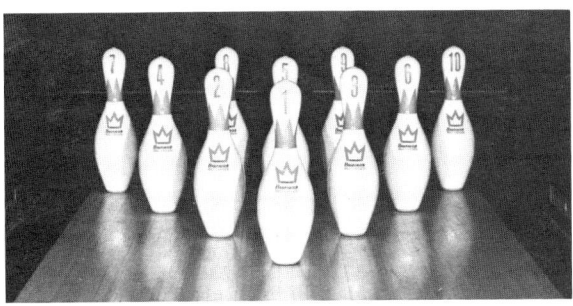

the 5-pin and slides it over in front of the 8-pin (RHB) then the 8-10 might result. (The LHB slides the 5-pin in front of the 9-pin, which it is supposed to take out, resulting in the 7-9). Unlike the taps mentioned previously, there is something you can do about pocket splits. Be sure you are delivering the ball at the correct angle to keep it in the pocket, and that you are giving it enough "lift" to drive into the pocket and to take out the 5-pin. Make sure that your ball is not "quitting" when it hits the pocket. Also, make sure you are getting enough roll on the ball, not sliding it too far, not using excessive speed, and that you are using the proper angle.

Let's return now to the perfect hit that does result in a strike. Notice that the strike hit has to be "more perfect" than most spare hits. Your point of aim is always the pocket and you always have 10 pins to knock down with one ball, whereas, you may have only one pin to knock down for a spare. To further add to your bowling skills, you should develop five different strike angles for the kinds of lane conditions you might have to adjust to!

You cannot hope that the lanes will be ideally suited to your "normal" strike angle. You must be ready to roll a strike ball that is suited to the way you find the lanes. Most good bowlers develop at least five strike ball angles, suited to lane conditions ranging from non-hooking to hooking; taking no hook at all to hooking strongly. This is what separates the great bowlers from the good ones. The good bowler might find lane conditions suited to the way he rolls his ball and score well. When the lane changes and he doesn't, his score drops sharply. The great bowler will read the lanes quickly and adjust his strike ball delivery to the condition of the lanes. To be able to do this, different strike angles are needed.

Exhibit 9 discusses the five strike angles most often used for various lane conditions. Exhibits 10 and 11 illustrate four common strike angles, showing the approximate approach positions and targets used for each angle.

Pocket hits produce more strikes and larger counts. This means that spares will have fewer pins in them and will be easier to convert. By hitting the pocket consistently your score will increase dramatically. The value of hitting the 1-3 pocket (RHB) or 1-2 pocket (LHB) can be brought into clearer focus with these facts: If you hit the pocket (RHB or LHB), the number of probable spares you leave will drop from 249 to only 101. In fact, the number of spares you will leave should drop to about 50 if you can hit the pocket consistently. And, many of these spares will have three or fewer pins in them.

Remember that the more strikes you get, the less spares you will have to shoot at. Also, a strike ball will come in handy on many spare leaves. Practice several strike angles and you will be well on your way towards converting most of the spares you leave.

EXHIBIT 9
The Five Strike Angles That Each Bowler Should Develop.

Five Strike Angles for the Right Handed Bowler

Angle	Target on the Lane*
The Deep Inside Angle	Approximately Boards 18-22
The Inside Angle (3rd Arrow Angle)	Approximately Boards 13-17
The 2nd Arrow Angle	Approximately Boards 8-12
The Outside Angle (1st Arrow Angle)	Approximately Boards 4-7
The Deep Outside Angle	Approximately Boards 1-3

Five Strike Angles for the Left Handed Bowler

Angle	Target on the Lane*
The Deep Outside Angle	Approximately Boards 1-3
The Outside Angle (1st Arrow Angle)	Approximately Boards 4-7
The 2nd Arrow Angle	Approximately Boards 8-12
The Inside Angle (3rd Arrow Angle)	Approximately Boards 13-17
The Deep Inside Angle	Approximately Boards 18-22

*The Boards are numbered from the right side of the lane for right handed bowlers, and from the left side for the left handed bowler. It is impossible to give the exact board for each strike angle. The way the ball is rolled, lane conditions, and other factors will determine which boards should be used. Most RHB use the 2nd Arrow Angle for strikes and left side spares; the 3rd Arrow for right side spares. Most LHB use the 1st Arrow Angle for strikes and right side spares, and the 3rd Arrow Angle for left side spares.

EXHIBIT 10
Four Common Strike Angles Used by *Right* Handed Bowlers in Adjusting to Lane Conditions.

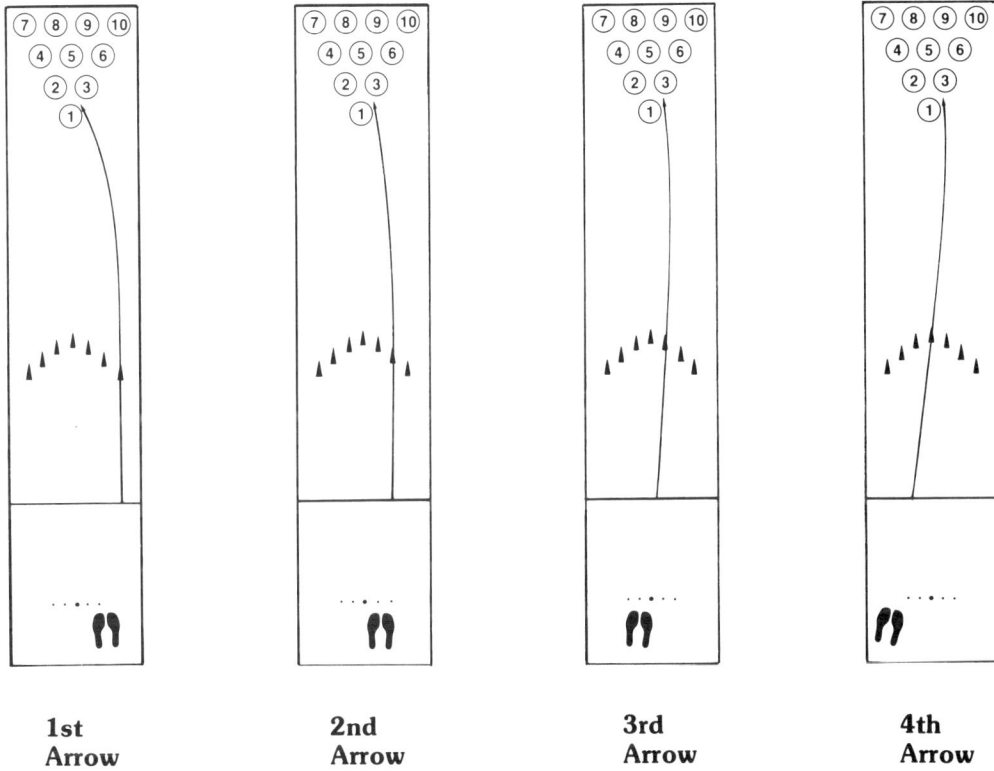

| 1st Arrow | 2nd Arrow | 3rd Arrow | 4th Arrow |

"Follow the ball." If the ball is going to the left then shift to the left on the approach. If the ball is going to the right then shift to the right. Or when the lanes are hooking, either shift your approach position to the left or move your target (point of aim) to the right. Reverse these last two adjustments on non-hooking lanes. Of course, many variations of these angles exist.

EXHIBIT 11
Four Common Strike Angles Used by *Left* Handed Bowlers in Adjusting to Lane Conditions.

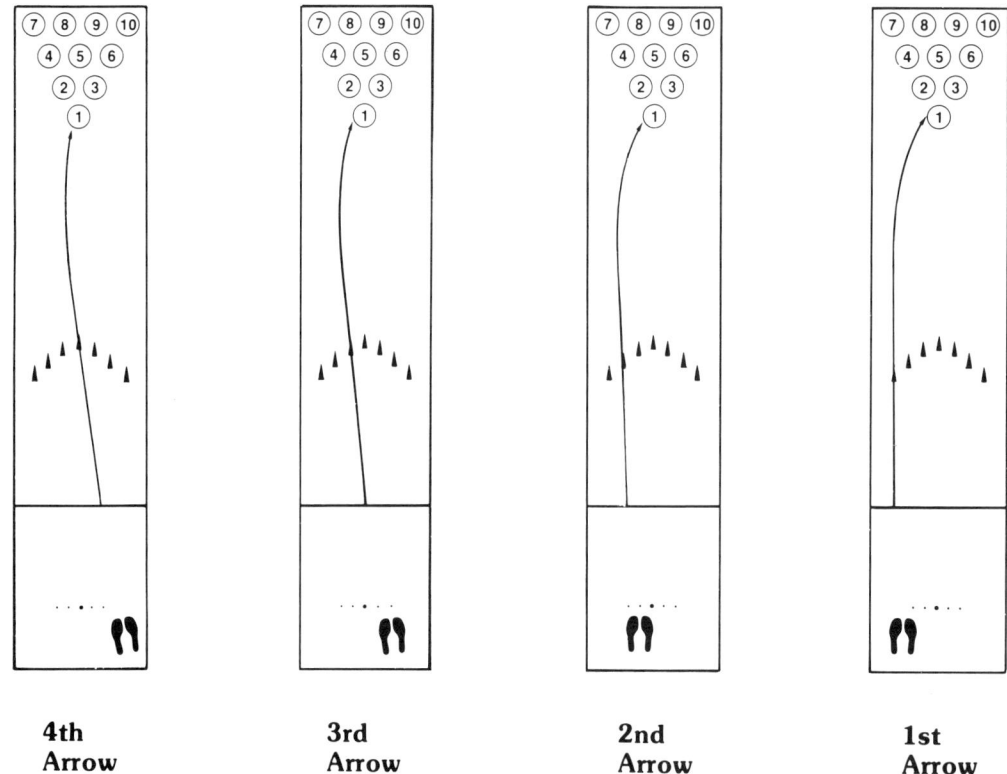

| 4th Arrow | 3rd Arrow | 2nd Arrow | 1st Arrow |

"Follow the Ball." If the ball is going to the right then shift your approach position to the right. If the ball is going too much to the left then shift left on the approach. Or when lanes are hooking, either shift your approach position to the right or move your target (point of aim) to the left. Reverse these adjustments on non-hooking lanes. Of course, many variations of these angles exist.

SUMMARY: COUNTDOWN ON ALL SPARES

"Concentrate on all spare leaves and you should make most of them."

Many spares are missed because a bowler becomes careless, not because he or she does not know how to make the spare. In fact, almost every time you miss a spare it will be because you did something wrong in your approach, release, delivery, aiming, etc. First you must know *what* to do to make a given spare and then you must learn *how* to do it.

There are 10 items to consider in preparing for any spare leave. These are:

1　Determine the key pin and point of contact.
2　Select the target on the lane and the required angle.
3　Select your approach position, taking into consideration lane condition, cross lane angles, chop possibilities, pin and ball deflection, etc.
4　Determine if special problems exist such as pins off spot, pin count, need to reduce or increase angle, etc.

These four decisions should be made before you step on the approach. Then:

5　Take your stance on the approach and face your target squarely.
6　Recheck your approach position, target, and point of contact.

7　Take a deep breath and count to 3 to avoid rushing.
8　Concentrate on executing the shot and deliver the ball.
9　Follow through and watch the ball cross over (or miss) your target.
10　Watch what happens to the ball and pins. If you miss, determine what you did wrong and try to correct that on the next spare.

The first four items should be considered while your ball is returning from the pit. Figure out what you have to do to make the spare *before* you step on the approach. This gives you more time to think and helps prevent you from rushing into the shot. Avoid rushing at all cost.

Remember what spares you have left so that you can determine what you are doing wrong (by not getting strikes). The spares you leave are an indication of what you are doing on your strike ball. Know what you did on each lane each time so that you can correct any errors immediately. Watch to see if the lanes are changing (drying out). Be prepared to adjust accordingly to take advantage of the lanes, not fight them.

These 10 points can and should become automatic for you. Practice them on all your spare leaves and your success rate with spares should increase rapidly. Concentrate on all spares and you should make most of them.

SECTION II
HOW TO CONVERT THE 249 PROBABLE SPARES

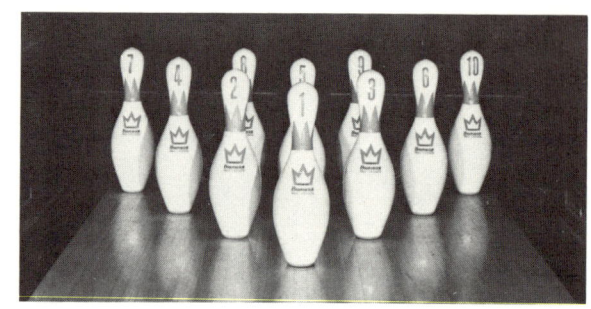

"The kind of spares you leave is an indication of your average."

This section contains the 249 probable spares which might be left by anyone who bowls. With few exceptions, every spare that you will ever leave in your entire bowling career is included here. Those that you will not leave are pictured in Section III.

The average bowler may hit the ten pin setup anywhere. He or she may leave a wide variety of spares. Some of these spares would seem strange to the high average bowler. The top bowlers are in or near the pocket (1-3 or 1-2) most of the time. They leave fewer types of spares, and generally with only one, two or three pins in them. They seldom miss the 1-pin, and their spare leaves often involve these four pins: 4-pin; 6-pin; 7-pin; and 10-pin. But even the best bowlers will miss the 1-pin and may leave any one of these 249 spares. It is not uncommon for a top bowler to bowl a gutter ball—it has happened on nationwide television! And, a professional bowler once knocked down *only* the 7 and 10 pins on the *first* ball!

Some of the spares included in this section might well have been classified as "rare." (The 2-3; 8-9; 2-7-9; and 3-8-10 splits are examples that come to mind.) If there was sufficient reason to include a spare in the probables, it was included. In this way we were able to illustrate all spares which a bowler might leave, and to demonstrate all of the principles from Section I.

In this section, the 249 probable spares have been organized into 10 groups—spares with one pin, two pins, etc. The group number appears in the center of each page.

Each group is in order by pin number. Therefore, it is easy to locate any spare. *How many pins* in the spare will tell you what group it is in, and the *actual numbers* of the pins will locate it in numerical sequence within the group. For example, the 1-2-8 spare has *three pins* in it. It is located in the *third group* of spares, following the 1-2-7 leave and immediately in front of the 1-2-9 spare. Try to locate some of the spares you typically leave and you will be able to locate any other spare in seconds.

We have tried to present all the information that you would ever need to know to make every spare. For each spare, this information is given: the numbers of the pins in the spare (i.e. the 1-2 spare, the 5-7 spare, etc.); the Key Pin in the spare (which may be an "imaginary" pin); the Spare Zone that should be used; the Contact Area on the key pin which gives the best chance to make the spare; the Approach Position and Target which gives the best angle to make the spare; the suggested method for the conversion; and if one exists, an alternative method; problems which might be presented by the spare, such as chop possibilities, unfavorable pin or ball deflection, etc., and references to similar or related spares. All of these items are written from both the Right Handed and Left Handed Bowlers points of view.

Each spare is discussed as a separate unit, although there is a great deal of similarity among the probable spares, especially the spare families (spares with the same key pin, contact area, and using the same approach position). At times we make reference to one or more similar spares, or to the same kind of spare but on the opposite side of the pin deck. For example, the 4-7 spare is similar to the 6-10 leave, but on the opposite side of the pin deck. The 4-7 is more of a chop possibility for the LHB, but the 6-10 is more of a chop possibility for the RHB. By relating the spares in this way, we hope to make it easier to understand all of the probable spares, thereby reducing the time required to know how to make all of them.

All 1,023 spares have been numbered in sequence—from 1 to 1,023. An S after the number indicates a Split. The number of each spare is in the top right corner of the spare, above the number for its opposite side spare. (See the 4-7 and 6-10.)

This book is more of a reference text than something to be read from cover to cover, starting on page 1. Each spare can be studied separately, in any order, and as part of a larger group (family) of similar spares. For example, many of the right side washouts are played exactly like the 1-2-10 spare. The left side washouts are played exactly like the 1-3-7 spare. Thus, by studying one spare as it relates to similar

ones you can cover all 249 probable spares very quickly.

Perhaps the quickest and most personalized way to use the book is to study those spares which you normally leave. Prepare a list of them and study each one well. See which ones can be grouped into families to simplify your studies. Also look for related spares and study them too. You may wish to use the spare numbers to prepare your list—and to make it easier to locate these spares.

You may find a way to make a spare that you often leave, that is different than what we suggest. If it works *consistently* then use that method for the conversion. Spare shooting is both an art as well as a science, and as your skill develops you can adjust the principles to suit your style of bowling—and lane conditions.

Some of the spare leaves which you may choose to shoot differently than we suggest include: 7; 10; 5-8; 5-9; 2-7-9; 3-9-10; 2-4-5; 3-5-6; 2-4-5-8; 3-5-6-9; 4-6-7-8-10; and 4-6-7-9-10. On most of these leaves we have indicated alternative methods to use.

Of course, you should read the material on all of the spares so that you can determine exactly how to convert any spare you might face *before* you face it. If you read this section well and the appropriate principles in Section I, you should be able to increase your average substantially. You should make most of your spare leaves. And, that is the purpose of the book.

IMPORTANT: *If you are a Right Handed Bowler (RHB) please read the part which immediately follows this page. This is written especially for the RHB and explains all of the material presented for each probable spare. It is essential that the RHB read this part to fully understand the probable spares section.*

If you are a Left Handed Bowler (LHB) please skip to the part written especially for the LHB. It is essential that the LHB read that part to understand the material on each probable spare, as it relates to the Left Handed Bowler. (It starts on page 41.)

Special Note to Right Handed Bowlers

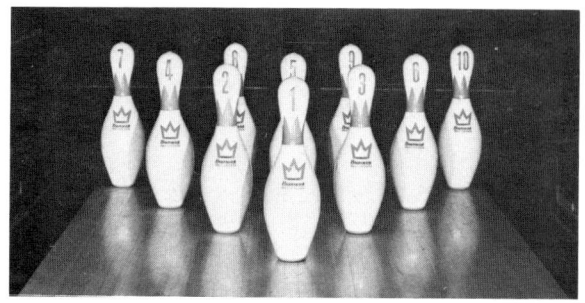

Important: *This note is for Right Handed Bowlers only. If you bowl left handed, please skip this part since it might be confusing to you. (The part following this is written for Left Handed Bowlers. See page 41.)*

Underneath the picture for each probable spare there is information regarding the proper Spare Zone, Contact Area and Approach Position and Targets for converting the spare. This note will explain the details behind that information.

CONTACT AREAS: The key pin in any spare must be hit in a certain spot or area to make the spare. We have determined that there are 9 Contact Areas on any pin which will cover all of the 249 probable spares. These 9 Contact Areas are illustrated on Exhibit 12.

When the Contact Area on a spare leave indicates "RIGHT on the 3-pin," such as in the 3-5-6 spare, the point of contact on the 3-pin is exactly where RIGHT is shown in Exhibit 12—not just anywhere on the right side of the 3-pin. Of course, you might make the spare by hitting slightly to the left or right of the suggested contact point. Therefore, we refer to contact AREAS and *not* contact POINTS. Try to hit the key pin in the spare setup at the impact point exactly as it is identified, and you will still have a small margin of error to make the spare.

SPARE ZONES: All of the 14 Spare Zones used in this book are illustrated in Exhibit 13. The 7 Basic Spare Zones call for right side hits on the key pin, and the 7 Head-On Spare Zones call for hits toward the center of the pin. Left side hits have been taken into account, as described in Exhibit 13. The 14 Spare Zones are as follows:

The 7 Basic Spare Zones refer to the normal way a Right Handed Bowler would plan to contact any key pin, on the right side coming into the pin. This is because the ball is hooking from right to left. A Left Handed Bowler would normally plan to contact the key pin coming into it from the left side, since the ball is hooking from the left. **IMPORTANT:** Therefore, the 1-pin zone for a RHB indicates a hit to the right side of the 1-pin, but the same spare zone would indicate a hit to the left side of the 1-pin for the LHB.

The 7 Head-On Spare Zones refer to hits on the key pin which are more to the center of the pin, including RIGHT CENTER, CENTER, and LEFT CENTER as defined on Exhibit 12. When the Head-On Spare Zone is indicated for any probable spare, this means that some small adjustment from the Basic Spare Zone is needed to make the spare. This will always be about a 1½ boards shift to the right of the Basic Spare Zone approach position when the 3-6-9 system is used, or a 1-board shift of the target to the left under the 2-4-6 system. These adjustments will be a little clearer after a discussion of both spare systems.

APPROACH POSITIONS AND TARGETS: *The 3-6-9 Spare System*

In Section I we discussed the 3-6-9 Spare System in detail. In this system, the approach position is changed by 3, 6, or 9 boards to the right from either the STRIKE POSITION or the 10-PIN POSITION. These two positions are determined by trial and error, and the other approach positions are merely the result of shifts to the right in 3-board units. Normally, the 2nd Arrow from the right is used for the

The 14 Spare Zones

The 7 Basic Spare Zones	*The 7 Head-On Spare Zones*
1-pin zone (RIGHT on the 1 or 5 pins)	Head-On 1-pin zone (Towards CENTER)
2-pin zone (RIGHT on the 2 or 8 pins)	Head-On 2-pin zone (Towards CENTER)
3-pin zone (RIGHT on the 3 or 9-pins)	Head-On 3-pin zone (Towards CENTER)
4-pin zone (RIGHT on the 4-pin)	Head-On 4-pin zone (Towards CENTER)
6-pin zone (RIGHT on the 6-pin)	Head-On 6-pin zone (Towards CENTER)
7-pin zone (RIGHT on the 7-pin)	Head-On 7-pin zone (Towards CENTER)
10-pin zone (RIGHT on the 10-pin)	Head-On 10-pin zone (Towards CENTER)

EXHIBIT 12
The Nine Specific Contact Areas
On Any Pin, Viewed from the Top.

These nine contact areas give the point of contact for all probable spares. Notice that Center includes Left Center and Right Center. The mid-point of each area is also given. You could hit slightly to the left or right of this mid-point and still make the spare. That is why we refer to Contact Areas and not Contact Points. There is a margin for error.

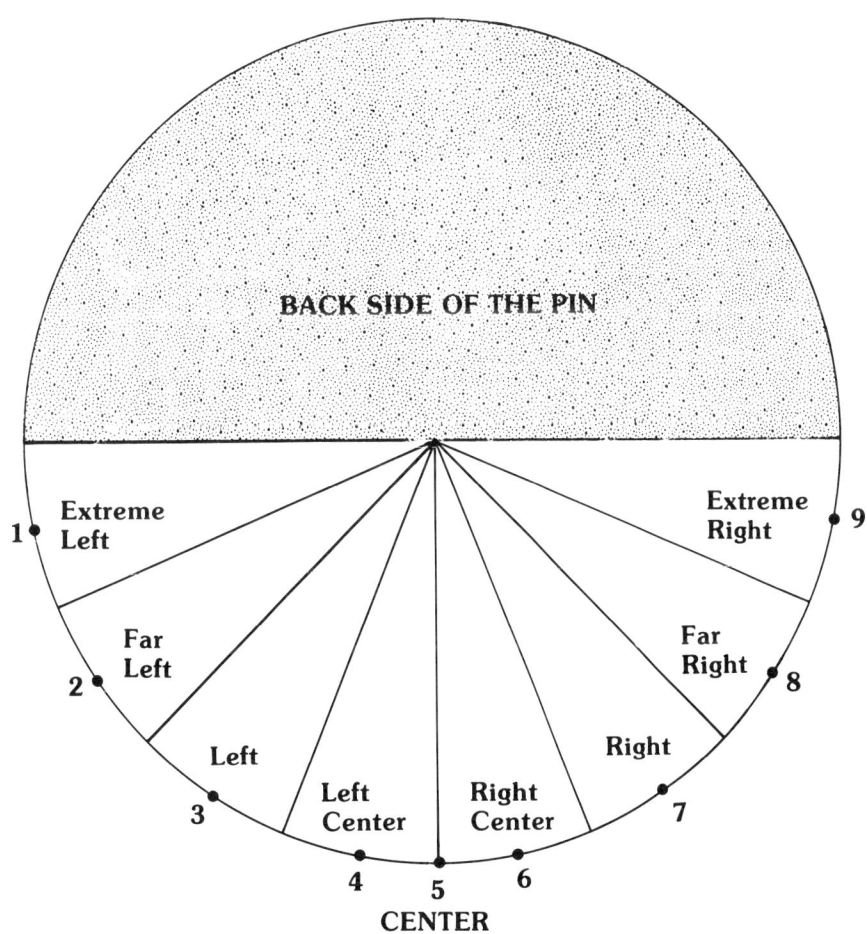

EXHIBIT 13
The 14 Spare Zones
for the *Right* Handed Bowler

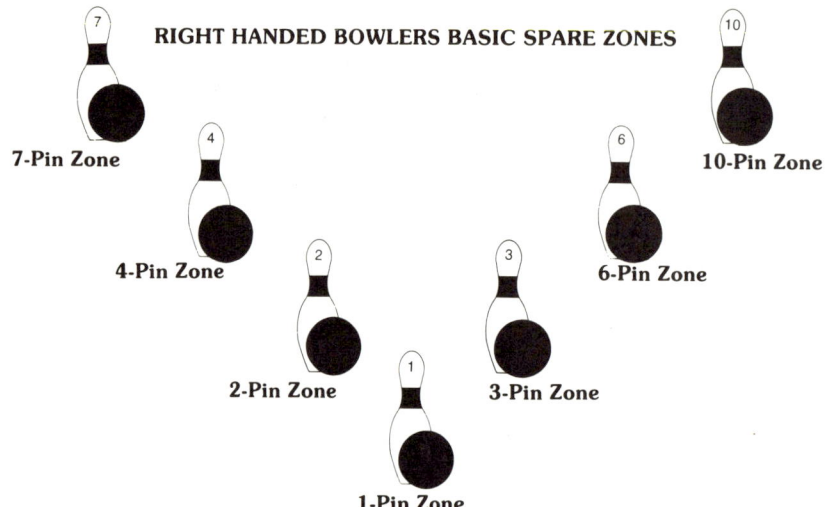

RIGHT HANDED BOWLERS BASIC SPARE ZONES

7-Pin Zone

4-Pin Zone

2-Pin Zone

1-Pin Zone

3-Pin Zone

6-Pin Zone

10-Pin Zone

The 7 Basic Spare Zones for the RHB call for hits on the right side, coming into the pins from the right. The 7 Head-On Spare Zones call for hits to the center of the pins. All *Left Side Hits use the Basic Spare Zones too.* A left side hit on the 1-pin is similar to a right side hit on the 2-pin, so the 2-pin zone is used for spares requiring a left side hit on the 1-pin. A left side hit on the 6-pin is similar to a right side hit on the 3-pin, so the 3-pin zone is used for spares needing a left hit on the 6-pin. Etc. Thus, these 14 Spare Zones cover all probable spares.

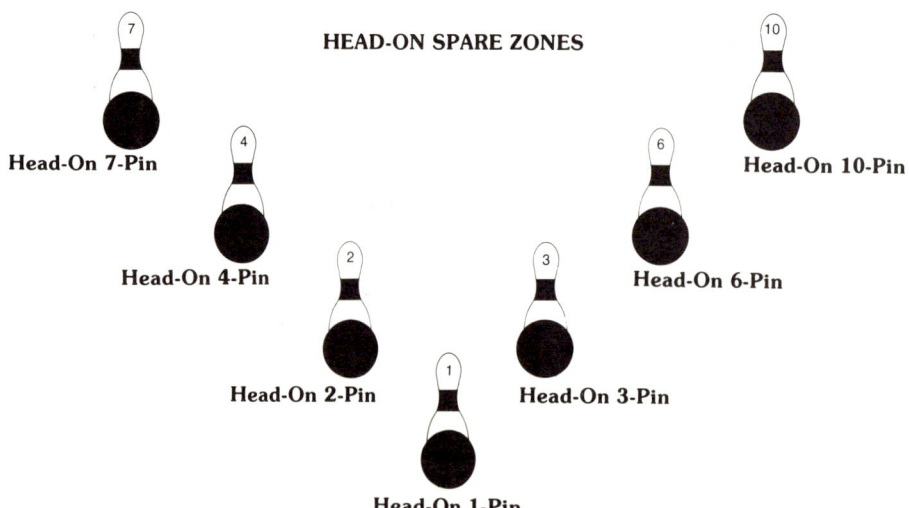

HEAD-ON SPARE ZONES

Head-On 7-Pin

Head-On 4-Pin

Head-On 2-Pin

Head-On 1-Pin

Head-On 3-Pin

Head-On 6-Pin

Head-On 10-Pin

36

for right handed bowlers only (cont'd)

strike ball and all left side spares. The 3rd Arrow is used for all right side spares. The 3-6-9 system results in Seven Basic Approach Positions:

The Seven Basic Approach Positions

7-pin position	Key Pin is the 7-pin
4-pin position	Key Pin is the 4-pin
2-pin position	Key Pin is the 2 or 8-pin

STRIKE POSITION   Key Pin is the 1 or 5-pin

3-pin position	Key Pin is the 3 or 9-pin
6-pin position	Key Pin is the 6-pin
10-pin position	Key Pin is the 10-pin

These seven approach positions are appropriate for spare leaves in which the key pin is to be contacted on either the right or left side; but not for Head-On hits. For example, a 3 board shift to the right of the 10-pin position is needed to hit the 6-pin on the right side. A 6 board shift is needed to hit the 3-pin on the right side. But what about a Head-On hit on the 6-pin? A shift to the right of 3 boards is not enough, while 6 boards is too much. A shift of 4½ boards would be just about the right amount of change in the approach position to hit the 6-pin head on,—assuming that you do not change the target on the lanes.

To explain further, a 3 board shift to the right of the STRIKE POSITION is used to hit the 2-pin on the right side (or the 1-pin on the left side). A 6 board shift to the right of the STRIKE POSITION is used to hit the 4-pin on the right side (or the 2-pin on the left side). Therefore, it follows that a 4½ board shift to the right would give the approach position to contact the 2-pin head-on! A 7½ board shift to the right would give the approach position to hit the 4-pin head-on. Thus, the Seven Basic Approach Positions can be *expanded* to include all possible hits on the key pin in the probable spares—right side, left side, and head-on. Exhibit 14 does exactly that. It expands the Seven Basic Spare Zones by 1½ board shifts between each of the 3, 6, and 9 board shifts in the spare system. *The result is 14 approach positions, one for each of the 14 Spare Zones.*

Exhibit 14 gives the appearance of a precise system for determining the approach position for every probable spare. You may have to make some adjustment, but you will have some basis to make the adjustment. You will note that the shifts are always to the right, and always in increments of 1½ boards. Therefore, it should be relatively easy to calculate any approach position from either the 10-PIN POSITION or the STRIKE POSITION. If the spare leave calls for a right or left side hit, then the approach position will be a shift of 3, 6, or 9 boards. If a Head-On hit is needed, then a further shift of 1½ boards to the right will have to be made. For example, if the spare calls for a Head-On 3-pin hit, shift 6 boards as required in the basic 3-6-9 system, then shift an additional 1½ boards (still to the right) for the Head-On hit. Once you learn the Seven Basic Approach Positions it is a simple matter to add the 1½ board shift to adjust for the Head-On hits.

APPROACH POSITIONS AND TARGETS: *The 2-4-6 Spare System*

Only two items will appear for any probable spare under "2-4-6 Spare System:" (1) Not Used on This Spare, or (2) Strike Position. If (1) appears, it means that the 2-4-6 System is not normally used on that spare. If (2) appears, then a target change will be indicated. If the 2-4-6 system is being used, the approach position must be the STRIKE POSITION.

The 2-4-6 Spare System is often used on left side spares when the strike ball is being played from the 1st Arrow, or near there. Shifting the approach position to the right is not practical, since it would require lofting the ball out over the channel. A change in the target is an easier and more practical adjustment to make for left side spares.

The target is shifted to the left as follows: a 2-board shift of the target to the left when the 2-pin is the key pin; a 4-board shift of the target to the left when the 4-pin is the key pin in the spare; and a 6-board shift of the target to the left when the key pin is the 7-pin. Right side spares are converted by using the 3-6-9 system, and changing your approach position as described above.

These target changes again assume that you will contact the key pin on the right side, coming into it from the right side. However, on some spare leaves a head-on hit is needed. Therefore, you may have to move your target more or less than the 2-4-6 boards as the basic system indicates. Essentially, the use of 1-board increments of shifting the target will give the correct shift for all left side spare leaves, whether a left side, right side, or head-on hit is needed.

A 1-board shift of the target to the left is suggested to hit the 1-pin head-on; a 3-board shift of the target to the left is suggested to hit the 2-pin head-on;

EXHIBIT 14
The Expanded 3-6-9 Spare System
For the *Right* Handed Bowler

The 7 Basic Spare Zones and 7 Head-On Spare Zones require 14 different positions on the approach—one for each zone. (Remember, the target does not change when you use the 3-6-9 Spare System, only the approach position changes.) These 14 approach positions can be determined by simply expanding the basic 3-6-9 Spare System to include all Head-On hits. Each approach position is still a movement to the right from either the STRIKE POSITION or the 10-PIN POSITION. As in the basic 3-6-9 system, these two positions must be found by trial and error, and all other approach positions are calculated as shown below.

SPARE ZONE	APPROACH POSITION FOR THAT SPARE ZONE	
*10-Pin Zone	*10-Pin Position:* DETERMINED BY TRIAL AND ERROR	
Head-On 10-Pin Zone	1½ Boards to Right of the 10-Pin Position	USE 10-PIN TARGET
*6-Pin Zone	3 Boards to Right of the 10-Pin Position	
Head-On 6-Pin Zone	4½ Boards to Right of the 10-Pin Position	
*3-Pin and 9-Pin Zone	6 Boards to Right of the 10-Pin Position	
Head-On 3-Pin & 9-Pin Zone	7½ Boards to Right of the 10-Pin Position	
*1-Pin and 5-Pin Zone	*Strike Position:* DETERMINED BY TRIAL AND ERROR	
Head-On 1-Pin & 5-Pin Zone	1½ Boards to Right of the Strike Position	USE STRIKE TARGET
*2-Pin and 8-Pin Zone	3 Boards to Right of the Strike Position	
Head-On 2-Pin & 8-Pin Zone	4½ Boards to Right of the Strike Position	
*4-Pin Zone	6 Boards to Right of the Strike Position	
Head-On 4-Pin Zone	7½ Boards to Right of the Strike Position	
*7-Pin Zone	9 Boards to Right of the Strike Position	
Head-On 7-Pin Zone	10½ Boards to Right of the Strike Position	

*These are the 7 Basic Approach Positions, using the 3-6-9 Spare System!

Notice that all adjustments are *to the right,* and in units of 1½ Boards. The target on the lane does not change, normally the 2nd Arrow from the right for the strike ball and left side spares, and the 3rd Arrow from the right for the 10-Pin and all right side spares. These targets and adjustments are approximates only. You must take lane conditions into consideration at all times. Also, remember to face your target on the lanes and walk toward that target.

for right handed bowlers only (cont'd)

a 5-board shift to hit the 4-pin head-on; and a 7-board shift of the target to the left to hit the 7-pin head-on. Thus, by *expanding* the basic 2-4-6 Spare System, all left side hits can be taken into consideration.

Exhibit 15 presents the *Expanded* 2-4-6 Spare System and gives additional adjustments for all left side hits. This expansion of the basic system gives the approximate target shift for all left side probable spares on which the 2-4-6 system might be used.

SUMMARY: This concludes the explanation of the Contact Areas, Spare Zones, and Approach Positions and Targets for the Right Handed Bowler. You should now be able to understand the material presented for each probable spare. However, it might be necessary to review this note from time to time until the material immediately comes to mind when you are faced with any given spare leave. When this happens, you will be well on your way to mastering all of the spares which you normally face on the lanes.

EXHIBIT 15
The Expanded 2-4-6 Spare System for the *Right* Handed Bowler

The 2-4-6 Spare System only refers to adjustments of the target (point of aim) by increments of 2 boards for left side spares. On some spare leaves an adjustment of more or less boards may be needed, depending upon the particular spare leave and any problems it might present (such as a chop possibility, unfavorable pin or ball deflection, etc.). The adjustments listed below are approximations only. The way you roll the ball, and other personal characteristics or preferences might suggest other adjustments. Use your Strike Position on the approach in all cases when you are using the 2-4-6 System. Point your feet and body at the target, and walk toward that target.

If The Spare Zone Is:	Shift the Target for Left Side Spares:
1-Pin Zone	Use the Strike Target Board
Head-On 1-Pin Zone	Shift Target 1 Board Left of the Strike Target
2-Pin Zone	*Shift Target 2 Boards Left of the Strike Target
Head-On 2-Pin Zone	Shift Target 3 Boards Left of the Strike Target
4-Pin Zone	*Shift Target 4 Boards Left of the Strike Target
Head-On 4-Pin Zone	Shift Target 5 Boards Left of the Strike Target
7-Pin Zone	*Shift Target 6 Boards Left of the Strike Target
Head-On 7-Pin Zone	Shift Target 7 Boards Left of the Strike Target

*These are the normal 2, 4, and 6-board adjustments suggested in the system. They have been expanded to provide guidelines for all left side spares, especially those requiring Head-On hits.

Note: A variation of the 2-4-6 System could be used for Right Side Spares, but we prefer to use the System for Left Side Spares only. Once your skill develops, you will be able to adjust any spare system to your style of bowling.

Special Note to Left Handed Bowlers

Important: *This note is for Left Handed Bowlers only. If you bowl Right Handed, please skip this part since it might be confusing to you. (The part preceding this is written for Right Handed Bowlers. See page 34.)*

Underneath the picture for each probable spare there is information regarding the proper Spare Zone, Contact Area, and Approach Position and Targets for converting the spare. This note will explain the details behind that information.

CONTACT AREAS: The key pin in any spare must be hit in a certain spot or area to make the spare. We have determined that there are 9 Contact Areas on any pin which will convert all of the 249 probable spares. These 9 Contact Areas are illustrated on Exhibit 16.

When the Contact Area on a spare leave indicates "LEFT on the 2-pin," such as in the 2-4-5 spare leave, the point of contact on the 2-pin is exactly where LEFT is shown in Exhibit 16—not just anywhere on the left side of the 2-pin. "RIGHT CENTER on the 1-pin" means the exact point of contact called RIGHT CENTER on the diagram. Of course, you might make the spare by hitting slightly to the left or right of the suggested contact point. Therefore, we refer to Contact Areas and *not* contact points. Try to hit the key pin in the spare setup at the impact point exactly as it is identified, and you still have a small margin of error to make the spare.

SPARE ZONES: All of the 14 Spare Zones used in this book are illustrated in Exhibit 17. The 7 Basic Spare Zones call for left side hits on the key pin, and

the 7 Head-On Spare Zones call for hits toward the center of the pin. Right side hits have been taken into account, as described in Exhibit 17. The 14 Spare Zones are listed below.

The 7 Basic Spare Zones refer to the normal way a Left Handed Bowler would plan to contact any key pin, on the left side coming into the pin. This is because the ball is hooking to the right, and coming from the left side of the lane. A Right Handed Bowler would normally plan to contact the key pin coming into it from the right side, since the ball is hooking from the right. **IMPORTANT:** Therefore, the 1-pin spare zone for the LHB indicates a hit to the left side of the 1-pin, but the same spare zone for the RHB would indicate a hit to the right side of the 1-pin.

The 7 Head-On Spare Zones refer to hits on the key pins which are more to the center of the pins, including RIGHT CENTER, LEFT CENTER and CENTER as defined on Exhibit 16. When the Head-On Spare Zone is indicated for any probable spare leave, it means that some small adjustment from the Basic Spare Zone is needed to make the spare. This adjustment will normally be about a 1½ board shift to the left of the Basic Spare Zone approach position when the 3-6-9 Spare System is being used, or a 1 board target change (to the right) if the 2-4-6 spare system is being used. These adjustments will be a little clearer after a discussion of both spare systems.

APPROACH POSITIONS AND TARGETS: *The 3-6-9 Spare System:*

In Section I we discussed the 3-6-9 system in some detail. You will recall that in this system the

The 14 Spare Zones

The 7 Basic Spare Zones
1-pin zone (LEFT on the 1 or 5 pins)
2-pin zone (LEFT on the 2 or 8 pins)
3-pin zone (LEFT on the 3 or 9-pins)
4-pin zone (LEFT on the 4-pin)
6-pin zone (LEFT on the 6-pin)
7-pin zone (LEFT on the 7-pin)
10-pin zone (LEFT on the 10-pin)

The 7 Head-On Spare Zones
Head-On 1-pin zone (Towards CENTER)
Head-On 2-pin zone (Towards CENTER)
Head-On 3-pin zone (Towards CENTER)
Head-On 4-pin zone (Towards CENTER)
Head-On 6-pin zone (Towards CENTER)
Head-On 7-pin zone (Towards CENTER)
Head-On 10-pin zone (Towards CENTER)

EXHIBIT 16
The Nine Specific Contact Areas On Any Pin, Viewed from the Top.

These nine Contact Areas are used to give the point of contact for all probable spares. Notice that Center includes Left Center and Right Center. The mid-point of each area is also given. You could hit slightly to the left or right of this mid-point and still make the spare. There is a margin for error.

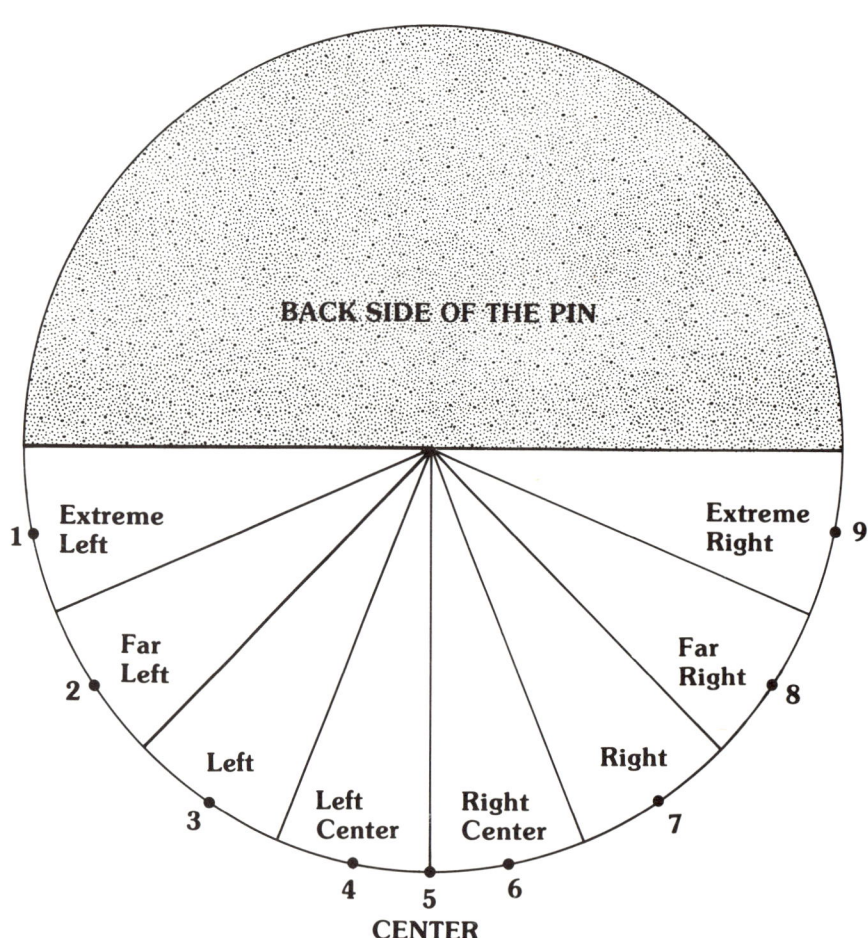

BACK SIDE OF THE PIN

Extreme Left — 1

Extreme Right — 9

Far Left — 2

Far Right — 8

Left — 3

Right — 7

Left Center — 4

Right Center — 6

5

CENTER

EXHIBIT 17
The 14 Spare Zones
for the *Left* Handed Bowler

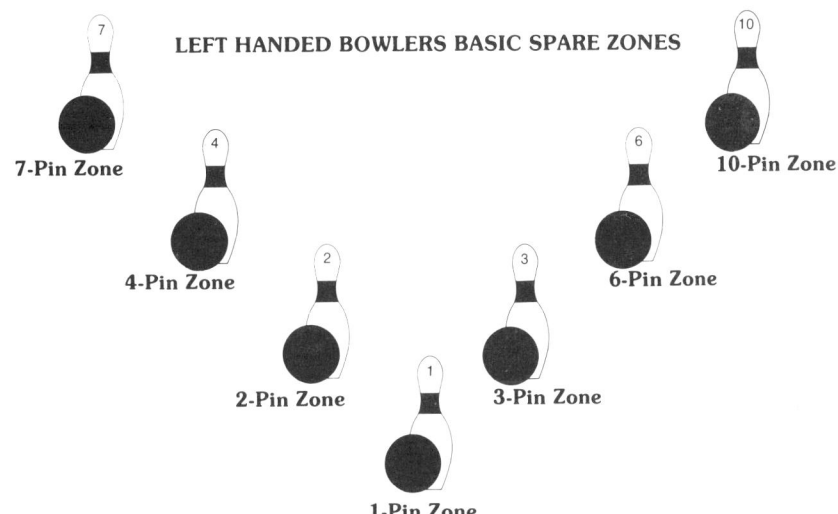

LEFT HANDED BOWLERS BASIC SPARE ZONES

7-Pin Zone

4-Pin Zone

2-Pin Zone

1-Pin Zone

3-Pin Zone

6-Pin Zone

10-Pin Zone

The 7 Basic Spare Zones for the LHB call for hits on the left side, coming into the pins from the left. The 7 Head-On Spare Zones call for hits to the center of the pins. All *Right side hits use the Basic Spare Zones too.* A right side hit on the 1-pin is similar to a left side hit on the 3-pin, so the 3-pin zone is used for spares requiring a right side hit on the 1-pin. A right side hit on the 4-pin is similar to a left side hit on the 2-pin, so the 2-pin zone is used for spares needing a right hit on the 4-pin. Etc. Thus, these 14 Spare Zones cover all probable spares.

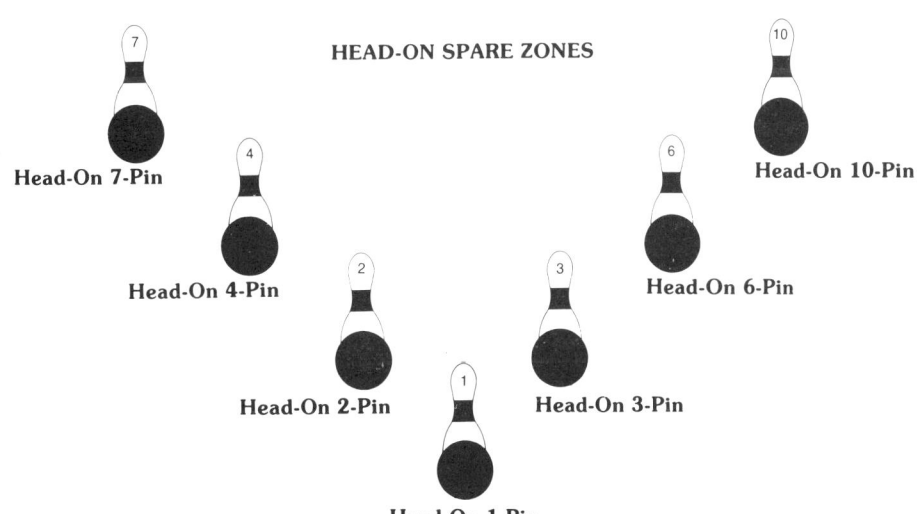

HEAD-ON SPARE ZONES

Head-On 7-Pin

Head-On 4-Pin

Head-On 2-Pin

Head-On 1-Pin

Head-On 3-Pin

Head-On 6-Pin

Head-On 10-Pin

approach position is changed by 3, 6 or 9 boards to the left of either the STRIKE POSITION or the 7-PIN POSITION. These two positions are determined by trial and error, using the suggestions in the Section I discussion of the system. All other approach positions were found by shifting to the left on the approach by 3-board units. The target on the lanes remained the same, normally the 2nd Arrow from the left side for the STRIKE POSITION and all right side spares, and the 3rd Arrow from the left side for all left side spares. The Seven Basic Approach Positions under the 3-6-9 system are:

The Seven Basic Approach Positions

7-pin position   Key Pin is the 7-pin
4-pin position   Key Pin is the 4-pin
2-pin position   Key Pin is the 2 or 8-pin

STRIKE POSITION   Key Pin is the 1 or 5-pin

3-pin position   Key Pin is the 3 or 9-pin
6-pin position   Key Pin is the 6-pin
10-pin position   Key Pin is the 10-pin

These Seven Basic Approach Positions are appropriate for spare leaves in which the key pin is to be contacted on either the right or left side, but not for Head-On hits. For example, a 3-board shift to the left of the 7-pin position is used to hit the 4-pin on the left side. A 6-board shift is used to hit the 2-pin on the left side. But what about a Head-On hit on the 4-pin? A shift of 3 boards is not enough, and 6 boards is too much. A shift of 4½ boards would seem to be just about the right amount of change in the approach position to hit the 4-pin head-on, assuming that you do not change the target on the lanes.

To explain further, a 3-board shift to the left of the STRIKE POSITION is used to hit the 3-pin on the left side (or the 1-pin on the right side). A 6-board shift in the approach position (to the left) is used to hit the 6-pin on the left side (or the 3-pin on the right side). Therefore, it follows that a 4½ board shift to the left would give the approach position needed to contact the 3-pin head-on. A 7½ board shift to the left would give the approach position needed to contact the 6-pin head-on.

Thus, the Seven Basic Approach Positions can be *expanded* to include all hits on the key pins in the probable spares—right side, left side, and head-on. Exhibit 18 does exactly that. *It expands the Seven Basic Approach Positions into 14 approach positions, one for each of the 14 Spare Zones.*

Exhibit 18 gives the appearance of a very precise system for determining the approach position for every

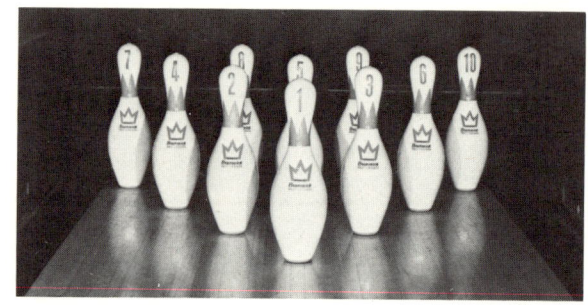

probable spare leave. You may have to make some further adjustments, but you will have some basis for making the adjustments.

Please note that all adjustments are made to the left, and in increments of 1½ boards. Therefore, it should be relatively easy to calculate any approach position from either the STRIKE POSITION or the 7-PIN POSITION. If the spare leave calls for a right or left hit, then the approach position will be a shift of 3, 6, or 9 boards, as in the basic system. If a Head-On hit is needed, then a further shift of 1½ boards will have to be made. For example, if the spare calls for a Head-On 2-pin hit, shift 6-boards to the left as in the basic system. Then shift an additional 1½ boards to the left for the Head-On hit. Once you learn the Seven Basic Approach Positions it is a relatively simple matter to add the 1½ board shift to adjust for the Head-On hits.

APPROACH POSITIONS AND TARGETS: *The 2-4-6 Spare System*

Only two items will appear for any probable spare under "Approach Position, 2-4-6 Spare System:" (1) Not Used on This Spare, or (2) Strike Position. If (1) appears, then the 2-4-6 System is not normally used on that spare. If (2) appears, then a target change will be indicated. If the 2-4-6 system is being used, then the approach position will be the Strike Position.

In Section I we discussed the 2-4-6 Spare System in some detail. You will recall that the system is used by Left Handed Bowlers who are using the 1st Arrow from the left for their strike ball. Shifting to the left to get the correct approach position for right side spares would not be practical. It would call for lofting the ball out over the channel. A *change in target for right side spares* is a more practical adjustment to make. Therefore, under the 2-4-6 Spare System all right side spares are shot from the STRIKE POSITION, with a 2-board shift of the target *to the right* when the key pin is the 3-pin; a 4-board shift of the target *to the right* when the 6-pin is the key pin; and a 6-board shift of the target *to the right* when the key pin is the 10-pin. Right side spares are handled by using the 3-6-9 system and shifting the approach position as explained previously.

EXHIBIT 18
The Expanded 3-6-9 Spare System
For the *Left* Handed Bowler

The 7 Basic Spare Zones and 7 Head-On Spare Zones require 14 different positions on the approach—one for each zone. (Remember, the target does not change when you use the 3-6-9 Spare System, only the approach position changes.) These 14 approach positions can be determined by simply expanding the basic 3-6-9 Spare System to include all Head-On hits. Each approach position is still a movement to the left from either the STRIKE POSITION or the 7-PIN POSITION. As in the basic 3-6-9 system, these two positions must be found by trial and error, and all other approach positions are calculated as shown below.

SPARE ZONE	APPROACH POSITION FOR THAT SPARE ZONE	
*7-Pin Zone	7-Pin Position: DETERMINED BY TRIAL AND ERROR	USE 7-PIN TARGET
Head-On 7-Pin Zone	1½ Boards to Left of 7-Pin Position	
*4-Pin Zone	3 Boards to Left of 7-Pin Position	
Head-On 4-Pin Zone	4½ Boards to Left of 7-Pin Position	
*2-Pin and 8-Pin Zone	6 Boards to Left of 7-Pin Position	
Head-On 2-Pin and 8-Pin Zone	7½ Boards to Left of 7-Pin Position	
*1-Pin and 5-Pin Zone	Strike Position: DETERMINED BY TRIAL AND ERROR	USE STRIKE TARGET
Head-On 1-Pin and 5-Pin Zone	1½ Boards to Left of Strike Position	
*3-Pin and 9-Pin Zone	3 Boards to Left of Strike Position	
Head-On 3-Pin and 9-Pin Zone	4½ Boards to Left of Strike Position	
*6-Pin Zone	6 Boards to Left of Strike Position	
Head-On 6-Pin Zone	7½ Boards to Left of Strike Position	
*10-Pin Zone	9 Boards to Left of Strike Position	
Head-On 10-Pin Zone	10½ Boards to Left of Strike Position	

*These are the 7 Basic Approach Positions, using the 3-6-9 Spare System!

Notice that all adjustments are *to the left,* and in units of 1½ boards. The target on the lane does not change, normally the 2nd Arrow from the left for the strike ball and right side spares, and the 3rd Arrow from the left for the 7-pin and all left side spares. These targets and adjustments are approximates only. You must take lane conditions into consideration at all times, and adjust for any unusual circumstances. Also, remember to face your target on the lanes and walk toward that target.

These shifts of the target generally result in left side hits on the 3-pin, the 6-pin, and the 10-pin. But what about Head-On hits? Shifting more or less than the 2-board increments is the answer.

Exhibit 19 describes the *Expanded* 2-4-6 Spare System, and gives additional adjustments for right side spares requiring Head-On as well as left or right side hits. This expansion of the system gives the approximate shift in the target for all right side spares.

SUMMARY: This concludes the explanation of the Contact Areas, Spare Zones, and Approach Positions and Targets for the Left Handed Bowlers. You should now be able to understand the material presented for each probable spare. However, it will probably be necessary to review this note from time to time until the material immediately comes to mind when you are faced with a given spare leave. When that happens you will be well on your way to converting a very high percentage of the spares which you normally leave.

EXHIBIT 19
The Expanded 2-4-6 Spare System for the *Left* Handed Bowler

The 2-4-6 Spare System only refers to adjustments of the target (point of aim) by increments of 2 boards for right side spares. On some spare leaves an adjustment of more or less boards may be needed, depending upon the particular spare leave and any problems it might present (such as a chop possibility, unfavorable pin or ball deflection, etc.). The adjustments listed below are approximations only. The way you roll the ball and other personal characteristics or preferences might suggest other adjustments. *Use your strike position on the approach in all cases when you are using the 2-4-6 System. Point your feet and body at the target, and walk toward that target.*

If The Spare Zone Is:	Shift The Target for Right Side Spares:
1-Pin Zone	Use the Strike Target Board
Head-On 1-Pin Zone	Shift Target 1 Board Right of the Strike Target
3-Pin Zone	*Shift Target 2 Boards Right of the Strike Target
Head-On 3-Pin Zone	Shift Target 3 Boards Right of the Strike Target
6-Pin Zone	*Shift Target 4 Boards Right of the Strike Target
Head-On 6-Pin Zone	Shift Target 5 Boards Right of the Strike Target
10-Pin Zone	*Shift Target 6 Boards Right of the Strike Target
Head-On 10-Pin Zone	Shift Target 7 Boards Right of the Strike Target

*These are the normal 2, 4, and 6-Board Adjustments suggested in the 2-4-6 spare system. They have been expanded to provide guidelines for all right side spares, especially those calling for Head-On hits.

Note: A variation of the 2-4-6 System could be used for Left Side Spares, but we prefer to use the system for Right Side Spares only. Once your skill develops, you will be able to adjust any spare system to your style of bowling.

SPARE: 1   Key Pin: **1-Pin**   Spare Number: **1**

Opposite Spare: None

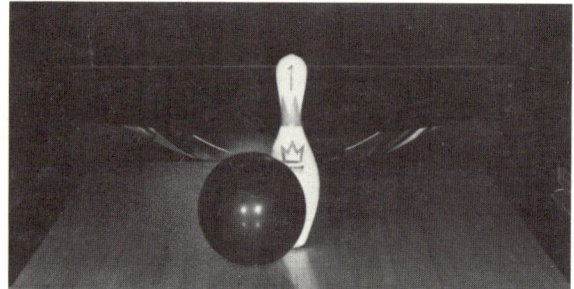 

LEFT HAND BOWLER: *See Page 41*
SPARE ZONE: 1-Pin Zone
CONTACT AREA: Left on 1-Pin
APPROACH POSITIONS AND TARGETS:
3-6-9 System: Strike Position—
                Strike Target
2-4-6 System: Strike Position—
                Strike Target

RIGHT HAND BOWLER: *See Page 34*
SPARE ZONE: 1-Pin Zone
CONTACT AREA: Right on 1-Pin
APPROACH POSITIONS AND TARGETS:
3-6-9 System: Strike Position—
                Strike Target
2-4-6 System: Strike Position—
                Strike Target

Best Way to Convert: (*Head-Pin*)(*King Pin*) These two hits illustrate the *1-Pin Spare Zone* used in this section for both the RHB and LHB. The RHB hits the 1-pin coming into it from the right side, and the LHB hits it coming into it from the left side. Some bowlers prefer to hit the 1-pin in the center. We do not dis- agree with this method for making this spare. But in order to cover the spare without making any adjustment from your normal strike position and target (and to illustrate the 1-Pin Spare Zones) we suggest covering the spare as shown above.

SPARE: 2   Key Pin: **2-Pin**   Spare Number: **2**

Opposite Spare: 3

LEFT HAND BOWLER: *See Page 41*
SPARE ZONE: 2-Pin Zone
CONTACT AREA: Left on 2-Pin
APPROACH POSITIONS AND TARGETS:
3-6-9 System: 2-Pin Position—
                7-Pin Target
2-4-6 System: Not Used on This Spare

RIGHT HAND BOWLER: *See Page 34*
SPARE ZONE: 2-Pin Zone
CONTACT AREA: Right on 2-Pin
APPROACH POSITIONS AND TARGETS:
3-6-9 System: 2-Pin Position—
                Strike Target
2-4-6 System: Strike Position—
                Move Target 2 Boards LEFT

Best Way to Convert: These two hits illustrate the *2-Pin Spare Zone* for both Left-Handed Bowlers and Right-Handed Bowlers. The RHB hits the 2-pin coming into it from the right side, and the LHB comes into it from the left side. This gives the maximum opportunity to cover this Single Pin Spare. Some bowlers prefer to hit the 2-pin more towards the cen- ter. We do not disagree with them, but prefer the hits shown above because these hits demonstrate the 2-Pin Spare Zone, and a similar hit is needed to cover many other spares. You might wish to practice hitting the 2-pin more towards the center, to prepare for those spares requiring such a hit . . . such as the 2-8 Spare.

SPARE: 3   Key Pin: **3-Pin**   Spare Number: **3**

LEFT HAND BOWLER: See Page 41
SPARE ZONE: 3-Pin Zone
CONTACT AREA: Left on 3-Pin
APPROACH POSITIONS AND TARGETS:
3-6-9 System: 3-Pin Position—
               Strike Target
2-4-6 System: Strike Position—
               Move Target 2 Boards RIGHT

RIGHT HAND BOWLER: See Page 34
SPARE ZONE: 3-Pin Zone
CONTACT AREA: Right on 3-Pin
APPROACH POSITIONS AND TARGETS:
3-6-9 System: 3-Pin Position—
               10-Pin Target
2-4-6 System: Not Used on This Spare

Best Way to Convert: These two hits illustrate the *3-Pin Spare Zone* which is used throughout this book. The RHB hits the 3-pin coming into it from the right, but the LHB hits it coming into it from the left. As with the other spares having only a single pin in them, some bowlers prefer to hit a Single Pin Leave more towards the center. We do not disagree with that method for making these spares, but prefer the hits shown above; that is, coming into the pins from the side. Of course, there are times when you want to hit the 3-pin more towards the center (for example, the 3-9 Spare). You might want to practice hitting it more towards the center when you leave it. Such practice should not cause you to miss the spare.

SPARE: 4   Key Pin: **4-Pin**   Spare Number: **4**

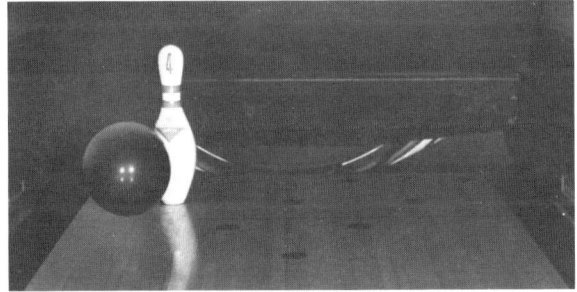

LEFT HAND BOWLER: See Page 41
SPARE ZONE: 4-Pin Zone
CONTACT AREA: Left on 4-Pin
APPROACH POSITIONS AND TARGETS:
3-6-9 System: 4-Pin Position—
               7-Pin Target
2-4-6 System: Not Used on This Spare

RIGHT HAND BOWLER: See Page 34
SPARE ZONE: 4-Pin Zone
CONTACT AREA: Right on 4-Pin
APPROACH POSITIONS AND TARGETS:
3-6-9 System: 4-Pin Position—
               Strike Target
2-4-6 System: Strike Position—
               Move Target 4 Boards LEFT

Best Way to Convert: These hits illustrate the *4-Pin Spare Zone*—for both RHB and LHB—which is used in this book. The RHB hits the 4-pin coming into it from the right side, but the LHB covers it by coming into it from the left side. Since the 4-pin is about 21 inches further back on the Pin Deck than the 1-pin, the tendency might be to hit the pin more towards the center. In fact, many bowlers prefer to cover the 4-pin this way. This is an acceptable way, since the Head-On 4-Pin Zone is used to cover several spares, and trying to hit the pin towards the center will not normally cause you to miss it.

SPARE: 5
Key Pin: 5-Pin
Spare Number: 5
Opposite Spare: None

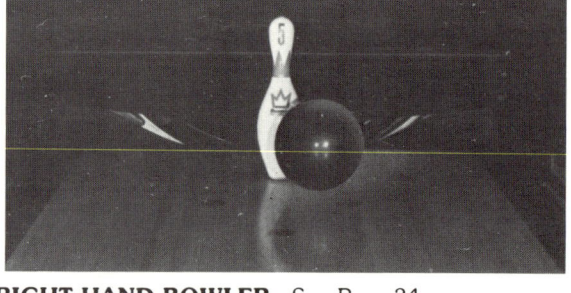

LEFT HAND BOWLER: *See Page 41*
SPARE ZONE: 1-Pin Zone
CONTACT AREA: Left on 5-Pin
APPROACH POSITIONS AND TARGETS:
3-6-9 System: Strike Position—
        Strike Target
2-4-6 System: Strike Position—
        Strike Target

RIGHT HAND BOWLER: *See Page 34*
SPARE ZONE: 1-Pin Zone
CONTACT AREA: Right on 5-Pin
APPROACH POSITIONS AND TARGETS:
3-6-9 System: Strike Position—
        Strike Target
2-4-6 System: Strike Position—
        Strike Target

Best Way to Convert: (*King Pin*) The 5-pin should be one of the easiest spares to make, since both the RHB and LHB have a target of about 13 inches. The pin is about 4½ inches wide at the contact area, and the ball is about 8½ inches in diameter. So, half the diameter of the ball (4¼ inches) on either side of the 5-pin, plus the width of the pin gives an area of about 13 boards to cover the 5-pin. We suggest that the LHB hit the 5-pin coming into it from the left side and the RHB hit is coming into it from the right side. Both could hit it more to the center. Since the 5-pin is about 21 inches directly behind the 1-pin, the 1-Pin Spare Zone is recommended. A 1-board move of the approach position towards center is often used.

SPARE: 6
Key Pin: 6-Pin
Spare Number: 6
Opposite Spare: 4

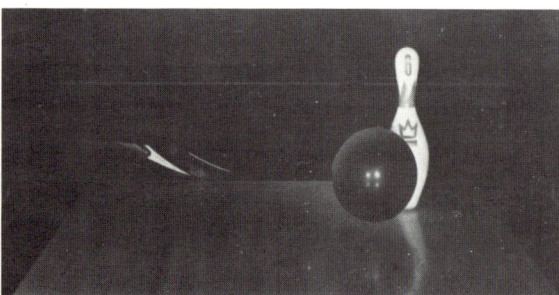

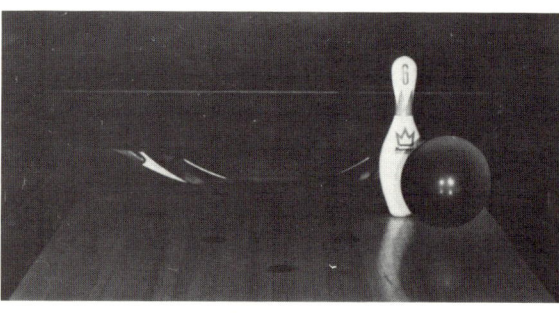

LEFT HAND BOWLER: *See Page 41*
SPARE ZONE: 6-Pin Zone
CONTACT AREA: Left on 6-Pin
APPROACH POSITIONS AND TARGETS:
3-6-9 System: 6-Pin Position—
        Strike Target
2-4-6 System: Strike Position—
        Move Target 4 Boards RIGHT

RIGHT HAND BOWLER: *See Page 34*
SPARE ZONE: 6-Pin Zone
CONTACT AREA: Right on 6-Pin
APPROACH POSITIONS AND TARGETS:
3-6-9 System: 6-Pin Position—
        10-Pin Target
2-4-6 System: Not Used on This Spare

Best Way to Convert: These two hits demonstrate the *6-Pin Spare Zone*—both for the RHB and LHB— which is used in this book. The RHB hits the 6-pin coming into it from the right side, but the LHB covers it by coming into it from the left side. Since the 6-pin is about 21 inches behind the 1-pin on the pin deck, the tendency might be to hit the pin more towards the center. Many bowlers prefer to cover the 6-pin this way. This is fine, since the Head-On 6-Pin Spare Zone is used to cover several spares, and trying to hit the pin towards the center should not normally cause you to miss it.

SPARE: 7   Key Pin: **7-Pin**   Spare Number: **7**

Opposite Spare: 10

LEFT HAND BOWLER: See Page 41
SPARE ZONE: Head-On 7-Pin Zone
CONTACT AREA: Center on 7-Pin
APPROACH POSITIONS AND TARGETS:
3-6-9 System: Head-On 7-Pin Position—
          7-Pin Target
2-4-6 System: Not Used on This Spare

RIGHT HAND BOWLER: See Page 34
SPARE ZONE: 7-Pin Zone
CONTACT AREA: Right on 7-Pin
APPROACH POSITIONS AND TARGETS:
3-6-9 System: 7-Pin Position—
          Strike Target
2-4-6 System: Strike Position—
          Move Target 6 Boards LEFT

Best Way to Convert: (*Mother-In-Law*) The 7-pin is the most "feared" Single Pin Spare for the LHB because the Channel (gutter) is so close. The 7-pin is a relatively easy spare for the RHB, and he or she should hit it coming into it from the right. The LHB should hit the 7-pin more towards the center. These two hits show the Head-On (LHB) and Basic (RHB) 7-Pin Spare Zones used in this book. (Actually, both the LHB and RHB could hit the 7-pin near the center!) The LHB should determine the approach position and target to cover the 7-pin PRIOR to EACH bowling session. Then the 3-6-9 Spare Shooting System can be used to cover all of the left side spares which might occur during the session.

SPARE: 8   Key Pin: **8-Pin**   Spare Number: **8**

Opposite Spare: 9

LEFT HAND BOWLER: See Page 41
SPARE ZONE: 2-Pin Zone
CONTACT AREA: Left on 8-Pin
APPROACH POSITIONS AND TARGETS:
3-6-9 System: 2-Pin Position—
          7-Pin Target
2-4-6 System: Not Used on This Spare

RIGHT HAND BOWLER: See Page 34
SPARE ZONE: 2-Pin Zone
CONTACT AREA: Right on 8-Pin
APPROACH POSITIONS AND TARGETS:
3-6-9 System: 2-Pin Position—
          Strike Target
2-4-6 System: Strike Position—
          Strike Target

Best Way to Convert: Since the 8-pin is directly behind the 2-pin, shooting for both pins is similar. The *2-Pin Spare Zone* is used. However, the 8-pin is over 21 inches further back on the Pin Deck. Some small adjustment in the target or approach position might have to be made to cover the 8-pin instead of the 2-pin. The LHB should try to hit the 8-pin coming into it from the left, but the RHB should hit it coming into it from the right. Hitting the 8-Pin Head-On is also acceptable, and will be the kind of hit needed to cover the difficult 2-8-Pin Leave.

SPARE: 9   Key Pin: **9-Pin**   Spare Number: **9**

Opposite Spare: **8**

9

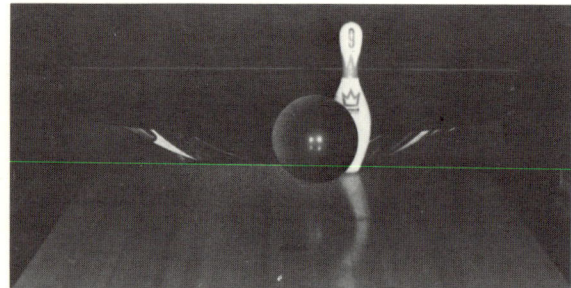 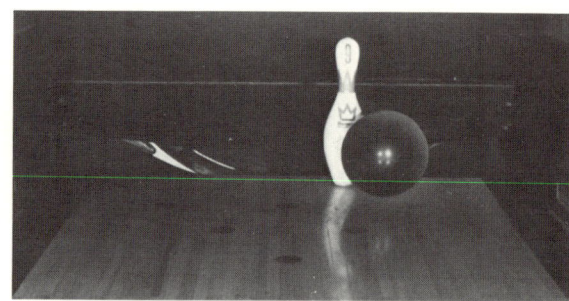

LEFT HAND BOWLER: See Page 41
SPARE ZONE: 3-Pin Zone
CONTACT AREA: Left on 9-Pin
APPROACH POSITIONS AND TARGETS:
3-6-9 System: 3-Pin Position—
                 Strike Target
2-4-6 System: Strike Position—
                 Strike Target

RIGHT HAND BOWLER: See Page 34
SPARE ZONE: 3-Pin Zone
CONTACT AREA: Right on 9-Pin
APPROACH POSITIONS AND TARGETS:
3-6-9 System: 3-Pin Position—
                 10-Pin Target
2-4-6 System: Not Used on This Spare

Best Way to Convert: Since the 9-pin is directly behind the 3-pin, shooting for both pins is similar. The *3-Pin Spare Zone* is used. Keep in mind, however that the 9-pin is over 21 inches further back on the Pin Deck. Some small adjustment in the target or approach position might have to be made to cover the 9-pin instead of the 3-pin. The RHB should hit the 9-pin coming into it from the right, but the LHB hits it coming into it from the left. Hitting the 9-Pin Head-On is also acceptable. This is the kind of hit needed to cover the difficult 3-9-Pin Tandem Leave.

1

SPARE: 10   Key Pin: **10-Pin**   Spare Number: **10**

Opposite Spare: **7**

10

LEFT HAND BOWLER: See Page 41
SPARE ZONE: 10-Pin Zone
CONTACT AREA: Left on 10-Pin
APPROACH POSITIONS AND TARGETS:
3-6-9 System: 10-Pin Position—
                 Strike Target
2-4-6 System: Strike Position—
                 Move Target 6 Boards RIGHT

RIGHT HAND BOWLER: See Page 34
SPARE ZONE: Head-On 10-Pin Zone
CONTACT AREA: Center on 10-Pin
APPROACH POSITIONS AND TARGETS:
3-6-9 System: Head-On 10-Pin Position—
                 10-Pin Target
2-4-6 System: Not Used on This Spare

Best Way to Convert: The 10-pin is the most "feared" Single Pin Spare for the RHB because the Channel (gutter) is so close. The 10-pin is relatively easy for the LHB, and he or she should hit it coming into it from the left. The RHB should hit the 10-pin more towards the center. These two hits demonstrate the Basic (LHB) and Head-On 10-Pin Spare Zones used in this book. (Actually, both the LHB and RHB could hit the 10-pin near the center!) The RHB should determine the approach position and target to cover the 10-pin PRIOR to EACH bowling session. Then, the 3-6-9 Spare Shooting System can be used to determine the best way to cover all of the right side spares which occur during the session.

SPARE: 1-2   Key Pin: **1-Pin**   Spare Number: **11**

Opposite Spare: 12

1
2

LEFT HAND BOWLER: See Page 41
SPARE ZONE: 1-Pin Zone
CONTACT AREA: Left on 1-Pin
APPROACH POSITIONS AND TARGETS:
3-6-9 System: Strike Position—
Strike Target
2-4-6 System: Strike Position—
Strike Target

RIGHT HAND BOWLER: See Page 34
SPARE ZONE: 1-Pin Zone
CONTACT AREA: Right on 1-Pin
APPROACH POSITIONS AND TARGETS:
3-6-9 System: Strike Position—
Strike Target
2-4-6 System: Strike Position—
Strike Target

Best Way to Convert: (*LHB Pocket*) (*Hole*) (*RHB Brooklyn Side*) This is one of six similar spares with chop possibilities for the LHB and giving the RHB an option to cover both pins with the ball. (The RHB can also chop, but it is less likely.) The LHB should hit the 1-pin on the left to cover both pins with the ball. The RHB should hit the 1-pin on the right, driving it into the 2-pin. The probability of a chop is not likely with both the pin and ball heading towards the 2-pin. The RHB could also cover both pins with the ball as shown for the LHB, and many prefer to do so. A full hit on the 1-pin could result in a chop for either bowler. (See the 2-4; 3-5; 4-7; 5-8; and 6-9 Spares which are played similarly.)

2

SPARE: 1-3   Key Pin: **1-Pin**   Spare Number: **12**

Opposite Spare: 11

1
3

LEFT HAND BOWLER: See Page 41
SPARE ZONE: 1-Pin Zone
CONTACT AREA: Left on 1-Pin
APPROACH POSITIONS AND TARGETS:
3-6-9 System: Strike Position—
Strike Target
2-4-6 System: Strike Position—
Strike Target

RIGHT HAND BOWLER: See Page 34
SPARE ZONE: 1-Pin Zone
CONTACT AREA: Right on 1-Pin
APPROACH POSITIONS AND TARGETS:
3-6-9 System: Strike Position—
Strike Target
2-4-6 System: Strike Position—
Strike Target

Best Way to Convert: (*Hole*)(*RHB Pocket*)(*LHB Brooklyn Side*) This is one of six similar Spare Leaves with chop possibilities for the RHB and giving the LHB an option to cover both pins with the ball or to hit the left side of the front pin. The RHB should hit the right side of the 1-pin to cover both pins with the ball. A full hit on the 1-pin might chop off the 1-pin. The LHB should hit the 1-pin on the left, driving that pin into the 3-pin. The probability of a chop is less with the ball and pin heading to the right. The LHB could also cover both pins with the ball by hitting the 1-pin on the right (see the RHB hit) and using the 3-Pin Spare Zone and 3-Pin Approach Position. (See the 2-5; 3-6; 4-8; 5-9; and 6-10 Spares.)

SPARE: 1-4   Key Pin: Imaginary **2-Pin**   Spare Number: **13**

Opposite Spare: 15

LEFT HAND BOWLER: *See Page 41*
SPARE ZONE: Head-On 2-Pin Zone
CONTACT AREA: Far Left on 1-Pin
APPROACH POSITIONS AND TARGETS:
3-6-9 System: Head-On 2-Pin Position—
           7-Pin Target
2-4-6 System: Not Used on This Spare

RIGHT HAND BOWLER: *See Page 34*
SPARE ZONE: Head-On 2-Pin Zone
CONTACT AREA: Far Left on 1-Pin
APPROACH POSITIONS AND TARGETS:
3-6-9 System: Head-On 2-Pin Position—
           Strike Target
2-4-6 System: Strike Position—
           Move Target 3 Boards LEFT

Best Way to Convert: The ball should cover both pins on this spare. Hit the 1-pin on the far left so that the ball will deflect to the left into the 4-pin. Ball deflection favors the RHB on this spare, since the ball is heading towards the left and must deflect left. The LHB should use the Head-On 2-Pin Approach Position to increase ball deflection off the 1-pin. This is not a split since the 1-pin is still standing.

SPARE: 1-5   Key Pin: **1-Pin**   Spare Number: **14**

Opposite Spare: None

LEFT HAND BOWLER: *See Page 41*
SPARE ZONE: Head-On 1-Pin Zone
CONTACT AREA: Center on 1-Pin
APPROACH POSITIONS AND TARGETS:
3-6-9 System: Head-On 1-Pin Position—
           Strike Target
2-4-6 System: Strike Position—
           Move Target 1 Board RIGHT

RIGHT HAND BOWLER: *See Page 34*
SPARE ZONE: Head-On 1-Pin Zone
CONTACT AREA: Center on 1-Pin
APPROACH POSITIONS AND TARGETS:
3-6-9 System: Head-On 1-Pin Position—
           Strike Target
2-4-6 System: Strike Position—
           Move Target 1 Board LEFT

Best Way to Convert: (*Double Wood*) (*Sleeper*)(*Tandem*)(*One in the Dark*) This is one of three similar Spare Leaves, all very difficult spares. The hit illustrates the Head-On 1-Pin Spare Zone, a hit needed to cover several difficult spare leaves. Hit the 1-Pin Head-On so that both the pin and ball drive back into the 5-pin. Hitting the 1-pin on either side may produce a miss, as the ball goes to one side of the 5-pin and the 1-pin goes by the opposite side. Many bowlers "shoot through" the 1-pin, aiming for the 5-pin. A ball heading for the center of the 5-pin will cover this tough spare. (See the 2-8 and 3-9-Pin Spares.)

SPARE: 1-6

Key Pin: Imaginary **3-Pin**

Spare Number: 15
Opposite Spare: 13

LEFT HAND BOWLER: See Page 41
SPARE ZONE: Head-On 3-Pin Zone
CONTACT AREA: Far Right on 1-Pin
APPROACH POSITIONS AND TARGETS:
3-6-9 System: Head-On 3-Pin Position—
                 Strike Target
2-4-6 System: Strike Position—
                 Move Target 3 Boards RIGHT

RIGHT HAND BOWLER: See Page 34
SPARE ZONE: Head-On 3-Pin Zone
CONTACT AREA: Far Right on 1-Pin
APPROACH POSITIONS AND TARGETS:
3-6-9 System: Head-On 3-Pin Position—
                 10-Pin Target
2-4-6 System: Not Used on This Spare

Best Way to Convert: The ball should cover both pins on this spare, which is *not* a split since the 1-pin is still standing. Hit the 1-pin on the far right so that the ball deflects to the right into the 6-pin. Ball deflection favors the LHB on this spare, since the ball is coming to the right and has to deflect to the right. The RHB should use the suggested Head-On 3-Pin Approach Position to increase ball deflection off the 1-pin.

SPARE: 1-7

Key Pin: **1-Pin**

Spare Number: 16
Opposite Spare: 19

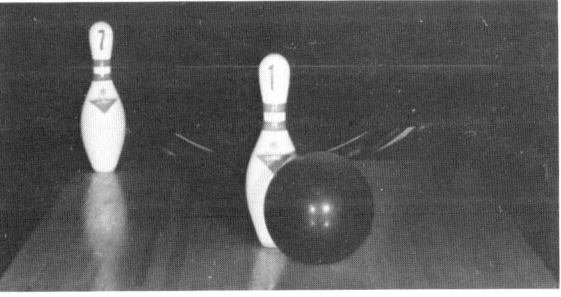

LEFT HAND BOWLER: See Page 41
SPARE ZONE: 3-Pin Zone
CONTACT AREA: Right on 1-Pin
APPROACH POSITIONS AND TARGETS:
3-6-9 System: 3-Pin Position—
                 Strike Target
2-4-6 System: Strike Position—
                 Move Target 2 Boards RIGHT

RIGHT HAND BOWLER: See Page 34
SPARE ZONE: 1-Pin Zone
CONTACT AREA: Right on 1-Pin
APPROACH POSITIONS AND TARGETS:
3-6-9 System: Strike Position—
                 Strike Target
2-4-6 System: Strike Position—
                 Strike Target

Best Way to Convert: (*Washout*) This is not a split since the 1-pin is still standing, but it is just as difficult as many splits. It is one of many Left Side Washouts, where the 2 and 4-pins are down and the 1 and 7-pins are standing. Accurate pin deflection is needed to make this spare. Hit the 1-pin on the right side and send it into the 7-pin. A far right hit on the 1-pin might send it off the kickback and into the 7-pin, but this method is less accurate and not recommended. Also, some RHB could hit the 1-pin on the left side and deflect the ball into the 7-pin. Too much ball deflection is needed, so this method is not recommended either.

SPARE: 1-8   Key Pin: **1-Pin**   Spare Number: **17**

Opposite Spare: **18**

LEFT HAND BOWLER: *See Page 41*
SPARE ZONE: 1-Pin Zone
CONTACT AREA: Left on 1-Pin
APPROACH POSITIONS AND TARGETS:
3-6-9 System: Strike Position—
Strike Target
2-4-6 System: Strike Position—
Strike Target

RIGHT HAND BOWLER: *See Page 34*
SPARE ZONE: Head-On 1-Pin Zone
CONTACT AREA: Right Center on 1-Pin
APPROACH POSITIONS AND TARGETS:
3-6-9 System: Head-On 1-Pin Position—
Strike Target
2-4-6 System: Strike Position—
Move Target 1 Board LEFT

Best Way to Convert: Cover both pins with the ball. Ball deflection is a big factor in this spare, especially for the RHB. The LHB should hit the 1-pin on the left side so that the ball continues on back into the 8-pin. The RHB should hit the 1-pin more to right center so that the ball and 1-pin will continue through and take out the 8-pin. A light hit on the right side for a LHB or RHB (or a full hit by the LHB) could result in a miss, with the 8-pin still standing. The RHB might "shoot through" the spare, by aiming for the 8-pin. Many LHB move 9 Boards to the left of their 7-Pin Position to increase ball deflection off the 1-pin.

SPARE: 1-9   Key Pin: **1-Pin**   Spare Number: **18**

Opposite Spare: **17**

LEFT HAND BOWLER: *See Page 41*
SPARE ZONE: Head-On 1-Pin Zone
CONTACT AREA: Left Center on 1-Pin
APPROACH POSITIONS AND TARGETS:
3-6-9 System: Head-On 1-Pin Position—
Strike Target
2-4-6 System: Strike Position—
Move Target 1 Board RIGHT

RIGHT HAND BOWLER: *See Page 34*
SPARE ZONE: 1-Pin Zone
CONTACT AREA: Right on 1-Pin
APPROACH POSITIONS AND TARGETS:
3-6-9 System: Strike Position—
Strike Target
2-4-6 System: Strike Position—
Strike Target

Best Way to Convert: Cover both pins with the ball. Ball deflection is a big factor in this spare, especially for the LHB. The RHB should hit the 1-pin on the right side so the ball will deflect slightly to the right and into the 9-pin. The LHB should hit the 1-pin more to left center to drive the ball and the pin back into the 9-pin. Many LHB "shoot through" the spare by aiming for the 9-pin, similar to the 3-9 Tandem Leave. A light hit on the left side of the 1-pin for a RHB or LHB (or a full hit by the RHB) could result in a miss with the 9-pin still standing. Many RHB shift 9 Boards to the right of their 10-Pin Position to increase ball deflection off the 1-pin.

SPARE: 1-10

LEFT HAND BOWLER: See Page 41
SPARE ZONE: 1-Pin Zone
CONTACT AREA: Left on 1-Pin
APPROACH POSITIONS AND TARGETS:
3-6-9 System: Strike Position—
          Strike Target
2-4-6 System: Strike Position—
          Strike Target

RIGHT HAND BOWLER: See Page 34
SPARE ZONE: 2-Pin Zone
CONTACT AREA: Left on 1-Pin
APPROACH POSITIONS AND TARGETS:
3-6-9 System: 2-Pin Position—
          Strike Target
2-4-6 System: Strike Position—
          Move Target 2 Boards LEFT

Best Way to Convert: (*Washout*) This is not a split since the 1-pin is still standing, but it is just as difficult as many splits. It is one of many Right Side Washouts, where the 3 and 6-pins are down and the 1 and 10-pins are up. An accurate hit is needed. Hit the 1-pin on the left side and send it into the 10-pin. (A far left hit might get the 10-pin off the kickback, but this way is not suggested.) Some LHB could hit the 1-pin on the far right and deflect the ball into the 10-pin. Too much ball deflection is needed, so this method is not recommended either.

SPARE: 2-3

LEFT HAND BOWLER: See Page 41
SPARE ZONE: Head-On 1-Pin Zone
CONTACT AREA: Between 2 and 3-Pins
APPROACH POSITIONS AND TARGETS:
3-6-9 System: Head-On 1-Pin Position—
          Strike Target
2-4-6 System: Strike Position—
          Move Target 1 Board RIGHT

RIGHT HAND BOWLER: See Page 34
SPARE ZONE: Head-On 1-Pin Zone
CONTACT AREA: Between 2 and 3-Pins
APPROACH POSITIONS AND TARGETS:
3-6-9 System: Head-On 1-Pin Position—
          Strike Target
2-4-6 System: Strike Position—
          Move Target 1 Board LEFT

Best Way to Convert: This is one of several similar spares requiring a hit directly between two pins standing beside each other. There is a little more than 7 inches gap between the pins, and the ball is just over 8½ inches in width. This leaves about 3/4 of an inch on either side of the ball to cover this split.* Try to "fit the ball" exactly between the 2 and 3-pins. As indicated, aim for an imaginary 1-pin. (See the 4-5; 5-6; 7-8; 8-9; and 9-10 similar Splits.) *To be precise: the gap is 7.23 inches; the ball is 8.59 inches wide; and there is .68 of an inch overlap to contact the two pins!*

SPARE: 2-4   Key Pin: **2-Pin**   Spare Number: **21**

LEFT HAND BOWLER: See Page 41
SPARE ZONE: 2-Pin Zone
CONTACT AREA: Left on 2-Pin
APPROACH POSITIONS AND TARGETS:
3-6-9 System: 2-Pin Position—
            7-Pin Target
2-4-6 System: Not Used on This Spare

RIGHT HAND BOWLER: See Page 34
SPARE ZONE: 2-Pin Zone
CONTACT AREA: Right on 2-Pin
APPROACH POSITIONS AND TARGETS:
3-6-9 System: 2-Pin Position—
            Strike Target
2-4-6 System: Strike Position—
            Move Target 2 Boards LEFT

Best Way to Convert: This is one of six similar spares with chop possibilities for the LHB and giving the RHB an option to cover both pins with the ball. (The RHB could also chop, but it is less likely.) The LHB should hit the 2-pin on the left to cover both pins with the ball. The RHB should hit the 2-pin on the right, driving it into the 4-pin. The probability of a chop is not likely with the pin and ball both heading towards the 4-pin. The RHB could cover both pins with the ball as shown for the LHB, and many prefer to do so. A full hit on the 2-pin could result in a chop for either bowler. (See the 1-2; 3-5; 4-7; 5-8; and 6-9 Spares.)

SPARE: 2-5   Key Pin: **2-Pin**   Spare Number: **22**

LEFT HAND BOWLER: See Page 41
SPARE ZONE: 2-Pin Zone
CONTACT AREA: Left on 2-Pin
APPROACH POSITIONS AND TARGETS:
3-6-9 System: 2-Pin Position—
            7-Pin Target
2-4-6 System: Not Used on This Spare

RIGHT HAND BOWLER: See Page 34
SPARE ZONE: 2-Pin Zone
CONTACT AREA: Right on 2-Pin
APPROACH POSITIONS AND TARGETS:
3-6-9 System: 2-Pin Position—
            Strike Target
2-4-6 System: Strike Position—
            Move Target 2 Boards LEFT

Best Way to Convert: This is one of six similar Spare Leaves with chop possibilities for the RHB. All give the LHB the option to cover both pins with the ball or to hit the left side of the front pin. The RHB should cover both pins with the ball by hitting the 2-pin on the right side. A hit too much to the center of the 2-pin might leave the 5-pin—a chop. The LHB should hit the 2-pin on the left and drive that pin into the 5-pin. There is little chance for a chop from this angle, although a light hit could bring a miss. The LHB could cover both pins with the ball by hitting the 2-pin on the right side, using the 1-Pin Spare Zone and Approach Position. (See the 1-3; 3-6; 4-8; 5-9; and 6-10 Spares.)

SPARE: 2-6   Key Pin: **2-Pin**   Spare Number: **23-S**

Opposite Spare: 28-S

LEFT HAND BOWLER: *See Page 41*
SPARE ZONE: Head-On 4-Pin Zone
CONTACT AREA: Far Left on 2-Pin
APPROACH POSITIONS AND TARGETS:
3-6-9 System: Head-On 4-Pin Position—
          7-Pin Target
2-4-6 System: Not Used on This Spare

RIGHT HAND BOWLER: *See Page 34*
SPARE ZONE: Head-On 4-Pin Zone
CONTACT AREA: Far Left on 2-Pin
APPROACH POSITIONS AND TARGETS:
3-6-9 System: Head-On 4-Pin Position—
          Strike Target
2-4-6 System: Strike Position—
          Move Target 5 Boards LEFT

Best Way to Convert: Keep Pin Count In Mind! Proper pin deflection and an accurate hit are both needed to make this difficult split. Try for this spare in the same way you would shoot for the 2-7 Baby Split, since a hit that would convert the 2-7 would probably cover this split. Hit the 2-pin on the far left as shown and slide it across the lane into the 6-pin. Make sure you hit the 2-pin to get maximum pin count should you miss the split. (See the 2-7 Baby Split below.)

SPARE: 2-7   Key Pin: Imaginary **4-Pin**   Spare Number: **24-S**

Opposite Spare: 34-S

LEFT HAND BOWLER: *See Page 41*
SPARE ZONE: Head-On 4-Pin Zone
CONTACT AREA: Far Left on 2-Pin
APPROACH POSITIONS AND TARGETS:
3-6-9 System: Head-On 4-Pin Position—
          7-Pin Target
2-4-6 System: Not Used on This Spare

RIGHT HAND BOWLER: *See Page 34*
SPARE ZONE: Head-On 4-Pin Zone
CONTACT AREA: Far Left on 2-Pin
APPROACH POSITIONS AND TARGETS:
3-6-9 System: Head-On 4-Pin Position—
          Strike Target
2-4-6 System: Strike Position—
          Move Target 5 Boards LEFT

Best Way to Convert: *(Baby Split-LHB)(Murphy)* The ball should cover both pins in this split. Hit the 2-pin on the far left side so the ball deflects to the left and into the 7-pin. Ball deflection favors the RHB, since a ball coming from the right and hitting the pin on the left side will deflect more than one coming from the left side. This gives the RHB a slight edge in being able to convert this Baby Split. On occasion the LHB will roll the ball between both pins without touching either one. (See the 3-10 Baby Split, where the LHB has a slight advantage.)

SPARE: 2-8   Key Pin: **2-Pin**   Spare Number: **25**

Opposite Spare: 33

LEFT HAND BOWLER: See Page 41
SPARE ZONE: Head-On 2-Pin Zone
CONTACT AREA: Center on 2-Pin
APPROACH POSITIONS AND TARGETS:
3-6-9 System: Head-On 2-Pin Position—
7-Pin Target
2-4-6 System: Not Used on This Spare

RIGHT HAND BOWLER: See Page 34
SPARE ZONE: Head-On 2-Pin Zone
CONTACT AREA: Center on 2-Pin
APPROACH POSITIONS AND TARGETS:
3-6-9 System: Head-On 2-Pin Position—
Strike Target
2-4-6 System: Strike Position—
Move Target 3 Boards LEFT

Best Way to Convert: *(Double Wood)* *(Sleeper)(Tandem)(One in the Dark)* This is one of three similar Spare Leaves, all needing very accurate hits. The hit illustrates the Head-On 2-Pin Spare Zone, a zone used to cover several difficult spares. Hit the 2-Pin Head-On so that both the pin and the ball drive back into the 8-pin. If the 2-pin is hit on either side, the ball may be deflected to one side of the 8-pin and the 2-pin will go by the other side—resulting in a miss. Many top bowlers "shoot through" the 2-pin, aiming for the 8-pin. A ball heading towards the center of the 8-pin will probably convert this difficult spare. (See the 1-5 and 3-9 Spares.)

SPARE: 2-9   Key Pin: RHB: **2-Pin**   Spare Number: **26-S**

LHB: Imaginary **5-Pin**   Opposite Spare: 32-S

LEFT HAND BOWLER: See Page 41
SPARE ZONE: Head-On 1-Pin Zone
CONTACT AREA: Far Right on 2-Pin
APPROACH POSITIONS AND TARGETS:
3-6-9 System: Head-On 1-Pin Position—
Strike Target
2-4-6 System: Strike Position—
Move Target 1 Board RIGHT

RIGHT HAND BOWLER: See Page 34
SPARE ZONE: Head-On 4-Pin Zone
CONTACT AREA: Left on 2-Pin
APPROACH POSITIONS AND TARGETS:
3-6-9 System: Head-On 4-Pin Position—
Strike Target
2-4-6 System: Strike Position—
Move Target 5 Boards LEFT

Best Way to Convert: This unusual split presents problems for the RHB. The LHB should hit the far right side of the 2-pin so the ball will deflect to the right into the 9-pin. The RHB could use the same hit, but ball deflection is working against him or her, and the 9-pin might not be covered with the ball. The RHB could (a) hit the 2-pin as shown and send it into the 9-pin, or (b) hit the 2-pin on the right side as shown for the LHB but use a left side approach. Slower ball speed would increase deflection off the 2-pin into the 9-pin.

SPARE: 2-10 Key Pin: **2-Pin** Spare Number: **27-S**

Opposite Spare: 31-S

LEFT HAND BOWLER: See Page 41
SPARE ZONE: Head-On 4-Pin Zone
CONTACT AREA: Far Left on 2-Pin
APPROACH POSITIONS AND TARGETS:
3-6-9 System: Head-On 4-Pin Position—
7-Pin Target
2-4-6 System: Not Used on This Spare

RIGHT HAND BOWLER: See Page 34
SPARE ZONE: Head-On 4-Pin Zone
CONTACT AREA: Far Left on 2-Pin
APPROACH POSITIONS AND TARGETS:
3-6-9 System: Head-On 4-Pin Position—
Strike Target
2-4-6 System: Strike Position—
Move Target 5 Boards LEFT

Best Way to Convert: Keep Pin Count In Mind! Proper pin deflection and a precise hit are needed to make this difficult split. It can be made and should be attempted. Play it as you would the 2-7 Baby Split. Hit the 2-pin on the far left as shown and slide it across the lane into the 10-pin. Make sure you hit the 2-pin in your attempt, so you will get maximum pin count should you not make the split. (See the 2-7 Baby Split.)

SPARE: 3-4 Key Pin: **3-Pin** Spare Number: **28-S**

Opposite Spare: 23-S

LEFT HAND BOWLER: See Page 41
SPARE ZONE: Head-On 6-Pin Zone
CONTACT AREA: Far Right on 3-Pin
APPROACH POSITIONS AND TARGETS:
3-6-9 System: Head-On 6-Pin Position—
Strike Target
2-4-6 System: Strike Position—
Move Target 5 Boards RIGHT

RIGHT HAND BOWLER: See Page 34
SPARE ZONE: Head-On 6-Pin Zone
CONTACT AREA: Far Right on 3-Pin
APPROACH POSITIONS AND TARGETS:
3-6-9 System: Head-On 6-Pin Position—
10-Pin Target
2-4-6 System: Not Used on This Spare

Best Way to Convert: Keep Pin Count In Mind! Proper pin deflection and a precise hit are needed to make this difficult split. Try for this spare in the same way you would shoot for the 3-10 Baby Split, since a hit that would make the 3-10 would probably cover this split. Hit the 3-pin on the far right as shown and slide it across into the 4-pin. Make sure you hit the 3-pin to get maximum pin count if you miss the spare. (See the 3-10 Split.)

SPARE: 3-5   Key Pin: **3-Pin**   Spare Number: **29**

Opposite Spare: 22

3
5

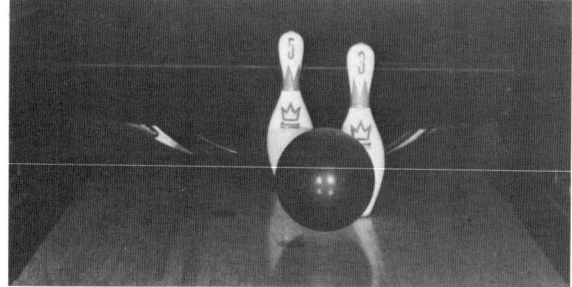

LEFT HAND BOWLER: See Page 41
SPARE ZONE: 3-Pin Zone
CONTACT AREA: Left on 3-Pin
APPROACH POSITIONS AND TARGETS:
3-6-9 System: 3-Pin Position—
          Strike Target
2-4-6 System: Strike Position—
          Move Target 2 Boards RIGHT

RIGHT HAND BOWLER: See Page 34
SPARE ZONE: 3-Pin Zone
CONTACT AREA: Right on 3-Pin
APPROACH POSITIONS AND TARGETS:
3-6-9 System: 3-Pin Position—
          10-Pin Target
2-4-6 System: Not Used on This Spare

Best Way to Convert: This is one of six similar Spare Leaves presenting chop possibilities for the LHB, and giving the RHB two methods for making the spare. The LHB should hit the 3-pin on the left to cover both pins with the ball. The RHB should hit the 3-pin on the right, driving it into the 5-pin. The prob- ability of a chop is not likely with the pin and ball both heading for the 5-pin. The RHB could also cover both pins with the ball as shown for the LHB, and many prefer to do this. A full hit on the 3-pin could result in a chop for either bowler. (See the 1-2; 2-4; 4-7; 5-8; and 6-9 Spares.)

2

SPARE: 3-6   Key Pin: **3-Pin**   Spare Number: **30**

Opposite Spare: 21

3
6

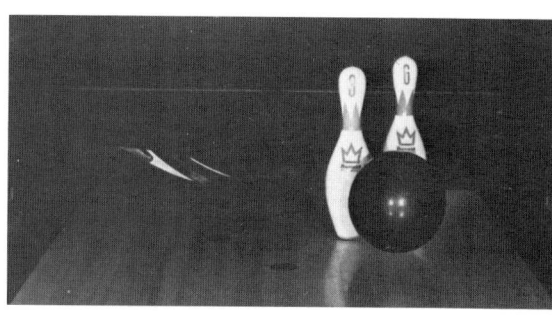

LEFT HAND BOWLER: See Page 41
SPARE ZONE: 3-Pin Zone
CONTACT AREA: Left on 3-Pin
APPROACH POSITIONS AND TARGETS:
3-6-9 System: 3-Pin Position—
          Strike Target
2-4-6 System: Strike Position—
          Move Target 2 Boards RIGHT

RIGHT HAND BOWLER: See Page 34
SPARE ZONE: 3-Pin Zone
CONTACT AREA: Right on 3-Pin
APPROACH POSITIONS AND TARGETS:
3-6-9 System: 3-Pin Position—
          10-Pin Target
2-4-6 System: Not Used on This Spare

Best Way to Convert: This is one of six similar leaves with two pins which have chop possibilities for the RHB. All give the LHB the option to cover both pins with the ball or to hit the left side of the front pin. The RHB should cover both pins with the ball by hitting the 3-pin on the right. A full hit on the 3-pin may result in a chop. The LHB should hit the 3-pin on the left to send it into the 6-pin. There is little chance for a chop using this angle and impact point, al- though a light hit on the left could leave the 6-pin. The LHB could cover both pins with the ball by also hitting the 3-pin on the right side and using the 6-Pin Spare Zone and Approach Position. (See the 1-3; 2-5; 4-8; 5-9; and 6-10 Spares.)

SPARE: 3-7   Key Pin: **3-Pin**   Spare Number: **31-S**

Opposite Spare: 27-S

LEFT HAND BOWLER: See Page 41
SPARE ZONE: Head-On 6-Pin Zone
CONTACT AREA: Far Right on 3-Pin
APPROACH POSITIONS AND TARGETS:
3-6-9 System: Head-On 6-Pin Position—
           Strike Target
2-4-6 System: Strike Position—
           Move Target 5 Boards RIGHT

RIGHT HAND BOWLER: See Page 34
SPARE ZONE: Head-On 6-Pin Zone
CONTACT AREA: Far Right on 3-Pin
APPROACH POSITIONS AND TARGETS:
3-6-9 System: Head-On 6-Pin Position—
           10-Pin Target
2-4-6 System: Not Used on This Spare

Best Way to Convert: Keep Pin Count In Mind! Proper pin deflection and an accurate hit are both needed to make this difficult split. It can be made and should be attempted. Play it as you would the 3-10 Baby Split. Hit the 3-pin on the far right as shown and slide it across the lane into the 7-pin. Make sure you hit the 3-pin on your attempt, so you will get maximum pin count should you miss the spare. (See the 3-10 Baby Split.)

SPARE: 3-8   Key Pin: RHB: Imaginary **5-Pin**   Spare Number: **32-S**

LHB: **3-Pin**   Opposite Spare: 26-S

LEFT HAND BOWLER: See Page 41
SPARE ZONE: Head-On 6-Pin Zone
CONTACT AREA: Right on 3-Pin
APPROACH POSITIONS AND TARGETS:
3-6-9 System: Head-On 6-Pin Position—
           Strike Target
2-4-6 System: Strike Position—
           Move Target 5 Boards RIGHT

RIGHT HAND BOWLER: See Page 34
SPARE ZONE: Head-On 1-Pin Zone
CONTACT AREA: Far Left on 3-Pin
APPROACH POSITIONS AND TARGETS:
3-6-9 System: Head-On 1-Pin Position—
           Strike Target
2-4-6 System: Strike Position—
           Move Target 1 Board LEFT

Best Way to Convert: This unusual split presents problems for the LHB. The RHB should hit the 3-pin on the far left as shown so the ball will deflect to the left into the 8-pin. The LHB could use the same hit, but ball deflection is working against him or her, and the 8-pin might not be taken out. The LHB could (a) hit the 3-pin on the right as shown to send it into the 8-pin, or (b) hit the 3-pin on the far left but shooting from the right side of the approach to increase ball deflection into the 8-pin. Slower ball speed would increase deflection off the 3-pin into the 8-pin.

SPARE: 3-9   Key Pin: **3-Pin**   Spare Number: **33**

Opposite Spare: 25

LEFT HAND BOWLER: See Page 41
SPARE ZONE: Head-On 3-Pin Zone
CONTACT AREA: Center on 3-Pin
APPROACH POSITIONS AND TARGETS:
3-6-9 System: Head-On 3-Pin Position—
　　　　　　　　Strike Target
2-4-6 System: Strike Position—
　　　　　　　　Move Target 3 Boards RIGHT

RIGHT HAND BOWLER: See Page 34
SPARE ZONE: Head-On 3-Pin Zone
CONTACT AREA: Center on 3-Pin
APPROACH POSITIONS AND TARGETS:
3-6-9 System: Head-On 3-Pin Position—
　　　　　　　　10-Pin Target
2-4-6 System: Not Used on This Spare

Best Way to Convert: (*Double Wood*) (*Sleeper*)(*Tandem*)(*One in the Dark*) This is one of three similar spares, all very difficult to make. The hit illustrates the Head-On 3-Pin Spare Zone, a hit used to cover several spares. Hit the 3-Pin directly in the center and drive the pin and ball back into the 9-pin. Hitting the 3-pin on either side may deflect the ball on one side of the 9-pin and the 3-pin on the other side, producing a miss. Many top bowlers "shoot through" the 3-pin, aiming for the 9-pin. A ball that would hit the 9-Pin Head-On will cover this difficult spare. (See the 1-5 and 2-8 Spares.)

SPARE: 3-10   Key Pin: Imaginary **6-Pin**   Spare Number: **34-S**

Opposite Spare: 24-S

LEFT HAND BOWLER: See Page 41
SPARE ZONE: Head-On 6-Pin Zone
CONTACT AREA: Far Right on 3-Pin
APPROACH POSITIONS AND TARGETS:
3-6-9 System: Head-On 6-Pin Position—
　　　　　　　　Strike Target
2-4-6 System: Strike Position—
　　　　　　　　Move Target 5 Boards RIGHT

RIGHT HAND BOWLER: See Page 34
SPARE ZONE: Head-On 6-Pin Zone
CONTACT AREA: Far Right on 3-Pin
APPROACH POSITIONS AND TARGETS:
3-6-9 System: Head-On 6-Pin Position—
　　　　　　　　10-Pin Target
2-4-6 System: Not Used on This Spare

Best Way to Convert: (*Baby Split-RHB*)(*Murphy*) The ball should cover both pins in this split. It is possible for the ball to go between the pins and not touch either one—for a RHB—but almost impossible for the LHB because of the angle of the ball. Hit the 3-pin on the far right side so the ball deflects to the right into the 10-pin. Ball deflection favors the LHB on this spare, giving the LHB a slight edge in converting this split. The RHB has the edge in making the opposite side 2-7 Baby Split. (See the 2-7 Split.)

SPARE: 4-5

Key Pin: Imaginary **2-Pin**

Spare Number: **35-S**

Opposite Spare: 41-S

LEFT HAND BOWLER: See Page 41
SPARE ZONE: Head-On 2-Pin Zone
CONTACT AREA: Between 4 and 5-Pins
APPROACH POSITIONS AND TARGETS:
3-6-9 System: Head-On 2-Pin Position—
          7-Pin Target
2-4-6 System: Not Used on This Spare

RIGHT HAND BOWLER: See Page 34
SPARE ZONE: Head-On 2-Pin Zone
CONTACT AREA: Between 4 and 5-Pins
APPROACH POSITIONS AND TARGETS:
3-6-9 System: Head-On 2-Pin Position—
          Strike Target
2-4-6 System: Strike Position—
          Move Target 3 Boards LEFT

Best Way to Convert: This is the second of six similar Splits having two pins standing beside each other. Try to fit the ball exactly between the 4 and 5-pins, aiming at an imaginary 2-pin. There is a little more than 7 inches gap between the pins, and the ball is just over 8½ inches in width. This leaves only about 3/4 of an inch on each side of the ball to make the split. Trying for this split will not cause you to lose pin count since you should get at least one of the pins. (See the 2-3; 5-6; 7-8; 8-9; and 9-10 Splits.)

SPARE: 4-6

Key Pin: RHB: **6-Pin**
LHB: **4-Pin**

Spare Number: **36-S**

Opposite Spare: None

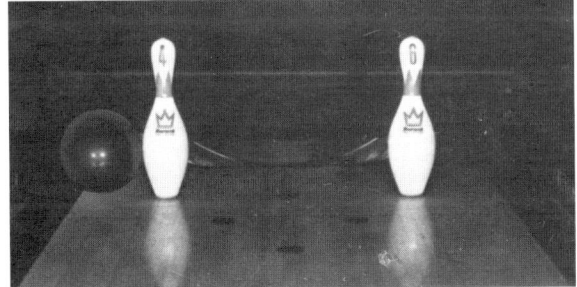 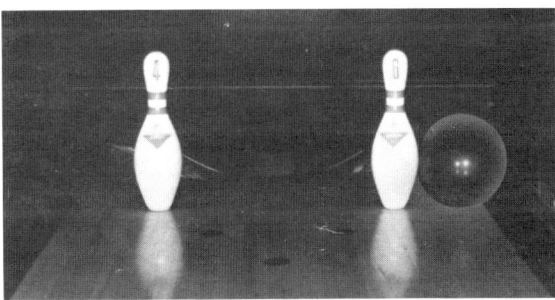

LEFT HAND BOWLER: See Page 41
SPARE ZONE: Head-On 7-Pin Zone
CONTACT AREA: Extreme Left on 4-Pin
APPROACH POSITIONS AND TARGETS:
3-6-9 System: Head-On 7-Pin Position—
          7-Pin Target
2-4-6 System: Not Used on This Spare

RIGHT HAND BOWLER: See Page 34
SPARE ZONE: Head-On 10-Pin Zone
CONTACT AREA: Extreme Right on 6-Pin
APPROACH POSITIONS AND TARGETS:
3-6-9 System: Head-On 10-Pin Position—
          10-Pin Target
2-4-6 System: Not Used on This Spare

Best Way to Convert: Keep Pin Count Firmly in Mind! This split should rarely be attempted; only when a spare is essential. To convert it, the RHB should try to slide the 6-pin across into the 4-pin. The LHB should try to slide the 4-pin into the 6-pin. This was achieved by a LHB on nationwide television exactly that way. Since it was a one-game match, the try was justified and rewarded! Another method is to drive either the 4 or 6-pin into the pit and hope for a lucky bounce out of the pit. Trying for a "nearly impossible" split could cause you to miss both pins. "Take one" is good advice on the 4-6. (Several bowlers have made this split *twice* in the same game, proving that it is not impossible.)

SPARE: 4-7   Key Pin: **4-Pin**   Spare Number: **37**

Opposite Spare: 49

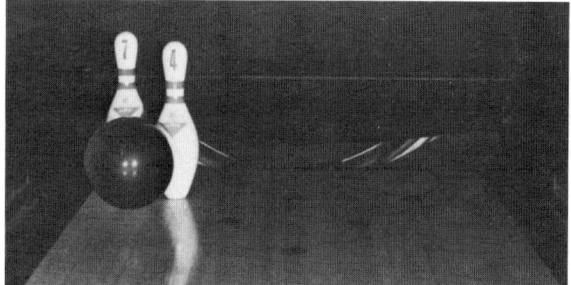 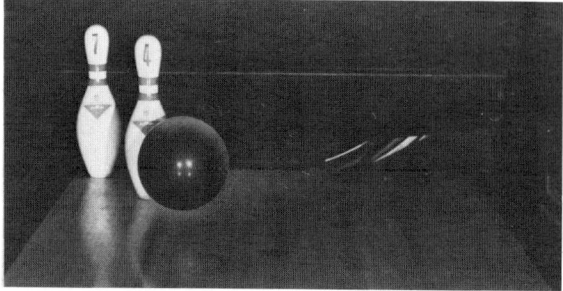

LEFT HAND BOWLER: See Page 41
SPARE ZONE: 4-Pin Zone
CONTACT AREA: Left on 4-Pin
APPROACH POSITIONS AND TARGETS:
3-6-9 System: 4-Pin Position—
             7-Pin Target
2-4-6 System: Not Used on This Spare

RIGHT HAND BOWLER: See Page 34
SPARE ZONE: 4-Pin Zone
CONTACT AREA: Right on 4-Pin
APPROACH POSITIONS AND TARGETS:
3-6-9 System: 4-Pin Position—
             Strike Target
2-4-6 System: Strike Position—
             Move Target 4 Boards LEFT

Best Way to Convert: This is another of the six similar Spare Leaves presenting chop possibilities for the LHB, and giving the RHB two methods for making the spare. The LHB should hit the 4-pin on the left to cover both pins with the ball. The RHB should hit the 4-pin on the right, driving it into the 7-pin. The probability of a chop is not likely with the 4-pin and the ball both heading for the 7-pin. The RHB could also cover both pins with the ball by hitting as shown for the LHB, and many prefer to do this. A full hit on the 4-pin could result in a chop for either bowler. (See the 1-2; 2-4; 3-5; 5-8; and 6-9 Spares.)

SPARE: 4-8   Key Pin: **4-Pin**   Spare Number: **38**

Opposite Spare: 48

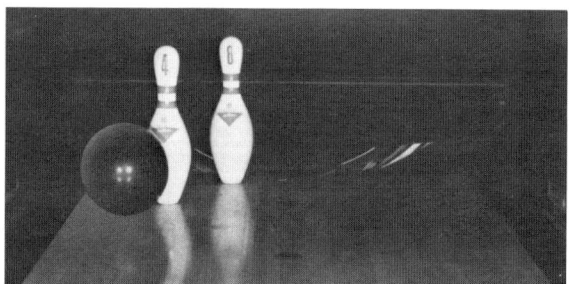 

LEFT HAND BOWLER: See Page 41
SPARE ZONE: 4-Pin Zone
CONTACT AREA: Left on 4-Pin
APPROACH POSITIONS AND TARGETS:
3-6-9 System: 4-Pin Position—
             7-Pin Target
2-4-6 System: Not Used on This Spare

RIGHT HAND BOWLER: See Page 34
SPARE ZONE: 4-Pin Zone
CONTACT AREA: Right on 4-Pin
APPROACH POSITIONS AND TARGETS:
3-6-9 System: 4-Pin Position—
             Strike Target
2-4-6 System: Strike Position—
             Move Target 4 Boards LEFT

Best Way to Convert: This is one of six similar Spare Leaves which have chop possibilities for the RHB and give the LHB the option to hit the front pin on the left side or to cover both pins with the ball. The RHB should cover both pins with the ball by hitting the 4-pin on the right. A full hit on the 4-pin might leave the 8-pin standing—a chop. The LHB should hit the 4-pin on the left to send it into the 8-pin. There is little chance of a chop using this angle, but a light hit left on the 4-pin might leave the 8-pin standing. Or, the LHB could cover both pins by hitting the 4-pin as shown for the RHB, using the 2-Pin Spare Zone and Approach Position. (See the 1-3; 2-5; 3-6; 5-9; and 6-10 Spares.)

SPARE: 4-9

Key Pin: 4-Pin

LEFT HAND BOWLER: See Page 41
SPARE ZONE: Head-On 7-Pin Zone
CONTACT AREA: Far Left on 4-Pin
APPROACH POSITIONS AND TARGETS:
3-6-9 System: Head-On 7-Pin Position—
7-Pin Target
2-4-6 System: Not Used on This Spare

RIGHT HAND BOWLER: See Page 34
SPARE ZONE: Head-On 7-Pin Zone
CONTACT AREA: Far Left on 4-Pin
APPROACH POSITIONS AND TARGETS:
3-6-9 System: Head-On 7-Pin Position—
Strike Target
2-4-6 System: Strike Position—
Move Target 7 Boards LEFT

Best Way to Convert: (*Forty-Niner*) Keep Pin Count In Mind! An accurate hit and proper pin deflection are both needed to convert this difficult split. It can be made and should be attempted. Hit the 4-pin on the far left side as shown in order to slide it across and into the 9-pin. Make sure you hit the 4-pin to get maximum pin count should you not convert the split.

SPARE: 4-10

Key Pin: 4-Pin

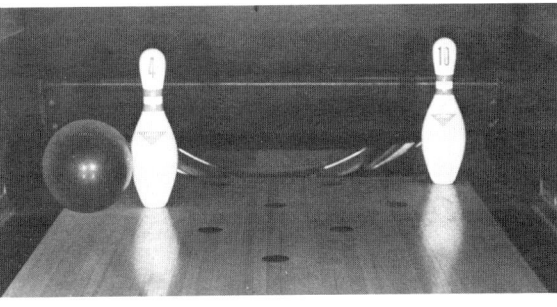

LEFT HAND BOWLER: See Page 41
SPARE ZONE: Head-On 7-Pin Zone
CONTACT AREA: Extreme Left on 4-Pin
APPROACH POSITIONS AND TARGETS:
3-6-9 System: Head-On 7-Pin Position—
7-Pin Target
2-4-6 System: Not Used on This Spare

RIGHT HAND BOWLER: See Page 34
SPARE ZONE: Head-On 7-Pin Zone
CONTACT AREA: Extreme Left on 4-Pin
APPROACH POSITIONS AND TARGETS:
3-6-9 System: Head-On 7-Pin Position—
Strike Target
2-4-6 System: Strike Position—
Move Target 7 Boards LEFT

Best Way to Convert: (*Pinochle*) Keep Pin Count In Mind! A great deal of pin deflection is needed to convert this most difficult split. But, it can be made and should be attempted. Hit the 4-pin on the extreme left side as illustrated and slide it across and into the 10-pin. Make sure you hit the 4-pin so that you will get the maximum count in case you miss the split.

SPARE: 5-6 | Key Pin: Imaginary **3-Pin** | Spare Number: **41-S**

Opposite Spare: 35-S

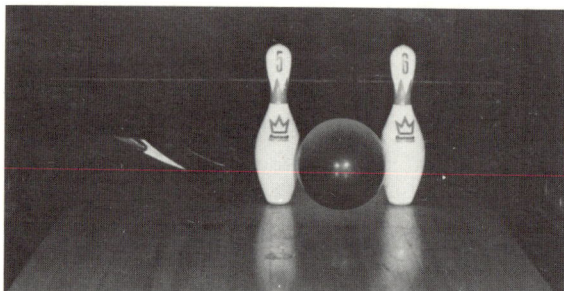

LEFT HAND BOWLER: See Page 41
SPARE ZONE: Head-On 3-Pin Zone
CONTACT AREA: Between 5 and 6-Pins
APPROACH POSITIONS AND TARGETS:
3-6-9 System: Head-On 3-Pin Position—
Strike Target
2-4-6 System: Strike Position—
Move Target 3 Boards RIGHT

RIGHT HAND BOWLER: See Page 34
SPARE ZONE: Head-On 3-Pin Zone
CONTACT AREA: Between 5 and 6-Pins
APPROACH POSITIONS AND TARGETS:
3-6-9 System: Head-On 3-Pin Position—
10-Pin Target
2-4-6 System: Not Used on This Spare

Best Way to Convert: This is another of the six Two-Pin Splits where the pins are standing beside each other. Try to fit the ball directly between the 5 and 6-pins by aiming at an imaginary 3-pin. There is about 3/4 of an inch on either side of the ball to convert the split, which means that a fairly accurate hit is needed to make it. Trying for this split will not cause you to lose any pin count since you should be able to get at least one of them. (See the 2-3; 4-5; 7-8; 8-9; and 9-10 Splits.)

SPARE: 5-7 | Key Pin: **5-Pin** | Spare Number: **42-S**

Opposite Spare: 45-S

LEFT HAND BOWLER: See Page 41
SPARE ZONE: Head-On 3-Pin Zone
CONTACT AREA: Far Right on 5-Pin
APPROACH POSITIONS AND TARGETS:
3-6-9 System: Head-On 3-Pin Position—
Strike Target
2-4-6 System: Strike Position—
Move Target 3 Boards RIGHT

RIGHT HAND BOWLER: See Page 34
SPARE ZONE: Head-On 3-Pin Zone
CONTACT AREA: Far Right on 5-Pin
APPROACH POSITIONS AND TARGETS:
3-6-9 System: Head-On 3-Pin Position—
10-Pin Target
2-4-6 System: Not Used on This Spare

Best Way to Convert: (*Kresge*) Keep Pin Count In Mind! Proper pin deflection and an accurate hit are both needed to make this difficult split. But it can be made and should be attempted. Hit the 5-pin on the far right side as shown and slide it across the lane into the 7-pin. Make sure you hit the 5-pin on your attempt so you will get maximum pin count should you miss the split. The RHB has a slight advantage on this split.

SPARE: 5-8   Key Pin: **5-Pin**   Spare Number: **43**

Opposite Spare: **44**

LEFT HAND BOWLER: See Page 41
SPARE ZONE: Head-On 2-Pin Zone
CONTACT AREA: Left on 5-Pin
APPROACH POSITIONS AND TARGETS:
3-6-9 System: Head-On 2-Pin Position—
            7-Pin Target
2-4-6 System: Not Used on This Spare

RIGHT HAND BOWLER: See Page 34
SPARE ZONE: 1-Pin Zone
CONTACT AREA: Right Center on 5-Pin
APPROACH POSITIONS AND TARGETS:
3-6-9 System: Strike Position—
            Strike Target
2-4-6 System: Strike Position—
            Strike Target

Best Way to Convert: This is another of the six similar Spare Leaves presenting chop possibilities for the LHB, and giving the RHB two methods for making the spare. The LHB should hit the 5-pin on the left to cover both pins with the ball. The RHB should hit the 5-pin on the right, driving it into the 8-pin. The probability of a chop is not likely with the 5-pin and the ball both heading for the 8-pin. The RHB could also cover both pins with the ball by hitting the 5-pin as shown for the LHB, and many prefer to do this. A full hit on the 5-pin could result in a chop for either bowler. (See the 1-2; 2-4; 3-5; 4-7; and 6-9 Spares.)

SPARE: 5-9   Key Pin: **5-Pin**   Spare Number: **44**

Opposite Spare: **43**

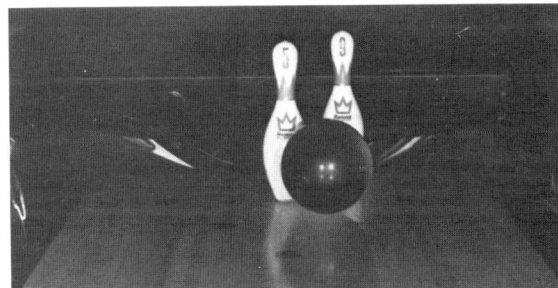

LEFT HAND BOWLER: See Page 41
SPARE ZONE: 1-Pin Zone
CONTACT AREA: Left Center on 5-Pin
APPROACH POSITIONS AND TARGETS:
3-6-9 System: Strike Position—
            Strike Target
2-4-6 System: Strike Position—
            Strike Target

RIGHT HAND BOWLER: See Page 34
SPARE ZONE: Head-On 3-Pin Zone
CONTACT AREA: Right on 5-Pin
APPROACH POSITIONS AND TARGETS:
3-6-9 System: Head-On 3-Pin Position—
            10-Pin Target
2-4-6 System: Not Used on This Spare

Best Way to Convert: This is one of six similar Spares which have chop possibilities for the RHB and give the LHB the option to hit the front pin on the left side or to cover both pins with the ball. The RHB should cover both pins with the ball by hitting the 5-pin on the right. A full hit on the 5-pin may leave the 9-pin—a chop. The LHB should hit the 5-pin on the left and send it into the 9-pin. There is little chance for a chop using this angle, but a light hit on the left side of the 5-pin might leave the 9-pin. Or, the LHB could cover both pins with the ball by hitting the 5-pin as shown for the RHB, using the Head-On 1-Pin Spare Zone and Strike Position. (See the 1-3; 2-5; 3-6; 4-8; and 6-10 Spares).

SPARE: 5-10

Key Pin: **5-Pin**

Spare Number: **45-S**

Opposite Spare: 42-S

5
10

LEFT HAND BOWLER: See Page 41
SPARE ZONE: Head-On 2-Pin Zone
CONTACT AREA: Far Left on 5-Pin
APPROACH POSITIONS AND TARGETS:
3-6-9 System: Head-On 2-Pin Position—
7-Pin Target
2-4-6 System: Not Used on This Spare

RIGHT HAND BOWLER: See Page 34
SPARE ZONE: Head-On 2-Pin Zone
CONTACT AREA: Far Left on 5-Pin
APPROACH POSITIONS AND TARGETS:
3-6-9 System: Head-On 2-Pin Position—
Strike Target
2-4-6 System: Strike Position—
Move Target 3 Boards LEFT

Best Way to Convert: (*Woolworth*) (*Dime Store*) Keep Pin Count In Mind! A precise hit and proper pin deflection are both needed to make this difficult split. But it can be made and should be attempted. Hit the 5-pin on the far left as shown and slide it across the lane into the 10-pin. Make sure you hit the 5-pin on your attempt so you will get maximum pin count if you miss the spare. The LHB has a slight advantage on this split.

2

SPARE: 6-7

Key Pin: **6-Pin**

Spare Number: **46-S**

Opposite Spare: 40-S

6
7

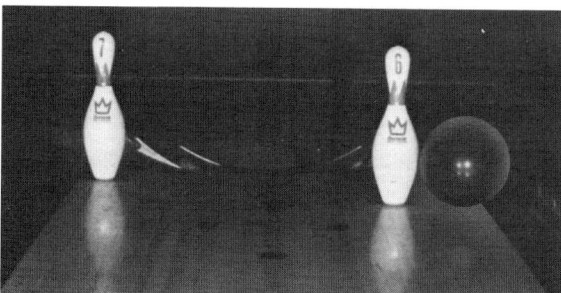

LEFT HAND BOWLER: See Page 41
SPARE ZONE: Head-On 10-Pin Zone
CONTACT AREA: Extreme Right on 6-Pin
APPROACH POSITIONS AND TARGETS:
3-6-9 System: Head-On 10-Pin Position—
Strike Target
2-4-6 System: Strike Position—
Move Target 7 Boards RIGHT

RIGHT HAND BOWLER: See Page 34
SPARE ZONE: Head-On 10-Pin Zone
CONTACT AREA: Extreme Right on 6-Pin
APPROACH POSITIONS AND TARGETS:
3-6-9 System: Head-On 10-Pin Position—
10-Pin Target
2-4-6 System: Not Used on This Spare

Best Way to Convert: (*Pinochle*) Keep Pin Count In Mind! An accurate hit and a great deal of pin deflection are required to convert this difficult split. But it can be made and should be attempted. Hit the 6-pin on the extreme right side as illustrated to slide it across the lane and into the 7-pin. Make sure you hit the 6-pin so that you will get maximum pin count should you fail to convert the split.

SPARE: 6-8

Key Pin: 6-Pin

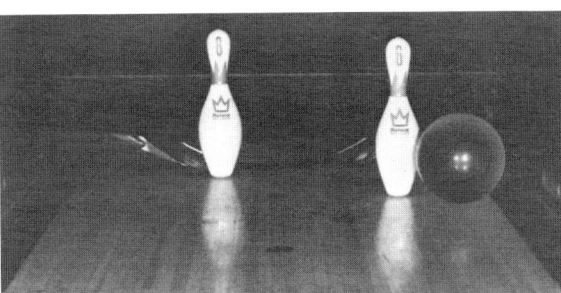

LEFT HAND BOWLER: See Page 41
SPARE ZONE: Head-On 10-Pin Zone
CONTACT AREA: Far Right on 6-Pin
APPROACH POSITIONS AND TARGETS:
3-6-9 System: Head-On 10-Pin Position—
                Strike Target
2-4-6 System: Strike Position—
                Move Target 7 Boards RIGHT

RIGHT HAND BOWLER: See Page 34
SPARE ZONE: Head-On 10-Pin Zone
CONTACT AREA: Far Right on 6-Pin
APPROACH POSITIONS AND TARGETS:
3-6-9 System: Head-On 10-Pin Position—
                10-Pin Target
2-4-6 System: Not Used on This Spare

Best Way to Convert: Keep Pin Count In Mind! Proper pin deflection and an accurate hit on the 6-pin are both needed to convert this difficult split. But it can be made and should be attempted. Hit the 6-pin on the far right side as shown and slide it across the lane into the 8-pin. Make sure you hit the 6-pin on your attempt so you will get maximum pin count should you not make the spare.

SPARE: 6-9

Key Pin: 6-Pin

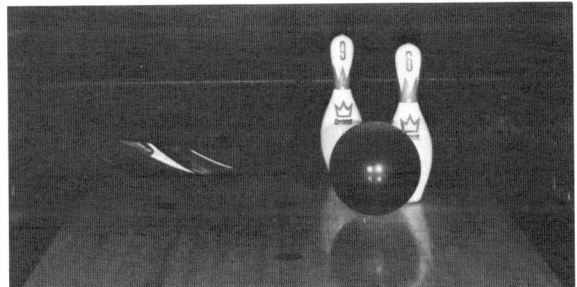

LEFT HAND BOWLER: See Page 41
SPARE ZONE: 6-Pin Zone
CONTACT AREA: Left on 6-Pin
APPROACH POSITIONS AND TARGETS:
3-6-9 System: 6-Pin Position—
                Strike Target
2-4-6 System: Strike Position
                Move Target 4 Boards RIGHT

RIGHT HAND BOWLER: See Page 34
SPARE ZONE: 6-Pin Zone
CONTACT AREA: Right on 6-Pin
APPROACH POSITIONS AND TARGETS:
3-6-9 System: 6-Pin Position—
                10-Pin Target
2-4-6 System: Not Used on This Spare

Best Way to Convert: This is another of the six similar Spare Leaves presenting chop possibilities for the LHB, and giving the RHB two methods for making the spare. The LHB should hit the 6-pin on the left side to cover both pins with the ball. The RHB should hit the 6-pin on the right side, driving it into the 9-pin. The probability of a chop is not likely with the 6-pin and the ball both heading for the 9-pin. Or the RHB could cover both pins with the ball as illustrated for the LHB, and many prefer to do this. A full hit on the 6-pin could result in a chop for either bowler. (See the 1-2; 2-4; 3-5; 4-7; and 5-8 Spares.)

SPARE: 6-10

Key Pin: 6-Pin

Spare Number: 49

Opposite Spare: 37

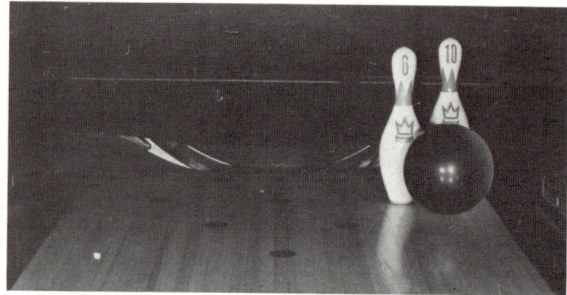

LEFT HAND BOWLER: See Page 41
SPARE ZONE: 6-Pin Zone
CONTACT AREA: Left on 6-Pin
APPROACH POSITIONS AND TARGETS:
3-6-9 System: 6-Pin Position—
    Strike Target
2-4-6 System: Strike Position—
    Move Target 4 Boards RIGHT

RIGHT HAND BOWLER: See Page 34
SPARE ZONE: 6-Pin Zone
CONTACT AREA: Right on 6-Pin
APPROACH POSITIONS AND TARGETS:
3-6-9 System: 6-Pin Position—
    10-Pin Target
2-4-6 System: Not Used on This Spare

Best Way to Convert: (*Quick Eight-LHB*) This is the last of six similar Spares presenting chop possibilities for the RHB and giving the LHB the option to hit the front pin on the left side or to cover both pins with the ball. The RHB should cover both pins with the ball by hitting the 6-pin on the right. A full hit on the 6-pin might leave the 10-pin—a chop. The LHB should hit the 6-pin on the left, sending it into the 10-pin. There is little chance for a chop with this angle, but a light hit on the left of the 6-pin might leave the 10-pin standing. Or, the LHB could cover the pins with the ball as shown for the RHB, using the 10-Pin Spare Zone and Approach Position. (See the 1-3; 2-5; 3-6; 4-8; 5-9 Spares.)

SPARE: 7-8

Key Pin: Imaginary 4-Pin

Spare Number: 50-S

Opposite Spare: 55-S

LEFT HAND BOWLER: See Page 41
SPARE ZONE: Head-On 4-Pin Zone
CONTACT AREA: Between 7 and 8-Pins
APPROACH POSITIONS AND TARGETS:
3-6-9 System: Head-On 4-Pin Position—
    7-Pin Target
2-4-6 System: Not Used on This Spare

RIGHT HAND BOWLER: See Page 34
SPARE ZONE: Head-On 4-Pin Zone
CONTACT AREA: Between 7 and 8-Pins
APPROACH POSITIONS AND TARGETS:
3-6-9 System: Head-On 4-Pin Position—
    Strike Target
2-4-6 System: Strike Position—
    Move Target 5 Boards LEFT

Best Way to Convert: This is another of the six splits having two pins standing beside each other. Try to fit the ball directly between the 7 and 8-pins by aiming at an imaginary 4-pin. There is about 3/4 of an inch on either side of the ball to convert the split, which means that an accurate hit is needed. Trying for this split should not cause you to lose any count since you should be able to get at least one of the pins. (See the 2-3; 4-5; 5-6; 8-9; and 9-10 Splits.)

SPARE: 7-9   Key Pin: **9-Pin**   Spare Number: **51-S**

Opposite Spare: 54-S

LEFT HAND BOWLER: See Page 41
SPARE ZONE: Head-On 6-Pin Zone
CONTACT AREA: Extreme Right on 9-Pin
APPROACH POSITIONS AND TARGETS:
3-6-9 System: Head-On 6-Pin Position—
                Strike Target
2-4-6 System: Strike Position—
                Move Target 5 Boards RIGHT

RIGHT HAND BOWLER: See Page 34
SPARE ZONE: Head-On 6-Pin Zone
CONTACT AREA: Extreme Right on 9-Pin
APPROACH POSITIONS AND TARGETS:
3-6-9 System: Head-On 6-Pin Position—
                10-Pin Target
2-4-6 System: Not Used on This Spare

Best Way to Convert: (*The Strike Split*) Keep Pin Count In Mind! The 7-9 is another of the "Railroad" Splits which should only be attempted when a spare is essential—even though it has been converted by one bowler in two consecutive frames! To convert the 7-9 Split, hit the 9-pin on the extreme right to slide it directly across into the 7-pin; or drive *either* pin into the pit and hope for a lucky bounce out of the pit. We recommend sliding the 9-pin into the 7-pin, or sending the 9-pin into the pit for the bounce. "Take one" is good advice for this split, to get maximum pin count.

SPARE: 7-10   Key Pin: RHB: **7-Pin**   Spare Number: **52-S**
                               LHB: **10-Pin**   Opposite Spare: None

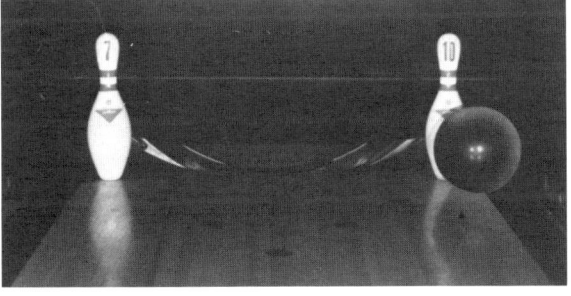

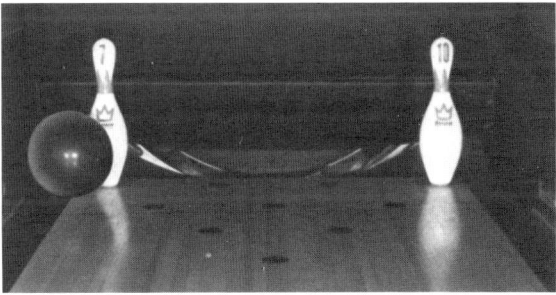

LEFT HAND BOWLER: See Page 41
SPARE ZONE: Head-On 10-Pin Zone
CONTACT AREA: Right on 10-Pin
APPROACH POSITIONS AND TARGETS:
3-6-9 System: Head-On 10-Pin Position—
                Strike Target
2-4-6 System: Strike Position—
                Move Target 7 Boards RIGHT

RIGHT HAND BOWLER: See Page 34
SPARE ZONE: Head-On 7-Pin Zone
CONTACT AREA: Left on 7-Pin
APPROACH POSITIONS AND TARGETS:
3-6-9 System: Head-On 7-Pin Position—
                Strike Target
2-4-6 System: Strike Position—
              Move Target 7 Boards LEFT

Best Way to Convert: (*Goal Posts*)(*Bed Posts*)(*Fence Posts*)(*Mule Ears*)(*Snake Eyes*) The 7-10 might be called the "granddaddy of the Railroad Splits." It should be "attempted," since the suggested attempt should not cost pin count. (However, don't expect to make it very often.) It has been made twice in the same game by several bowlers; and it is converted almost 3,000 times each bowling season!! The LHB should drive the 10-pin into the pit and hope for a lucky bounce to take out the 7-pin. The RHB should drive the 7-pin into the pit for a lucky bounce into the 10-pin. (Pick the one that is easier for you.) "Take one" is good advice when you face the 7-10 Split.

SPARE: 8-9   Key Pin: Imaginary 5-Pin   Spare Number: 53-S

Opposite Spare: None

8
9

LEFT HAND BOWLER: See Page 41
SPARE ZONE: 1-Pin Zone
CONTACT AREA: Between 8 and 9-Pins
APPROACH POSITIONS AND TARGETS:
3-6-9 System: Strike Position—
Strike Target
2-4-6 System: Strike Position—
Strike Target

RIGHT HAND BOWLER: See Page 34
SPARE ZONE: 1-Pin Zone
CONTACT AREA: Between 8 and 9-Pins
APPROACH POSITIONS AND TARGETS:
3-6-9 System: Strike Position—
Strike Target
2-4-6 System: Strike Position—
Strike Target

Best Way to Convert: This spare could really be included in the "Rare Spares Section." It is included here since it is the only Two-Pin Spare that might properly be considered as "Rare." (The 2-3 Spare runs a close "second.") The ball should hit directly between the 8 and 9-pins by aiming at an imaginary 5-pin. There is about 3/4 of an inch on either side of the ball to convert the split, which means an accurate hit is needed. As with all similar splits, trying for it should not cause you to lose pin count, since you should be able to get at least one of the pins. The Spare Zones and Approach Positions take into consideration that this split is over 30 inches behind the 1-pin. (See the 2-3; 4-5; 5-6; 7-8; and 9-10 Splits.)

2

SPARE: 8-10   Key Pin: 8-Pin   Spare Number: 54-S

Opposite Spare: 51-S

8
10

LEFT HAND BOWLER: See Page 41
SPARE ZONE: Head-On 4-Pin Zone
CONTACT AREA: Extreme Left on 8-Pin
APPROACH POSITIONS AND TARGETS:
3-6-9 System: Head-On 4-Pin Position—
7-Pin Target
2-4-6 System: Not Used on This Spare

RIGHT HAND BOWLER: See Page 34
SPARE ZONE: Head-On 4-Pin Zone
CONTACT AREA: Extreme Left on 8-Pin
APPROACH POSITIONS AND TARGETS:
3-6-9 System: Head-On 4-Pin Position—
Strike Target
2-4-6 System: Strike Position—
Move Target 5 Boards LEFT

Best Way to Convert: (*Strike Split*) (*Cincinnati*) Keep Pin Count In Mind! The 8-10 is still another of the "Railroads" which should only be attempted when a spare is essential—even though it has been *converted twice* by a bowler in the *same* game. To convert it, hit the 8-pin on the extreme left side to slide it directly across into the 10-pin (don't try sliding the 10-pin into 8-pin) or drive *either* one of the pins into the pit and hope for a lucky bounce out of the pit. We recommend sliding the 8-pin into the 10-pin, or driving the 8-pin into the pit for the bounce. "Take one" is good advice on the 8-10 Split, to get maximum pin count.

SPARE: 9-10

Key Pin: Imaginary **6-Pin**

Spare Number: **55-S**

Opposite Spare: 50-S

LEFT HAND BOWLER: See Page 41
SPARE ZONE: Head-On 6-Pin Zone
CONTACT AREA: Between 9 and 10-Pins
APPROACH POSITIONS AND TARGETS:
3-6-9 System: Head-On 6-Pin Position—
Strike Target
2-4-6 System: Strike Position—
Move Target 5 Boards RIGHT

RIGHT HAND BOWLER: See Page 34
SPARE ZONE: Head-On 6-Pin Zone
CONTACT AREA: Between 9 and 10-Pins
APPROACH POSITIONS AND TARGETS:
3-6-9 System: Head-On 6-Pin Position—
10-Pin Target
2-4-6 System: Not Used on This Spare

Best Way to Convert: This is the last of the six similar splits, all having two-pins standing side by side. Try to fit the ball directly between the 9 and 10-pins by aiming for an imaginary 6-pin. There is about 3/4 of an inch on either side of the ball to convert the split, which means that an accurate hit is required. Trying for this split should not cause you to lose any pin count, since you should be able to get at least one of the pins on the try. (See the 2-3; 4-5; 5-6; 7-8; and 8-9 Splits.)

2

SPARE: 1-2-3 Key Pin: **1-Pin** Spare Number: **56**

Opposite Spare: None

1
2
3

LEFT HAND BOWLER: *See Page 41*
SPARE ZONE: 1-Pin Zone
CONTACT AREA: Left on 1-Pin
APPROACH POSITIONS AND TARGETS:
3-6-9 System: Strike Position—
　　　　　　　　Strike Target
2-4-6 System: Strike Position—
　　　　　　　　Strike Target

RIGHT HAND BOWLER: *See Page 34*
SPARE ZONE: 1-Pin Zone
CONTACT AREA: Right on 1-Pin
APPROACH POSITIONS AND TARGETS:
3-6-9 System: Strike Position—
　　　　　　　　Strike Target
2-4-6 System: Strike Position—
　　　　　　　　Strike Target

Best Way to Convert: This is one of five similar "three pin clusters" which present possible chops for both the RHB and LHB. (The other four are listed below.) The RHB should hit the 1-3 Pocket, driving the 1-pin into the 2-pin. However, the LHB should hit the 1-2 Pocket, sending the 1-pin into the 3-pin. Hitting the 1-pin too much to the center (too full) could leave either the 2-pin (LHB) or 3-pin (RHB) standing —a chop. This particular Spare Leave gives both the LHB and RHB an opportunity to practice their strike ball, since each one is trying for a "pocket hit" in order to cover the spare. (See the 2-4-5; 3-5-6; 4-7-8; and 6-9-10 Spare Clusters.)

3

SPARE: 1-2-4 Key Pin: **1-Pin** Spare Number: **57**

Opposite Spare: 66

1
2
4

LEFT HAND BOWLER: *See Page 41*
SPARE ZONE: Head-On 2-Pin Zone
CONTACT AREA: Left on 1-Pin
APPROACH POSITIONS AND TARGETS:
3-6-9 System: Head-On 2-Pin Position—
　　　　　　　　7-Pin Target
2-4-6 System: Not Used on This Spare

RIGHT HAND BOWLER: *See Page 34*
SPARE ZONE: 2-Pin Zone
CONTACT AREA: Left on 1-Pin
APPROACH POSITIONS AND TARGETS:
3-6-9 System: 2-Pin Position—
　　　　　　　　Strike Target
2-4-6 System: Strike Position—
　　　　　　　　Move Target 2 Boards LEFT

Best Way to Convert: This is one of four similar Spare Leaves presenting chop possibilities for both the RHB and LHB. (See the list below.) A full hit on the 1-pin might "chop off" the 1-pin and leave the 2 and 4-pins standing. Hit the 1-pin on the left side as shown, so the ball will deflect to the left into the 2 and 4-pins. Ball deflection is working for the RHB, so the LHB should use the Head-On 2-Pin Approach Position to *increase ball deflection* off the 1 and 2-pins. The LHB could also play this spare from the Strike Position, and let the 2-pin take out the 4-pin as on a strike hit. (See the 1-3-6; 2-4-7; and 3-6-10 Spares.)

SPARE: 1-2-5   Key Pin: **1-Pin**   Spare Number: **58**

Opposite Spare: 65

LEFT HAND BOWLER: See Page 41
SPARE ZONE: Head-On 1-Pin Zone
CONTACT AREA: Left Center on 1-Pin
APPROACH POSITIONS AND TARGETS:
3-6-9 System: Head-On 1-Pin Position—
                    Strike Target
2-4-6 System: Strike Position—
                    Move Target 1 Board RIGHT

RIGHT HAND BOWLER: See Page 34
SPARE ZONE: Head-On 1-Pin Zone
CONTACT AREA: Right Center on 1-Pin
APPROACH POSITIONS AND TARGETS:
3-6-9 System: Head-On 1-Pin Position—
                    Strike Target
2-4-6 System: Strike Position—
                    Move Target 1 Board LEFT

Best Way to Convert: Cover all three pins with the ball! This is one of six similar leaves having three pins in them, with a Sleeper Pin, and with chop possibilities for both the RHB and LHB. (See the list below.) In each case a high hit on the front pin is needed. The RHB should convert this one by hitting the 1-pin to the right of center, driving the ball back into the 2 and 5-pins. (Either the ball or the 1-pin will take out the 2-pin.) The LHB should hit the 1-pin just to the left of center so the ball will continue through and take out both the 2 and 5-pins. Some of the top bowlers would "shoot through" this spare by aiming for the Sleeper Pin—the 5-pin. (See the 1-3-5; 2-4-8; 2-5-8; 3-5-9; 3-6-9 Spare Leaves.)

SPARE: 1-2-7   Key Pin: **1-Pin**   Spare Number: **60**

Opposite Spare: 70

LEFT HAND BOWLER: See Page 41
SPARE ZONE: Head-On 2-Pin Zone
CONTACT AREA: Far Left on 1-Pin
APPROACH POSITIONS AND TARGETS:
3-6-9 System: Head-On 2-Pin Position—
                    7-Pin Target
2-4-6 System: Not Used on This Spare

RIGHT HAND BOWLER: See Page 34
SPARE ZONE: Head-On 2-Pin Zone
CONTACT AREA: Far Left on 1-Pin
APPROACH POSITIONS AND TARGETS:
3-6-9 System: Head-On 2-Pin Position—
                    Strike Target
2-4-6 System: Strike Position—
                    Move Target 3 Boards LEFT

Best Way to Convert: Ball deflection should be used to make this spare, but pin deflection could be used by the LHB. The RHB should hit the far left side of the 1-pin so the ball will deflect into the 2-pin and then even further into the 7-pin. The RHB can do this since ball deflection is favorable on this leave. The LHB should also try for the same hit and deflection, using the Head-On 2-Pin Approach Position to reduce the angle of the shot and increase ball deflection off the 1-pin and the 2-pin. Or the LHB could cover the 1-pin and 2-pin with the ball as in a strike hit and deflect the 2-pin into the 7-pin. A slightly high hit is needed if this method is used. (See the 1-3-10 Spare.)

SPARE: 1-2-8 Key Pin: 1-Pin Spare Number: 61
Opposite Spare: 69

LEFT HAND BOWLER: See Page 41
SPARE ZONE: 1-Pin Zone
CONTACT AREA: Left on 1-Pin
APPROACH POSITIONS AND TARGETS:
3-6-9 System: Strike Position—
        Strike Target
2-4-6 System: Strike Position—
        Strike Target

RIGHT HAND BOWLER: See Page 34
SPARE ZONE: 2-Pin Zone
CONTACT AREA: Left on 1-Pin
APPROACH POSITIONS AND TARGETS:
3-6-9 System: 2-Pin Position—
        Strike Target
2-4-6 System: Strike Position—
        Move Target 2 Boards LEFT

Best Way to Convert: Cover all three pins with the ball! The 8-Pin Sleeper makes this a difficult spare. Many of the better bowlers "shoot through" this spare, that is, aim for the 8-pin. Hit the 1-pin on the left side as shown to send both the 2-pin and the ball back into the 8-pin. Ball and pin deflection must both be considered on this spare, requiring a fairly precise hit to avoid leaving the 8-pin standing. Some LHB use the Head-On 2-Pin Approach Position to increase ball deflection off the 1-pin, giving the ball a better angle to cover the 8-pin. Using the 3-6-9 Spare System, this would require a 7½ Board Shift to the LEFT of the 7-Pin Position.

SPARE: 1-2-9 Key Pin: 1-Pin Spare Number: 62
Opposite Spare: 68

LEFT HAND BOWLER: See Page 41
SPARE ZONE: 3-Pin Zone
CONTACT AREA: Right on 1-Pin
APPROACH POSITIONS AND TARGETS:
3-6-9 System: 3-Pin Position—
        Strike Target
2-4-6 System: Strike Position—
        Move Target 2 Boards RIGHT

RIGHT HAND BOWLER: See Page 34
SPARE ZONE: 1-Pin Zone
CONTACT AREA: Right on 1-Pin
APPROACH POSITIONS AND TARGETS:
3-6-9 System: Strike Position—
        Strike Target
2-4-6 System: Strike Position—
        Strike Target

Best Way to Convert: The 9-pin makes this a difficult spare, with chop possibilities. It is slightly easier for the RHB because ball deflection is favorable. The RHB should hit the 1-pin on the right so it takes out the 2-pin and the ball takes out the 9-pin. The LHB should try for the same hit, perhaps slightly more towards right center, and cover the pins in the same manner. A hit to the center or to the left side of the 1-pin might result in a miss which leaves the 2 or 9-pin. Some RHB shift 7½ Boards to the RIGHT of the 10-Pin Approach Position to get better deflection of the ball off the 1-pin into the 9-pin.

SPARE: 1-2-10

Key Pin: 1-Pin

LEFT HAND BOWLER: See Page 41
SPARE ZONE: 1-Pin Zone
CONTACT AREA: Left on 1-Pin
APPROACH POSITIONS AND TARGETS:
3-6-9 System: Strike Position—
    Strike Target
2-4-6 System: Strike Position—
    Strike Target

RIGHT HAND BOWLER: See Page 34
SPARE ZONE: Head-On 2-Pin Zone
CONTACT AREA: Left on 1-Pin
APPROACH POSITIONS AND TARGETS:
3-6-9 System: Head-On 2-Pin Position—
    Strike Target
2-4-6 System: Strike Position—
    Move Target 3 Boards LEFT

Best Way to Convert: (*Washout*) This is one of many Right Side Washouts, needing a rather precise hit to convert. (A washout on the right side occurs when the 3 and 6-pins are down and the 1 and 10-pins are standing. A Left Side Washout occurs when the 2 and 4-pins are down and the 1 and 7-pins are still up.) Hit the 1-pin on the left to send it into the 10-pin as the ball takes out the 2-pin. The 1-pin should contact the 10-pin directly, although it more often contacts the 10-pin off the kickback. This is not a split since the 1-pin is still standing.

SPARE: 1-3-5

Key Pin: 1-Pin

LEFT HAND BOWLER: See Page 41
SPARE ZONE: Head-On 1-Pin Zone
CONTACT AREA: Left Center on 1-Pin
APPROACH POSITIONS AND TARGETS:
3-6-9 System: Head-On 1-Pin Position—
    Strike Target
2-4-6 System: Strike Position—
    Move Target 1 Board RIGHT

RIGHT HAND BOWLER: See Page 34
SPARE ZONE: Head-On 1-Pin Zone
CONTACT AREA: Right Center on 1-Pin
APPROACH POSITIONS AND TARGETS:
3-6-9 System: Head-On 1-Pin Position—
    Strike Target
2-4-6 System: Strike Position—
    Move Target 1 Board LEFT

Best Way to Convert: Cover all three pins with the ball! This is one of six similar Three-Pin Spares all having a Sleeper Pin and presenting chop possibilities for both the RHB and LHB. (See the list with the 1-2-5 Spare.) In each case a high hit is needed on the front pin. The LHB should convert this spare by hitting the 1-pin to the left of center, driving the ball back into the 3 and 5-pins. The RHB should hit the 1-pin to the right of center so the ball will also contact the 3 and 5-pins similar to a strike hit. Some of the best bowlers aim for the 5-pin when they shoot at this spare.

SPARE: 1-3-6

Key Pin: 1-Pin

Spare Number: 66

Opposite Spare: 57

LEFT HAND BOWLER: See Page 41
SPARE ZONE: 3-Pin Zone
CONTACT AREA: Right on 1-Pin
APPROACH POSITIONS AND TARGETS:
3-6-9 System: 3-Pin Position—
Strike Target
2-4-6 System: Strike Position—
Move Target 2 Boards RIGHT

RIGHT HAND BOWLER: See Page 34
SPARE ZONE: Head-On 3-Pin Zone
CONTACT AREA: Right on 1-Pin
APPROACH POSITIONS AND TARGETS:
3-6-9 System: Head-On 3-Pin Position—
10-Pin Target
2-4-6 System: Not Used on This Spare

Best Way to Convert: This is another of the similar leaves with three pins, all presenting chop possibilities for both the RHB and LHB. A full hit on the 1-pin or a light hit on the extreme left side might "chop off" the 1 and 3-pins, and leave the 6-pin standing. The LHB should cover all the pins with the ball, hitting the 1-pin on the right as shown, so the ball deflects to the right and into the 3 and 6-pins. The RHB should use the Head-On 3-Pin Approach Position to *increase ball deflection* off the 1 and 3-pins. The RHB could also play this spare from the Strike Position, and let the 3-pin take out the 6-pin as in a strike ball hit. (See the 1-2-4; 2-4-7; and 3-6-10 Spares.)

SPARE: 1-3-7

Key Pin: 1-Pin

Spare Number: 67

Opposite Spare: 63

LEFT HAND BOWLER: See Page 41
SPARE ZONE: Head-On 3-Pin Zone
CONTACT AREA: Right on 1-Pin
APPROACH POSITIONS AND TARGETS:
3-6-9 System: Head-On 3-Pin Position—
Strike Target
2-4-6 System: Strike Position—
Move Target 3 Boards RIGHT

RIGHT HAND BOWLER: See Page 34
SPARE ZONE: 1-Pin Zone
CONTACT AREA: Right on 1-Pin
APPROACH POSITIONS AND TARGETS:
3-6-9 System: Strike Position—
Strike Target
2-4-6 System: Strike Position—
Strike Target

Best Way to Convert: (*Washout*) This is one of many washouts on the left side which requires an accurate hit on the 1-pin to convert. It is not a split since the 1-pin is up. It is more difficult than some splits since very precise pin deflection is needed to make it. Hit the 1-pin on the right side as illustrated, so the ball takes out the 1 and 3-pins as the 1-pin slides over into the 7-pin. A far right hit on the 1-pin might send the 1-pin off the kickback into the 7-pin, but it is best not to rely upon this kind of pin action. A direct hit on the 7-pin is better strategy than an indirect *possible* hit off the kickback.

SPARE: 1-3-8

Key Pin: **1-Pin**

LEFT HAND BOWLER: *See Page 41*
SPARE ZONE: 1-Pin Zone
CONTACT AREA: Left on 1-Pin
APPROACH POSITIONS AND TARGETS:
3-6-9 System: Strike Position—
              Strike Target
2-4-6 System: Strike Position—
              Strike Target

RIGHT HAND BOWLER: *See Page 34*
SPARE ZONE: 2-Pin Zone
CONTACT AREA: Left on 1-Pin
APPROACH POSITIONS AND TARGETS:
3-6-9 System: 2-Pin Position—
              Strike Target
2-4-6 System: Strike Position—
              Move Target 2 Boards LEFT

Best Way to Convert: The 8-pin makes this a difficult spare, with chop possibilities. It is slightly easier for the LHB because ball deflection is favorable. The LHB should hit the 1-pin on the left, so it takes out the 3-pin and the ball takes out the 8-pin. The RHB should try for a similar hit, perhaps slightly more towards right center, and cover the pins in the same way. A hit to the center, or to the right side of the 1-pin, might leave the 8-pin standing. Some LHB shift 9 boards to the left of their 7-Pin Approach Position to get better deflection of the ball off the 1-pin into the 8-pin using the 7-pin target.

SPARE: 1-3-9

Key Pin: **1-Pin**

LEFT HAND BOWLER: *See Page 41*
SPARE ZONE: 3-Pin Zone
CONTACT AREA: Right on 1-Pin
APPROACH POSITIONS AND TARGETS:
3-6-9 System: 3-Pin Position—
              Strike Target
2-4-6 System: Strike Position—
              Move Target 2 Boards RIGHT

RIGHT HAND BOWLER: *See Page 34*
SPARE ZONE: 1-Pin Zone
CONTACT AREA: Right on 1-Pin
APPROACH POSITIONS AND TARGETS:
3-6-9 System: Strike Position—
              Strike Target
2-4-6 System: Strike Position—
              Strike Target

Best Way to Convert: Cover all three pins with the ball! The 9-Pin Sleeper makes this a difficult spare with chop possibilities. Many of the better bowlers shoot through the spare, that is, aim for the 9-pin (as in the 3-9 Tandem Leave). Hit the 1-pin on the right side as shown to send both the ball and the 3-pin back into the 9-pin. Both ball and pin deflection must be considered on this spare, requiring a precise hit to avoid leaving the 9-pin standing. Some RHB use the Head-On 3-Pin Approach Position to increase ball deflection off the 1-pin, giving the ball a better angle to cover the 9-pin. Using the 3-6-9 Spare System, this would require a 7½ Board Shift to the RIGHT of the 10-Pin Position using the 10-pin target.

SPARE: 1-3-10   Key Pin: **1-Pin**   Spare Number: **70**

Opposite Spare: 60

1
3
10

LEFT HAND BOWLER: See Page 41
SPARE ZONE: Head-On 3-Pin Zone
CONTACT AREA: Far Right on 1-Pin
APPROACH POSITIONS AND TARGETS:
3-6-9 System: Head-On 3-Pin Position—
　　　　　　Strike Target
2-4-6 System: Strike Position—
　　　　　　Move Target 3 Boards RIGHT

RIGHT HAND BOWLER: See Page 34
SPARE ZONE: Head-On 3-Pin Zone
CONTACT AREA: Far Right on 1-Pin
APPROACH POSITIONS AND TARGETS:
3-6-9 System: Head-On 3-Pin Position—
　　　　　　10-Pin Target
2-4-6 System: Not Used on This Spare

Best Way to Convert: Ball deflection should be used to make this spare, but pin deflection could be used by the RHB. The LHB should hit the 1-pin on the far right side so the ball will deflect into the 3-pin and then even further into the 10-pin. The LHB can do this since ball deflection is working for him or her. The RHB should also try for the same hit, using the Head-On 3-Pin Approach Position as shown. This will reduce the angle of the shot and increase ball deflection off the 1 and 3-pins. Or the RHB could cover the 1-pin and 3-pin with the ball as in a strike hit and deflect the 3-pin into the 10-pin. A slightly high hit is needed if this method is used. (See the 1-2-7 Spare.)

3

SPARE: 1-4-7   Key Pin: Imaginary **2-Pin**   Spare Number: **73**

Opposite Spare: 85

1
4
7

LEFT HAND BOWLER: See Page 41
SPARE ZONE: Head-On 2-Pin Zone
CONTACT AREA: Far Left on 1-Pin
APPROACH POSITIONS AND TARGETS:
3-6-9 System: Head-On 2-Pin Position—
　　　　　　7-Pin Target
2-4-6 System: Not Used on This Spare

RIGHT HAND BOWLER: See Page 34
SPARE ZONE: Head-On 2-Pin Zone
CONTACT AREA: Far Left on 1-Pin
APPROACH POSITIONS AND TARGETS:
3-6-9 System: Head-On 2-Pin Position—
　　　　　　Strike Target
2-4-6 System: Strike Position—
　　　　　　Move Target 3 Boards LEFT

Best Way to Convert: Ball and pin deflection favor the RHB on this difficult spare, which is not a split since the 1-pin is still standing. Hit the 1-pin on the far left so the ball deflects to the left and into the 4-pin, which should take out the 7-pin. The RHB might cover all pins with the ball, since the ball is heading towards the left and deflecting to the left off the 1-pin. The LHB has to use the 4-pin to take out the 7-pin. Hitting the 1-pin on the right side might cover the spare, but this method is not recommended. The LHB should use the Head-On 2-Pin Approach Position to increase ball deflection off the 1-pin into the 4-pin.

SPARE: 1-4-10   Key Pin: Imaginary **2-Pin**   Spare Number: **76**

Opposite Spare: 82

LEFT HAND BOWLER: See Page 41
SPARE ZONE: Head-On 2-Pin Zone
CONTACT AREA: Left on 1-Pin
APPROACH POSITIONS AND TARGETS:
3-6-9 System: Head-On 2-Pin Position—
7-Pin Target
2-4-6 System: Not Used on This Spare

RIGHT HAND BOWLER: See Page 34
SPARE ZONE: Head-On 2-Pin Zone
CONTACT AREA: Left on 1-Pin
APPROACH POSITIONS AND TARGETS:
3-6-9 System: Head-On 2-Pin Position—
Strike Target
2-4-6 System: Strike Position—
Move Target 3 Boards LEFT

Best Way to Convert: (*Washout*) This is another Right Side Washout needing a precise hit and good ball and pin deflection to make it. It is not a split with the 1-pin standing. Hit the 1-pin on the left as shown to send it into the 10-pin directly, or off the kickback. The ball should deflect to the left and into the 4-pin. Ball deflection favors the RHB on this washout, so the LHB should use the Head-On 2-Pin Approach Position to increase ball deflection off the 1-pin into the 4-pin.

SPARE: 1-5-7   Key Pin: **1-Pin**   Spare Number: **78**

Opposite Spare: 81

LEFT HAND BOWLER: See Page 41
SPARE ZONE: Head-On 1-Pin Zone
CONTACT AREA: Center on 1-Pin
APPROACH POSITIONS AND TARGETS:
3-6-9 System: Head-On 1-Pin Position—
Strike Target
2-4-6 System: Strike Position—
Move Target 1 Board RIGHT

RIGHT HAND BOWLER: See Page 34
SPARE ZONE: 1-Pin Zone
CONTACT AREA: Right on 1-Pin
APPROACH POSITIONS AND TARGETS:
3-6-9 System: Strike Position—
Strike Target
2-4-6 System: Strike Position
Strike Target

Best Way to Convert: Very accurate pin deflection is needed to make this spare, which is not a split since the 1-pin is standing! The RHB should hit the 1-pin on the right to send it into the 7-pin, as the ball drives through and takes out the 5-pin. The LHB, however, must hit the 1-pin more to the center and hope for favorable deflection of the 1-pin off the 5-pin. Keep pin count in mind and try to get at least the 1 and 5-pins should you not make the spare conversion.

SPARE: 1-5-8   Key Pin: **1-Pin**   Spare Number: **79**

Opposite Spare: 80

LEFT HAND BOWLER: *See Page 41*
SPARE ZONE: 1-Pin Zone
CONTACT AREA: Left on 1-Pin
APPROACH POSITIONS AND TARGETS:
3-6-9 System: Strike Position—
Strike Target
2-4-6 System: Strike Position—
Strike Target

RIGHT HAND BOWLER: *See Page 34*
SPARE ZONE: Head-On 1-Pin Zone
CONTACT AREA: Right Center on 1-Pin
APPROACH POSITIONS AND TARGETS:
3-6-9 System: Head-On 1-Pin Position—
Strike Target
2-4-6 System: Strike Position—
Move Target 1 Board LEFT

Best Way to Convert: Cover all three pins with the ball. The RHB should hit the 1-pin to the right of center, driving it back towards the 8-pin as the ball continues through to the 5-pin. If the 1-pin misses the 8-pin, either the 5-pin or the ball should get it. Some of the better RHB "shoot through" this spare by aiming for the 8-pin. The LHB should hit the 1-pin on the left side, sending the ball back into the 5 and 8-pins. It is a little easier for the LHB to cover all three pins with the ball because the ball is coming from the left side. The LHB might favor a slightly high hit on the left side of the 1-pin to be sure the ball takes out the 5-Pin Sleeper

---

SPARE: 1-5-9   Key Pin: **1-Pin**   Spare Number: **80**

Opposite Spare: 79

LEFT HAND BOWLER: *See Page 41*
SPARE ZONE: Head-On 1-Pin Zone
CONTACT AREA: Left Center on 1-Pin
APPROACH POSITIONS AND TARGETS:
3-6-9 System: Head-On 1-Pin Position—
Strike Target
2-4-6 System: Strike Position—
Move Target 1 Board RIGHT

RIGHT HAND BOWLER: *See Page 34*
SPARE ZONE: 1-Pin Zone
CONTACT AREA: Right on 1-Pin
APPROACH POSITIONS AND TARGETS:
3-6-9 System: Strike Position—
Strike Target
2-4-6 System: Strike Position—
Strike Target

Best Way to Convert: Cover all three pins with the ball! It is slightly easier for the RHB to cover these three pins with the ball, because the ball is coming from the right side and can cleanly contact them as in a perfect strike ball. (The LHB has the advantage on the 1-5-8 Spare.) The RHB should hit the 1-pin on the right side as indicated, sending the ball back into the 5 and 9-pins. The LHB should hit the 1-pin just to the left of center, so the 1-pin and the ball drive back into the 5-pin and 9-pin. Some of the better LHB "shoot through" this spare by aiming for the 9-pin. The RHB might favor a slightly high hit on the right side of the 1-pin to be sure the ball takes out the 5-Pin Sleeper.

SPARE: 1-5-10   Key Pin: **1-Pin**   Spare Number: **81**

Opposite Spare: 78

LEFT HAND BOWLER: See Page 41
SPARE ZONE: 1-Pin Zone
CONTACT AREA: Left on 1-Pin
APPROACH POSITIONS AND TARGETS:
3-6-9 System: Strike Position—
                     Strike Target
2-4-6 System: Strike Position—
                     Strike Target

RIGHT HAND BOWLER: See Page 34
SPARE ZONE: Head-On 1-Pin Zone
CONTACT AREA: Center on 1-Pin
APPROACH POSITIONS AND TARGETS:
3-6-9 System: Head-On 1-Pin Position—
                     Strike Target
2-4-6 System: Strike Position—
                     Move Target 1 Board LEFT

Best Way to Convert: Very accurate pin deflection is needed to make this difficult spare, which is not a split since the 1-pin is standing. The LHB should hit the 1-pin on the left side as shown, sending it into the 10-pin directly or off the kickback. The ball should drive through and take out the 5-pin. The RHB, on the other hand, must hit the 1-pin more to the center and hope for favorable pin deflection off the 5-pin. Keep pin count in mind and try to get at least the 1 and 5-pins should you not make this very difficult spare.

SPARE: 1-6-7   Key Pin: Imaginary **3-Pin**   Spare Number: **82**

Opposite Spare: 76

LEFT HAND BOWLER: See Page 41
SPARE ZONE: Head-On 3-Pin Zone
CONTACT AREA: Right on 1-Pin
APPROACH POSITIONS AND TARGETS:
3-6-9 System: Head-On 3-Pin Position—
                     Strike Target
2-4-6 System: Strike Position—
                     Move Target 3 Boards RIGHT

RIGHT HAND BOWLER: See Page 34
SPARE ZONE: Head-On 3-Pin Zone
CONTACT AREA: Right on 1-Pin
APPROACH POSITIONS AND TARGETS:
3-6-9 System: Head-On 3-Pin Position—
                     10-Pin Target
2-4-6 System: Not Used on This Spare

Best Way to Convert: (*Washout*) This is another of the Left Side Washouts requiring a precise hit and good ball and pin deflection to cover the spare. It is not a split since the 1-pin is standing. Hit the 1-pin on the right as illustrated and send it directly into the 7-pin. (It might make the 7-pin off the kickback, but don't try for it this way.) The ball should deflect to the right and into the 6-pin. Ball deflection favors the LHB on this washout, so the RHB should use the Head-On 3-Pin Approach Position to reduce the angle of the shot and increase ball deflection off the 1-pin into the 6-pin.

SPARE: 1-6-10

Key Pin: Imaginary 3-Pin

Spare Number: 85

Opposite Spare: 73

1
6
10

LEFT HAND BOWLER: *See Page 41*
SPARE ZONE: Head-On 3-Pin Zone
CONTACT AREA: Far Right on 1-Pin
APPROACH POSITIONS AND TARGETS:
3-6-9 System: Head-On 3-Pin Position—
Strike Target
2-4-6 System: Strike Position—
Move Target 3 Boards RIGHT

RIGHT HAND BOWLER: *See Page 34*
SPARE ZONE: Head-On 3-Pin Zone
CONTACT AREA: Far Right on 1-Pin
APPROACH POSITIONS AND TARGETS:
3-6-9 System: Head-On 3-Pin Position—
10-Pin Target
2-4-6 System: Not Used on This Spare

Best Way to Convert: Ball and pin deflection favor the LHB on this difficult spare, which is not a split since the 1-pin is still standing. Hit the 1-pin on the far right side as shown so that the ball will deflect to the right and into the 6-pin, which should take out the 10-pin. The LHB may cover all three pins with the ball since the ball is heading towards the right

and deflecting to the right off the 1-pin. The RHB has to use the 6-pin to take out the 10-pin. Hitting the 1-pin on the left side might make this spare, but it is not recommended. The RHB should use the Head-On 3-Pin Approach Position to increase ball deflection off the 1-pin into the 6-pin.

3

SPARE: 2-4-5

Key Pin: 2-Pin

Spare Number: 99

Opposite Spare: 126

2
4
5

LEFT HAND BOWLER: *See Page 41*
SPARE ZONE: 2-Pin Zone
CONTACT AREA: Left on 2-Pin
APPROACH POSITIONS AND TARGETS:
3-6-9 System: 2-Pin Position—
7-Pin Target
2-4-6 System: Not Used on This Spare

RIGHT HAND BOWLER: *See Page 34*
SPARE ZONE: 2-Pin Zone
CONTACT AREA: Right on 2-Pin
APPROACH POSITIONS AND TARGETS:
3-6-9 System: 2-Pin Position—
Strike Target
2-4-6 System: Strike Position—
Move Target 2 Boards LEFT

Best Way to Convert: This is one of five similar "Three Pin Clusters" which have chop possibilities for both the RHB and LHB. (The others are listed below.) This spare is more of a chop problem for the RHB because of the deeper angle of the ball coming from the right side. The RHB should hit the 2-pin on the right as shown, sending it into the 4-pin. The

LHB should hit the 2-pin on the left side, sending it into the 5-pin. A hit too full on the 2-pin, or too much on either side could leave either the 4 or 5-pin standing. Some RHB prefer to play this spare from the left side of the approach to reduce the angle, thereby reducing the possibility of a chop. (See the 1-2-3; 3-5-6; 4-7-8; and 6-9-10 Spares.)

SPARE: 2-4-7

Key Pin: **2-Pin**

Spare Number: **101**

Opposite Spare: 134

LEFT HAND BOWLER: *See Page 41*
SPARE ZONE: 2-Pin Zone
CONTACT AREA: Left on 2-Pin
APPROACH POSITIONS AND TARGETS:
3-6-9 System: 2-Pin Position—
7-Pin Target
2-4-6 System: Not Used on This Spare

RIGHT HAND BOWLER: *See Page 34*
SPARE ZONE: 4-Pin Zone
CONTACT AREA: Left on 2-Pin
APPROACH POSITIONS AND TARGETS:
3-6-9 System: 4-Pin Position—
Strike Target
2-4-6 System: Strike Position—
Move Target 4 Boards LEFT

Best Way to Convert: This is another of the four similar leaves with three pins, all presenting chop possibilities for both the RHB and LHB. (See the list below.) A full hit on the 2-pin or a light hit on the extreme right side might "chop off" the 2 and 4-pins and leave the 7-pin standing. The RHB should cover all three pins with the ball, hitting the 2-pin on the left side so the ball deflects to the left into the 4 and 7-pins. The LHB should try for the same hit and ball deflection, using the 2-Pin Approach Position to *reduce the angle* of the shot and *increase ball deflection* off the 2 and 4-pins. Or, the LHB could hit more to the left side of the 2-pin so the 4-pin (instead of the ball) takes out the 7-pin. (See the 1-2-4; 1-3-6; and 3-6-10.)

SPARE: 2-4-8

Key Pin: **2-Pin**

Spare Number: **102**

Opposite Spare: 133

LEFT HAND BOWLER: See Page 41
SPARE ZONE: Head-On 2-Pin Zone
CONTACT AREA: Left Center on 2-Pin
APPROACH POSITIONS AND TARGETS:
3-6-9 System: Head-On 2-Pin Position—
7-Pin Target
2-4-6 System: Not Used on This Spare

RIGHT HAND BOWLER: See Page 34
SPARE ZONE: 2-Pin Zone
CONTACT AREA: Right Center on 2-Pin
APPROACH POSITIONS AND TARGETS:
3-6-9 System: 2-Pin Position—
Strike Target
2-4-6 System: Strike Position—
Move Target 2 Boards LEFT

Best Way to Convert: Cover all three pins with the ball! This is one of six similar spares having three pins in them, with a Sleeper Pin, and with chop possibilities for both the RHB and LHB. (See the list with the 1-2-5 Spare.) The RHB should convert this spare by hitting the 2-pin to the right of center, sending the ball back into the 4 and 8-pins. Either the ball or the 2-pin will take out the 4-pin. The LHB should hit the 2-pin to the left of center so the ball can continue through and take out both the 4 and 8-pins. Some of the best bowlers "shoot through" this spare by aiming for the Sleeper 8-Pin.

SPARE: 2-4-10   Key Pin: **2-Pin**   Spare Number: **104-S**

Opposite Spare: **131-S**

2
4
10

LEFT HAND BOWLER: See Page 41
SPARE ZONE: Head-On 4-Pin Zone
CONTACT AREA: Far Left on 2-Pin
APPROACH POSITIONS AND TARGETS:
3-6-9 System: Head-On 4-Pin Position—
        7-Pin Target
2-4-6 System: Not Used on This Spare

RIGHT HAND BOWLER: See Page 34
SPARE ZONE: Head-On 4-Pin Zone
CONTACT AREA: Far Left on 2-Pin
APPROACH POSITIONS AND TARGETS:
3-6-9 System: Head-On 4-Pin Position—
        Strike Target
2-4-6 System: Strike Position—
        Move Target 5 Boards LEFT

Best Way to Convert: Keep Pin Count In Mind! A precise hit and proper pin deflection are needed on this difficult split. Play it as you would the 2-10 or 2-7 Splits. Hit the 2-pin on the far left as illustrated and slide the 2-pin across the lane into the 10-pin, as the ball takes out the 4-pin. Make sure you hit the 2-pin in your conversion attempt so you will get maximum pin count if you miss the split. (See the 2-7 and 2-10 Splits.)

3

SPARE: 2-5-7   Key Pin: Imaginary **4-Pin**   Spare Number: **106-S**

Opposite Spare: **130-S**

2
5
7

LEFT HAND BOWLER: See Page 41
SPARE ZONE: Head-On 4-Pin Zone
CONTACT AREA: Far Left on 2-Pin
APPROACH POSITIONS AND TARGETS:
3-6-9 System: Head-On 4-Pin Position—
        7-Pin Target
2-4-6 System: Not Used on This Spare

RIGHT HAND BOWLER: See Page 34
SPARE ZONE: Head-On 4-Pin Zone
CONTACT AREA: Far Left on 2-Pin
APPROACH POSITIONS AND TARGETS:
3-6-9 System: Head-On 4-Pin Position—
        Strike Target
2-4-6 System: Strike Position—
        Move Target 5 Boards LEFT

Best Way to Convert: This spare should be played exactly like the 2-7 Baby Split, except that you need to hit a little more of the 2-pin so that it can take out the 5-pin. Ball deflection favors the RHB on this split, so the LHB should use the Head-On 4-Pin Approach Position to increase ball deflection off the 2-pin. Both the RHB and LHB should hit the 2-pin on the far left side so that the ball deflects to the left into the 7-pin as the 2-pin takes out the 5-pin. Since ball deflection favors the RHB, the LHB has to contact the 2-pin slightly further to the left than the RHB does. Hitting the 2-pin on the right side could also make this split; this method is not recommended. (See the 2-7 Split.)

SPARE: 2-5-8

Key Pin: **2-Pin**

Spare Number: **107**

Opposite Spare: 129

LEFT HAND BOWLER: See Page 41
SPARE ZONE: Head-On 2-Pin Zone
CONTACT AREA: Left Center on 2-Pin
APPROACH POSITIONS AND TARGETS:
3-6-9 System: Head-On 2-Pin Position—
7-Pin Target
2-4-6 System: Not Used on This Spare

RIGHT HAND BOWLER: See Page 34
SPARE ZONE: 2-Pin Zone
CONTACT AREA: Right Center on 2-Pin
APPROACH POSITIONS AND TARGETS:
3-6-9 System: 2-Pin Position—
Strike Target
2-4-6 System: Strike Position—
Move Target 2 Boards LEFT

Best Way to Convert: Cover all three pins with the ball! This is another of the six similar Three-Pin Clusters all with a Sleeper Pin, and presenting chop possibilities for the RHB and LHB. (See the list with the 1-2-5 Spare.) The LHB should convert this spare by hitting the 2-pin to the left of center as shown, driving the ball back into the 5 and 8-pins. The 2-pin should take out the 5-pin. The RHB should hit the 2-pin to the right of center, so the ball will also contact the 5 and 8-pins. Some of the top bowlers aim for the 8-pin and "shoot through" this spare to avoid a chop.

SPARE: 2-7-8

Key Pin: RHB: **2-Pin**
LHB: Imaginary **4-Pin**

Spare Number: **114-S**

Opposite Spare: 140-S

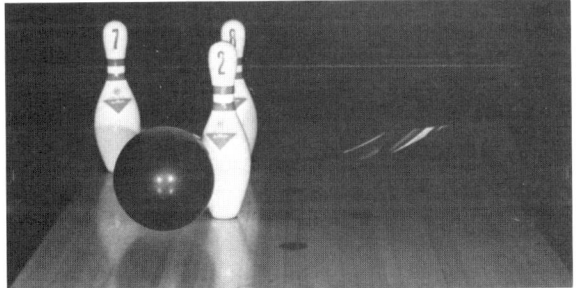

LEFT HAND BOWLER: See Page 41
SPARE ZONE: Head-On 4-Pin Zone
CONTACT AREA: Far Left on 2-Pin
APPROACH POSITIONS AND TARGETS:
3-6-9 System: Head-On 4-Pin Position—
7-Pin Target
2-4-6 System: Not Used on This Spare

RIGHT HAND BOWLER: See Page 34
SPARE ZONE: 2-Pin Zone
CONTACT AREA: Right on 2-Pin
APPROACH POSITIONS AND TARGETS:
3-6-9 System: 2-Pin Position—
Strike Target
2-4-6 System: Strike Position—
Move Target 2 Boards LEFT

Best Way to Convert: (*Baby Split with Company*) Keep Pin Count In Mind! Ball and pin deflection favor the RHB on this split, making it more difficult for the LHB to convert. The RHB should hit the 2-pin on the right as shown, driving it into the 7-pin as the ball continues through and takes out the 8-pin. The LHB should hit the 2-pin on the extreme left and try to deflect the ball directly between the 7 and 8-pins. Obviously, a very precise hit is needed to make the spare. Be sure to hit the 2-pin on the conversion attempt to get maximum pin count should you miss the spare. Some LHB use a Left Side Approach Position to reduce ball deflection off the 2-pin.

SPARE: 2-7-9

Key Pin: **2-Pin**

Spare Number: **115-S**

Opposite Spare: 139-S

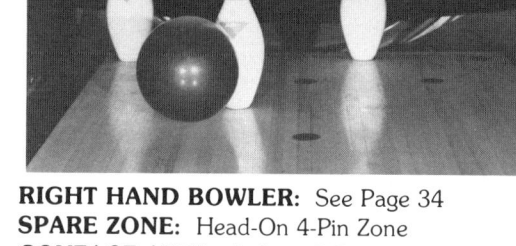

LEFT HAND BOWLER: See Page 41
SPARE ZONE: 1-Pin Zone
CONTACT AREA: Right on 2-Pin
APPROACH POSITIONS AND TARGETS:
3-6-9 System: Strike Position—
Strike Target
2-4-6 System: Strike Position—
Strike Target

RIGHT HAND BOWLER: See Page 34
SPARE ZONE: Head-On 4-Pin Zone
CONTACT AREA: Left on 2-Pin
APPROACH POSITIONS AND TARGETS:
3-6-9 System: Head-On 4-Pin Position—
Strike Target
2-4-6 System: Strike Position—
Move Target 5 Boards LEFT

Best Way to Convert: (*Left Side Triangle*) This unusual split and the opposite side 3-8-10 could just as easily have been included in the "Rare Spares Section." But, both splits occur with some degree of regularity and illustrate the need for proper ball and pin deflection on the same split, so it is included with the Probable Spares. The LHB takes advantage of ball

deflection by hitting the 2-pin on the *right*, sending it into the 7-pin as the ball deflects into the 9-pin. The RHB takes advantage of ball deflection by hitting the 2-pin on the *left*, sending it into the 9-pin as the ball deflects into the 7-pin. Fairly accurate hits are needed by both the RHB and LHB. (See the 3-8-10-Pin Split.)

SPARE: 2-7-10

Key Pin: Imaginary **4-Pin**

Spare Number: **116-S**

Opposite Spare: 137-S

LEFT HAND BOWLER: See Page 41
SPARE ZONE: Head-On 4-Pin Zone
CONTACT AREA: Far Left on 2-Pin
APPROACH POSITIONS AND TARGETS:
3-6-9 System: Head-On 4-Pin Position—
7-Pin Target
2-4-6 System: Not Used on This Spare

RIGHT HAND BOWLER: See Page 34
SPARE ZONE: Head-On 4-Pin Zone
CONTACT AREA: Far Left on 2-Pin
APPROACH POSITIONS AND TARGETS:
3-6-9 System: Head-On 4-Pin Position—
Strike Target
2-4-6 System: Strike Position—
Move Target 5 Boards LEFT

Best Way to Convert: (*Christmas Tree*)(*Faith-Hope-Charity*) Pin and ball deflection, and an accurate hit are both required to convert this difficult split. But it can be made and should be attempted. Play it as if only the 2-7 Baby Split were standing since the same hit is needed. Hit the 2-pin on the far left side to slide

it across the lane into the 10-pin, directly or off the kickback, as the ball deflects to the left into the 7-pin. Make sure you hit the 2-pin to get maximum pin count should you not make the split. (See the 2-7 Split.)

SPARE: 2-8-10   Key Pin: **2-Pin**   Spare Number: **118-S**

Opposite Spare: 136-S

LEFT HAND BOWLER: See Page 41
SPARE ZONE: Head-On 4-Pin Zone
CONTACT AREA: Far Left on 2-Pin
APPROACH POSITIONS AND TARGETS:
3-6-9 System: Head-On 4-Pin Position—
     7-Pin Target
2-4-6 System: Not Used on This Spare

RIGHT HAND BOWLER: See Page 34
SPARE ZONE: Head-On 2-Pin Zone
CONTACT AREA: Center on 2-Pin
APPROACH POSITIONS AND TARGETS:
3-6-9 System: Head-On 2-Pin Position—
     Strike Target
2-4-6 System: Strike Position—
     Move Target 3 Boards LEFT

Best Way to Convert: Keep Pin Count In Mind! This is an extremely difficult split, but more so for the RHB. The LHB should hit the 2-pin on the far left as shown, sending it across the lane into the 10-pin, as the ball drives through to barely hit the 8-pin on the extreme left side. The RHB should hit the 2-pin more to the center, driving it back into the 8-pin and hoping for pin deflection to the right to take out the 10-pin (or a lucky bounce out of the pit). The LHB could also use this center 2-pin hit. Notice that the RHB cannot use a far left hit on the 2-pin and cover the 8-pin with the ball, because the ball would deflect too much to the left. Some LHB move to the far left side of the approach on this spare.

SPARE: 3-5-6   Key Pin: **3-Pin**   Spare Number: **126**

Opposite Spare: 99

LEFT HAND BOWLER: See Page 41
SPARE ZONE: 3-Pin Zone
CONTACT AREA: Left on 3-Pin
APPROACH POSITIONS AND TARGETS:
3-6-9 System: 3-Pin Position—
     Strike Target
2-4-6 System: Strike Position—
     Move Target 2 Boards RIGHT

RIGHT HAND BOWLER: See Page 34
SPARE ZONE: 3-Pin Zone
CONTACT AREA: Right on 3-Pin
APPROACH POSITIONS AND TARGETS:
3-6-9 System: 3-Pin Position—
     10-Pin Target
2-4-6 System: Not Used on This Spare

Best Way to Convert: This is another of the "Three Pin Clusters" presenting chop possibilities for both the RHB and LHB. This one is more of a problem for the LHB, because of the deeper angle of the ball coming from the left side. The RHB should hit the 3-pin on the right side, sending it into the 5-pin, as the ball takes out the 6-pin. The LHB hits the 3-pin on the left side, sending it into the 6-pin as the ball takes out the 5-pin. A hit too full on the 3-pin, or too light on either side, might leave either the 5-pin or 6-pin still standing. Some LHB prefer to ignore the "Cross Lane Principal," and shoot this spare from the right side of the approach. This reduces the chances for a chop.

SPARE: 3-5-9   Key Pin: **3-Pin**   Spare Number: **129**

Opposite Spare: 107

**3
5
9**

LEFT HAND BOWLER: See Page 41
SPARE ZONE: 3-Pin Zone
CONTACT AREA: Left Center on 3-Pin
APPROACH POSITIONS AND TARGETS:
  3-6-9 System: 3-Pin Position—
          Strike Target
  2-4-6 System: Strike Position—
          Move Target 2 Boards RIGHT

RIGHT HAND BOWLER: See Page 34
SPARE ZONE: Head-On 3-Pin Zone
CONTACT AREA: Right Center on 3-Pin
APPROACH POSITIONS AND TARGETS:
  3-6-9 System: Head-On 3-Pin Position—
          10-Pin Target
  2-4-6 System: Not Used on This Spare

Best Way to Convert: Cover all three pins with the ball! This is one of the six similar spares having three pins in them, with a Sleeper Pin, and with chop possibilities for both the RHB and LHB. (See the list following the 1-2-5 Spare.) The RHB should cover this spare by hitting the 3-pin to the right of center, send- ing the ball back into the 5 and 9-pins. Either the ball or the 3-pin will take out the 5-pin. The LHB should hit the 3-pin to the left of center as shown, so the ball will continue through and take out the 5 and 9-pins. Most of the better bowlers "shoot through" this spare by aiming for the Sleeper 9-Pin.

3

SPARE: 3-5-10   Key Pin: Imaginary **6-Pin**   Spare Number: **130-S**

Opposite Spare: 106-S

**3
5
10**

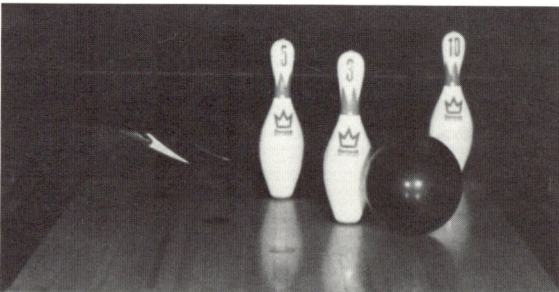

LEFT HAND BOWLER: See Page 41
SPARE ZONE: Head-On 6-Pin Zone
CONTACT AREA: Far Right on 3-Pin
APPROACH POSITIONS AND TARGETS:
  3-6-9 System: Head-On 6-Pin Position—
          Strike Target
  2-4-6 System: Strike Position—
          Move Target 5 Boards RIGHT

RIGHT HAND BOWLER: See Page 34
SPARE ZONE: Head-On 6-Pin Zone
CONTACT AREA: Far Right on 3-Pin
APPROACH POSITIONS AND TARGETS:
  3-6-9 System: Head-On 6-Pin Position—
          10-Pin Target
  2-4-6 System: Not Used on This Spare

Best Way to Convert: This split should be played exactly like the 3-10 Baby Split, except that you need to hit a little more of the 3-pin so that it can take out the 5-pin. Ball deflection favors the LHB on this split, so the RHB should use the Head-On 6-Pin Approach Position to increase ball deflection off the 3-pin. Both the RHB and LHB should hit the 3-pin on the far right side as shown so that the ball deflects to the right into the 10-pin, and the 3-pin takes out the 5-pin. Since ball deflection favors the LHB, the RHB has to contact the 3-pin slightly more to the right than the LHB does. Hitting the 3-pin on the left side could also make this split. This method is not recom- mended, particularly not for the LHB.

SPARE: 3-6-7

Key Pin: **3-Pin**

Spare Number: **131-S**

Opposite Spare: 104-S

LEFT HAND BOWLER: *See Page 41*
SPARE ZONE: Head-On 6-Pin Zone
CONTACT AREA: Far Right on 3-Pin
APPROACH POSITIONS AND TARGETS:
3-6-9 System: Head-On 6-Pin Position—
                    Strike Target
2-4-6 System: Strike Position—
                    Move Target 5 Boards RIGHT

RIGHT HAND BOWLER: See Page 34
SPARE ZONE: Head-On 6-Pin Zone
CONTACT AREA: Far Right on 3-Pin
APPROACH POSITIONS AND TARGETS:
3-6-9 System: Head-On 6-Pin Position—
                    10-Pin Target
2-4-6 System: Not Used on This Spare

Best Way to Convert: Keep Pin Count In Mind! A precise hit and proper pin deflection are both needed to make this difficult split. Play it the same way you would go for the 3-10 Baby Split, or the 3-7 Split. Hit the 3-pin on the far right side as shown and slide it across the lane into the 7-pin, as the ball takes out the 6-pin. Make sure you hit the 3-pin on your conversion attempt so you will get maximum pin count if you miss the split. (See the 3-10 and 3-7 Splits.)

SPARE: 3-6-9

Key Pin: **3-Pin**

Spare Number: **133**

Opposite Spare: 102

LEFT HAND BOWLER: *See Page 41*
SPARE ZONE: 3-Pin Zone
CONTACT AREA: Left Center on 3-Pin
APPROACH POSITIONS AND TARGETS:
3-6-9 System: 3-Pin Position—
                    Strike Target
2-4-6 System: Strike Position—
                    Move Target 2 Boards RIGHT

RIGHT HAND BOWLER: See Page 34
SPARE ZONE: Head-On 3-Pin Zone
CONTACT AREA: Right Center on 3-Pin
APPROACH POSITIONS AND TARGETS:
3-6-9 System: Head-On 3-Pin Position—
                    10-Pin Target
2-4-6 System: Not Used on This Spare

Best Way to Convert: Cover all three pins with the ball! This is another of the six similar spares all having three pins, a Sleeper Pin, and presenting chop possibilities for both the RHB and LHB. (See the list with the 1-2-5 Spare.) The RHB should cover this spare by hitting the 3-pin to the right of center as shown, so the ball will continue through and take out both the 6 and 9-pins. The LHB should hit the 3-pin just to the left of center, driving the ball back into the 6 and 9-pins. (The 3-pin will probably take out the 6-pin.) Many of the top bowlers "shoot through" this spare by aiming for the Sleeper 9-Pin.

SPARE: 3-6-10   Key Pin: **3-Pin**   Spare Number: **134**

Opposite Spare: 101

3
6
10

LEFT HAND BOWLER: See Page 41
SPARE ZONE: 6-Pin Zone
CONTACT AREA: Right on 3-Pin
APPROACH POSITIONS AND TARGETS:
3-6-9 System: 6-Pin Position—
　　　　　　　　Strike Target
2-4-6 System: Strike Position—
　　　　　　　　Move Target 4 Boards RIGHT

RIGHT HAND BOWLER: See Page 34
SPARE ZONE: 3-Pin Zone
CONTACT AREA: Right on 3-Pin
APPROACH POSITIONS AND TARGETS:
3-6-9 System: 3-Pin Position—
　　　　　　　　10-Pin Target
2-4-6 System: Not Used on This Spare

Best Way to Convert: (*Poison Ivy*) This is another of the four similar leaves with three pins, and all presenting chop possibilities for both the RHB and LHB. A full hit on the 3-pin or a light hit on the extreme left side could chop off the 3 and 6-pins and leave the 10-pin standing. (This is considered one of the most difficult "Non-Split" Spares for even the best bowl- ers!) The LHB should cover all three pins with the ball, hitting the 3-pin on the right side and deflecting the ball into the 6 and 10-pins. The RHB should try for a similar hit and ball deflection, using the 3-Pin Approach Position to *increase ball deflection* off the 3 and 6-pins. Or, the RHB could hit the 3 and 6-pins with the ball and send the 6-pin into the 10-pin.

3

SPARE: 3-7-9   Key Pin: **3-Pin**   Spare Number: **136-S**

Opposite Spare: 118-S

3
7
9

LEFT HAND BOWLER: See Page 41
SPARE ZONE: Head-On 3-Pin Zone
CONTACT AREA: Center on 3-Pin
APPROACH POSITIONS AND TARGETS:
3-6-9 System: Head-On 3-Pin Position—
　　　　　　　　Strike Target
2-4-6 System: Strike Position—
　　　　　　　　Move Target 3 Boards RIGHT

RIGHT HAND BOWLER: See Page 34
SPARE ZONE: Head-On 6-Pin Zone
CONTACT AREA: Far Right on 3-Pin
APPROACH POSITIONS AND TARGETS:
3-6-9 System: Head-On 6-Pin Position—
　　　　　　　　10-Pin Target
2-4-6 System: Not Used on This Spare

Best Way to Convert: Keep Pin Count In Mind! This is an extremely difficult split, but more so for the LHB. The RHB should hit the 3-pin on the far right to deflect it across the lane into the 7-pin, as the ball continues through and barely hits the 9-pin on the right side. The LHB should hit the 3-pin on the center, driving it back into the 9-pin and hope for pin count. deflection to the left to take out the 7-pin, or a lucky bounce out of the pit. The RHB could also use this method, and some do. Notice that the LHB cannot use the ball to take out the 9-pin on a conversion attempt as shown for the RHB, because the ball would deflect too much to the right. Some RHB move to the far right side of the approach on this spare.

SPARE: 3-7-10   Key Pin: Imaginary **6-Pin**   Spare Number: **137-S**

Opposite Spare: 116-S

LEFT HAND BOWLER: See Page 41
SPARE ZONE: Head-On 6-Pin Zone
CONTACT AREA: Far Right on 3-Pin
APPROACH POSITIONS AND TARGETS:
3-6-9 System: Head-On 6-Pin Position—
                Strike Target
2-4-6 System: Strike Position—
                Move Target 5 Boards RIGHT

RIGHT HAND BOWLER: See Page 34
SPARE ZONE: Head-On 6-Pin Zone
CONTACT AREA: Far Right on 3-Pin
APPROACH POSITIONS AND TARGETS:
3-6-9 System: Head-On 6-Pin Position—
                10-Pin Target
2-4-6 System: Not Used on This Spare

Best Way to Convert: (*Christmas Tree*)(*Faith-Hope-Charity*) Pin and ball deflection, and an accurate hit are required to convert this difficult split. It can be made and should be attempted. Play it as if only the 3-10 Baby Split were standing, since the same hit is needed. Hit the 3-pin on the far right as shown to slide it across the lane into the 7-pin, directly or off the kickback, as the ball deflects to the right into the 10-pin. Be sure to hit the 3-pin to get maximum pin count should you not make the split. (See the 3-10 Split.)

SPARE: 3-8-10   Key Pin: **3-Pin**   Spare Number: **139-S**

Opposite Spare: 115-S

LEFT HAND BOWLER: See Page 41
SPARE ZONE: Head-On 6-Pin Zone
CONTACT AREA: Right on 3-Pin
APPROACH POSITIONS AND TARGETS:
3-6-9 System: Head-On 6-Pin Position—
                Strike Target
2-4-6 System: Strike Position—
                Move Target 5 Boards RIGHT

RIGHT HAND BOWLER: See Page 34
SPARE ZONE: 1-Pin Zone
CONTACT AREA: Left on 3-Pin
APPROACH POSITIONS AND TARGETS:
3-6-9 System: Strike Position—
                Strike Target
2-4-6 System: Strike Position—
                Strike Target

Best Way to Convert: (*Right Side Triangle.*) This unusual split and the opposite side 2-7-9 could just as easily have been classified as "Rare." But both splits occur with some degree of regularity and illustrate the need for proper ball and pin deflection on the same spare, so it is included with the Probable Spares. The RHB takes advantage of ball deflection by hitting the 3-pin on the *left*, sending that pin into the 10-pin as the ball deflects into the 8-pin. The LHB takes advantage of ball deflection by hitting the 3-pin on the *right*, sending that pin into the 8-pin as the ball deflects to the right into the 10-pin. An accurate hit is needed by both the LHB and RHB to cover this difficult split. (See the 2-7-9 Split.)

SPARE: 3-9-10

Key Pin: RHB: Imaginary **6-Pin**
LHB: **3-Pin**

Spare Number: **140-S**

Opposite Spare: 114-S

3
9
10

LEFT HAND BOWLER: See Page 41
SPARE ZONE: 3-Pin Zone
CONTACT AREA: Left on 3-Pin
APPROACH POSITIONS AND TARGETS:
3-6-9 System: 3-Pin Position—
Strike Target
2-4-6 System: Strike Position—
Move Target 2 Boards RIGHT

RIGHT HAND BOWLER: See Page 34
SPARE ZONE: Head-On 6-Pin Zone
CONTACT AREA: Far Right on 3-Pin
APPROACH POSITIONS AND TARGETS:
3-6-9 System: Head-On 6-Pin Position—
10-Pin Target
2-4-6 System: Not Used on This Spare

Best Way to Convert: (*Baby Split With Company*) Keep Pin Count In Mind! Pin and ball deflection favor the LHB on this split, making it more difficult for the RHB to convert. The LHB should hit the 3-pin on the left side, driving it into the 10-pin as the ball takes out the 9-pin. The RHB should hit the 3-pin on the extreme right side and try to deflect the ball directly between the 9 and 10-pins. The RHB needs a very precise hit to make the spare. Either the RHB or LHB might miss this split by hitting the 3-pin too full, or too much on the left side. Be sure to hit the 3-pin on the spare attempt to get maximum pin count. Many RHB use a Right Side Approach Position to reduce ball deflection off the 3-pin.

3

SPARE: 4-5-7

Key Pin: Imaginary **2-Pin**

Spare Number: **142-S**

Opposite Spare: 159-S

4
5
7

LEFT HAND BOWLER: See Page 41
SPARE ZONE: Head-On 2-Pin Zone
CONTACT AREA: Between 4 and 5-Pins
APPROACH POSITIONS AND TARGETS:
3-6-9 System: Head-On 2-Pin Position—
7-Pin Target
2-4-6 System: Not Used on This Spare

RIGHT HAND BOWLER: See Page 34
SPARE ZONE: Head-On 2-Pin Zone
CONTACT AREA: Between 4 and 5-Pins
APPROACH POSITIONS AND TARGETS:
3-6-9 System: Head-On 2-Pin Position—
Strike Target
2-4-6 System: Strike Position—
Move Target 3 Boards LEFT

Best Way to Convert: This is similar to the 4-5 Split, but with the 7-pin standing. Thus, it is a much more difficult split since you could make the 4-5 portion of the split and leave the 7-pin. Try to hit directly between the 4 and 5-pins, ever so slightly more to the 4-pin side. The 4-pin might take out the 7-pin directly or off the kickback. Aim for an imaginary 2-pin, hitting "it" head-on. Since pin count is always important, make sure you hit the 4-pin to get maximum pin count should you miss the spare. (See the 4-5 Split.)

SPARE: 4-5-8   Key Pin: Imaginary **2-Pin**   Spare Number: **143-S**

Opposite Spare: 158-S

LEFT HAND BOWLER: See Page 41
SPARE ZONE: Head-On 2-Pin Zone
CONTACT AREA: Between 4 and 5-Pins
APPROACH POSITIONS AND TARGETS:
3-6-9 System: Head-On 2-Pin Position—
           7-Pin Target
2-4-6 System: Not Used on This Spare

RIGHT HAND BOWLER: See Page 34
SPARE ZONE: Head-On 2-Pin Zone
CONTACT AREA: Between 4 and 5-Pins
APPROACH POSITIONS AND TARGETS:
3-6-9 System: Head-On 2-Pin Position—
           Strike Target
2-4-6 System: Strike Position—
           Move Target 3 Boards LEFT

Best Way to Convert: This split is the same as the 4-5-Pin Split but with the 8-pin also standing. It is no more difficult than the 4-5 since any hit between the 4 and 5-pins will take out the 8-pin. Try to hit directly between the 4 and 5-pins, aiming for an imaginary 2-pin that you wish to hit head-on. As with all similar spares there is about 3/4 of an inch on either side of the ball to convert the split. Trying for this split should not run the risk of losing pin count, since a reasonable effort should get at least two of the three pins.

SPARE: 4-5-10   Key Pin: Imaginary **2-Pin**   Spare Number: **145-S**

Opposite Spare: 156-S

LEFT HAND BOWLER: See Page 41
SPARE ZONE: Head-On 2-Pin Zone
CONTACT AREA: Between 4 and 5-Pins
APPROACH POSITIONS AND TARGETS:
3-6-9 System: Head-On 2-Pin Position—
           7-Pin Target
2-4-6 System: Not Used on This Spare

RIGHT HAND BOWLER: See Page 34
SPARE ZONE: Head-On 2-Pin Zone
CONTACT AREA: Between 4 and 5-Pins
APPROACH POSITIONS AND TARGETS:
3-6-9 System: Head-On 2-Pin Position—
           Strike Target
2-4-6 System: Strike Position
           Move Target 3 Boards LEFT

Best Way to Convert: This split is a combination of the 4-5 Split and the 5-10 Split. Both are difficult. This one should be attempted in the same manner as the 4-5-Pin Split. Aim for an imaginary 2-pin which you want to hit head-on and try to contact directly between the 4 and 5-pins. With any luck the 5-pin might slide to the right and take out the 10-pin. However, it is possible to make the 4-5 and leave the 10-pin standing. Since there is only 3/4 of an inch on either side of the ball to contact the 4 and 5-pins, an accurate hit is needed. (See the 4-5 Split.)

SPARE: 4-6-7   Key Pin: **4-Pin**   Spare Number: **146-S**
Opposite Spare: 149-S

4
6
7

LEFT HAND BOWLER: See Page 41
SPARE ZONE: Head-On 7-Pin Zone
CONTACT AREA: Extreme Left on 4-Pin
APPROACH POSITIONS AND TARGETS:
3-6-9 System: Head-On 7-Pin Position—
          7-Pin Target
2-4-6 System: Not Used on This Spare

RIGHT HAND BOWLER: See Page 34
SPARE ZONE: Head-On 7-Pin Zone
CONTACT AREA: Extreme Left on 4-Pin
APPROACH POSITIONS AND TARGETS:
3-6-9 System: Head-On 7-Pin Position—
          Strike Target
2-4-6 System: Strike Position—
          Move Target 7 Boards LEFT

Best Way to Convert: Keep Pin Count In Mind! This split is another of the "Railroads" which should only be seriously attempted when a spare is essential. To convert it, hit the 4-pin on the extreme left side to slide it directly across into the 6-pin, as the ball takes out the 7-pin. Another way is to drive the 4 and 7-pins into the pit and hope for a lucky bounce out of the pit to get the 6-pin. "Take two" is good advice when faced with this split, to get maximum pin count. (See the 4-6-10 Split below.)

3

SPARE: 4-6-10   Key Pin: **6-Pin**   Spare Number: **149-S**
Opposite Spare: 146-S

4
6
10

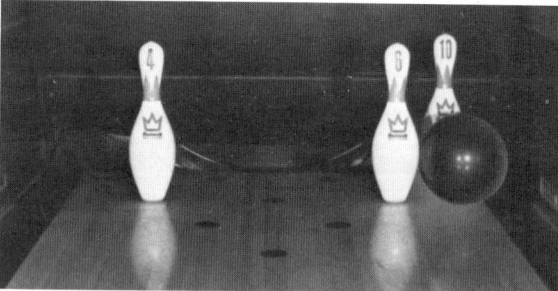

LEFT HAND BOWLER: See Page 41
SPARE ZONE: Head-On 10-Pin Zone
CONTACT AREA: Extreme Right on 6-Pin
APPROACH POSITIONS AND TARGETS:
3-6-9 System: Head-On 10-Pin Position—
          Strike Target
2-4-6 System: Strike Position—
          Move Target 7 Boards RIGHT

RIGHT HAND BOWLER: See Page 34
SPARE ZONE: Head-On 10-Pin Zone
CONTACT AREA: Extreme Right on 6-Pin
APPROACH POSITIONS AND TARGETS:
3-6-9 System: Head-On 10-Pin Position—
          10-Pin Target
2-4-6 System: Not Used on This Spare

Best Way to Convert: Keep Pin Count In Mind! This split is another of the "Railroads" which should only be seriously attempted when a spare is essential. To convert it, hit the 6-pin on the extreme right side to slide it directly across into the 4-pin, as the ball takes out the 10-pin. Another way to make the split is to drive both the 6 and 10-pins into the pit and hope for a lucky bounce out of the pit to take out the 4-pin. "Take two" is good advice when faced with this extremely difficult split, to get maximum pin count.

SPARE: 4-7-8   Key Pin: **4-Pin**   Spare Number: **150**

Opposite Spare: 171

LEFT HAND BOWLER: See Page 41
SPARE ZONE: 4-Pin Zone
CONTACT AREA: Left on 4-Pin
APPROACH POSITIONS AND TARGETS:
3-6-9 System: 4-Pin Position—
                         7-Pin Target
2-4-6 System: Not Used on This Spare

RIGHT HAND BOWLER: See Page 34
SPARE ZONE: 4-Pin Zone
CONTACT AREA: Right on 4-Pin
APPROACH POSITIONS AND TARGETS:
3-6-9 System: 4-Pin Position—
                         Strike Target
2-4-6 System: Strike Position—
                         Move Target 4 Boards LEFT

Best Way to Convert: This is another of the five similar "Three Pin Clusters" presenting chop possibilities for both the RHB and LHB. This spare is more of a problem for the RHB because of the wider angle of the ball coming from the right side. The RHB should hit the 4-pin on the right as shown, sending it into the 7-pin as the ball covers the 8-pin. The LHB, however, hits the 4-pin on the left side, sending it into the 8-pin as the ball takes out the 7-pin. A hit too full on the 4-pin, or too much to the left or right on it, may leave the 7-pin or the 8-pin. Some RHB shoot this spare from the left side, reducing the angle and the potential for a chop. (See the 1-2-3; 2-4-5; 3-5-6; and 6-9-10.)

SPARE: 4-7-9   Key Pin: **4-Pin**   Spare Number: **151-S**

Opposite Spare: 170-S

LEFT HAND BOWLER: See Page 41
SPARE ZONE: Head-On 7-Pin Zone
CONTACT AREA: Far Left on 4-Pin
APPROACH POSITIONS AND TARGETS:
3-6-9 System: Head-On 7-Pin Position—
                         7-Pin Target
2-4-6 System: Not Used on This Spare

RIGHT HAND BOWLER: See Page 34
SPARE ZONE: Head-On 7-Pin Zone
CONTACT AREA: Far Left on 4-Pin
APPROACH POSITIONS AND TARGETS:
3-6-9 System: Head-On 7-Pin Position—
                         Strike Target
2-4-6 System: Strike Position—
                         Move Target 7 Boards LEFT

Best Way to Convert: Keep Pin Count In Mind! This split is exactly like the 4-9 Split but with the 7-pin also standing. It is played exactly like the 4-9 Split. An accurate hit and proper pin deflection are both needed to make the spare. It can be made and should be attempted. Hit the 4-pin on the far left side as illustrated and slide it across into the 9-pin as the ball takes out the 7-pin. Make sure you hit the 4-pin on your attempt to get maximum pin count if you should not convert the split. (See the 4-9 Split.)

SPARE: 4-7-10 Key Pin: **4-Pin** Spare Number: **152-S**

Opposite Spare: 168-S

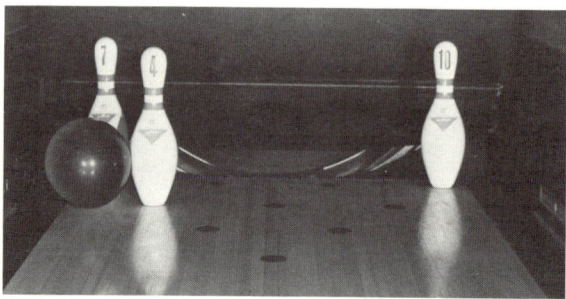

LEFT HAND BOWLER: See Page 41
SPARE ZONE: Head-On 7-Pin Zone
CONTACT AREA: Extreme Left on 4-Pin
APPROACH POSITIONS AND TARGETS:
3-6-9 System: Head-On 7-Pin Position—
   7-Pin Target
2-4-6 System: Not Used on This Spare

RIGHT HAND BOWLER: See Page 34
SPARE ZONE: Head-On 7-Pin Zone
CONTACT AREA: Extreme Left on 4-Pin
APPROACH POSITIONS AND TARGETS:
3-6-9 System: Head-On 7-Pin Position—
   Strike Target
2-4-6 System: Strike Position—
   Move Target 7 Boards LEFT

Best Way to Convert: (*Pinochle With Seven*) Keep Pin Count In Mind! This split is just like the 4-10 Split, but with the 7-pin also standing. A great deal of pin deflection and an accurate hit are needed to convert this difficult split. But it can be made and should be attempted. Hit the 4-pin on the extreme left side as illustrated and slide it across the lane into the 10-pin. The ball will then take out the 7-pin. Make sure you hit the 4-pin to get maximum pin count should you miss the spare. (See the 4-10 Split.)

SPARE: 4-8-10 Key Pin: **4-Pin** Spare Number: **154-S**

Opposite Spare: 167-S

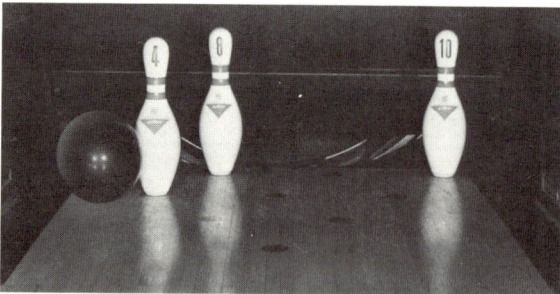

LEFT HAND BOWLER: See Page 41
SPARE ZONE: Head-On 7-Pin Zone
CONTACT AREA: Far Left on 4-Pin
APPROACH POSITIONS AND TARGETS:
3-6-9 System: Head-On 7-Pin Position—
   7-Pin Target
2-4-6 System: Not Used on This Spare

RIGHT HAND BOWLER: See Page 34
SPARE ZONE: Head-On 7-Pin Zone
CONTACT AREA: Far Left on 4-Pin
APPROACH POSITIONS AND TARGETS:
3-6-9 System: Head-On 7-Pin Position—
   Strike Target
2-4-6 System: Strike Position—
   Move Target 7 Boards LEFT

Best Way to Convert: Keep Pin Count In Mind! This very difficult split can be made and should be attempted, since you should not lose pin count in your attempt. However, accurate pin deflection is required. Hit the 4-pin on the far left as illustrated, so that it hits the 8-pin and deflects across the lane into the 10-pin. Make sure you hit the 4-pin to get maximum pin count should you miss the spare. Either the 4-pin or the 8-pin might take out the 10-pin for a spare. If pin count is vital, only shoot for the 4-8 pins.

SPARE: 4-9-10

Key Pin: **4-Pin**

Spare Number: **155-S**

Opposite Spare: 166-S

LEFT HAND BOWLER: See Page 41
SPARE ZONE: Head-On 7-Pin Zone
CONTACT AREA: Far Left on 4-Pin
APPROACH POSITIONS AND TARGETS:
   3-6-9 System: Head-On 7-Pin Position—
       7-Pin Target
   2-4-6 System: Not Used on This Spare

RIGHT HAND BOWLER: See Page 34
SPARE ZONE: Head-On 7-Pin Zone
CONTACT AREA: Far Left on 4-Pin
APPROACH POSITIONS AND TARGETS:
   3-6-9 System: Head-On 7-Pin Position—
       Strike Target
   2-4-6 System: Strike Position—
       Move Target 7 Boards LEFT

Best Way to Convert: Keep Pin Count In Mind! This split is played exactly like the 4-9 Split, but having the 10-pin also standing makes it much more difficult to convert. Hit the 4-pin on the far left side and slide it across into the 9-pin. Then either the 9-pin or the 4-pin might take out the 10-pin. If the 4-pin hits the 9-pin in the front, the 4-pin will probably deflect to the right into the 10-pin. A precise hit and proper pin deflection are essential on this split. Be sure you hit the 4-pin to get maximum pin count should you not make the spare. (See the 4-9 Split.)

SPARE: 5-6-7

Key Pin: Imaginary **3-Pin**

Spare Number: **156-S**

Opposite Spare: 145-S

LEFT HAND BOWLER: See Page 41
SPARE ZONE: Head-On 3-Pin Zone
CONTACT AREA: Between 5 and 6-Pins
APPROACH POSITIONS AND TARGETS:
   3-6-9 System: Head-On 3-Pin Position—
       Strike Target
   2-4-6 System: Strike Position—
       Move Target 3 Boards RIGHT

RIGHT HAND BOWLER: See Page 34
SPARE ZONE: Head-On 3-Pin Zone
CONTACT AREA: Between 5 and 6-Pins
APPROACH POSITIONS AND TARGETS:
   3-6-9 System: Head-On 3-Pin Position—
       10-Pin Target
   2-4-6 System: Not Used on This Spare

Best Way to Convert: This split is a combination of the 5-6-Pin Split and the 5-7-Pin Split. Both are difficult. This one should be attempted in the same way as the 5-6 Split. Aim for an imaginary 3-pin which you want to hit head-on and try to contact directly between the 5 and 6-pins. Hopefully the 5-pin will slide to the left and take out the 7-pin. It is possible, however, to make the 5-6 portion of this split and leave the 7-pin. Since there is only a 3/4 inch area on either side of the ball to contact the 5 and 6-pins, a very accurate hit is needed. (See the 5-6 Split.)

SPARE: 5-6-9

Key Pin: Imaginary **3-Pin**

Spare Number: **158-S**

Opposite Spare: 143-S

5
6
9

LEFT HAND BOWLER: See Page 41
SPARE ZONE: Head-On 3-Pin Zone
CONTACT AREA: Between 5 and 6-Pins
APPROACH POSITIONS AND TARGETS:
3-6-9 System: Head-On 3-Pin Position—
Strike Target
2-4-6 System: Strike Position—
Move Target 3 Boards RIGHT

RIGHT HAND BOWLER: See Page 34
SPARE ZONE: Head-On 3-Pin Zone
CONTACT AREA: Between 5 and 6-Pins
APPROACH POSITIONS AND TARGETS:
3-6-9 System: Head-On 3-Pin Position—
10-Pin Target
2-4-6 System: Not Used on This Spare

Best Way to Convert: This split is exactly like the 5-6 Split, but with the 9-pin also standing. It is no more difficult than the 5-6 since any hit between the 5 and 6-pins will take out the 9-pin. Try to hit directly between the 5 and 6-pins, aiming for an imaginary 3-pin which you want to hit head-on. As with all similar spares there is about 3/4 of an inch on either side of the ball to convert the split. Trying for this split should not risk losing pin count since a reasonable effort should get at least two of the three pins.

3

SPARE: 5-6-10

Key Pin: Imaginary **3-Pin**

Spare Number: **159-S**

Opposite Spare: 142-S

5
6
10

LEFT HAND BOWLER: See Page 41
SPARE ZONE: Head-On 3-Pin Zone
CONTACT AREA: Between 5 and 6-Pins
APPROACH POSITIONS AND TARGETS:
3-6-9 System: Head-On 3-Pin Position—
Strike Target
2-4-6 System: Strike Position—
Move Target 3 Boards RIGHT

RIGHT HAND BOWLER: See Page 34
SPARE ZONE: Head-On 3-Pin Zone
CONTACT AREA: Between 5 and 6-Pins
APPROACH POSITIONS AND TARGETS:
3-6-9 System: Head-On 3-Pin Position—
10-Pin Target
2-4-6 System: Not Used on This Spare

Best Way to Convert: This split is similar to the 5-6 Split, but with the 10-pin also standing. Thus, it is a more difficult split. You could make the 5 and 6-pins, yet leave the 10-pin. Try to hit directly between the 5 and 6-pins, ever so slightly more to the 6-pin side. The 6-pin might take out the 10-pin directly or off the kickback. Aim for an imaginary 3-pin, trying to hit "it" head-on. Since pin count is always important, make sure you hit the 6-pin to get maximum pin count should you miss the spare. (See the 5-6 Split.)

SPARE: 5-7-9   Key Pin: **5-Pin**   Spare Number: **161-S**

Opposite Spare: 164-S

LEFT HAND BOWLER: See Page 41
SPARE ZONE: Head-On 3-Pin Zone
CONTACT AREA: Far Right on 5-Pin
APPROACH POSITIONS AND TARGETS:
3-6-9 System: Head-On 3-Pin Position—
Strike Target
2-4-6 System: Strike Position—
Move Target 3 Boards RIGHT

RIGHT HAND BOWLER: See Page 34
SPARE ZONE: Head-On 3-Pin Zone
CONTACT AREA: Far Right on 5-Pin
APPROACH POSITIONS AND TARGETS:
3-6-9 System: Head-On 3-Pin Position—
10-Pin Target
2-4-6 System: Not Used on This Spare

Best Way to Convert: Keep Pin Count In Mind! This split is played exactly like the 5-7 Split, since the 9-pin does not make it any more difficult than the 5-7. Hit the 5-pin on the far right side as shown, sliding it across the lane into the 7-pin as the ball takes out the 9-pin. A precise hit and proper pin deflection are both needed to convert this split. Make sure you hit the 5-pin on your attempt in order to get maximum pin count should you miss the spare. (See the 5-7 Split.)

SPARE: 5-7-10   Key Pin: **5-Pin**   Spare Number: **162-S**

Opposite Spare: None

LEFT HAND BOWLER: See Page 41
SPARE ZONE: Head-On 2-Pin Zone
CONTACT AREA: Far Left on 5-Pin
APPROACH POSITIONS AND TARGETS:
3-6-9 System: Head-On 2-Pin Position—
7-Pin Target
2-4-6 System: Not Used on This Spare

RIGHT HAND BOWLER: See Page 34
SPARE ZONE: Head-On 3-Pin Zone
CONTACT AREA: Far Right on 5-Pin
APPROACH POSITIONS AND TARGETS:
3-6-9 System: Head-On 3-Pin Position—
10-Pin Target
2-4-6 System: Not Used on This Spare

Best Way to Convert: (*Lily*)(*Three Stooges*)(*Hart, Schaffner, and Marx*) There has been only one authenticated conversion of the 5-7-10 Split. Others have no doubt made it. On this split, getting even two pins is a task. The LHB should try for the 5-10. The RHB should try for the 5-7. However, try for the two pins which you feel you can make most easily. Perhaps the 5-pin will take out the 7 or 10-pin, bounce off the kickback, and slide across the lane into the remaining pin. Or, a pin could come out of the pit! Hit the 5-pin on your try, to get maximum pin count on this almost impossible split. (The 5-7-10 has been made on the *first* ball! Of course, this did not count as a split conversion.)

SPARE: 5-8-10 Key Pin: **5-Pin** Spare Number: **164-S**

Opposite Spare: 161-S

5
8
10

LEFT HAND BOWLER: See Page 41
SPARE ZONE: Head-On 2-Pin Zone
CONTACT AREA: Far Left on 5-Pin
APPROACH POSITIONS AND TARGETS:
3-6-9 System: Head-On 2-Pin Position—
7-Pin Target
2-4-6 System: Not Used on This Spare

RIGHT HAND BOWLER: See Page 34
SPARE ZONE: Head-On 2-Pin Zone
CONTACT AREA: Far Left on 5-Pin
APPROACH POSITIONS AND TARGETS:
3-6-9 System: Head-On 2-Pin Position—
Strike Target
2-4-6 System: Strike Position—
Move Target 3 Boards LEFT

Best Way to Convert: Keep Pin Count In Mind! This split is played exactly like the 5-10 Split, since the 8-pin does not make it any more difficult. A precise hit and proper pin deflection are needed to make the spare. Hit the 5-pin on the far left as illustrated and slide it across the lane into the 10-pin. The ball then takes out the 8-pin. Make sure you hit the 5-pin on your attempt so that you will get maximum pin count should you miss the spare. (See the 5-10 Split.)

3

SPARE: 6-7-8 Key Pin: **6-Pin** Spare Number: **166-S**

Opposite Spare: 155-S

6
7
8

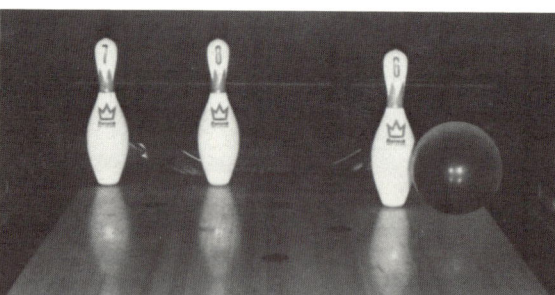

LEFT HAND BOWLER: See Page 41
SPARE ZONE: Head-On 10-Pin Zone
CONTACT AREA: Far Right on 6-Pin
APPROACH POSITIONS AND TARGETS:
3-6-9 System: Head-On 10-Pin Position—
Strike Target
2-4-6 System: Strike Position—
Move Target 7 Boards RIGHT

RIGHT HAND BOWLER: See Page 34
SPARE ZONE: Head-On 10-Pin Zone
CONTACT AREA: Far Right on 6-Pin
APPROACH POSITIONS AND TARGETS:
3-6-9 System: Head-On 10-Pin Position—
10-Pin Target
2-4-6 System: Not Used on This Spare

Best Way to Convert: Keep Pin Count In Mind! This split is attempted in the same manner as the 6-8 Split, but having the 7-pin standing makes it a lot more difficult to convert. Hit the 6-pin on the far right side as shown to slide it across into the 8-pin. Then either the 6-pin or the 8-pin might take out the 7-pin. If the 6-pin hits the 8-pin in the front it might then deflect to the left into the 7-pin. Both a precise hit and very good pin deflection are needed to make this conversion. Be sure you hit the 6-pin on your attempt, so you will get maximum pin count should you miss the spare. (See the 6-8 Split.)

SPARE: 6-7-9 Key Pin: 6-Pin Spare Number: 167-S

Opposite Spare: 154-S

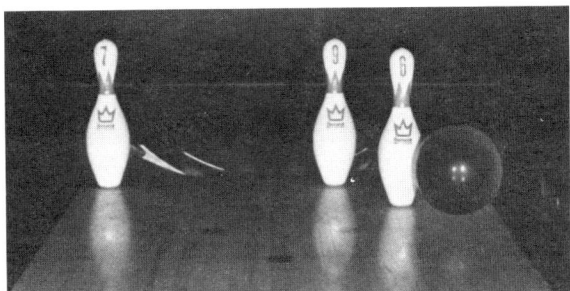

LEFT HAND BOWLER: See Page 41
SPARE ZONE: Head-On 10-Pin Zone
CONTACT AREA: Far Right on 6-Pin
APPROACH POSITIONS AND TARGETS:
3-6-9 System: Head-On 10-Pin Position—
　　　　　　　　Strike Target
2-4-6 System: Strike Position—
　　　　　　　　Move Target 7 Boards RIGHT

RIGHT HAND BOWLER: See Page 34
SPARE ZONE: Head-On 10-Pin Zone
CONTACT AREA: Far Right on 6-Pin
APPROACH POSITIONS AND TARGETS:
3-6-9 System: Head-On 10-Pin Position—
　　　　　　　　10-Pin Target
2-4-6 System: Not Used on This Spare

Best Way to Convert: Keep Pin Count In Mind! This very difficult split can be made and should be attempted, since you should not lose pin count in your attempt. However, accurate pin deflection is needed. Hit the 6-pin on the far right as shown, so that it hits the 9-pin and deflects across the lane into the 7-pin.

Make sure you hit the 6-pin to get maximum pin count if you should miss the split. Even a center hit on the 6-pin might deflect the 9-pin across the lane and into the 7-pin. If Pin Count is vital only try for 6-9 pins.

SPARE: 6-7-10 Key Pin: 6-Pin Spare Number: 168-S

Opposite Spare: 152-S

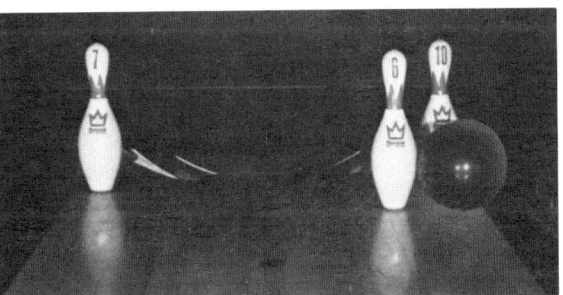

LEFT HAND BOWLER: See Page 41
SPARE ZONE: Head-On 10-Pin Zone
CONTACT AREA: Extreme Right on 6-Pin
APPROACH POSITIONS AND TARGETS:
3-6-9 System: Head-On 10-Pin Position—
　　　　　　　　Strike Target
2-4-6 System: Strike Position—
　　　　　　　　Move Target 7 Boards RIGHT

RIGHT HAND BOWLER: See Page 34
SPARE ZONE: Head-On 10-Pin Zone
CONTACT AREA: Extreme Right on 6-Pin
APPROACH POSITIONS AND TARGETS:
3-6-9 System: Head-On 10-Pin Position—
　　　　　　　　10-Pin Target
2-4-6 System: Not Used on This Spare

Best Way to Convert: (*Pinochle With Ten*) Keep Pin Count In Mind! This wide split is exactly like the 6-7 Split, but with the 10-pin also standing. Play for it exactly as you would the 6-7 Split. A great deal of pin deflection and an accurate hit are needed. But, the split can be made and should be attempted. Hit the 6-pin on the extreme right side as shown in the picture to slide it across the lane into the 7-pin. The ball will take out the 10-pin. Make sure you hit the 6-pin to get maximum pin count should you fail to convert the split. (See the 6-7 Split.)

SPARE: 6-8-10

Key Pin: **6-Pin**

6
8
10

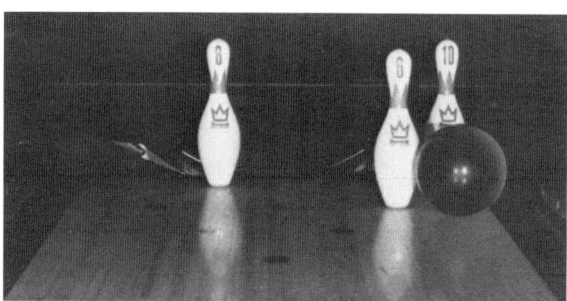

LEFT HAND BOWLER: See Page 41
SPARE ZONE: Head-On 10-Pin Zone
CONTACT AREA: Far Right on 6-Pin
APPROACH POSITIONS AND TARGETS:
3-6-9 System: Head-On 10-Pin Position—
          Strike Target
2-4-6 System: Strike Position—
          Move Target 7 Boards RIGHT

RIGHT HAND BOWLER: See Page 34
SPARE ZONE: Head-On 10-Pin Zone
CONTACT AREA: Far Right on 6-Pin
APPROACH POSITIONS AND TARGETS:
3-6-9 System: Head-On 10-Pin Position—
          10-Pin Target
2-4-6 System: Not Used on This Spare

Best Way to Convert: Keep Pin Count In Mind! This split is attempted in exactly the same manner as the 6-8 Split, since the 10-pin does not make it any more difficult than the 6-8 conversion. An accurate hit on the 6-pin and proper pin deflection are still needed to make this difficult split. Hit the 6-pin on the far right side as shown to slide it into the 8-pin as the ball takes out the 10-pin. Make sure you hit the 6-pin on your conversion try, so you will get maximum pin count if you miss the split. (See the 6-8 Split.)

3

SPARE: 6-9-10

Key Pin: **6-Pin**

6
9
10

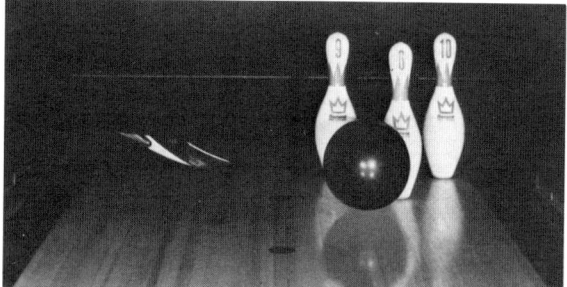

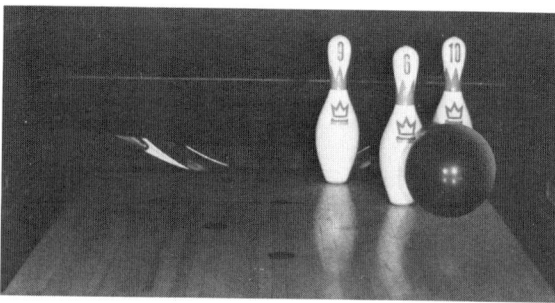

LEFT HAND BOWLER: See Page 41
SPARE ZONE: 6-Pin Zone
CONTACT AREA: Left on 6-Pin
APPROACH POSITIONS AND TARGETS:
3-6-9 System: 6-Pin Position—
          Strike Target
2-4-6 System: Strike Position—
          Move Target 4 Boards RIGHT

RIGHT HAND BOWLER: See Page 34
SPARE ZONE: 6-Pin Zone
CONTACT AREA: Right on 6-Pin
APPROACH POSITIONS AND TARGETS:
3-6-9 System: 6-Pin Position—
          10-Pin Target
2-4-6 System: Not Used on This Spare

Best Way to Convert: This is the last of the "Three Pin Clusters" which present chop problems for both the RHB and LHB. This spare is more of a chop problem for the LHB because of the wider angle of the ball coming into the pin cluster from the left. The RHB should hit the 6-pin on the right as shown, sending it into the 9-pin as the ball takes out the 10-pin. The LHB hits the 6-pin on the left side, sending it into the 10-pin and taking the 9-pin with the ball. A hit too full or too light on either side of the 6-pin might leave either the 9- or 10-pin. Some LHB play this spare from the right side of the approach, to reduce the angle and the possibility of a chop. (See the 1-2-3; 2-4-5; 3-5-6; and 4-7-8 Spares.)

SPARE: 7-8-10

LEFT HAND BOWLER: See Page 41
SPARE ZONE: Head-On 4-Pin Zone
CONTACT AREA: Between 7 and 8-Pins
APPROACH POSITIONS AND TARGETS:
3-6-9 System: Head-On 4-Pin Position—
7-Pin Target
2-4-6 System: Not Used on This Spare

RIGHT HAND BOWLER: See Page 34
SPARE ZONE: Head-On 4-Pin Zone
CONTACT AREA: Between 7 and 8-Pins
APPROACH POSITIONS AND TARGETS:
3-6-9 System: Head-On 4-Pin Position—
Strike Target
2-4-6 System: Strike Position—
Move Target 5 Boards LEFT

Best Way to Convert: This split is attempted in exactly the same way as the 7-8-Pin Split, but is far more difficult because the 10-pin is also standing. This split can be made and should be attempted, since you should not lose any pin count trying for a conversion. (But, getting two pins is about the best you can realistically hope for.) Aim for an imaginary 4-pin and try to fit the ball directly between the 7 and 8-pins, favoring the 7-pin very slightly. Hopefully the 8-pin will either slide to the right and take out the 10-pin or will get it by bouncing out of the pit. (See the 7-8 Split, and 7-9-10 Split below.)

SPARE: 7-9-10

LEFT HAND BOWLER: See Page 41
SPARE ZONE: Head-On 6-Pin Zone
CONTACT AREA: Between 9 and 10-Pins
APPROACH POSITIONS AND TARGETS:
3-6-9 System: Head-On 6-Pin Position—
Strike Target
2-4-6 System: Strike Position—
Move Target 5 Boards RIGHT

RIGHT HAND BOWLER: See Page 34
SPARE ZONE: Head-On 6-Pin Zone
CONTACT AREA: Between 9 and 10-Pins
APPROACH POSITIONS AND TARGETS:
3-6-9 System: Head-On 6-Pin Position—
10-Pin Target
2-4-6 System: Not Used on This Spare

Best Way to Convert: This split is attempted in exactly the same manner as the 9-10-Pin Split, but is far more difficult because the 7-pin is also standing. The split can be made and should be attempted, since you should not lose any pin count in your attempt. (But, getting two pins is about the best you can realistically hope for.) Aim for an imaginary 6-pin which you want to hit head-on, and try to fit the ball directly between the 9 and 10-pins—favoring the 10-pin ever so slightly. Hopefully the 9-pin will slide to the left and take out the 7-pin or will get it by bouncing out of the pit. (See the 9-10 Split.)

SPARE: 1-2-3-4   Key Pin: **1-Pin**   Spare Number: **176**

Opposite Spare: **178**

LEFT HAND BOWLER: See Page 41
SPARE ZONE: Head-On 2-Pin Zone
CONTACT AREA: Left on 1-Pin
APPROACH POSITIONS AND TARGETS:
3-6-9 System: Head-On 2-Pin Position—
                7-Pin Target
2-4-6 System: Not Used on This Spare

RIGHT HAND BOWLER: See Page 34
SPARE ZONE: 2-Pin Zone
CONTACT AREA: Left on 1-Pin
APPROACH POSITIONS AND TARGETS:
3-6-9 System: 2-Pin Position—
                Strike Target
2-4-6 System: Strike Position—
                Move Target 2 Boards LEFT

Best Way to Convert: This spare presents chop possibilities for both the RHB and LHB. A full hit on the 1-pin or extreme hit on either side could result in a miss. The RHB should hit the 1-pin on the left side as shown, taking out the 1-2-4-pins with the ball as the 1-pin takes out the 3-pin. (Ball deflection works for the RHB.) The LHB should hit the 1-pin on the left side too, trying for the same pin and ball deflection. However, since ball deflection does not favor the LHB, the Head-On 2-Pin Approach Position should be used to *reduce the angle* and *increase ball deflection* off the 1-pin. A 1-2 Pocket Hit from the Strike Position could also be used by the LHB, sending the 2-pin into the 4-pin as the 1-pin takes out the 3-pin.

SPARE: 1-2-3-5   Key Pin: **1-Pin**   Spare Number: **177**

Opposite Spare: **None**

LEFT HAND BOWLER: See Page 41
SPARE ZONE: Head-On 1-Pin Zone
CONTACT AREA: Left Center on 1-Pin
APPROACH POSITIONS AND TARGETS:
3-6-9 System: Head-On 1-Pin Position—
                Strike Target
2-4-6 System: Strike Position—
                Move Target 1 Board RIGHT

RIGHT HAND BOWLER: See Page 34
SPARE ZONE: Head-On 1-Pin Zone
CONTACT AREA: Right Center on 1-Pin
APPROACH POSITIONS AND TARGETS:
3-6-9 System: Head-On 1-Pin Position—
                Strike Target
2-4-6 System: Strike Position—
                Move Target 1 Board LEFT

Best Way to Convert: This is one of three similar clusters of four pins, and presenting chop possiblities for both the RHB and LHB. (The other two are listed below.) A center hit on the 1-pin, could leave the 2-pin or 3-pin stainding. The RHB should hit the 1-pin to the right of center, so that the ball will have enough "drive" to take out the 5-pin. The ball covers the 1-3-5-pins and the 1-pin takes out the 2-pin. The LHB should hit the 1-pin to the left of center, to carry the 1-2 and 5-pins with the ball as the 1-pin takes out the 3-pin. (See the 2-4-5-8 and 3-5-6-9 Spares.)

1
2
3
6

LEFT HAND BOWLER: See Page 41
SPARE ZONE: 3-Pin Zone
CONTACT AREA: Right on 1-Pin
APPROACH POSITIONS AND TARGETS:
3-6-9 System: 3-Pin Position—
Strike Target
2-4-6 System: Strike Position—
Move Target 2 Boards RIGHT

RIGHT HAND BOWLER: See Page 34
SPARE ZONE: Head-On 3-Pin Zone
CONTACT AREA: Right on 1-Pin
APPROACH POSITIONS AND TARGETS:
3-6-9 System: Head-On 3-Pin Position—
10-Pin Target
2-4-6 System: Not Used on This Spare

Best Way to Convert: This spare presents chop possibilities for both the RHB and LHB. A full hit on the 1-pin or light hit on either side could result in a miss. The LHB should hit the 1-pin on the right as shown, covering the 1-3-6-pins with the ball as the 1-pin takes out the 2-pin. The RHB should hit the 1-pin in the same way and try for the same pin and ball deflection. However, since ball deflection is working against the RHB, the Head-On 3-Pin Approach Position should be used to *reduce the angle* of the shot and *increase ball deflection* off the 1-pin. The RHB could also hit the 1-3 pocket, and send the 3-pin into the 6-pin as the 1-pin takes out the 2-pin.

4

1
2
3
7

LEFT HAND BOWLER: See Page 41
SPARE ZONE: 3-Pin Zone
CONTACT AREA: Right on 1-Pin
APPROACH POSITIONS AND TARGETS:
3-6-9 System: 3-Pin Position—
Strike Target
2-4-6 System: Strike Position—
Move Target 2 Boards RIGHT

RIGHT HAND BOWLER: See Page 34
SPARE ZONE: 2-Pin Zone
CONTACT AREA: Left on 1-Pin
APPROACH POSITIONS AND TARGETS:
3-6-9 System: 2-Pin Position—
Strike Target
2-4-6 System: Strike Position—
Move Target 2 Boards LEFT

Best Way to Convert: This difficult spare is not a split since the 1-pin is standing. Both the RHB and LHB are given two choices to convert the spare. The two hits are illustrated above. The RHB could hit the 1-pin on the left side, deflecting the ball into the 2 and 7-pins as the 1-pin takes out the 3-pin. Ball deflection is working for the RHB on this spare. The LHB could hit the 1-pin on the right side as shown, covering the 1 and 3-pins with the ball as the 2-pin (and 1-pin) are sent after the 7-pin. Or, the LHB could hit the 1-2 Pocket and the RHB the 1-3 Pocket to cover the spare with the same pin deflection as on a perfect strike hit. (Both Pocket Hits should be slightly high on the 1-pin.) We prefer the hits as shown.

SPARE: 1-2-3-10   Key Pin: **1-Pin**   Spare Number: **182**
Opposite Spare: 179

1
2
3
10

LEFT HAND BOWLER: *See Page 41*
SPARE ZONE: 3-Pin Zone
CONTACT AREA: Right on 1-Pin
APPROACH POSITIONS AND TARGETS:
3-6-9 System: 3-Pin Position—
Strike Target
2-4-6 System: Strike Position—
Move Target 2 Boards RIGHT

RIGHT HAND BOWLER: *See Page 34*
SPARE ZONE: 2-Pin Zone
CONTACT AREA: Left on 1-Pin
APPROACH POSITIONS AND TARGETS:
3-6-9 System: 2-Pin Position—
Strike Target
2-4-6 System: Strike Position—
Move Target 2 Boards LEFT

Best Way to Convert: This difficult spare is not a split since the 1-pin is standing. Both the RHB and LHB are given two choices to convert this spare. The two hits are illustrated above. The RHB could hit the 1-pin on the left side to cover the 1 and 2-pins with the ball, as the 3-pin (and 1-pin) are deflected to the right to take out the 10-pin. The LHB could hit the 1-pin on the right side to deflect the ball into the 1-3 and 10-pins as the 1-pin takes out the 2-pin. Or, the LHB could hit the 1-2 Pocket, and the RHB hit the 1-3 Pocket to cover the spare with the same pin deflection as on a perfect strike hit. (Both Pocket Hits should be slightly high on the 1-pin.) We prefer the hits pictured above.

4

SPARE: 1-2-4-5   Key Pin: **1-Pin**   Spare Number: **183**
Opposite Spare: 210

1
2
4
5

LEFT HAND BOWLER: *See Page 41*
SPARE ZONE: 1-Pin Zone
CONTACT AREA: Left on 1-Pin
APPROACH POSITIONS AND TARGETS:
3-6-9 System: Strike Position—
Strike Target
2-4-6 System: Strike Position—
Strike Target

RIGHT HAND BOWLER: *See Page 34*
SPARE ZONE: 1-Pin Zone
CONTACT AREA: Right on 1-Pin
APPROACH POSITIONS AND TARGETS:
3-6-9 System: Strike Position—
Strike Target
2-4-6 System: Strike Position—
Strike Target

Best Way to Convert: The 5-Pin "Sleeper" makes this spare difficult, since the 5-pin should be carried by the ball. There are chop possibilities, and a hit too full or too light on either side of the 1-pin could result in a miss. The LHB should hit the 1-pin on the left to cover the 1-2-5 pins with the ball. The 2-pin takes out the 4-pin. The RHB should hit the 1-pin on the right to cover the 1 and 5-pins with the ball. The 2-pin should take out the 4-pin. A high hit on the 1-pin by the LHB would give the ball a little more opportunity to carry the 5-pin. Such a hit by the RHB might leave the 4-pin standing, but the spare can be made this way.

LEFT HAND BOWLER: See Page 41
SPARE ZONE: Head-On 2-Pin Zone
CONTACT AREA: Left on 1-Pin
APPROACH POSITIONS AND TARGETS:
3-6-9 System: Head-On 2-Pin Position—
           7-Pin Target
2-4-6 System: Not Used on This Spare

RIGHT HAND BOWLER: See Page 34
SPARE ZONE: 2-Pin Zone
CONTACT AREA: Left on 1-Pin
APPROACH POSITIONS AND TARGETS:
3-6-9 System: 2-Pin Position—
           Strike Target
2-4-6 System: Strike Position—
           Move Target 2 Boards LEFT

Best Way to Convert: (*Left Clothesline*) This is the first of two "Clothesline Leaves." (See the 1-3-6-10) Both the LHB and RHB are able to cover all four pins with the ball but ball deflection favors the RHB on this spare. The LHB uses the Head-On 2-Pin Approach Position to increase ball deflection towards the 4-pin. Hitting the 1-pin on the right side might cover the spare, but this method is not recommended. Many LHB use the Strike Position and Strike Target on this spare. A 1-2 pocket hit is needed, sending the 2-pin into the 4-pin, and both into the 7-pin.

4

LEFT HAND BOWLER: See Page 41
SPARE ZONE: Head-On 2-Pin Zone
CONTACT AREA: Left on 1-Pin
APPROACH POSITIONS AND TARGETS:
3-6-9 System: Head-On 2-Pin Position—
           7-Pin Target
2-4-6 System: Not Used on This Spare

RIGHT HAND BOWLER: See Page 34
SPARE ZONE: 2-Pin Zone
CONTACT AREA: Left on 1-Pin
APPROACH POSITIONS AND TARGETS:
3-6-9 System: 2-Pin Position—
           Strike Target
2-4-6 System: Strike Position—
           Move Target 2 Boards LEFT

Best Way to Convert: This is one of the few spares with four pins in which it is possible to cover all the pins with the ball. The 8-pin makes this leave very difficult. Ball deflection favors the RHB, so the LHB should shift right on the approach to increase ball deflection off the 1 and 2-pins. Both the RHB and LHB should hit the 1-pin on the left side. Then the 2-pin and the ball should be sent back into the 8-pin, as either the ball or the 2-pin takes out the 4-pin. Some LHB play this spare from the Strike Position, using the Strike Target.

SPARE: 1-2-4-9   Key Pin: **1-Pin**   Spare Number: **187**

Opposite Spare: 216

1
2
4
9

LEFT HAND BOWLER: See Page 41
SPARE ZONE: 3-Pin Zone
CONTACT AREA: Right on 1-Pin
APPROACH POSITIONS AND TARGETS:
3-6-9 System: 3-Pin Position—
       Strike Target
2-4-6 System: Strike Position—
       Move Target 2 Boards RIGHT

RIGHT HAND BOWLER: See Page 34
SPARE ZONE: 1-Pin Zone
CONTACT AREA: Right on 1-Pin
APPROACH POSITIONS AND TARGETS:
3-6-9 System: Strike Position—
       Strike Target
2-4-6 System: Strike Position—
       Strike Target

Best Way to Convert: This spare is played exactly like the 1-2-9, but the 4-pin makes it more likely to produce a miss. The RHB should hit the 1-pin on the right side, sending it into the 2 and 4-pins as the ball continues on to take out the 9-pin. The LHB tries for a similar hit and the same pin and ball deflection. A Left Center hit on the 1-pin could cover this spare for either a LHB or RHB, and some bowlers prefer such a method. An accurate hit is needed. We prefer the hit as shown.

4

SPARE: 1-2-4-10   Key Pin: **1-Pin**   Spare Number: **188**

Opposite Spare: 215

1
2
4
10

LEFT HAND BOWLER: See Page 41
SPARE ZONE: Head-On 2-Pin Zone
CONTACT AREA: Left on 1-Pin
APPROACH POSITIONS AND TARGETS:
3-6-9 System: Head-On 2-Pin Position—
       7-Pin Target
2-4-6 System: Not Used on This Spare

RIGHT HAND BOWLER: See Page 34
SPARE ZONE: Head-On 2-Pin Zone
CONTACT AREA: Left on 1-Pin
APPROACH POSITIONS AND TARGETS:
3-6-9 System: Head-On 2-Pin Position—
       Strike Target
2-4-6 System: Strike Position—
       Move Target 3 Boards LEFT

Best Way to Convert: (*Washout*) This is another of the many Right Side Washouts. It is not a split with the 1-pin standing, but it is as difficult as many splits. Having the 4-pin standing makes it a little more difficult for the LHB. Hit the 1-pin on the left as shown and send it directly into the 10-pin. The 1-pin might take out the 10-pin off the kickback, but a direct hit is recommended. For the LHB, the ball or the 2-pin could take out the 4-pin. The LHB could shoot this from the Strike Postion or the Head-On 2-Pin Approach Position. Ball deflection is better from the Head-On 2-Pin Position, but the contact area on the 1-pin is larger from the Strike Position.

SPARE: 1-2-5-7   Key Pin: **1-Pin**   Spare Number: **190**

Opposite Spare: 214

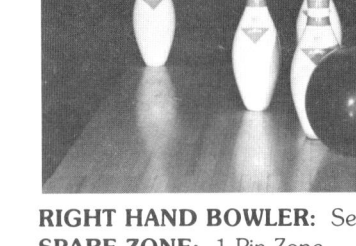

LEFT HAND BOWLER: See Page 41
SPARE ZONE: Head-On 1-Pin Zone
CONTACT AREA: Left Center on 1-Pin
APPROACH POSITIONS AND TARGETS:
3-6-9 System: Head-On 1-Pin Position—
Strike Target
2-4-6 System: Strike Position
Move Target 1 Board RIGHT

RIGHT HAND BOWLER: See Page 34
SPARE ZONE: 1-Pin Zone
CONTACT AREA: Right on 1-Pin
APPROACH POSITIONS AND TARGETS:
3-6-9 System: Strike Position—
Strike Target
2-4-6 System: Strike Position—
Strike Target

Best Way to Convert: The 7-Pin and the 5-Pin "Sleeper" make this a very difficult spare to convert. It is not a split since the 1-pin is standing. Proper pin deflection and an accurate hit are needed. The RHB should hit the 1-pin on the right to cover the 1 and 5-pins with the ball. The 1-pin should send the 2-pin into the 7-pin, as either one covers it. The LHB should hit the 1-pin to the left center, to cover the 1-2 and 5-pins with the ball. The 2-pin should be deflected to the left into the 7-pin. The LHB needs a more exact hit than the RHB since pin deflection favors the RHB on this spare.

4

SPARE: 1-2-5-8   Key Pin: **1-Pin**   Spare Number: **191**

Opposite Spare: 213

LEFT HAND BOWLER: See Page 41
SPARE ZONE: 1-Pin Zone
CONTACT AREA: Left on 1-Pin
APPROACH POSITIONS AND TARGETS:
3-6-9 System: Strike Position—
Strike Target
2-4-6 System: Strike Position—
Strike Target

RIGHT HAND BOWLER: See Page 34
SPARE ZONE: Head-On 1-Pin Zone
CONTACT AREA: Right Center on 1-Pin
APPROACH POSITIONS AND TARGETS:
3-6-9 System: Head-On 1-Pin Position—
Strike Target
2-4-6 System: Strike Position—
Move Target 1 Board LEFT

Best Way to Convert: (*Complete LHB Pocket*) These are the four pins which the LHB should cover with the ball on a perfect strike hit. Thus, this spare should be covered by the LHB exactly as if shooting for a strike. However, a high hit on the 1-pin might be all right, since the four corner pins are not standing (the 4-6-7 and 10-pins). The RHB should hit the 1-pin right of center to cover the 1 and 5-pins with the ball as the 1 takes out the 2-pin and the 5 takes out the 8-pin. The ball could take out all four pins on a Center hit on the 1-pin by the RHB, and this method might also be used.

SPARE: 1-2-5-9   Key Pin: 1-Pin   Spare Number: 192

Opposite Spare: 212

1
2
5
9

LEFT HAND BOWLER: See Page 41
SPARE ZONE: Head-On 1-Pin Zone
CONTACT AREA: Left Center on 1-Pin
APPROACH POSITIONS AND TARGETS:
3-6-9 System: Head-On 1-Pin Position—
                Strike Target
2-4-6 System: Strike Position—
                Move Target 1 Board RIGHT

RIGHT HAND BOWLER: See Page 34
SPARE ZONE: 1-Pin Zone
CONTACT AREA: Right on 1-Pin
APPROACH POSITIONS AND TARGETS:
3-6-9 System: Strike Position—
                Strike Target
2-4-6 System: Strike Position—
                Strike Target

Best Way to Convert: The 5 and 9-pins make this spare a difficult one. The LHB should hit the 1-pin on the left center to cover the 1-2-5-pins with the ball, as the 5-pin or the 1-pin takes out the 9-pin. The RHB hits the 1-pin on the right to cover the 1-5 and 9-pins with the ball as the 2-pin is taken out by the 1-pin. A precise hit is needed, with good pin and ball deflection. A right center hit by the RHB would give the ball a better opportunity to carry the 5-pin, so many RHB prefer this hit.

4

SPARE: 1-2-7-8   Key Pin: 1-Pin   Spare Number: 198

Opposite Spare: 224

1
2
7
8

LEFT HAND BOWLER: See Page 41
SPARE ZONE: Head-On 2-Pin Zone
CONTACT AREA: Left on 1-Pin
APPROACH POSITIONS AND TARGETS:
3-6-9 System: Head-On 2-Pin Position—
                7-Pin Target
2-4-6 System: Not Used on This Spare

RIGHT HAND BOWLER: See Page 34
SPARE ZONE: 2-Pin Zone
CONTACT AREA: Left Center on 1-Pin
APPROACH POSITIONS AND TARGETS:
3-6-9 System: 2-Pin Position—
                Strike Target
2-4-6 System: Strike Position—
                Move Target 2 Boards LEFT

Best Way to Convert: Ball and pin deflection favor the RHB on this spare, which means the LHB needs a more precise hit to make the spare. The RHB should hit the 1-pin to the left center as shown, sending the 2-pin back into the 8-pin as the ball deflects to the left into the 7-pin. Or the ball could cover the 1-2-8-pins and the 2-pin sent to the left into the 7-pin. The LHB hits the 1-pin on the left to cover the 1-2-7-pins with the ball. The 2-pin is sent back into the 8-pin. (Notice that both can use ball deflection to cover the 7-pin, but that it is much more difficult for the LHB.) A high or extreme right hit on the 1-pin will probably leave the 7 or 8-pin (or both) still standing.

SPARE: 1-2-7-9   Key Pin: **1-Pin**   Spare Number: **199**

Opposite Spare: 223

LEFT HAND BOWLER: See Page 41
SPARE ZONE: 3-Pin Zone
CONTACT AREA: Right on 1-Pin
APPROACH POSITIONS AND TARGETS:
3-6-9 System: 3-Pin Position—
　　　　　　　Strike Target
2-4-6 System: Strike Position—
　　　　　　　Move Target 2 Boards RIGHT

RIGHT HAND BOWLER: See Page 34
SPARE ZONE: 1-Pin Zone
CONTACT AREA: Right on 1-Pin
APPROACH POSITIONS AND TARGETS:
3-6-9 System: Strike Position—
　　　　　　　Strike Target
2-4-6 System: Strike Position—
　　　　　　　Strike Target

Best Way to Convert: This spare is similar to the 1-2-9 Leave, but the 7-pin makes it more difficult. It is not a split since the 1-pin is up. An accurate hit and precise pin deflection are needed to make it. Both the LHB and RHB should hit the 1-pin on the right as shown, covering the 1 and 9-pins with the ball. The 1-pin and the 2-pin should be sent towards the 7-pin. (See the 1-2-9 Spare.)

SPARE: 1-2-7-10   Key Pin: **1-Pin**   Spare Number: **200**

Opposite Spare: 221

LEFT HAND BOWLER: See Page 41
SPARE ZONE: Head-On 2-Pin Zone
CONTACT AREA: Left on 1-Pin
APPROACH POSITIONS AND TARGETS:
3-6-9 System: Head-On 2-Pin Position—
　　　　　　　7-Pin Target
2-4-6 System: Not Used on This Spare

RIGHT HAND BOWLER: See Page 34
SPARE ZONE: Head-On 2-Pin Zone
CONTACT AREA: Left on 1-Pin
APPROACH POSITIONS AND TARGETS:
3-6-9 System: Head-On 2-Pin Position—
　　　　　　　Strike Target
2-4-6 System: Strike Position—
　　　　　　　Move Target 3 Boards LEFT

Best Way to Convert: (*Washout*) This is another of the Right Side Washouts needing an accurate hit and good ball and pin deflection to make the spare. It is not a split because the 1-pin is standing. The 7-pin makes this a very difficult Washout to convert. The LHB should hit the 1-pin on the left to send it into the 10-pin. The ball takes out the 2-pin and deflects to the left into the 7-pin. A precise hit is needed. The RHB also hits the 1-pin on the left as shown to drive the 1-pin into the 10-pin. The ball should hit the 2-pin and deflect into the 7-pin. Fortunately, ball deflection is working for the RHB. For both the RHB and LHB the 1-pin might take out the 10-pin off the kickback, but a direct hit should be attempted.

SPARE: 1-2-8-9   Key Pin: **1-Pin**   Spare Number: **201**

Opposite Spare: **222**

LEFT HAND BOWLER: See Page 41
SPARE ZONE: Head-On 1-Pin Zone
CONTACT AREA: Left Center on 1-Pin
APPROACH POSITIONS AND TARGETS:
3-6-9 System: Head-On 1-Pin Position—
Strike Target
2-4-6 System: Strike Position—
Move Target 1 Board RIGHT

RIGHT HAND BOWLER: See Page 34
SPARE ZONE: Head-On 1-Pin Zone
CONTACT AREA: Right Center on 1-Pin
APPROACH POSITIONS AND TARGETS:
3-6-9 System: Head-On 1-Pin Position—
Strike Target
2-4-6 System: Strike Position—
Move Target 1 Board LEFT

Best Way to Convert: A very accurate hit is needed to cover this difficult spare. It is slightly easier for the RHB because ball and pin deflection are favorable. The RHB should hit the 1-pin on the right center, to cover the 1 and 9-pins with the ball. The 1-pin should deflect off the 2-pin into the 8-pin. The LHB should hit the 1-pin to the left center, covering the 1-2 and 8- pins with the ball. The 1-pin should be sent back into the 9-pin. (Many RHB prefer this acceptable method.) Some LHB cover this spare exactly as described for RHB, and often from the Right Side of the Approach. Still other LHB use the Head-On 2-Pin Approach Position and still hit the 1-pin on the left center as indicated.

SPARE: 1-2-8-10   Key Pin: **1-Pin**   Spare Number: **202**

Opposite Spare: **220**

LEFT HAND BOWLER: See Page 41
SPARE ZONE: 1-Pin Zone
CONTACT AREA: Left on 1-Pin
APPROACH POSITIONS AND TARGETS:
3-6-9 System: Strike Position—
Strike Target
2-4-6 System: Strike Position—
Strike Target

RIGHT HAND BOWLER: See Page 34
SPARE ZONE: 2-Pin Zone
CONTACT AREA: Left on 1-Pin
APPROACH POSITIONS AND TARGETS:
3-6-9 System: 2-Pin Position—
Strike Target
2-4-6 System: Strike Position—
Move Target 2 Boards LEFT

Best Way to Convert: (*Washout*) This is still another of the many Right Side Washouts needing accurate pin and ball deflection to make the spare. Having the 8-Pin Sleeper makes this Washout slightly more difficult for the LHB. Play this spare exactly like the 1-2-8 Spare Leave. Hit the 1-pin on the left side as shown, sending the 1-pin to the right directly into the 10-pin. (Don't try for a bounce off the kickback, although this may happen.) The ball and 2-pin should head back into the 8-Pin Sleeper. (See the 1-2-8 Spare.)

SPARE: 1-3-5-6

Key Pin: **1-Pin**

LEFT HAND BOWLER: See Page 41
SPARE ZONE: 1-Pin Zone
CONTACT AREA: Left on 1-Pin
APPROACH POSITIONS AND TARGETS:
3-6-9 System: Strike Position—
Strike Target
2-4-6 System: Strike Position—
Strike Target

RIGHT HAND BOWLER: See Page 34
SPARE ZONE: 1-Pin Zone
CONTACT AREA: Right on 1-Pin
APPROACH POSITIONS AND TARGETS:
3-6-9 System: Strike Position—
Strike Target
2-4-6 System: Strike Position—
Strike Target

Best Way to Convert: The 5-Pin Sleeper makes this a very difficult spare, since the ball should cover the 5-pin. The RHB should hit the 1-pin on the right (or right center) to cover the 1-3-5-pins with the ball, as the 3-pin takes out the 6-pin. The LHB should hit the 1-pin on the left as shown, to cover the 1 and 5-pins with the ball. The 1-pin should send the 3-pin into the 6-pin. An accurate hit and proper pin deflection are essential for this spare. A center or right center hit on the 1-pin by the LHB might also cover this spare, but a very accurate hit is necessary.

4

SPARE: 1-3-5-8

Key Pin: **1-Pin**

LEFT HAND BOWLER: See Page 41
SPARE ZONE: 1-Pin Zone
CONTACT AREA: Left on 1-Pin
APPROACH POSITIONS AND TARGETS:
3-6-9 System: Strike Position—
Strike Target
2-4-6 System: Strike Position—
Strike Target

RIGHT HAND BOWLER: See Page 34
SPARE ZONE: Head-On 1-Pin Zone
CONTACT AREA: Right Center on 1-Pin
APPROACH POSITIONS AND TARGETS:
3-6-9 System: Head-On 1-Pin Position—
Strike Target
2-4-6 System: Strike Position
Move Target 1 Board LEFT

Best Way to Convert: The 5 and 8-pins make this spare a difficult one. The RHB should hit the 1-pin on the right side, to cover the 1-3-5-pins with the ball, as either the 1 or 5-pin takes out the 8-pin. The LHB should hit the 1-pin on the left side, covering the 1-5-8-pins with the ball as the 1-pin takes out the 3-pin. An accurate hit and good pin and ball deflection are needed to make the spare. A left center hit by the LHB would give the ball more opportunity to take out the 5-pin, so many LHB prefer this hit.

SPARE: 1-3-5-9   Key Pin: **1-Pin**   Spare Number: **213**

Opposite Spare: 191

LEFT HAND BOWLER: See Page 41
SPARE ZONE: Head-On 1-Pin Zone
CONTACT AREA: Left Center on 1-Pin
APPROACH POSITIONS AND TARGETS:
3-6-9 System: Head-On 1-Pin Position—
Strike Target
2-4-6 System: Strike Position—
Move Target 1 Board RIGHT

RIGHT HAND BOWLER: See Page 34
SPARE ZONE: 1-Pin Zone
CONTACT AREA: Right on 1-Pin
APPROACH POSITIONS AND TARGETS:
3-6-9 System: Strike Position—
Strike Target
2-4-6 System: Strike Position—
Strike Target

Best Way to Convert: (*Complete RHB Pocket*) These are the four pins which the RHB should cover with the ball on a perfect strike hit. Thus, this spare should be converted by the RHB exactly as if shooting for a strike. However, a high hit on the 1-pin might be all right, since the corner pins are not standing (the 4-6-7 and 10-pins). The LHB should hit the 1-pin left of center to cover the 1 and 5-pins with the ball, as the 1 takes out the 3-pin and the 5 takes out the 9-pin. The ball could take out all four pins on a Center hit on the 1-pin by the LHB, and this method might also be used.

SPARE: 1-3-5-10   Key Pin: **1-Pin**   Spare Number: **214**

Opposite Spare: 190

LEFT HAND BOWLER: See Page 41
SPARE ZONE: 1-Pin Zone
CONTACT AREA: Left on 1-Pin
APPROACH POSITIONS AND TARGETS:
3-6-9 System: Strike Position—
Strike Target
2-4-6 System: Strike Position—
Strike Target

RIGHT HAND BOWLER: See Page 34
SPARE ZONE: Head-On 1-Pin Zone
CONTACT AREA: Right Center on 1-Pin
APPROACH POSITIONS AND TARGETS:
3-6-9 System: Head-On 1-Pin Position—
Strike Target
2-4-6 System: Strike Position—
Move Target 1 Board LEFT

Best Way to Convert: The 10-Pin and the 5-Pin "Sleeper" make this a very difficult spare to convert. It is not a split since the 1-pin is standing. The RHB needs a more exact hit than the LHB since pin deflection favors the LHB. The LHB should hit the 1-pin on the left side to cover the 1 and 5-pins with the ball. The 1 and 3-pins should be sent into the 10-pin; either one taking it out. The RHB should hit the right center of the 1-pin, covering the 1-3-5-pins with the ball. The 3-pin should be deflected to the right into the 10-pin.

SPARE: 1-3-6-7

Key Pin: 1-Pin

LEFT HAND BOWLER: See Page 41
SPARE ZONE: Head-On 3-Pin Zone
CONTACT AREA: Right on 1-Pin
APPROACH POSITIONS AND TARGETS:
3-6-9 System: Head-On 3-Pin Position—
    Strike Target
2-4-6 System: Strike Position—
    Move Target 3 Boards RIGHT

RIGHT HAND BOWLER: See Page 34
SPARE ZONE: Head-On 3-Pin Zone
CONTACT AREA: Right on 1-Pin
APPROACH POSITIONS AND TARGETS:
3-6-9 System: Head-On 3-Pin Position—
    10-Pin Target
2-4-6 System: Not Used on This Spare

Best Way to Convert: (*Washout*) This is another of the many Left Side Washouts, which needs a precise hit on the 1-pin to convert. It is played exactly like the 1-7, the 1-3-7, and similar Leaves. Of course it is not a split with the 1-pin still standing. Hit the 1-pin on the right side as shown to send it into the 7-pin, as the ball takes out the 1-3 and 6-pins. Ball deflection favors the LHB on this spare, so the RHB should use the Head-On 3-Pin Approach Position to increase ball deflection off the 1-pin into the 3 and 6-pins. However, the contact area on the 1-pin is greater from the Strike Position. A far right hit on the 1-pin might get the 7-pin off the kickback, but this method is not recommended. (See the 1-3-7 Spare.)

SPARE: 1-3-6-8

Key Pin: 1-Pin

LEFT HAND BOWLER: See Page 41
SPARE ZONE: 1-Pin Zone
CONTACT AREA: Left on 1-Pin
APPROACH POSITIONS AND TARGETS:
3-6-9 System: Strike Position—
    Strike Target
2-4-6 System: Strike Position—
    Strike Target

RIGHT HAND BOWLER: See Page 34
SPARE ZONE: 2-Pin Zone
CONTACT AREA: Left on 1-Pin
APPROACH POSITIONS AND TARGETS:
3-6-9 System: 2-Pin Position—
    Strike Target
2-4-6 System: Strike Position—
    Move Target 2 Boards LEFT

Best Way to Convert: This spare is played exactly like the 1-3-8, but the 6-pin makes it more likely to produce a miss. The LHB should hit the 1-pin on the left side, sending it into the 3 and 6-pins as the ball continues on to cover the 8-pin. The RHB tries for the same hit and the same pin and ball deflection. A Right Center hit on the 1-pin by either a RHB or LHB could make this spare, and some bowlers prefer this method. An accurate hit is needed. We prefer the hit as shown.

SPARE: 1-3-6-9   Key Pin: 1-Pin   Spare Number: 217

Opposite Spare: 186

1
3
6
9

LEFT HAND BOWLER: See Page 41
SPARE ZONE: 3-Pin Zone
CONTACT AREA: Right on 1-Pin
APPROACH POSITIONS AND TARGETS:
3-6-9 System: 3-Pin Position—
            Strike Target
2-4-6 System: Strike Position—
            Move Target 2 Boards RIGHT

RIGHT HAND BOWLER: See Page 34
SPARE ZONE: Head-On 3-Pin Zone
CONTACT AREA: Right on 1-Pin
APPROACH POSITIONS AND TARGETS:
3-6-9 System: Head-On 3-Pin Position—
            10-Pin Target
2-4-6 System: Not Used on This Spare

Best Way to Convert: This is one of the few spares with four pins in which it is possible to cover all the pins with the ball. The 9-Pin "Sleeper" makes it very difficult to convert. Ball deflection favors the LHB, so the RHB should shift left on the approach to increase ball deflection off the 1 and 3-pins. Both the LHB and RHB should hit the 1-pin on the right side. Then the 3-pin and the ball should be sent back into the 9-pin, as either the ball or the 3-pin takes out the 6-pin. Some RHB play this spare from the Strike Position, using the Strike Target.

4

SPARE: 1-3-6-10   Key Pin: 1-Pin   Spare Number: 218

Opposite Spare: 185

1
3
6
10

LEFT HAND BOWLER: See Page 41
SPARE ZONE: 3-Pin Zone
CONTACT AREA: Right on 1-Pin
APPROACH POSITIONS AND TARGETS:
3-6-9 System: 3-Pin Position—
            Strike Target
2-4-6 System: Strike Position—
            Move Target 2 Boards RIGHT

RIGHT HAND BOWLER: See Page 34
SPARE ZONE: Head-On 3-Pin Zone
CONTACT AREA: Right on 1-Pin
APPROACH POSITIONS AND TARGETS:
3-6-9 System: Head-On 3-Pin Position—
            10-Pin Target
2-4-6 System: Not Used on This Spare

Best Way to Convert: (*Right Clothesline*) This is the second of two "Clothesline Leaves." (See the 1-2-4-7.) Both the RHB and LHB are able to cover all four pins with the ball but ball deflection favors the LHB. The RHB uses the Head-On 3-Pin Position to take advantage of ball deflection. Hitting the 1-pin on the left side might cover this spare, but it is not recommended. Many RHB use the Strike Position and Strike Target on this leave. The RHB hits the 1-3 pocket as in a strike hit, sending the 3-pin into the 6-pin which covers the 10-pin.

LEFT HAND BOWLER: *See Page 41*
SPARE ZONE: 3-Pin Zone
CONTACT AREA: Right on 1-Pin
APPROACH POSITIONS AND TARGETS:
3-6-9 System: 3-Pin Position—
       Strike Target
2-4-6 System: Strike Position—
       Move Target 2 Boards RIGHT

RIGHT HAND BOWLER: *See Page 34*
SPARE ZONE: 1-Pin Zone
CONTACT AREA: Right on 1-Pin
APPROACH POSITIONS AND TARGETS:
3-6-9 System: Strike Position—
       Strike Target
2-4-6 System: Strike Position—
       Strike Target

Best Way to Convert: (*Washout*) This is another of the Left Side Washouts requiring accurate pin deflection to cover the spare. Having the 9-Pin Sleeper also makes ball deflection a factor to consider and increases the difficulty of the spare for the RHB. Play this exactly like the 1-3-9 Spare. Hit the 1-pin on the right side as shown, sending the 1-pin into the 7-pin, as the ball and 3-pin head back into the 9-pin. The 1-pin might take out the 7-pin off the kickback, but try for a direct hit instead. (See the 1-3-9 Spare.)

4

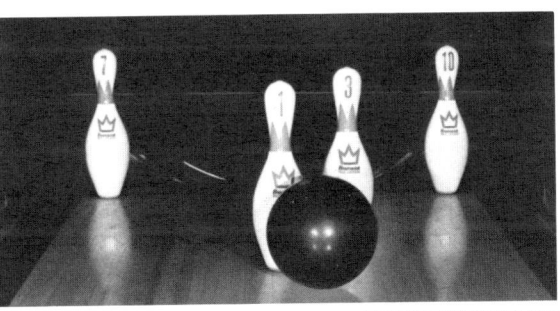

LEFT HAND BOWLER: *See Page 41*
SPARE ZONE: Head-On 3-Pin Zone
CONTACT AREA: Right on 1-Pin
APPROACH POSITIONS AND TARGETS:
3-6-9 System: Head-On 3-Pin Position—
       Strike Target
2-4-6 System: Strike Position—
       Move Target 3 Boards RIGHT

RIGHT HAND BOWLER: *See Page 34*
SPARE ZONE: Head-On 3-Pin Zone
CONTACT AREA: Right on 1-Pin
APPROACH POSITIONS AND TARGETS:
3-6-9 System: Head-On 3-Pin Position—
       10-Pin Target
2-4-6 System: Not Used on This Spare

Best Way to Convert: (*Washout*) This is another Left Side Washout requiring a precise hit and accurate ball and pin deflection to cover it. It is not a split because the 1-pin is standing. The 10-pin makes this washout very difficult. The RHB should hit the 1-pin on the right as shown, sending it into the 7-pin directly (although the 1-pin might take out the 7-pin off the kickback). The ball should be deflected to the right and into the 10-pin. The LHB should also hit the 1-pin on the right, sending it into the 7-pin. The ball should take out the 3-pin and deflect to the right into the 10-pin. Fortunately, ball deflection is working for the LHB. The RHB needs a more accurate hit, and good ball deflection.

SPARE: 1-3-8-9
Key Pin: 1-Pin

1
3
8
9

LEFT HAND BOWLER: See Page 41
SPARE ZONE: Head-On 1-Pin Zone
CONTACT AREA: Left Center on 1-Pin
APPROACH POSITIONS AND TARGETS:
3-6-9 System: Head-On 1-Pin Position—
Strike Target
2-4-6 System: Strike Position—
Move Target 1 Board RIGHT

RIGHT HAND BOWLER: See Page 34
SPARE ZONE: Head-On 1-Pin Zone
CONTACT AREA: Right Center on 1-Pin
APPROACH POSITIONS AND TARGETS:
3-6-9 System: Head-On 1-Pin Position—
Strike Target
2-4-6 System: Strike Position—
Move Target 1 Board LEFT

Best Way to Convert: A very accurate hit is needed to make this difficult spare. It is a little easier for the LHB because ball and pin deflection are favorable. The LHB should hit the 1-pin to the left center, sending the 1-pin into the 3-pin and then into the 9-pin. The ball covers the 8-pin. The RHB should hit the 1-pin to the right of center, covering the 1-3 and 9-pins with the ball, as the 1-pin is sent directly back into the 8-pin. Some RHB try for this spare exactly as the LHB does, and often from the left side of the approach. Still other RHBs use the Head-On 3-Pin Approach Position but still hit the 1-pin on the right center as shown in the picture.

4

SPARE: 1-3-8-10
Key Pin: 1-Pin

1
3
8
10

LEFT HAND BOWLER: See Page 41
SPARE ZONE: 1-Pin Zone
CONTACT AREA: Left on 1-Pin
APPROACH POSITIONS AND TARGETS:
3-6-9 System: Strike Position—
Strike Target
2-4-6 System: Strike Position—
Strike Target

RIGHT HAND BOWLER: See Page 34
SPARE ZONE: 2-Pin Zone
CONTACT AREA: Left on 1-Pin
APPROACH POSITIONS AND TARGETS:
3-6-9 System: 2-Pin Position—
Strike Target
2-4-6 System: Strike Position—
Move Target 2 Boards LEFT

Best Way to Convert: This spare is similar to the 1-3-8, and is played the same way. The 10-pin makes it more difficult. This spare is not a split with the 1-pin standing. A precise hit and accurate pin deflection are needed to convert the spare. Hit the 1-pin on the left side as shown, covering the 1 and 8-pins with the ball. The 1 and 3-pins should be sent into the 10-pin and one of them should take it out. A right center hit on the 1-pin can make this spare, but this method is not recommended.

SPARE: 1-3-9-10   Key Pin: **1-Pin**

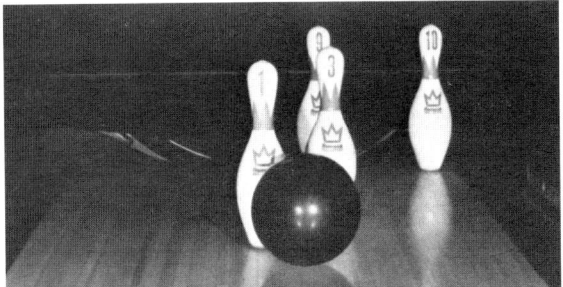

LEFT HAND BOWLER: See Page 41
SPARE ZONE: 3-Pin Zone
CONTACT AREA: Right Center on 1-Pin
APPROACH POSITIONS AND TARGETS:
3-6-9 System: 3-Pin Position—
　　　　　　　　Strike Target
2-4-6 System: Strike Position—
　　　　　　　　Move Target 2 Boards RIGHT

RIGHT HAND BOWLER: See Page 34
SPARE ZONE: Head-On 3-Pin Zone
CONTACT AREA: Right on 1-Pin
APPROACH POSITIONS AND TARGETS:
3-6-9 System: Head-On 3-Pin Position—
　　　　　　　　10-Pin Target
2-4-6 System: Not Used on This Spare

Best Way to Convert: Ball and pin deflection favor the LHB on this spare, which means that the RHB needs a more exact hit to make the spare. The LHB should hit the 1-pin to the right of center as shown, sending the 3-pin back into the 9-pin as the ball deflects to the right into the 10-pin. Or the ball could cover the 1-3 and 9-pins as the 3-pin takes out the 10-pin. The RHB should hit the 1-pin on the right to cover the 1-3-10-pins with the ball. The 3-pin is sent back into the 9-pin. (Notice that both can use ball deflection to cover the 10-pin, but that it is more difficult for the RHB.) A full or light hit on the left side of the 1-pin will probably leave the 9 or 10-pin (or both) still standing.

4

SPARE: 1-4-7-9   Key Pin: **1-Pin**

LEFT HAND BOWLER: See Page 41
SPARE ZONE: 3-Pin Zone
CONTACT AREA: Right on 1-Pin
APPROACH POSITIONS AND TARGETS:
3-6-9 System: 3-Pin Position—
　　　　　　　　Strike Target
2-4-6 System: Strike Position—
　　　　　　　　Move Target 2 Boards RIGHT

RIGHT HAND BOWLER: See Page 34
SPARE ZONE: 1-Pin Zone
CONTACT AREA: Right on 1-Pin
APPROACH POSITIONS AND TARGETS:
3-6-9 System: Strike Position—
　　　　　　　　Strike Target
2-4-6 System: Strike Position
　　　　　　　　Strike Target

Best Way to Convert: Ball and pin deflection are both factors in this difficult spare. It is slightly easier for the RHB since ball and pin deflection favor a Right Side Hit. Both bowlers should hit the 1-pin on the right as shown, taking out the 1 and 9-pins with the ball. The 1-pin should be sent into the 4-pin and either the 1 or 4-pin should take out the 7-pin. Some RHB use a left center hit on the 1-pin, driving it into the 9-pin. The ball deflects into the 4 and 7-pins. Of course, this is not a split since the 1-pin is standing.

SPARE: 1-4-7-10   Key Pin: Imaginary **2-Pin**   Spare Number: **236**

Opposite Spare: 252

1
4
7
10

LEFT HAND BOWLER: *See Page 41*
SPARE ZONE: Head-On 2-Pin Zone
CONTACT AREA: Left on 1-Pin
APPROACH POSITIONS AND TARGETS:
3-6-9 System: Head-On 2-Pin Position—
7-Pin Target
2-4-6 System: Not Used on This Spare

RIGHT HAND BOWLER: *See Page 34*
SPARE ZONE: Head-On 2-Pin Zone
CONTACT AREA: Left on 1-Pin
APPROACH POSITIONS AND TARGETS:
3-6-9 System: Head-On 2-Pin Position—
Strike Target
2-4-6 System: Strike Position—
Move Target 3 Boards LEFT

Best Way to Convert: (*Washout*) This is a Right Side Washout needing a very precise hit and good ball and pin deflection to convert the spare. It is not a split with the 1-pin standing. Hit the 1-pin on the left as shown to send it into the 10-pin directly. It may take out the 10-pin off the kickback, but should not be played this way. The ball should deflect to the left and into the 4-pin to drive it into the 7-pin. Ball deflection favors the RHB on this Leave, so the LHB should use the Head-On 2-Pin Approach Position to increase ball deflection off the 1-pin into the 4-pin. Some LHB elect a right hit on the 1-pin and deflect the ball into the 10-pin. We do not recommend this way.

4

SPARE: 1-5-7-8   Key Pin: **1-Pin**   Spare Number: **244**

Opposite Spare: 249

1
5
7
8

LEFT HAND BOWLER: *See Page 41*
SPARE ZONE: Head-On 1-Pin Zone
CONTACT AREA: Center on 1-Pin
APPROACH POSITIONS AND TARGETS:
3-6-9 System: Head-On 1-Pin Position—
Strike Target
2-4-6 System: Strike Position—
Move Target 1 Board RIGHT

RIGHT HAND BOWLER: *See Page 34*
SPARE ZONE: 1-Pin Zone
CONTACT AREA: Right on 1-Pin
APPROACH POSITIONS AND TARGETS:
3-6-9 System: Strike Position—
Strike Target
2-4-6 System: Strike Position—
Strike Target

Best Way to Convert: The 7-pin makes this spare extremely difficult, especially for the LHB. A precise hit and almost perfect pin deflection are needed to make the spare. The RHB should hit the 1-pin on the right and send it into the 7-pin. The ball should have enough "drive" to take out the 5-pin and send it into the 8-pin. The LHB, however, must hit the 1-pin in the center and hope that it will deflect off the 5 or 8-pin into the 7-pin. The ball should continue into the 5-pin. The ball, 1-pin, or 5-pin might take out the 8-pin. (Some RHBs use this center hit on the 1-pin too.) Hitting the 1-pin too light on either side could result in a miss, so a high hit is preferred.

SPARE: 1-5-7-9

Key Pin: **1-Pin**

LEFT HAND BOWLER: See Page 41
SPARE ZONE: Head-On 1-Pin Zone
CONTACT AREA: Center on 1-Pin
APPROACH POSITIONS AND TARGETS:
3-6-9 System: Head-On 1-Pin Position—
　　　　　　　　Strike Target
2-4-6 System: Strike Position—
　　　　　　　　Move Target 1 Board RIGHT

RIGHT HAND BOWLER: See Page 34
SPARE ZONE: 1-Pin Zone
CONTACT AREA: Right on 1-Pin
APPROACH POSITIONS AND TARGETS:
3-6-9 System: Strike Position—
　　　　　　　　Strike Target
2-4-6 System: Strike Position—
　　　　　　　　Strike Target

Best Way to Convert: The 7-pin makes this spare extremely difficult, especially for the LHB. A precise hit and accurate pin deflection are needed for the spare. The RHB should hit the 1-pin on the right to send it into the 7-pin. The ball should have enough "drive" to continue on and take out the 5-pin and then the 9-pin. The LHB, however, must hit the 1-pin in the center and hope that it will deflect off the 5-pin into the 7-pin. The ball continues on to take out the 9-pin. (Some RHBs use this center hit too.) Hitting the 1-pin too light on either side would leave the 5-pin standing, so a high hit is necessary.

SPARE: 1-5-8-9

Key Pin: **1-Pin**

LEFT HAND BOWLER: See Page 41
SPARE ZONE: Head-On 1-Pin Zone
CONTACT AREA: Left Center on 1-Pin
APPROACH POSITIONS AND TARGETS:
3-6-9 System: Head-On 1-Pin Position—
　　　　　　　　Strike Target
2-4-6 System: Strike Position—
　　　　　　　　Move Target 1 Board RIGHT

RIGHT HAND BOWLER: See Page 34
SPARE ZONE: Head-On 1-Pin Zone
CONTACT AREA: Right Center on 1-Pin
APPROACH POSITIONS AND TARGETS:
3-6-9 System: Head-On 1-Pin Position—
　　　　　　　　Strike Target
2-4-6 System: Strike Position -
　　　　　　　　Move Target 1 Board LEFT

Best Way to Convert: Pin and ball deflection are important factors on this unusual (not rare) Leave. The RHB should hit the 1-pin to the right of center, driving it back towards the 8-pin. The ball should continue through to hit the 5 and 9-pins, as the 5-pin also is sent for the 8-pin. The LHB should hit the 1-pin to the left of center, driving it back towards the 9-pin. The ball should continue through to hit the 5 and 8-pins, with the 5-pin also being sent to take out the 9-pin. Some bowlers prefer to hit the 1-pin head-on, driving it, the 5-pin, and ball straight back to take out the 8 and 9-pins. This is an acceptable way to make this spare.

SPARE: 1-5-8-10   Key Pin: **1-Pin**   Spare Number: **248**

Opposite Spare: 245

1
5
8
10

LEFT HAND BOWLER: *See Page 41*
SPARE ZONE: 1-Pin Zone
CONTACT AREA: Left on 1-Pin
APPROACH POSITIONS AND TARGETS:
3-6-9 System: Strike Position—
               Strike Target
2-4-6 System: Strike Position—
               Strike Target

RIGHT HAND BOWLER: *See Page 34*
SPARE ZONE: Head-On 1-Pin Zone
CONTACT AREA: Center on 1-Pin
APPROACH POSITIONS AND TARGETS:
3-6-9 System: Head-On 1-Pin Position—
               Strike Target
2-4-6 System: Strike Position—
               Move Target 1 Board LEFT

Best Way to Convert: The 10-pin makes this spare extremely difficult, especially for the RHB. A precise hit and accurate pin deflection are essential to make this spare. The LHB should hit the 1-pin on the left to send it into the 10-pin. The ball should have enough "drive" to continue on and take out the 5-pin and then the 8-pin. The RHB, however, must hit the 1-pin in the center and hope that it will deflect off the 5-pin into the 10-pin. The ball continues on to take out the 8-pin. (Some LHBs use this center hit too.) Hitting the 1-pin too light on either side would leave the 5-pin standing, so a high hit is necessary.

4

SPARE: 1-5-9-10   Key Pin: **1-Pin**   Spare Number: **249**

Opposite Spare: 244

1
5
9
10

LEFT HAND BOWLER: *See Page 41*
SPARE ZONE: 1-Pin Zone
CONTACT AREA: Left on 1-Pin
APPROACH POSITIONS AND TARGETS:
3-6-9 System: Strike Position—
               Strike Target
2-4-6 System: Strike Position—
               Strike Target

RIGHT HAND BOWLER: *See Page 34*
SPARE ZONE: Head-On 1-Pin Zone
CONTACT AREA: Center on 1-Pin
APPROACH POSITIONS AND TARGETS:
3-6-9 System: Head-On 1-Pin Position—
               Strike Target
2-4-6 System: Strike Position—
               Move Target 1 Board LEFT

Best Way to Convert: The 10-pin makes this spare extremely difficult, especially for the RHB. A precise hit and almost perfect pin deflection are needed to make the spare. The LHB should hit the 1-pin on the left and send it into the 10-pin. The ball should continue through to hit the 5-pin and send it into the 9-pin. The RHB, however, must hit the 1-pin in the center and hope for a deflection to the right into the 10-pin. The ball, the 1-pin, or the 5-pin might take out the 9-pin. (Some LHBs use the center hit on the 1-pin too.) Hitting the 1-pin too light on either side might leave the 5-pin standing, so a high hit is necessary.

SPARE: 1-6-7-10 Key Pin: Imaginary **3-Pin** Spare Number: **252**

Opposite Spare: 236

LEFT HAND BOWLER: *See Page 41*
SPARE ZONE: Head-On 3-Pin Zone
CONTACT AREA: Right on 1-Pin
APPROACH POSITIONS AND TARGETS:
3-6-9 System: Head-On 3-Pin Position—
        Strike Target
2-4-6 System: Strike Position—
        Move Target 3 Boards RIGHT

RIGHT HAND BOWLER: *See Page 34*
SPARE ZONE: Head-On 3-Pin Zone
CONTACT AREA: Right on 1-Pin
APPROACH POSITIONS AND TARGETS:
3-6-9 System: Head-On 3-Pin Position—
        10-Pin Target
2-4-6 System: Not Used on This Spare

Best Way to Convert: (*Washout*) This is still another of the Left Side Washouts requiring a precise hit and good ball and pin deflection for making the spare. It is not a split because the 1-pin is standing. Hit the 1-pin on the right side to send it directly into the 7-pin. It might take out the 7-pin off the kickback, but try for a direct hit instead. The ball should deflect to the right and into the 6-pin, driving it into the 10-pin. Ball deflection favors the LHB on this washout, so the RHB should use the Head-On 3-Pin Approach Position to increase ball deflection off the 1-pin into the 6-pin.

SPARE: 1-6-8-10 Key Pin: **1-Pin** Spare Number: **254**

Opposite Spare: 235

LEFT HAND BOWLER: *See Page 41*
SPARE ZONE: 1-Pin Zone
CONTACT AREA: Left on 1-Pin
APPROACH POSITIONS AND TARGETS:
3-6-9 System: Strike Position—
        Strike Target
2-4-6 System: Strike Position—
        Strike Target

RIGHT HAND BOWLER: *See Page 34*
SPARE ZONE: 2-Pin Zone
CONTACT AREA: Left on 1-Pin
APPROACH POSITIONS AND TARGETS:
3-6-9 System: 2-Pin Position—
        Strike Target
2-4-6 System: Strike Position—
        Move Target 2 Boards LEFT

Best Way to Convert: Ball and pin deflection are both factors in this difficult spare, which is not a split since the 1-pin is standing. It is slightly easier for the LHB, since ball and pin deflection favor a hit from the left side. Both bowlers should hit the 1-pin on the left side as shown, covering the 1 and 8-pins with the ball. The 1-pin should be sent into the 6-pin, and either the 1 or 6-pin should take out the 10-pin. Some LHB use a right center hit on the 1-pin, driving it into the 8-pin. The ball deflects into the 6 and 10-pins.

SPARE: 2-4-5-7   Key Pin: **2-Pin**   Spare Number: **282**

Opposite Spare: 334

LEFT HAND BOWLER: See Page 41
SPARE ZONE: 2-Pin Zone
CONTACT AREA: Left on 2-Pin
APPROACH POSITIONS AND TARGETS:
3-6-9 System: 2-Pin Position—
             7-Pin Target
2-4-6 System: Not Used on This Spare

RIGHT HAND BOWLER: See Page 34
SPARE ZONE: 4-Pin Zone
CONTACT AREA: Left on 2-Pin
APPROACH POSITIONS AND TARGETS:
3-6-9 System: 4-Pin Position—
             Strike Target
2-4-6 System: Strike Position—
             Move Target 4 Boards LEFT

Best Way to Convert: Chop possibilities exist for both the RHB and LHB on this spare, but more so for the RHB. A precise hit is needed. Ball and pin deflection favor the RHB. Hit the 2-pin on the left side as shown. For the RHB the ball should cover the 2-4-7-pins and the 2 should take out the 5-pin. The ball might also cover the 2-4-7-pins for the LHB, or the 4- pin could take out the 7-pin because ball deflection is a little more difficult for the LHB. Using the 2-Pin Approach Position would reduce the angle and increase ball deflection. Hitting the 2-pin too full or too light on either side could result in a miss. (Some RHB prefer to hit the 2-pin on the right side, as in a 2-5 Leave, using the 2-Pin Approach Position.)

SPARE: 2-4-5-8   Key Pin: **2-Pin**   Spare Number: **283**

Opposite Spare: 333

LEFT HAND BOWLER: See Page 41
SPARE ZONE: 2-Pin Zone
CONTACT AREA: Left Center on 2-Pin
APPROACH POSITIONS AND TARGETS:
3-6-9 System: 2-Pin Position—
             7-Pin Target
2-4-6 System: Not Used on This Spare

RIGHT HAND BOWLER: See Page 34
SPARE ZONE: 2-Pin Zone
CONTACT AREA: Right Center on 2-Pin
APPROACH POSITIONS AND TARGETS:
3-6-9 System: 2-Pin Position—
             Strike Target
2-4-6 System: Strike Position—
             Move Target 2 Boards LEFT

Best Way to Convert: *(Bucket)(Dinner Bucket)(Dinner Pail)* This is one of three similar Leaves with chop possibilities for both the RHB and LHB. The "Sleeper" 8-Pin presents the problem. An accurate hit that covers the 8-pin with the ball is required to cover the spare. The RHB should hit the 2-pin to the right of center, taking out the 2-5 and 8-pins with the ball as the 2-pin takes out the 4-pin. The LHB hits the 2-pin to the left of center, taking out the 2-4 and 8-pins with the ball as the 2-pin takes out the 5-pin. Some RHB shoot this spare from the left side of the approach to reduce chop possibilities, which can occur with a high hit on the 2-pin. (See the 1-2-3-5 and 3-5-6-9 Spares.)

SPARE: 2-4-5-10   Key Pin: **2-Pin**   Spare Number: **285-S**

Opposite Spare: 331-S

LEFT HAND BOWLER: See Page 41
SPARE ZONE: 2-Pin Zone
CONTACT AREA: Left on 2-Pin
APPROACH POSITIONS AND TARGETS:
3-6-9 System: 2-Pin Position—
                 7-Pin Target
2-4-6 System: Not Used on This Spare

RIGHT HAND BOWLER: See Page 34
SPARE ZONE: Head-On 4-Pin Zone
CONTACT AREA: Left on 2-Pin
APPROACH POSITIONS AND TARGETS:
3-6-9 System: Head-On 4-Pin Position—
                 Strike Target
2-4-6 System: Strike Position—
                 Move Target 5 Boards LEFT

Best Way to Convert: Keep Pin Count In Mind! Proper pin deflection is needed to make this difficult split. Hit the 2-pin on the left side as shown and try to deflect the 2-pin or the 5-pin across the lane into the 10-pin. The ball will take out the 4-pin. A left center hit on the 2-pin would probably insure getting three pins (the 2-4-5) and might send the 5-pin into the 10-pin. Be sure you hit the 2-pin on your conversion attempt to get maximum pin count should you not make the spare. (See the opposite side 3-5-6-7 Spare.)

SPARE: 2-4-6-7   Key Pin: **2-Pin**   Spare Number: **286-S**

Opposite Spare: 324-S

LEFT HAND BOWLER: See Page 41
SPARE ZONE: Head-On 4-Pin Zone
CONTACT AREA: Far Left on 2-Pin
APPROACH POSITIONS AND TARGETS:
3-6-9 System: Head-On 4-Pin Position—
                 7-Pin Target
2-4-6 System: Not Used on This Spare

RIGHT HAND BOWLER: See Page 34
SPARE ZONE: Head-On 4-Pin Zone
CONTACT AREA: Far Left on 2-Pin
APPROACH POSITIONS AND TARGETS:
3-6-9 System: Head-On 4-Pin Position—
                 Strike Target
2-4-6 System: Strike Position—
                 Move Target 5 Boards LEFT

Best Way to Convert: Keep Pin Count In Mind! An accurate hit, and good ball and pin deflection are all needed to make this difficult split. Ball deflection favors the RHB. The RHB should hit the far left side of the 2-pin, sliding it across the lane into the 6-pin. The ball should then take out the 4 and 7-pins. The LHB should hit the 2-pin in the same place and hope that the same pin and ball deflection take place; or that the 4-pin takes out the 7-pin. Using the Head-On 4-Pin Approach Position should reduce the angle for the LHB and increase ball deflection off the 2-pin and 4-pin. Try for this split exactly like playing for the 2-7 Baby Split. Be sure you hit the 2-pin to get maximum pin count if you miss the split.

SPARE: 2-4-6-10   Key Pin: **2-Pin**   Spare Number: **289-S**

Opposite Spare: 321-S

2
4
6
10

LEFT HAND BOWLER: See Page 41
SPARE ZONE: Head-On 4-Pin Zone
CONTACT AREA: Far Left on 2-Pin
APPROACH POSITIONS AND TARGETS:
3-6-9 System: Head-On 4-Pin Position—
7-Pin Target
2-4-6 System: Not Used on This Spare

RIGHT HAND BOWLER: See Page 34
SPARE ZONE: Head-On 4-Pin Zone
CONTACT AREA: Far Left on 2-Pin
APPROACH POSITIONS AND TARGETS:
3-6-9 System: Head-On 4-Pin Position—
Strike Target
2-4-6 System: Strike Position—
Move Target 5 Boards LEFT

Best Way to Convert: Keep Pin Count In Mind! This split is similar to the 2-4-6-7-10-split but without the 7-pin. It is a little easier, but still a difficult split to make. An accurate hit on the 2-pin and proper pin deflection are needed to produce a spare. Hit the 2-pin on the far left side as shown to slide it across into the 6-pin. The ball will take out the 4-pin, and the 2-pin or 6-pin might take out the 10-pin. Make sure you hit the 2-pin on your attempt. This should give you maximum pin count if you fail to make the conversion. (See the 2-4-6-7-10 Split.)

4

SPARE: 2-4-7-8   Key Pin: **2-Pin**   Spare Number: **290**

Opposite Spare: 346

2
4
7
8

LEFT HAND BOWLER: See Page 41
SPARE ZONE: Head-On 2-Pin Zone
CONTACT AREA: Left Center on 2-Pin
APPROACH POSITIONS AND TARGETS:
3-6-9 System: Head-On 2-Pin Position—
7-Pin Target
2-4-6 System: Not Used on This Spare

RIGHT HAND BOWLER: See Page 34
SPARE ZONE: 2-Pin Zone
CONTACT AREA: Right on 2-Pin
APPROACH POSITIONS AND TARGETS:
3-6-9 System: 2-Pin Position—
Strike Target
2-4-6 System: Strike Position—
Move Target 2 Boards LEFT

Best Way to Convert: The 8-Pin Sleeper makes this a very difficult spare, with chop possibilities. Hitting the 2-pin too full or too light on either side could result in a miss. The RHB should hit the 2-pin on the right to cover it and the 8-pin with the ball. The 2-pin should send the 4 into the 7-pin. The LHB should hit the 2-pin on the left center to cover the 2-4 and 8-pins with the ball. The 4-pin should take out the 7-pin. A fairly accurate hit is needed for the spare, with both ball and pin deflection favoring the RHB. Some RHB prefer to hit the 2-pin toward center or left center.

SPARE: 2-4-7-10　　Key Pin: 2-Pin　　Spare Number: 292-S

Opposite Spare: 343-S

LEFT HAND BOWLER: See Page 41
SPARE ZONE: Head-On 4-Pin Zone
CONTACT AREA: Far Left on 2-Pin
APPROACH POSITIONS AND TARGETS:
3-6-9 System: Head-On 4-Pin Position—
　　　　　　　7-Pin Target
2-4-6 System: Not Used on This Spare

RIGHT HAND BOWLER: See Page 34
SPARE ZONE: Head-On 4-Pin Zone
CONTACT AREA: Far Left on 2-Pin
APPROACH POSITIONS AND TARGETS:
3-6-9 System: Head-On 4-Pin Position—
　　　　　　　Strike Target
2-4-6 System: Strike Position—
　　　　　　　Move Target 5 Boards LEFT

Best Way to Convert: Keep Pin Count In Mind! An accurate hit, and proper ball and pin deflection are required to make this difficult split. It is similar to the 2-4-10, but the 7-pin makes it slightly more difficult for the LHB. Hit the 2-pin on the far left as shown, and slide it across into the 10-pin. The ball should deflect to the left and take out the 2-4 and 7-pins. Ball deflection is working for the RHB but against the LHB. The LHB should use the Head-On 4-Pin Approach Position to increase ball deflection off the 2 and 4-pins to cover the 7-pin. Be sure to hit the 2-pin on your conversion try, to get maximum pin count should you fail to convert the split. (See the 2-4-10 Split.)

SPARE: 2-4-8-10　　Key Pin: 2-Pin　　Spare Number: 294-S

Opposite Spare: 342-S

LEFT HAND BOWLER: See Page 41
SPARE ZONE: Head-On 4-Pin Zone
CONTACT AREA: Far Left on 2-Pin
APPROACH POSITIONS AND TARGETS:
3-6-9 System: Head-On 4-Pin Position—
　　　　　　　7-Pin Target
2-4-6 System: Not Used on This Spare

RIGHT HAND BOWLER: See Page 34
SPARE ZONE: Head-On 4-Pin Zone
CONTACT AREA: Far Left on 2-Pin
APPROACH POSITIONS AND TARGETS:
3-6-9 System: Head-On 4-Pin Position—
　　　　　　　Strike Target
2-4-6 System: Strike Position—
　　　　　　　Move Target 5 Boards LEFT

Best Way to Convert: Keep Pin Count In Mind! This extremely difficult split can be made, but if pin count is essential, *take three*. Both pin and ball deflection are critical on this split. The RHB should hit the 2-pin on the far left, sliding it across into the 10-pin. The ball takes out the 4-pin which could hit the extreme left side of the 8-pin. The LHB makes the same hit to the far left on the 2-pin, sending it into the 10-pin. Then, either the ball or the 4-pin might take out the 8-pin. Notice that the RHB can not cover the 8-pin with the ball on the conversion attempt because the ball is deflected too much to the left, not driving to the right as with the LHB. If pin count is critical, only play for the 2-4-8-pins. (See the 2-4-8 Spare.)

SPARE: 2-5-7-8   Key Pin: **2-Pin**   Spare Number: **300-S**

Opposite Spare: 340-S

2
5
7
8

LEFT HAND BOWLER: See Page 41
SPARE ZONE: Head-On 2-Pin Zone
CONTACT AREA: Left Center on 2-Pin
APPROACH POSITIONS AND TARGETS:
3-6-9 System: Head-On 2-Pin Position—
                   7-Pin Target
2-4-6 System: Not Used on This Spare

RIGHT HAND BOWLER: See Page 34
SPARE ZONE: 2-Pin Zone
CONTACT AREA: Right on 2-Pin
APPROACH POSITIONS AND TARGETS:
3-6-9 System: 2-Pin Position—
                   Strike Target
2-4-6 System: Strike Position—
                   Move Target 2 Boards LEFT

Best Way to Convert: Keep Pin Count In Mind! Ball and pin deflection favor the RHB on this Leave, which means that the LHB needs a more precise hit to convert the split. The RHB should hit the 2-pin on the right to drive it into the 7-pin, as the ball continues through and takes out the 5 and 8-pins. The LHB should hit more towards the center of the 2-pin and try to deflect it off the 5-pin or 8-pin into the 7-pin. The ball covers the 2-5 and 8-pins. The LHB could play this split exactly like the 2-7 Baby Split, but a very precise hit is needed, and the possibility of leaving the 8-pin or 5-pin is very great. Make sure you hit the 2-pin on your conversion attempt, to get maximum pin count should you miss the spare.

4

SPARE: 2-6-7-10   Key Pin: Imaginary **4-Pin**   Spare Number: **308-S**

Opposite Spare: 327-S

2
6
7
10

LEFT HAND BOWLER: See Page 41
SPARE ZONE: Head-On 4-Pin Zone
CONTACT AREA: Far Left on 2-Pin
APPROACH POSITIONS AND TARGETS:
3-6-9 System: Head-On 4-Pin Position—
                   7-Pin Target
2-4-6 System: Not Used on This Spare

RIGHT HAND BOWLER: See Page 34
SPARE ZONE: Head-On 4-Pin Zone
CONTACT AREA: Far Left on 2-Pin
APPROACH POSITIONS AND TARGETS:
3-6-9 System: Head-On 4-Pin Position—
                   Strike Target
2-4-6 System: Strike Position—
                   Move Target 5 Boards LEFT

Best Way to Convert: Keep Pin Count In Mind! An accurate hit, and precise pin and ball deflection are all needed to make this difficult split. Play it as you would the 2-7 Baby Split or the 2-6 Split. Hit the 2-pin on the far left and slide it across the lane into the 6-pin. The ball should deflect to the left into the 7-pin, and either the 2-pin or the 6-pin might take out the 10-pin. Ball deflection works for the RHB on this split, so the LHB should use the Head-On 4-Pin Approach Position to increase ball deflection off the 2-pin into the 7-pin. Be sure to hit the 2-pin on your conversion try, to get maximum pin count if you miss the split. Of course, if you need only two pins go for the 6-10-pins. (See the 2-7 and 2-6 Splits.)

SPARE: 2-7-8-10   Key Pin: RHB: **2-Pin**   Spare Number: **313-S**

LHB: Imaginary **4-Pin**   Opposite Spare: 349-S

LEFT HAND BOWLER: See Page 41
SPARE ZONE: Head-On 4-Pin Zone
CONTACT AREA: Far Left on 2-Pin
APPROACH POSITIONS AND TARGETS:
3-6-9 System: Head-On 4-Pin Position—
7-Pin Target
2-4-6 System: Not Used on This Spare

RIGHT HAND BOWLER: See Page 34
SPARE ZONE: Head-On 2-Pin Zone
CONTACT AREA: Center on 2-Pin
APPROACH POSITIONS AND TARGETS:
3-6-9 System: Head-On 2-Pin Position—
Strike Target
2-4-6 System: Strike Position—
Move Target 3 Boards LEFT

Best Way to Convert: (*Christmas Tree With Package*) Ball deflection makes this split much easier for the LHB, but still a very difficult split. The LHB should hit the 2-pin on the far left side to send it across the lane into the 10-pin. The ball should deflect slightly to the left and directly between the 7 and 8-pins. The RHB should hit the 2-pin slightly left of center, driving that pin back into the 8-pin and hope for pin deflection to the right into the 10-pin. The ball should deflect to the left into the 7-pin, because the ball is driving left and ball deflection is favorable. If pin count is vital, the RHB should play for three pins by hitting the 2-pin on the right as in the 2-7-8 Split. (See the 2-7-8 Split.)

SPARE: 2-7-9-10   Key Pin: Imaginary **4-Pin**   Spare Number: **314-S**

Opposite Spare: 348-S

LEFT HAND BOWLER: See Page 41
SPARE ZONE: Head-On 4-Pin Zone
CONTACT AREA: Left on 2-Pin
APPROACH POSITIONS AND TARGETS:
3-6-9 System: Head-On 4-Pin Position—
7-Pin Target
2-4-6 System: Not Used on This Spare

RIGHT HAND BOWLER: See Page 34
SPARE ZONE: Head-On 4-Pin Zone
CONTACT AREA: Left on 2-Pin
APPROACH POSITIONS AND TARGETS:
3-6-9 System: Head-On 4-Pin Position—
Strike Target
2-4-6 System: Strike Position—
Move Target 5 Boards LEFT

Best Way to Convert: Keep Pin Count In Mind! This unusual split might more properly belong in the rares, but it does occur with some frequency. Play for it like the 2-7-10 Split. Hit the 2-pin on the left as shown, sending it into the 9-pin. The ball should deflect to the left into the 7-pin, as the 2-pin or 9-pin deflects into the 10-pin. Of course, accurate pin deflection is essential. Ball deflection favors the RHB on this split, so the LHB should use the Head-On 4-Pin Approach Position to increase ball deflection off the 2-pin into the 7-pin. (See the 2-7-10 Split.)

SPARE: 3-4-6-7
Key Pin: 3-Pin

3
4
6
7

LEFT HAND BOWLER: See Page 41
SPARE ZONE: Head-On 6-Pin Zone
CONTACT AREA: Far Right on 3-Pin
APPROACH POSITIONS AND TARGETS:
3-6-9 System: Head-On 6-Pin Position—
　　　　　　　Strike Target
2-4-6 System: Strike Position—
　　　　　　　Move Target 5 Boards RIGHT

RIGHT HAND BOWLER: See Page 34
SPARE ZONE: Head-On 6-Pin Zone
CONTACT AREA: Far Right on 3-Pin
APPROACH POSITIONS AND TARGETS:
3-6-9 System: Head-On 6-Pin Position—
　　　　　　　10-Pin Target
2-4-6 System: Not Used on This Spare

Best Way to Convert: Keep Pin Count In Mind! This split is similar to the 3-4-6-7-10 but without the 10-pin. It is a little easier, although still a difficult split. An accurate hit on the 3-pin and proper pin deflection are needed. Hit the 3-pin on the far right as shown to slide it across into the 4-pin. The ball will take out the 6-pin, and the 3-pin or 4-pin might take out the 7-pin. Make sure you hit the 3-pin to get maximum pin count in case you miss the split. (See the 3-4-6-7-10 Split.)

4

SPARE: 3-4-6-10
Key Pin: 3-Pin

3
4
6
10

LEFT HAND BOWLER: See Page 41
SPARE ZONE: Head-On 6-Pin Zone
CONTACT AREA: Far Right on 3-Pin
APPROACH POSITIONS AND TARGETS:
3-6-9 System: Head-On 6-Pin Position—
　　　　　　　Strike Target
2-4-6 System: Strike Position—
　　　　　　　Move Target 5 Boards RIGHT

RIGHT HAND BOWLER: See Page 34
SPARE ZONE: Head-On 6-Pin Zone
CONTACT AREA: Far Right on 3-Pin
APPROACH POSITIONS AND TARGETS:
3-6-9 System: Head-On 6-Pin Position—
　　　　　　　10-Pin Target
2-4-6 System: Not Used on This Spare

Best Way to Convert: Keep Pin Count In Mind! An accurate hit, and precise ball and pin deflection are needed to make this difficult split. Try for it as you would for the 3-10 Baby Split. The LHB should hit the 3-pin on the far right side and slide it across into the 4-pin; the ball should then take out the 6 and 10-pins, too. (Ball deflection is favorable for the LHB.) The RHB should hit the 3-pin in the same place and hope for the same pin and ball deflection, or that the 6-pin will take out the 10-pin. Using the Head-On 6-Pin Approach Position will reduce the angle and increase ball deflection for the RHB. Make sure you hit the 3-pin on the attempt to get maximum pin count should the split be missed. (See the 3-10 Split.)

SPARE: 3-4-7-10   Key Pin: Imaginary **6-Pin**   Spare Number: **327-S**

Opposite Spare: 308-S

LEFT HAND BOWLER: See Page 41
SPARE ZONE: Head-On 6-Pin Zone
CONTACT AREA: Far Right on 3-Pin
APPROACH POSITIONS AND TARGETS:
3-6-9 System: Head-On 6-Pin Position—
            Strike Target
2-4-6 System: Strike Position—
            Move Target 5 Boards RIGHT

RIGHT HAND BOWLER: See Page 34
SPARE ZONE: Head-On 6-Pin Zone
CONTACT AREA: Far Right on 3-Pin
APPROACH POSITIONS AND TARGETS:
3-6-9 System: Head-On 6-Pin Position—
            10-Pin Target
2-4-6 System: Not Used on This Spare

Best Way to Convert: Keep Pin Count In Mind! An accurate hit, and pin and ball deflection are all needed to make this difficult split. Play it as you would the 3-10 Baby Split, or the 3-4 Split. Hit the 3-pin on the far right and slide it across into the 4-pin. The ball should deflect to the right into the 10-pin, and either the 3-pin or the 4-pin might take out the 7-pin. Ball deflection favors the LHB, so the RHB should use the Head-On 6-Pin Approach Position to increase ball deflection off the 3-pin. Be sure you hit the 3-pin on your conversion attempt to get maximum pin count in case you miss the split. Of course, if you need only two pins you would go for the 4-7 pins. (See the 3-10 and 3-4 Splits.)

SPARE: 3-5-6-7   Key Pin: **3-Pin**   Spare Number: **331-S**

Opposite Spare: 285-S

LEFT HAND BOWLER: See Page 41
SPARE ZONE: Head-On 6-Pin Zone
CONTACT AREA: Right on 3-Pin
APPROACH POSITIONS AND TARGETS:
3-6-9 System: Head-On 6-Pin Position—
            Strike Target
2-4-6 System: Strike Position—
            Move Target 5 Boards RIGHT

RIGHT HAND BOWLER: See Page 34
SPARE ZONE: 3-Pin Zone
CONTACT AREA: Right on 3-Pin
APPROACH POSITIONS AND TARGETS:
3-6-9 System: 3-Pin Position—
            10-Pin Target
2-4-6 System: Not Used on This Spare

Best Way to Convert: Keep Pin Count In Mind! Proper pin deflection is needed to convert this difficult split. But it can be made and should be attempted. Hit the 3-pin on the right as shown and try to deflect the 3-pin or 5-pin across the lane into the 7-pin. A right center hit on the 3-pin would probable insure getting three pins (the 3-5-6) and might send the 5-pin into the 7-pin. Be sure you hit the 3-pin on your conversion attempt to get maximum pin count should you not make the spare. (See the opposite side 2-4-5-10 Split.)

SPARE: 3-5-6-9 Key Pin: **3-Pin** Spare Number: **333**

Opposite Spare: **283**

3
5
6
9

LEFT HAND BOWLER: See Page 41
SPARE ZONE: 3-Pin Zone
CONTACT AREA: Left Center on 3-Pin
APPROACH POSITIONS AND TARGETS:
3-6-9 System: 3-Pin Position—
Strike Target
2-4-6 System: Strike Position—
Move Target 2 Boards RIGHT

RIGHT HAND BOWLER: See Page 34
SPARE ZONE: Head-On 3-Pin Zone
CONTACT AREA: Right Center on 3-Pin
APPROACH POSITIONS AND TARGETS:
3-6-9 System: Head-On 3-Pin Position—
10-Pin Target
2-4-6 System: Not Used on This Spare

Best Way to Convert: (*Bucket*)(*Dinner Pail*)(*Dinner Bucket*) This is another of the three similar Leaves with four pins, and presenting chop possibilities for both the RHB and LHB. The 9-Pin Sleeper presents the problem. A precise hit that covers the 9-pin with the ball is needed. The RHB should hit the 3-pin to the right of center to take out the 3-6 and 9-pins with the ball, as the 3-pin takes out the 5-pin. The LHB hits the 3-pin to the left of center, taking out the 3-5-9-pins with the ball, as the 3-pin takes out the 6-pin. Some LHB shoot this spare from the right side of the approach to *reduce the angle* and *reduce chop possibilities,* which can occur with a high hit on the 3-pin. (See the 2-4-5-8 and 1-2-3-5 Spares.)

SPARE: 3-5-6-10 Key Pin: **3-Pin** Spare Number: **334**

Opposite Spare: **282**

4

3
5
6
10

LEFT HAND BOWLER: See Page 41
SPARE ZONE: 6-Pin Zone
CONTACT AREA: Right on 3-Pin
APPROACH POSITIONS AND TARGETS:
3-6-9 System: 6-Pin Position—
Strike Target
2-4-6 System: Strike Position—
Move Target 4 Boards RIGHT

RIGHT HAND BOWLER: See Page 34
SPARE ZONE: 3-Pin Zone
CONTACT AREA: Right on 3-Pin
APPROACH POSITIONS AND TARGETS:
3-6-9 System: 3-Pin Position—
10-Pin Target
2-4-6 System: Not Used on This Spare

Best Way to Convert: Chop possibilities exist for both the RHB and LHB on this spare, but more so for the LHB. A precise hit is needed. Ball and pin deflection favor the LHB. The LHB should hit the 3-pin on the right, covering the 3-6-10-pins with the ball as the 3-pin takes out the 5-pin. The RHB should try for the same hit and ball deflection. However, to increase ball deflection off the 3 and 6-pins the 3-Pin Approach Position should be used. Hitting the 3-pin too full could result in a chop. Some LHB prefer to hit the 3-pin on the left side, as in a 3-5 Leave, using the 3-Pin Approach Position.

SPARE: 3-5-9-10   Key Pin: **3-Pin**   Spare Number: **340-S**

Opposite Spare: 300-S

LEFT HAND BOWLER: See Page 41
SPARE ZONE: 3-Pin Zone
CONTACT AREA: Left on 3-Pin
APPROACH POSITIONS AND TARGETS:
3-6-9 System: 3-Pin Position—
　　　　　　　Strike Target
2-4-6 System: Strike Position—
　　　　　　　Move Target 2 Boards RIGHT

RIGHT HAND BOWLER: See Page 34
SPARE ZONE: Head-On 3-Pin Zone
CONTACT AREA: Right Center on 3-Pin
APPROACH POSITIONS AND TARGETS:
3-6-9 System: Head-On 3-Pin Position—
　　　　　　　10-Pin Target
2-4-6 System: Not Used on This Spare

Best Way to Convert: Keep Pin Count In Mind! Ball and pin deflection favor the LHB on this split, which means the RHB needs a more accurate hit for the spare. The LHB should hit the 3-pin on the left as shown to drive it into the 10-pin. The ball should continue through and take out the 5 and 9-pins. The RHB should hit more to the right center of the 3-pin to deflect it off the 5 or 9-pin into the 10-pin. The ball covers the 3-5 and 9-pins. The RHB could play this spare exactly like the 3-10 Baby Split, but a very precise hit is needed and the possibility of leaving the 5-pin or 9-pin (or both) is great. Make sure you hit the 3-pin on your conversion attempt, in order to get maximum pin count should you not make the spare.

SPARE: 3-6-7-9   Key Pin: **3-Pin**   Spare Number: **342-S**

Opposite Spare: 294-S

LEFT HAND BOWLER: See Page 41
SPARE ZONE: Head-On 6-Pin Zone
CONTACT AREA: Far Right on 3-Pin
APPROACH POSITIONS AND TARGETS:
3-6-9 System: Head-On 6-Pin Position—
　　　　　　　Strike Target
2-4-6 System: Strike Position—
　　　　　　　Move Target 5 Boards RIGHT

RIGHT HAND BOWLER: See Page 34
SPARE ZONE: Head-On 6-Pin Zone
CONTACT AREA: Far Right on 3-Pin
APPROACH POSITIONS AND TARGETS:
3-6-9 System: Head-On 6-Pin Position—
　　　　　　　10-Pin Target
2-4-6 System: Not Used on This Spare

Best Way to Convert: Keep Pin Count In Mind! This extremely difficult split can be made, but if pin count is essential, take three if you can. Both pin and ball deflection are critical on this split. The RHB should hit the 2-pin on the far right to slide it across into the 7-pin. The ball or the 6-pin might take out the 9-pin. The LHB makes the same hit to the far right on the 3-pin, sending it across the lanes into the 7-pin. The ball takes out the 6-pin which might hit the 9-pin on the extreme right side. Notice that the LHB can not cover the 9-pin with the ball on the conversion attempt because the ball is deflecting too much to the right, not driving to the left as with the RHB. If pin count is critical, only play for the 3-6-9-pins.

SPARE: 3-6-7-10   Key Pin: **3-Pin**   Spare Number: **343-S**

Opposite Spare: 292-S

3
6
7
10

LEFT HAND BOWLER: See Page 41
SPARE ZONE: Head-On 6-Pin Zone
CONTACT AREA: Far Right on 3-Pin
APPROACH POSITIONS AND TARGETS:
3-6-9 System: Head-On 6-Pin Position—
      Strike Target
2-4-6 System: Strike Position—
      Move Target 5 Boards RIGHT

RIGHT HAND BOWLER: See Page 34
SPARE ZONE: Head-On 6-Pin Zone
CONTACT AREA: Far Right on 3-Pin
APPROACH POSITIONS AND TARGETS:
3-6-9 System: Head-On 6-Pin Position—
      10-Pin Target
2-4-6 System: Not Used on This Spare

Best Way to Convert: Keep Pin Count In Mind! An accurate hit, and proper ball and pin deflection are needed to make this difficult split. It is similar to the 3-6-7, but the 10-pin makes it slightly more difficult for the RHB. Hit the 3-pin on the far right as shown and slide it across the lane into the 7-pin. The ball should deflect to the right and take out the 3-6 and 10-pins. Ball deflection is working for the LHB but against the RHB on this spare. The RHB should use the Head-On 6-Pin Approach Position to increase ball deflection off the 3 and 6-pins to cover the 10-pin. Be sure to hit the 3-pin on your spare attempt, to get maximum pin count if you miss the split. (See the 3-6-7 Split.)

4

SPARE: 3-6-9-10   Key Pin: **3-Pin**   Spare Number: **346**

Opposite Spare: 290

3
6
9
10

LEFT HAND BOWLER: See Page 41
SPARE ZONE: 3-Pin Zone
CONTACT AREA: Left on 3-Pin
APPROACH POSITIONS AND TARGETS:
3-6-9 System: 3-Pin Position—
      Strike Target
2-4-6 System: Strike Position—
      Move Target 2 Boards RIGHT

RIGHT HAND BOWLER: See Page 34
SPARE ZONE: Head-On 3-Pin Zone
CONTACT AREA: Right Center on 3-Pin
APPROACH POSITIONS AND TARGETS:
3-6-9 System: Head-On 3-Pin Position—
      10-Pin Target
2-4-6 System: Not Used on This Spare

Best Way to Convert: The 9-Pin Sleeper makes this a very difficult spare, with chop possibilities. Hitting the 3-pin too full could result in a chop. The LHB should hit the 3-pin on the left to cover it and the 9-pin with the ball. The 3-pin should send the 6-pin into the 10-pin. The RHB should hit the 3-pin on the right center as shown, covering the 3-6 and 9-pins with the ball. The 6-pin should take out the 10-pin. An accurate hit is needed by both the RHB and LHB to make this spare, with both ball and pin deflection favoring the LHB. Some LHB prefer to hit the 3-pin toward center or right center.

SPARE: 3-7-8-10

LEFT HAND BOWLER: *See Page 41*
SPARE ZONE: Head-On 6-Pin Zone
CONTACT AREA: Right on 3-Pin
APPROACH POSITIONS AND TARGETS:
3-6-9 System: Head-On 6-Pin Position—
              Strike Target
2-4-6 System: Strike Position—
              Move Target 5 Boards RIGHT

RIGHT HAND BOWLER: *See Page 34*
SPARE ZONE: Head-On 6-Pin Zone
CONTACT AREA: Right on 3-Pin
APPROACH POSITIONS AND TARGETS:
3-6-9 System: Head-On 6-Pin Position—
              10-Pin Target
2-4-6 System: Not Used on This Spare

Best Way to Convert: Keep Pin Count In Mind! This unusual split might be more properly classified as "Rare," but it does occur with some frequency. Play it like the 3-7-10 Split. Hit the 3-pin on the right as shown, sending it into the 8-pin. The 3-pin or the 8-pin might deflect to the left into the 7-pin. The ball should deflect to the right and into the 10-pin. Ball deflection favors the LHB on this split. The RHB should reduce the angle of the shot by using the Head-On 6-Pin Approach Position. This should increase ball deflection off the 3-pin into the 10-pin. (See the 3-7-10 Split.)

SPARE: 3-7-9-10

LEFT HAND BOWLER: *See Page 41*
SPARE ZONE: Head-On 3-Pin Zone
CONTACT AREA: Center on 3-Pin
APPROACH POSITIONS AND TARGETS:
3-6-9 System: Head-On 3-Pin Position—
              Strike Target
2-4-6 System: Strike Position—
              Move Target 3 Boards RIGHT

RIGHT HAND BOWLER: *See Page 34*
SPARE ZONE: Head-On 6-Pin Zone
CONTACT AREA: Far Right on 3-Pin
APPROACH POSITIONS AND TARGETS:
3-6-9 System: Head-On 6-Pin Position—
              10-Pin Target
2-4-6 System: Not Used on This Spare

Best Way to Convert: (*Christmas Tree With Package*) Ball deflection makes this split much easier for the RHB, but still a very difficult split. The RHB should hit the 3-pin on the far right to send it into the 7-pin. The ball should deflect to the right slightly and go directly between the 9 and 10-pins. The LHB should hit the 3-pin towards the center, driving it back into the 9-pin and hope for a deflection to the left into the 7-pin. The ball should deflect to the right into the 10-pin, because the ball is coming from the left and ball deflection is favorable. If pin count is vital, the LHB should play for three pins by hitting the 3-pin on the left as in the 3-9-10 Split. (See the 3-9-10 Split.)

SPARE: 4-5-7-8   Key Pin: Imaginary **2-Pin**   Spare Number: **355-S**

Opposite Spare: 376-S

4
5
7
8

LEFT HAND BOWLER: See Page 41
SPARE ZONE: Head-On 2-Pin Zone
CONTACT AREA: Between 4 and 5-Pins
APPROACH POSITIONS AND TARGETS:
3-6-9 System: Head-On 2-Pin Position—
                 7-Pin Target
2-4-6 System: Not Used on This Spare

RIGHT HAND BOWLER: See Page 34
SPARE ZONE: Head-On 2-Pin Zone
CONTACT AREA: Between 4 and 5-Pins
APPROACH POSITIONS AND TARGETS:
3-6-9 System: Head-On 2-Pin Position—
                 Strike Target
2-4-6 System: Strike Position—
                 Move Target 3 Boards LEFT

Best Way to Convert: Play for this split exactly as you would the 4-5, the 4-5-7, or the 4-5-8 Split. The presence of the 7-pin makes the split very difficult. Aim for an imaginary 2-pin that you want to hit head-on, and try to contact directly between the 4 and 5-pins. Slightly favor the 4-pin side, so the 4-pin has a chance to take out the 7-pin directly or off the kickback. Since pin count is always important, make sure you hit the 4-pin on your try for a conversion. This will give you the best chance to cover the 4-7 and 8-pins should you not make the split conversion.

4

SPARE: 4-5-7-10   Key Pin: Imaginary **2-Pin**   Spare Number: **357-S**

Opposite Spare: 373-S

4
5
7
10

LEFT HAND BOWLER: See Page 41
SPARE ZONE: Head-On 2-Pin Zone
CONTACT AREA: Between 4 and 5-Pins
APPROACH POSITIONS AND TARGETS:
3-6-9 System: Head-On 2-Pin Position—
                 7-Pin Target
2-4-6 System: Not Used on This Spare

RIGHT HAND BOWLER: See Page 34
SPARE ZONE: Head-On 2-Pin Zone
CONTACT AREA: Between 4 and 5-Pins
APPROACH POSITIONS AND TARGETS:
3-6-9 System: Head-On 2-Pin Position—
                 Strike Target
2-4-6 System: Strike Position—
                 Move Target 3 Boards LEFT

Best Way to Convert: This unusual (not Rare) split is a combination of the 4-5-7 and 4-5-10 Splits. Having both the 7 and 10-pins standing makes this a very difficult split. But it can be made and should be attempted. Try to hit directly between the 4 and 5-pins, so the 5-pin will slide to the right and take out the 10-pin and the 4-pin will take out the 7-pin directly or off the kickback. The 4-pin is very important on this split. Hitting it should give you at least two pins on your conversion attempt; and pin count is always important. (See the 4-5 Split.)

140

SPARE: 4-6-7-8   Key Pin: **4-Pin**   Spare Number: **361-S**

Opposite Spare: 366-S

LEFT HAND BOWLER: See Page 41
SPARE ZONE: Head-On 7-Pin Zone
CONTACT AREA: Far Left on 4-Pin
APPROACH POSITIONS AND TARGETS:
3-6-9 System: Head-On 7-Pin Position—
           7-Pin Target
2-4-6 System: Not Used on This Spare

RIGHT HAND BOWLER: See Page 34
SPARE ZONE: Head-On 7-Pin Zone
CONTACT AREA: Far Left on 4-Pin
APPROACH POSITIONS AND TARGETS:
3-6-9 System: Head-On 7-Pin Position—
           Strike Target
2-4-6 System: Strike Position—
           Move Target 7 Boards LEFT

Best Way to Convert: This is another of the six splits requiring *forward* pin deflection (or a lucky bounce) to convert. (See the list with the 4-6-7-9-10 Split.) An effort should be made to make this split since you should get at least three pins and might get lucky enough to make the spare. Hit the 4-pin on the far left side as shown, to try to deflect it off the front of the 8-pin and into the 6-pin. Or, just try for the Three Pin Cluster on the left and hope for a lucky bounce out of the pit. "Take three" is good advice on this difficult split, since pin count is always important. (Some bowlers prefer to play this similar to the 6-7-8 Split, hitting the 6-pin on the far right. We do not recommend this method, although it could work.)

SPARE: 4-6-7-9   Key Pin: **4-Pin**   Spare Number: **362-S**

Opposite Spare: 365-S

LEFT HAND BOWLER: See Page 41
SPARE ZONE: Head-On 7-Pin Zone
CONTACT AREA: Far Left on 4-Pin
APPROACH POSITIONS AND TARGETS:
3-6-9 System: Head-On 7-Pin Position—
           7-Pin Target
2-4-6 System: Not Used on This Spare

RIGHT HAND BOWLER: See Page 34
SPARE ZONE: Head-On 7-Pin Zone
CONTACT AREA: Far Left on 4-Pin
APPROACH POSITIONS AND TARGETS:
3-6-9 System: Head-On 7-Pin Position—
           Strike Target
2-4-6 System: Strike Position—
           Move Target 7 Boards LEFT

Best Way to Convert: This is another of the six splits requiring *forward* pin deflection (or a lucky bounce) to convert. (See the list with the 4-6-7-9-10 Split.) An effort should be made to convert this split, since you might get three pins, and could even be lucky enough to make all four. Hit the 4-pin on the far left to slide it across into the 9-pin. Either the 4-pin or 9-pin might fall forward enough to take out the 6-pin. The 4-7 or 6-9-pins might be driven into the pit and bounce out to knock down the other two pins. Make sure you get at least two pins on this very difficult split. Pin count is important.

SPARE: 4-6-7-10

Key Pin: RHB: **6-Pin**

LHB: **4-Pin**

Spare Number: **363-S**

Opposite Spare: None

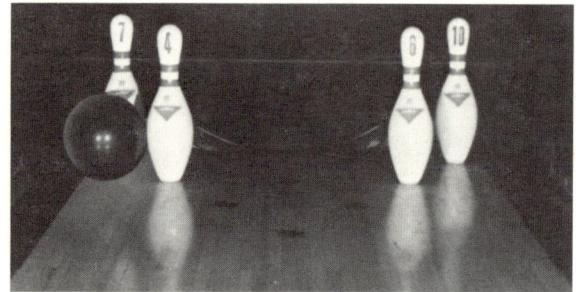

LEFT HAND BOWLER: See Page 41
SPARE ZONE: Head-On 7-Pin Zone
CONTACT AREA: Extreme Left on 4-Pin
APPROACH POSITIONS AND TARGETS:
3-6-9 System: Head-On 7-Pin Position—
7-Pin Target
2-4-6 System: Not Used on This Spare

RIGHT HAND BOWLER: See Page 34
SPARE ZONE: Head-On 10-Pin Zone
CONTACT AREA: Extreme Right on 6-Pin
APPROACH POSITIONS AND TARGETS:
3-6-9 System: Head-On 10-Pin Position—
10-Pin Target
2-4-6 System: Not Used on This Spare

Best Way to Convert: (*Big Four*)(*Golden Gate*) (*Double Pinochle*)(*Big Ears*) This extremely difficult split is made about 3,000 times each bowling season, and has been made by one bowler twice in a single game. Yet, three pins might be the best to hope for on this split, and "take two" might be good advice when pin count is really important. The split can be converted by: (1) sliding the 4-pin across to take out the 6 and 10-pins as the ball takes out the 7-pin; (2) sliding the 6-pin across to take out the 4 and 7-pins as the ball takes out the 10-pin; or (3) driving two pins into the pit and hope for a lucky bounce out of the pit to take out the other two pins. Keep pin count in mind and get maximum count when you leave this split.

SPARE: 4-6-8-10

Key Pin: **6-Pin**

Spare Number: **365-S**

Opposite Spare: 362-S

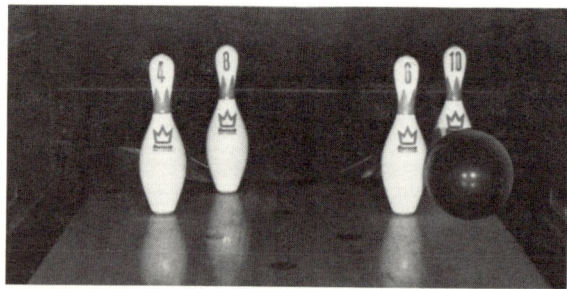

LEFT HAND BOWLER: See Page 41
SPARE ZONE: Head-On 10-Pin Zone
CONTACT AREA: Far Right on 6-Pin
APPROACH POSITIONS AND TARGETS:
3-6-9 System: Head-On 10-Pin Position—
Strike Target
2-4-6 System: Strike Position—
Move Target 7 Boards RIGHT

RIGHT HAND BOWLER: See Page 34
SPARE ZONE: Head-On 10-Pin Zone
CONTACT AREA: Far Right on 6-Pin
APPROACH POSITIONS AND TARGETS:
3-6-9 System: Head-On 10-Pin Position—
10-Pin Target
2-4-6 System: Not Used on This Spare

Best Way to Convert: This is another of the six splits requiring *forward* pin deflection (or a lucky bounce) to convert. See the list with the 4-6-7-9-10 Split. Some effort should be made to convert this one, since you might get three pins, and could even be lucky enough to make all four. Hit the 6-pin on the far right side and send it across into the 8-pin. Either the 6 or 8-pin might fall forward and cover the 4-pin. The 4-8 or 6-10 could be driven into the pit and bounce out to take the other two pins down. Make sure you get at least two pins on this very difficult split. Pin count is important.

SPARE: 4-6-9-10   Key Pin: **4-Pin**   Spare Number: **366-S**

Opposite Spare: 361-S

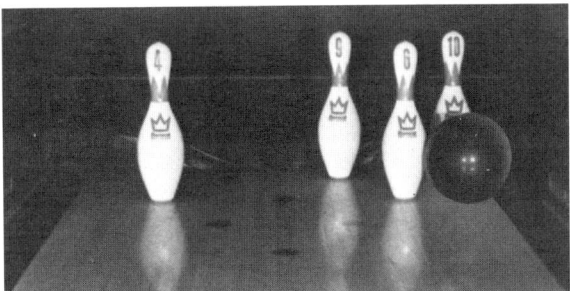

4
6
9
10

LEFT HAND BOWLER: See Page 41
SPARE ZONE: Head-On 10-Pin Zone
CONTACT AREA: Far Right on 6-Pin
APPROACH POSITIONS AND TARGETS:
3-6-9 System: Head-On 10-Pin Position—
                      Strike Target
2-4-6 System: Strike Position—
                      Move Target 7 Boards RIGHT

RIGHT HAND BOWLER: See Page 34
SPARE ZONE: Head-On 10-Pin Zone
CONTACT AREA: Far Right on 6-Pin
APPROACH POSITIONS AND TARGETS:
3-6-9 System: Head-On 10-Pin Position—
                      10-Pin Target
2-4-6 System: Not Used on This Spare

Best Way to Convert: This is another of the six splits requiring *forward* pin deflection (or a lucky bounce) to convert. (See the list with the 4-6-7-9-10 Split.) An effort should be made to make this split, since you should get at least three pins in the attempt and might get lucky enough to make the spare. Hit the 6-pin on the far right side to try to deflect it off the front of the 9-pin and into the 4-pin. Or, just try for the Three Pin Cluster and hope for a lucky bounce out of the pit. "Take three" is good advice on this difficult split, since pin count is important. (Some bowlers prefer to play this similar to the 4-9-10 Split, hitting the 4-pin on the far left. We do not recommend this method, although it could work.)

SPARE: 4-7-8-10   Key Pin: **4-Pin**   Spare Number: **368-S**

Opposite Spare: 383-S

4

4
7
8
10

LEFT HAND BOWLER: See Page 41
SPARE ZONE: Head-On 7-Pin Zone
CONTACT AREA: Far Left on 4-Pin
APPROACH POSITIONS AND TARGETS:
3-6-9 System: Head-On 7-Pin Position—
                      7-Pin Target
2-4-6 System: Not Used on This Spare

RIGHT HAND BOWLER: See Page 34
SPARE ZONE: Head-On 7-Pin Zone
CONTACT AREA: Far Left on 4-Pin
APPROACH POSITIONS AND TARGETS:
3-6-9 System: Head-On 7-Pin Position—
                      Strike Target
2-4-6 System: Strike Position—
                      Move Target 7 Boards LEFT

Best Way to Convert: Keep Pin Count In Mind! This split is played exactly like the 4-8-10 Split. The 7-pin does not make this Leave any more difficult than the 4-8-10. Try for a conversion, since you should not lose any pin count in your attempt. A precise hit and proper pin deflection are needed. Hit the 4-pin on the far left as shown, sending it into the 8-pin and across the lane into the 10-pin, as the ball takes out the 7-pin. Make sure you hit the 4-pin on your conversion attempt, to get maximum pin count should you miss the spare. (See the 4-8-10 Split.)

SPARE: 4-7-9-10

Key Pin: **4-Pin**

Spare Number: 369-S

Opposite Spare: 382-S

4
7
9
10

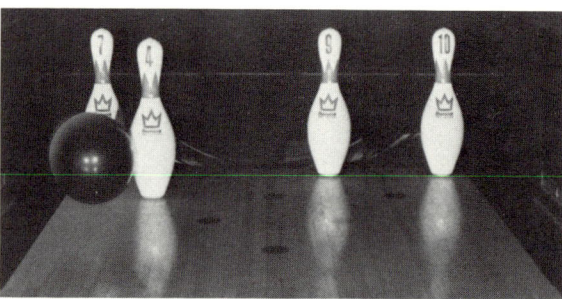

LEFT HAND BOWLER: See Page 41
SPARE ZONE: Head-On 7-Pin Zone
CONTACT AREA: Far Left on 4-Pin
APPROACH POSITIONS AND TARGETS:
3-6-9 System: Head-On 7-Pin Position—
7-Pin Target
2-4-6 System: Not Used on This Spare

RIGHT HAND BOWLER: See Page 34
SPARE ZONE: Head-On 7-Pin Zone
CONTACT AREA: Far Left on 4-Pin
APPROACH POSITIONS AND TARGETS:
3-6-9 System: Head On 7 Pin Position—
Strike Target
2-4-6 System: Strike Position—
Move Target 7 Boards LEFT

Best Way to Convert: Keep Pin Count In Mind! This split is played exactly like the 4-9-10 since the presence of the 7-pin does not make this spare any more difficult. Hit the 4-pin on the far left side to slide it across into the 9-pin. The ball takes out the 7-pin and either the 4 or 9-pin might take out the 10-pin. Ob-

viously a precise hit on the 4-pin and proper pin deflection are required to convert this difficult split. Make sure you hit the 4-pin on your attempt, so you will get maximum pin count if you miss the spare. (See the 4-9-10 Split.)

4

SPARE: 5-6-7-10

Key Pin: Imaginary **3-Pin**

Spare Number: 373-S

Opposite Spare: 357-S

5
6
7
10

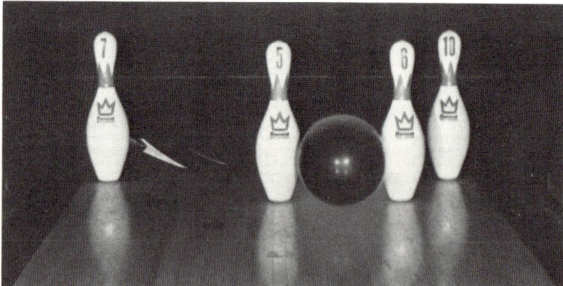

LEFT HAND BOWLER: See Page 41
SPARE ZONE: Head-On 3-Pin Zone
CONTACT AREA: Between 5 and 6-Pins
APPROACH POSITIONS AND TARGETS:
3-6-9 System: Head-On 3-Pin Position—
Strike Target
2-4-6 System: Strike Position—
Move Target 3 Boards RIGHT

RIGHT HAND BOWLER: See Page 34
SPARE ZONE: Head-On 3-Pin Zone
CONTACT AREA: Between 5 and 6-Pins
APPROACH POSITIONS AND TARGETS:
3-6-9 System: Head-On 3-Pin Position—
10-Pin Target
2-4-6 System: Not Used on This Spare

Best Way to Convert: This unusual (but not Rare) split is a combination of the 5-6-10 and 5-6-7 Splits. Having both the 7 and 10-pins standing makes this a very difficult split to convert. But it can be made and should be attempted. Try to hit directly between the 5 and 6-pins, so the 5-pin will slide across the lane and

take out the 7-pin, and the 6-pin will take out the 10-pin directly or off the kickback. A very accurate hit is necessary. The 6-pin is very important on this split. Hitting it should give you at least two pins on your conversion attempt; and pin count is always important. (See the 5-6 Split.)

SPARE: 5-6-9-10

Key Pin: Imaginary **3-Pin**

Spare Number: **376-S**

Opposite Spare: 355-S

LEFT HAND BOWLER: See Page 41
SPARE ZONE: Head-On 3-Pin Zone
CONTACT AREA: Between 5 and 6-Pins
APPROACH POSITIONS AND TARGETS:
3-6-9 System: Head-On 3-Pin Position—
　　　　　　Strike Target
2-4-6 System: Strike Position—
　　　　　　Move Target 3 Boards RIGHT

RIGHT HAND BOWLER: See Page 34
SPARE ZONE: Head-On 3-Pin Zone
CONTACT AREA: Between 5 and 6-Pins
APPROACH POSITIONS AND TARGETS:
3-6-9 System: Head-On 3-Pin Position—
　　　　　　10-Pin Target
2-4-6 System: Not Used on This Spare

Best Way to Convert: Play for this split exactly as you would the 5-6, the 5-6-10 or the 5-6-9 Split. The presence of the 10-pin makes the split very difficult. Aim for an imaginary 3-pin that you would like to hit head-on. Try to contact directly between the 5 and 6-pins, slightly favoring the 6-pin. This will give the 6-pin a chance to take out the 10-pin directly, or off the kickback. Since pin count is important, particularly on splits, make sure you hit the 6-pin on your attempt for a conversion. This will give you the best chance to cover the 6-9 and 10-pins should you not make the split conversion.

SPARE: 6-7-8-10

Key Pin: **6-Pin**

Spare Number: **382-S**

Opposite Spare: 369-S

LEFT HAND BOWLER: See Page 41
SPARE ZONE: Head-On 10-Pin Zone
CONTACT AREA: Far Right on 6-Pin
APPROACH POSITIONS AND TARGETS:
3-6-9 System: Head-On 10-Pin Position—
　　　　　　Strike Target
2-4-6 System: Strike Position—
　　　　　　Move Target 7 Boards RIGHT

RIGHT HAND BOWLER: See Page 34
SPARE ZONE: Head-On 10-Pin Zone
CONTACT AREA: Far Right on 6-Pin
APPROACH POSITIONS AND TARGETS:
3-6-9 System: Head-On 10-Pin Position—
　　　　　　10-Pin Target
2-4-6 System: Not Used on This Spare

Best Way to Convert: Keep Pin Count In Mind! This split is attempted in exactly the same way as the 6-7-8 Split, since the 10-pin does not make this split more difficult to convert than the 6-7-8 Leave. An accurate hit on the 6-pin and very precise pin deflection are both needed to make the conversion for a spare. Hit the 6-pin on the far right as shown to slide that pin into the 8-pin. The ball takes out the 10-pin. Hopefully, either the 6-pin or the 8-pin will take out the 7-pin. Make sure you hit the 6-pin on your conversion attempt, to get maximum pin count should you miss the spare. (See the 6-7-8 Split.)

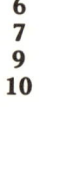

6
7
9
10

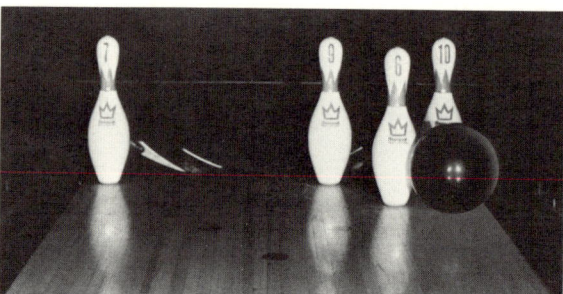

LEFT HAND BOWLER: See Page 41
SPARE ZONE: Head-On 10-Pin Zone
CONTACT AREA: Far Right on 6-Pin
APPROACH POSITIONS AND TARGETS:
3-6-9 System: Head On 10 Pin Position—
          Strike Target
2-4-6 System: Strike Position—
          Move Target 7 Boards RIGHT

RIGHT HAND BOWLER: See Page 34
SPARE ZONE: Head-On 10-Pin Zone
CONTACT AREA: Far Right on 6-Pin
APPROACH POSITIONS AND TARGETS:
3-6-9 System: Head-On 10-Pin Position—
          10-Pin Target
2-4-6 System: Not Used on This Spare

Best Way to Convert: Keep Pin Count In Mind! This spare is played just like the 6-7-9 Split, since the 10-pin does not make it any more difficult than that split. Try for the conversion, since you should not lose any pin count in your attempt. Hit the 6-pin on the far right side, sending it into the 9-pin and across the lane into the 7-pin, as the ball covers the 10-pin. A precise hit and proper pin deflection are needed. Make sure you hit the 6-pin on your conversion attempt, to get maximum pin count if you fail to convert the split. (See the 6-7-9 Split.)

4

1
2
3
4
5

LEFT HAND BOWLER: See Page 41
SPARE ZONE: 1-Pin Zone
CONTACT AREA: Left on 1-Pin
APPROACH POSITIONS AND TARGETS:
3-6-9 System: Strike Position—
               Strike Target
2-4-6 System: Strike Position—
               Strike Target

RIGHT HAND BOWLER: See Page 34
SPARE ZONE: 1-Pin Zone
CONTACT AREA: Right on 1-Pin
APPROACH POSITIONS AND TARGETS:
3-6-9 System: Strike Position—
               Strike Target
2-4-6 System: Strike Position—
               Strike Target

Best Way to Convert: Shooting for this spare should be exactly like shooting for a strike for both the RHB and LHB. The RHB should hit the 1-3 Pocket as shown, so the ball takes out the 1-3-5-pins, and the 2-pin takes out the 4-pin. The LHB hits the 1-2 Pocket so the ball covers the 1-2-5-pins, and the 2-pin takes out the 4-pin, while the 1-pin takes out the 3-pin. The 5-pin is very important in this spare, since the ball should hit it to take it out, rather than rely upon pin deflection. Of course, a full or light hit on the 1-pin could result in a miss.

5

1
2
3
4
7

LEFT HAND BOWLER: See Page 41
SPARE ZONE: Head-On 2-Pin Zone
CONTACT AREA: Left on 1-Pin
APPROACH POSITIONS AND TARGETS:
3-6-9 System: Head-On 2-Pin Position—
               7-Pin Target
2-4-6 System: Not Used on This Spare

RIGHT HAND BOWLER: See Page 34
SPARE ZONE: 2-Pin Zone
CONTACT AREA: Left on 1-Pin
APPROACH POSITIONS AND TARGETS:
3-6-9 System: 2-Pin Position—
               Strike Target
2-4-6 System: Strike Position—
               Move Target 2 Boards LEFT

Best Way to Convert: Both the RHB and LHB should hit the 1-pin on the left as shown. The RHB might cover the 1-2-4-7 "Clothesline" with the ball as the 1-pin takes out the 3-pin. Or, the 4-pin might take out the 7-pin. The LHB may get the same pin and ball deflection as the RHB, but more likely the 4-pin will take out the 7-pin. To increase ball deflection off the 1 and 2-pins, the LHB should use the Head-On 2-Pin Approach Position. Some LHB and RHB use the Strike Position to get the same pin deflection as on a perfect strike hit—The LHB hitting the 1-2 Pocket and the RHB hitting the 1-3 Pocket.

SPARE: 1-2-3-4-9   Key Pin: **1-Pin**   Spare Number: **390**

Opposite Spare: 398

1
2
3
4
9

LEFT HAND BOWLER: See Page 41
SPARE ZONE: 3-Pin Zone
CONTACT AREA: Right on 1-Pin
APPROACH POSITIONS AND TARGETS:
3-6-9 System: 3-Pin Position—
         Strike Target
2-4-6 System: Strike Position—
         Move Target 2 Boards RIGHT

RIGHT HAND BOWLER: See Page 34
SPARE ZONE: 1-Pin Zone
CONTACT AREA: Right on 1-Pin
APPROACH POSITIONS AND TARGETS:
3-6-9 System: Strike Position—
         Strike Target
2-4-6 System: Strike Position—
         Strike Target

Best Way to Convert: This spare requires an accurate hit and proper pin and ball deflection. Both the RHB and LHB should hit the 1-pin on the right as shown to cover the 1-3 and 9-pins with the ball. The 1-pin should send the 2-pin into the 4-pin. Either the 3-pin or the ball should cover the 9-pin.

5

SPARE: 1-2-3-5-6   Key Pin: **1-Pin**   Spare Number: **392**

Opposite Spare: 386

1
2
3
5
6

LEFT HAND BOWLER: See Page 41
SPARE ZONE: 1-Pin Zone
CONTACT AREA: Left on 1-Pin
APPROACH POSITIONS AND TARGETS:
3-6-9 System: Strike Position—
         Strike Target
2-4-6 System: Strike Position—
         Strike Target

RIGHT HAND BOWLER: See Page 34
SPARE ZONE: 1-Pin Zone
CONTACT AREA: Right on 1-Pin
APPROACH POSITIONS AND TARGETS:
3-6-9 System: Strike Position—
         Strike Target
2-4-6 System: Strike Position—
         Strike Target

Best Way to Convert: Shooting for this spare should be exactly like shooting for a strike for both the RHB and LHB. The RHB should hit the 1-3 Pocket as shown to cover the 1-3-5-pins with the ball, as the 1-pin takes out the 2-pin, and the 3-pin takes out the 6-pin. The LHB hits the 1-2 pocket to cover the 1-2 and 5-pins with the ball, as the 1-pin takes out the 3-pin, sending it into the 6-pin. The "5-Pin Sleeper" is very important on this spare since the ball must take it out. This requires a good "Driving Hit" on the 1-pin for both the LHB and RHB.

SPARE: 1-2-3-5-7   Key Pin: **1-Pin**   Spare Number: **393**

Opposite Spare: 396

1
2
3
5
7

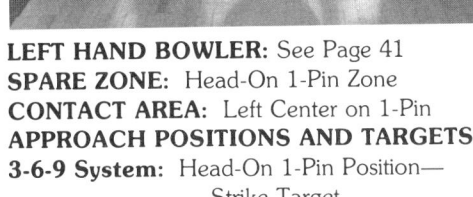

LEFT HAND BOWLER: See Page 41
SPARE ZONE: Head-On 1-Pin Zone
CONTACT AREA: Left Center on 1-Pin
APPROACH POSITIONS AND TARGETS:
3-6-9 System: Head-On 1-Pin Position—
       Strike Target
2-4-6 System: Strike Position—
       Move Target 1 Board RIGHT

RIGHT HAND BOWLER: See Page 34
SPARE ZONE: 1-Pin Zone
CONTACT AREA: Right on 1-Pin
APPROACH POSITIONS AND TARGETS:
3-6-9 System: Strike Position—
       Strike Target
2-4-6 System: Strike Position—
       Strike Target

Best Way to Convert: The 5-pin and 7-pin make this a difficult Spare Leave. The 5-pin should be covered by the ball, and pin deflection is needed to take out the 7-pin. The RHB hits the 1-3 Pocket to cover the 1-3-5-pins with the ball, and sending the 2-pin into the 7-pin. (A high hit on the 1-pin might send the 2-pin into the kickback and then into the 7-pin, but this method is not recommended.) The LHB hits the 1-2 Pocket as shown, to cover the 1-2-5-pins with the ball. The 1-pin takes out the 3-pin; and the 2-pin is sent into the 7-pin. A slightly more accurate hit is needed by the LHB to cover this spare, since pin deflection favors the RHB.

5

SPARE: 1-2-3-5-10   Key Pin: **1-Pin**   Spare Number: **396**

Opposite Spare: 393

1
2
3
5
10

LEFT HAND BOWLER: See Page 41
SPARE ZONE: 1-Pin Zone
CONTACT AREA: Left on 1-Pin
APPROACH POSITIONS AND TARGETS:
3-6-9 System: Strike Position—
       Strike Target
2-4-6 System: Strike Position—
       Strike Target

RIGHT HAND BOWLER: See Page 34
SPARE ZONE: Head-On 1-Pin Zone
CONTACT AREA: Right Center on 1-Pin
APPROACH POSITIONS AND TARGETS:
3-6-9 System: Head-On 1-Pin Position—
       Strike Target
2-4-6 System: Strike Position—
       Move Target 1 Board LEFT

Best Way to Convert: The 5-pin and 10-pin make this a difficult spare. The 5-pin should be covered by the ball, but pin deflection is needed to take out the 10-pin. The LHB covers the 1-2-5-pins with the ball, and sends the 3-pin into the 10-pin. (The 1-pin might also take it out.) The RHB hits the 1-3 Pocket to cover the 1-3-5-pins with the ball. The 1-pin takes out the 2-pin; the 3-pin should be deflected to the right into the 10-pin. A more accurate hit is needed by the RHB on this spare, since pin deflection favors the LHB. Both the 1 and 3-pins are sent to take out the 10-pin by the LHB, but only the 3-pin can be deflected by the RHB to cover the 10-pin.

SPARE: 1-2-3-6-8   Key Pin: **1-Pin**   Spare Number: **398**

Opposite Spare: 390

1
2
3
6
8

LEFT HAND BOWLER: *See Page 41*
SPARE ZONE: 1-Pin Zone
CONTACT AREA: Left on 1-Pin
APPROACH POSITIONS AND TARGETS:
3-6-9 System: Strike Position—
    Strike Target
2-4-6 System: Strike Position—
    Strike Target

RIGHT HAND BOWLER: *See Page 34*
SPARE ZONE: 2-Pin Zone
CONTACT AREA: Left on 1-Pin
APPROACH POSITIONS AND TARGETS:
3-6-9 System: 2-Pin Position—
    Strike Target
2-4-6 System: Strike Position—
    Move Target 2 Boards LEFT

Best Way to Convert: This Leave requires proper pin deflection and an accurate hit to make the spare. Both the LHB and RHB should hit the 1-pin on the left as shown, covering the 1-2-8-pins with the ball.

The 1 and 3-pins should be sent to take out the 6-pin. Either the ball or the 2-pin should take out the 8-Pin "Sleeper."

5

SPARE: 1-2-3-6-10   Key Pin: **1-Pin**   Spare Number: **400**

Opposite Spare: 388

1
2
3
6
10

LEFT HAND BOWLER: *See Page 41*
SPARE ZONE: 3-Pin Zone
CONTACT AREA: Right on 1-Pin
APPROACH POSITIONS AND TARGETS:
3-6-9 System: 3-Pin Position—
    Strike Target
2-4-6 System: Strike Position—
    Move Target 2 Boards RIGHT

RIGHT HAND BOWLER: *See Page 34*
SPARE ZONE: Head-On 3-Pin Zone
CONTACT AREA: Right on 1-Pin
APPROACH POSITIONS AND TARGETS:
3-6-9 System: Head-On 3-Pin Position—
    10-Pin Target
2-4-6 System: Not Used on This Spare

Best Way to Convert: Ball deflection favors the LHB on this spare. The LHB should hit the 1-pin on the right, covering the 1-3-6-10-pins with the ball as the 1-pin takes out the 2-pin. The RHB also hits the 1-pin as shown, and may get the same pin and ball deflection if the Head-On 3-Pin Approach Position is

used. Or, the 6-pin might take out the 10-pin. Some RHB and LHB use the Strike Position on this spare and try for the same pin deflection as in a perfect strike hit—the RHB hitting the 1-3 Pocket and the LHB hitting the 1-2 Pocket. We recommend the hit pictured above.

SPARE: 1-2-3-7-9

Key Pin: **1-Pin**

Spare Number: 402
Opposite Spare: 405

LEFT HAND BOWLER: See Page 41
SPARE ZONE: 3-Pin Zone
CONTACT AREA: Right on 1-Pin
APPROACH POSITIONS AND TARGETS:
3-6-9 System: 3-Pin Position—
Strike Target
2-4-6 System: Strike Position—
Move Target 2 Boards RIGHT

RIGHT HAND BOWLER: See Page 34
SPARE ZONE: 1-Pin Zone
CONTACT AREA: Right on 1-Pin
APPROACH POSITIONS AND TARGETS:
3-6-9 System: Strike Position—
Strike Target
2-4-6 System: Strike Position—
Strike Target

Best Way to Convert: This is a difficult spare requiring an accurate hit and proper pin deflection. The RHB should hit the 1-pin on the right, covering the 1-3-9-pins with the ball. The 1 and 2-pin should be sent to the left to take out the 7-pin. The LHB uses the same hit to get the same ball and pin deflection. Either the 3-pin or the ball should take out the 9-Pin "Sleeper."

SPARE: 1-2-3-8-10

Key Pin: **1-Pin**

Spare Number: 405
Opposite Spare: 402

LEFT HAND BOWLER: See Page 41
SPARE ZONE: 1-Pin Zone
CONTACT AREA: Left on 1-Pin
APPROACH POSITIONS AND TARGETS:
3-6-9 System: Strike Position—
Strike Target
2-4-6 System: Strike Position
Strike Target

RIGHT HAND BOWLER: See Page 34
SPARE ZONE: 2-Pin Zone
CONTACT AREA: Left on 1-Pin
APPROACH POSITIONS AND TARGETS:
3-6-9 System: 2-Pin Position—
Strike Target
2-4-6 System: Strike Position—
Move Target 2 Boards LEFT

Best Way to Convert: This difficult Leave requires an accurate hit and proper pin deflection to make the spare. The RHB and LHB should hit the 1-pin on the left side, covering the 1-2 and 8-pins with the ball. Either the 1 or 3-pin should take out the 10-pin, and the ball or the 2-pin should take out the 8-Pin "Sleeper."

SPARE: 1-2-4-5-7   Key Pin: **1-Pin**   Spare Number: **408**

Opposite Spare: 460

1
2
4
5
7

LEFT HAND BOWLER: See Page 41
SPARE ZONE: 1-Pin Zone
CONTACT AREA: Left on 1-Pin
APPROACH POSITIONS AND TARGETS:
3-6-9 System: Strike Position—
      Strike Target
2-4-6 System: Strike Position—
      Strike Target

RIGHT HAND BOWLER: See Page 34
SPARE ZONE: 1-Pin Zone
CONTACT AREA: Right on 1-Pin
APPROACH POSITIONS AND TARGETS:
3-6-9 System: Strike Position—
      Strike Target
2-4-6 System: Strike Position—
      Strike Target

Best Way to Convert: The 5-Pin "Sleeper" makes this spare very difficult. The 5-pin must be carried with the ball, so a good solid hit on the 1-pin is necessary. The RHB hits the 1-pin on the right side as shown, taking out the 1 and 5-pin with the ball. The 1-2-4-7 "Clothesline" should fall in "Domino Fash-

ion" if pin deflection is successful. The LHB hits the 1-pin on the left side, covering the 1-2 and 5-pin with the ball. The 2-pin takes out the 4-pin, and either of these two pins should take out the 7-pin. Some RHB prefer a "high left center" hit to cover this spare, to insure a good pin count in case of a miss.

5

SPARE: 1-2-4-7-9   Key Pin: **1-Pin**   Spare Number: **417**

Opposite Spare: 471

1
2
4
7
9

LEFT HAND BOWLER: See Page 41
SPARE ZONE: 3-Pin Zone
CONTACT AREA: Right on 1-Pin
APPROACH POSITIONS AND TARGETS:
3-6-9 System: 3-Pin Position—
      Strike Target
2-4-6 System: Strike Position—
      Move Target 2 Boards RIGHT

RIGHT HAND BOWLER: See Page 34
SPARE ZONE: 1-Pin Zone
CONTACT AREA: Right on 1-Pin
APPROACH POSITIONS AND TARGETS:
3-6-9 System: Strike Position—
      Strike Target
2-4-6 System: Strike Position—
      Strike Target

Best Way to Convert: A precise hit and good pin deflection are needed to make this spare. Both the RHB and LHB should hit the 1-pin on the right, covering the 1 and 9-pin with the ball. The 1-2-4-7-

pins should fall in "Domino Fashion" if pin deflection works well. Some bowlers prefer a "high left center" hit on the 1-pin to get maximum pin count. We suggest the hit shown above.

SPARE: 1-2-4-7-10   Key Pin: 1-Pin   Spare Number: 418

Opposite Spare: 469

LEFT HAND BOWLER: See Page 41
SPARE ZONE: Head-On 2-Pin Zone
CONTACT AREA: Left on 1-Pin
APPROACH POSITIONS AND TARGETS:
3-6-9 System: Head-On 2-Pin Position—
            7-Pin Target
2-4-6 System: Not Used on This Spare

RIGHT HAND BOWLER: See Page 34
SPARE ZONE: Head-On 2-Pin Zone
CONTACT AREA: Left on 1-Pin
APPROACH POSITIONS AND TARGETS:
3-6-9 System: Head-On 2-Pin Position—
            Strike Target
2-4-6 System: Strike Position—
            Move Target 3 Boards LEFT

Best Way to Convert: (*Washout*) This is another of the Right Side Washouts, needing accurate pin deflection to convert. It is not a split with the 1-pin standing. It is played exactly like the 1-2-4-10 Spare. Hit the 1-pin on the left to send it directly into the 10-pin (although it usually takes out the 10-pin off the kickback). The ball should deflect to the left and take out the 1-2-4-7 "Clothesline" if the Head-On 2-Pin Position is used. Or, the ball could take out the 1 and 2-pin, as the 4-pin takes out the 7-pin. The LHB could take out the 1 and 2-pins with the ball and rely upon the 4-pin to take out the 7-pin, using the Strike Position and Strike Target.

SPARE: 1-2-5-8-9   Key Pin: 1-Pin   Spare Number: 429

Opposite Spare: 464

LEFT HAND BOWLER: See Page 41
SPARE ZONE: Head-On 1-Pin Zone
CONTACT AREA: Left Center on 1-Pin
APPROACH POSITIONS AND TARGETS:
3-6-9 System: Head-On 1-Pin Position—
            Strike Target
2-4-6 System: Strike Position—
            Move Target 1 Board RIGHT

RIGHT HAND BOWLER: See Page 34
SPARE ZONE: Head-On 1-Pin Zone
CONTACT AREA: Right Center on 1-Pin
APPROACH POSITIONS AND TARGETS:
3-6-9 System: Head-On 1-Pin Position—
            Strike Target
2-4-6 System: Strike Position—
            Move Target 1 Board LEFT

Best Way to Convert: It is very important for the ball to "Carry" the 5-pin on this Leave, so a "High Hit" is suggested for both the LHB and RHB. The RHB hits the 1-pin to the right of center; as the 1-pin takes out the 2-pin the ball takes out the 5 and 9-pins; the 5-pin takes out the 8-pin. The LHB hits the 1-pin high to take out the 1-2-5-8-pins with the ball, as the 5-pin takes out the 9-pin. A normal 1-2 Pocket Hit for the LHB could have the same result, just as a normal 1-3 Pocket Hit could also make the spare for the RHB.

SPARE: 1-2-7-8-10   Key Pin: **1-Pin**   Spare Number: **439**

Opposite Spare: 475

1
2
7
8
10

LEFT HAND BOWLER: See Page 41
SPARE ZONE: Head-On 2-Pin Zone
CONTACT AREA: Left on 1-Pin
APPROACH POSITIONS AND TARGETS:
3-6-9 System: Head-On 2-Pin Position—
         7-Pin Target
2-4-6 System: Not Used on This Spare

RIGHT HAND BOWLER: See Page 34
SPARE ZONE: Head-On 2-Pin Zone
CONTACT AREA: Left on 1-Pin
APPROACH POSITIONS AND TARGETS:
3-6-9 System: Head-On 2-Pin Position—
         Strike Target
2-4-6 System: Strike Position—
         Move Target 3 Boards LEFT

Best Way to Convert: (*Washout*) This is one of the most difficult of the Washouts since both the 7 and 10-pins are standing. A very exact hit and accurate pin deflection are needed to make this spare. (It is not a split with the 1-pin up!) The RHB should cover the 1-2 and 7-pins with the ball; as the 1-pin takes out the 10-pin, the 2-pin takes out the 8-Pin Sleeper. The LHB should cover the 1-2 and 8-pins with the ball, as the 1-pin takes out the 10-pin and the 2-pin takes out the 7-pin. Or, the LHB might cover the 1-2 and 7-pins with the ball, because the Head-On 2-Pin Position is used.

5

SPARE: 1-3-5-6-10   Key Pin: **1-Pin**   Spare Number: **460**

Opposite Spare: 408

1
3
5
6
10

LEFT HAND BOWLER: See Page 41
SPARE ZONE: 1-Pin Zone
CONTACT AREA: Left on 1-Pin
APPROACH POSITIONS AND TARGETS:
3-6-9 System: Strike Position—
         Strike Target
2-4-6 System: Strike Position—
         Strike Target

RIGHT HAND BOWLER: See Page 34
SPARE ZONE: 1-Pin Zone
CONTACT AREA: Right on 1-Pin
APPROACH POSITIONS AND TARGETS:
3-6-9 System: Strike Position—
         Strike Target
2-4-6 System: Strike Position—
         Strike Target

Best Way to Convert: The 5-Pin "Sleeper" makes this Leave very difficult. It must be covered by the ball, so a good solid hit on the 1-pin is needed. The LHB hits the 1-pin on the left as shown, taking out the 1 and 5-pins with the ball. The 1-3-6-10 "Clothesline" should fall in "Domino Fashion" if pin deflection is successful. The RHB hits the 1-pin on the right, covering the 1-3 and 5-pins with the ball. The 3-pin takes out the 6-pin, and either of these two pins should take out the 10-pin. Some LHB prefer a "high right center" hit to cover this spare, to insure a good count in case the spare is missed.

SPARE: 1-3-5-8-9   Key Pin: **1-Pin**   Spare Number: **464**

Opposite Spare: **429**

1
3
5
8
9

LEFT HAND BOWLER: *See Page 41*
SPARE ZONE: Head-On 1-Pin Zone
CONTACT AREA: Left Center on 1-Pin
APPROACH POSITIONS AND TARGETS:
3-6-9 System: Head-On 1-Pin Position—
        Strike Target
2-4-6 System: Strike Position—
        Move Target 1 Board RIGHT

RIGHT HAND BOWLER: See Page 34
SPARE ZONE: Head-On 1-Pin Zone
CONTACT AREA: Right Center on 1-Pin
APPROACH POSITIONS AND TARGETS:
3-6-9 System: Head-On 1-Pin Position—
        Strike Target
2-4-6 System: Strike Position—
        Move Target 1 Board LEFT

Best Way to Convert: It is very important for the ball to "Carry" the 5-pin so a "High Hit" is suggested for both the RHB and LHB. However, a normal 1-2 Pocket Hit (LHB) or 1-3 Pocket Hit (RHB) could cover this spare. The RHB hits the 1-3 Pocket to cover the 1- 3-5 and 9-pins with the ball—the same four pins covered by the ball in a perfect strike. The 5-pin takes out the 8-pin. The LHB hits the 1-pin slightly high to take out the 1-5-8-pins with the ball. The 1-pin takes out the 3-pin and the 5-pin takes out the 9-pin.

5

SPARE: 1-3-6-7-10   Key Pin: **1-Pin**   Spare Number: **469**

Opposite Spare: **418**

1
3
6
7
10

LEFT HAND BOWLER: See Page 41
SPARE ZONE: Head-On 3-Pin Zone
CONTACT AREA: Right on 1-Pin
APPROACH POSITIONS AND TARGETS:
3-6-9 System: Head-On 3-Pin Position—
        Strike Target
2-4-6 System: Strike Position—
        Move Target 3 Boards RIGHT

RIGHT HAND BOWLER: See Page 34
SPARE ZONE: Head-On 3-Pin Zone
CONTACT AREA: Right on 1-Pin
APPROACH POSITIONS AND TARGETS:
3-6-9 System: Head-On 3-Pin Position—
        10-Pin Target
2-4-6 System: Not Used on This Spare

Best Way to Convert: *(Washout)* This is still another of the Left Side Washouts. It is played exactly like the 1-3-6-7 Spare. Of course, it is not a split with the 1-pin standing. Hit the right side of the 1-pin as shown, so the 1-pin will be sent after the 7-pin— either getting it directly or off the kickback. The ball will take out the 1 and 3-pins, as the 3-pin sends the 6-pin into the 10-pin. Or, the ball may cover the 1-3-6 and 10-pins. The RHB should use the Head-On 3-Pin Approach Position to increase ball deflection for covering the 1-3-6 and 10-pins with the ball.

SPARE: 1-3-6-8-10   Key Pin: **1-Pin**   Spare Number: **471**

Opposite Spare: 417

1
3
6
8
10

LEFT HAND BOWLER: See Page 41
SPARE ZONE: 1-Pin Zone
CONTACT AREA: Left on 1-Pin
APPROACH POSITIONS AND TARGETS:
3-6-9 System: Strike Position—
Strike Target
2-4-6 System: Strike Position—
Strike Target

RIGHT HAND BOWLER: See Page 34
SPARE ZONE: 2-Pin Zone
CONTACT AREA: Left on 1-Pin
APPROACH POSITIONS AND TARGETS:
3-6-9 System: 2-Pin Position—
Strike Target
2-4-6 System: Strike Position—
Move Target 2 Boards LEFT

Best Way to Convert: A precise hit and good pin deflection are needed to make this difficult spare. Both the RHB and LHB should hit the 1-pin on the left, covering the 1 and 8-pins with the ball. The 1-3-6-10-pins should fall in "Domino Fashion" if pin deflection works well. Some RHB and LHB prefer a "high right center" hit to get maximum pin count if the spare is missed. We suggest the hit shown above.

5

SPARE: 1-3-7-9-10   Key Pin: **1-Pin**   Spare Number: **475**

Opposite Spare: 439

1
3
7
9
10

LEFT HAND BOWLER: See Page 41
SPARE ZONE: Head-On 3-Pin Zone
CONTACT AREA: Right on 1-Pin
APPROACH POSITIONS AND TARGETS:
3-6-9 System: Head-On 3-Pin Position—
Strike Target
2-4-6 System: Strike Position—
Move Target 3 Boards RIGHT

RIGHT HAND BOWLER: See Page 34
SPARE ZONE: Head-On 3-Pin Zone
CONTACT AREA: Right on 1-Pin
APPROACH POSITIONS AND TARGETS:
3-6-9 System: Head-On 3-Pin Position—
10-Pin Target
2-4-6 System: Not Used on This Spare

Best Way to Convert: (*Washout*) This is one of the most difficult of the Washouts since both the 7 and 10-pins are standing. A very precise hit and accurate pin and ball deflection are needed to make this spare. (It is not a split since the 1-pin is standing!) The LHB should cover the 1-3 and 10-pins with the ball, as the 1-pin takes out the 7-pin directly or off the kickback, and the 3-pin takes out the 9-Pin Sleeper. The RHB should cover the 1-3 and 9-pins with the ball, as the 1-pin takes out the 7-pin, and the 3-pin or the ball takes out the 10-pin. Or, the RHB might cover the 1-3 and 10-pins with the ball, by using the Head-On 3-Pin Position.

SPARE: 1-4-5-7-8   Key Pin: **1-Pin**   Spare Number: **481**

Opposite Spare: **502**

LEFT HAND BOWLER: See Page 41
SPARE ZONE: 1-Pin Zone
CONTACT AREA: Left on 1-Pin
APPROACH POSITIONS AND TARGETS:
3-6-9 System: Strike Position—
        Strike Target
2-4-6 System: Strike Position—
        Strike Target

RIGHT HAND BOWLER: See Page 34
SPARE ZONE: 1-Pin Zone
CONTACT AREA: Right on 1-Pin
APPROACH POSITIONS AND TARGETS:
3-6-9 System: Strike Position—
        Strike Target
2-4-6 System: Strike Position—
        Strike Target

Best Way to Convert: A very precise hit and proper pin deflection are needed to make this difficult and unusual spare. It is not a split since the 1-pin is standing, and it is more difficult for the LHB since pin deflection favors the RHB. The RHB should hit the 1-pin on the right to send it into the 4-pin, hoping that either pin will take out the 7-pin. The ball continues through the hit to take out the 5-pin and send it into the 8-pin. The LHB should hit the 1-pin on the left and try to deflect to the left to hit directly between the 4 and 5-pins. The ball takes out the 8-pin and the 4-pin should take out the 7-pin, directly or off the kickback.

5

SPARE: 1-5-6-9-10   Key Pin: **1-Pin**   Spare Number: **502**

Opposite Spare: **481**

LEFT HAND BOWLER: See Page 41
SPARE ZONE: 1-Pin Zone
CONTACT AREA: Left on 1-Pin
APPROACH POSITIONS AND TARGETS:
3-6-9 System: Strike Position—
        Strike Target
2-4-6 System: Strike Position—
        Strike Target

RIGHT HAND BOWLER: See Page 34
SPARE ZONE: 1-Pin Zone
CONTACT AREA: Right on 1-Pin
APPROACH POSITIONS AND TARGETS:
3-6-9 System: Strike Position—
        Strike Target
2-4-6 System: Strike Position—
        Strike Target

Best Way to Convert: A very precise hit and proper pin deflection are needed to make this difficult and unusual spare. It is not a split since the 1-pin is standing, and it is more difficult for the RHB since pin deflection favors the LHB. The LHB should hit the 1-pin on the left to send it into the 6-pin, trying to have either pin take out the 10-pin. The ball continues through to take out the 5-pin and send it into the 9-pin. The RHB should hit the right side of the 1-pin and try to deflect to the right to hit directly between the 5 and 6-pins. The ball takes out the 9-pin and the 6-pin should take out the 10-pin directly or off the kickback.

SPARE: 1-5-7-8-9   Key Pin: **1-Pin**   Spare Number: **503**

Opposite Spare: 506

1
5
7
8
9

LEFT HAND BOWLER: See Page 41
SPARE ZONE: Head-On 1-Pin Zone
CONTACT AREA: Center on 1-Pin
APPROACH POSITIONS AND TARGETS:
3-6-9 System: Head-On 1-Pin Position—
       Strike Target
2-4-6 System: Strike Position—
       Move Target 1 Board RIGHT

RIGHT HAND BOWLER: See Page 34
SPARE ZONE: 1-Pin Zone
CONTACT AREA: Right on 1-Pin
APPROACH POSITIONS AND TARGETS:
3-6-9 System: Strike Position—
       Strike Target
2-4-6 System: Strike Position—
       Strike Target

Best Way to Convert: A very precise hit and proper pin deflection are needed to make this unusual and very difficult spare. It is much more difficult for the LHB since pin deflection favors the RHB. The RHB should hit the 1-pin on the right to send it into the 7-pin. The ball should continue through the hit to take out the 5 and 9-pins, as the 5-pin takes out the 8-pin.

The LHB, however, should hit the 1-pin to the center, driving it back into the 5 and 8-pins and trying for deflection to the left into the 7-pin. The ball continues through to take out the 9-pin. A light hit on either side of the 1-pin would probably result in a miss, so a center hit on the 1-pin is preferred.

5

SPARE: 1-5-8-9-10   Key Pin: **1-Pin**   Spare Number: **506**

Opposite Spare: 503

1
5
8
9
10

LEFT HAND BOWLER: See Page 41
SPARE ZONE: 1-Pin Zone
CONTACT AREA: Left on 1-Pin
APPROACH POSITIONS AND TARGETS:
3-6-9 System: Strike Position—
       Strike Target
2-4-6 System: Strike Position—
       Strike Target

RIGHT HAND BOWLER: See Page 34
SPARE ZONE: Head-On 1-Pin Zone
CONTACT AREA: Center on 1-Pin
APPROACH POSITIONS AND TARGETS:
3-6-9 System: Head-On 1-Pin Position—
       Strike Target
2-4-6 System: Strike Position—
       Move Target 1 Board LEFT

Best Way to Convert: A very precise hit and proper pin deflection are needed to make this very difficult and unusual spare. It is much more difficult for the RHB since pin deflection favors the LHB. The LHB should hit the 1-pin on the left side to send it into the 10-pin. The ball should continue through the hit to take out the 5 and 8-pins, as the 5-pin takes out the 9-

pin. The RHB, however, should hit the 1-pin to the center, driving it back into the 5 and 9-pins and trying for deflection to the right into the 10-pin. The ball continues through to take out the 8-pin. A light hit on either side of the 1-pin would probably result in a miss, so a center hit on the 1-pin gives a better chance for the spare.

SPARE: 2-4-5-7-8   Key Pin: **2-Pin**   Spare Number: **551**

Opposite Spare: 607

LEFT HAND BOWLER: *See Page 41*
SPARE ZONE: Head-On 2-Pin Zone
CONTACT AREA: Left Center on 2-Pin
APPROACH POSITIONS AND TARGETS:
3-6-9 System: Head-On 2-Pin Position—
           7-Pin Target
2-4-6 System: Not Used on This Spare

RIGHT HAND BOWLER: See Page 34
SPARE ZONE: 2-Pin Zone
CONTACT AREA: Right on 2-Pin
APPROACH POSITIONS AND TARGETS:
3-6-9 System: 2-Pin Position—
           Strike Target
2-4-6 System: Strike Position—
           Move Target 2 Boards LEFT

Best Way to Convert: A precise hit that will carry the 8-pin is required to cover this difficult spare. The RHB should hit the 2-pin on the right side, but enough for the ball to drive through and take out the 2-5 and 8-pins. The 2-pin sends the 4 into the 7-pin. The LHB hits the 2-pin on the left center to carry the 2-4 and 8-pins with the ball. The 4-pin takes out the 7-pin and the 2 takes out the 5-pin. Hitting too full on the 2-pin could result in a chop for either the RHB or LHB. The RHB has a slight advantage in carrying the 8-pin on this spare, since the Leave is on the left side of the Pin Deck and the ball is coming into the pins at a greater angle from the right.

SPARE: 2-4-5-8-10   Key Pin: **2-Pin**   Spare Number: **555-S**

Opposite Spare: 603-S

5

LEFT HAND BOWLER: See Page 41
SPARE ZONE: Head-On 2-Pin Zone
CONTACT AREA: Left Center on 2-Pin
APPROACH POSITIONS AND TARGETS:
3-6-9 System: Head-On 2-Pin Position—
           7-Pin Target
2-4-6 System: Not Used on This Spare

RIGHT HAND BOWLER: See Page 34
SPARE ZONE: Head-On 2-Pin Zone
CONTACT AREA: Center on 2-Pin
APPROACH POSITIONS AND TARGETS:
3-6-9 System: Head-On 2-Pin Position—
           Strike Target
2-4-6 System: Strike Position—
           Move Target 3 Boards LEFT

Best Way to Convert: Keep Pin Count In Mind! Even getting four pins of this split is going to be difficult, and will take an accurate hit on the 2-pin. The RHB should hit the 2-pin towards the center, to cover the 2-4-8-pins with the ball. Hopefully the 5-pin (or 2-pin) will be deflected to the right and into the 10-pin. The LHB should hit the 2-pin just to the left of center to cover the 2-4-8 with the ball too. The 5-pin or 2-pin should be deflected to the right and into the 10-pin. Be sure you hit the 2-pin on your conversion attempt, to get maximum pin count if you do not make the spare. (Some RHB prefer a hit exactly like that shown for the LHB.)

SPARE: 2-4-6-7-10   Key Pin: 2-Pin   Spare Number: 559-S

Opposite Spare: 594-S

2
4
6
7
10

LEFT HAND BOWLER: See Page 41
SPARE ZONE: Head-On 4-Pin Zone
CONTACT AREA: Far Left on 2-Pin
APPROACH POSITIONS AND TARGETS:
3-6-9 System: Head On 4-Pin Position—
7-Pin Target
2-4-6 System: Not Used on This Spare

RIGHT HAND BOWLER: See Page 34
SPARE ZONE: Head-On 4-Pin Zone
CONTACT AREA: Far Left on 2-Pin
APPROACH POSITIONS AND TARGETS:
3-6-9 System: Head-On 4-Pin Position—
Strike Target
2-4-6 System: Strike Position—
Move Target 5 Boards LEFT

Best Way to Convert: Keep Pin Count In Mind! Proper pin and ball deflection are both needed, as well as an accurate hit on the 2-pin, to make this difficult split. It is similar to the 2-4-6-10 Split. This split should be attempted almost like the 2-7 or the 2-4-6 Split. Hit the 2-pin on the far left side and slide it across into the 6-pin. The ball should take out the 2-4 and 7-pins, and the 2-pin or 6-pin might take out the 10-pin. Ball deflection favors the RHB on this split, so the LHB should use the Head-On 4-Pin Approach Position to increase ball deflection off the 2 and 4-pins. (Perhaps the 4-pin instead of the ball will take out the 7-pin.) Be sure to hit the 2-pin on your try to get maximum pin count.

SPARE: 2-4-7-8-10   Key Pin: 2-Pin   Spare Number: 564-S

Opposite Spare: 614-S

5

2
4
7
8
10

LEFT HAND BOWLER: See Page 41
SPARE ZONE: Head-On 4-Pin Zone
CONTACT AREA: Far Left on 2-Pin
APPROACH POSITIONS AND TARGETS:
3-6-9 System: Head-On 4-Pin Position—
7-Pin Target
2-4-6 System: Not Used on This Spare

RIGHT HAND BOWLER: See Page 34
SPARE ZONE: Head-On 4-Pin Zone
CONTACT AREA: Far Left on 2-Pin
APPROACH POSITIONS AND TARGETS:
3-6-9 System: Head-On 4-Pin Position—
Strike Target
2-4-6 System: Strike Position—
Move Target 5 Boards LEFT

Best Way to Convert: Keep Pin Count In Mind! Pin and ball deflection plus an accurate hit are needed to make this very difficult split. The 8-pin presents the problem. Hit the 2-pin on the far left as shown, sending it into the 10-pin. The ball should cover the 2-4-7-pins, and either the 4-pin or the ball should take out the 8-pin—for the LHB. But the RHB will have to rely upon the 4-pin to take out the 8-pin since the ball is deflecting away from the 8-pin. Using the Head-On 4-Pin Approach Position, the RHB should get enough ball deflection to cover the 2-4-7-pins with the ball, and the 4-pin can take out the 8-pin. (The authors saw this split converted by a RHB, with the 4 taking out the 8-pin.)

SPARE: 2-4-7-9-10   Key Pin: **2-Pin**   Spare Number: **565-S**

Opposite Spare: 613-S

LEFT HAND BOWLER: See Page 41
SPARE ZONE: Head-On 4-Pin Zone
CONTACT AREA: Far Left on 2-Pin
APPROACH POSITIONS AND TARGETS:
  3-6-9 System: Head-On 4-Pin Position—
                   7-Pin Target
  2-4-6 System: Not Used on This Spare

RIGHT HAND BOWLER: See Page 34
SPARE ZONE: Head-On 4-Pin Zone
CONTACT AREA: Far Left on 2-Pin
APPROACH POSITIONS AND TARGETS:
  3-6-9 System: Head-On 4-Pin Position—
                   Strike Target
  2-4-6 System: Strike Position—
                 Move Target 5 Boards LEFT

Best Way to Convert: Keep Pin Count In Mind! This unusual spare might more properly be in the rares, but it does occur with some regularity. It is played exactly like the 2-7-9 or 2-7-9-10 Split. Hit the 2-pin on the far left to send it into the 9-pin. Either the 2-pin or 9-pin might take out the 10-pin. Then, the RHB should cover the 2-4-7-pins with the ball because of favorable ball deflection. The LHB may cover the 2-4-7-pins with the ball, or the 4-pin could take out the 7-pin. To increase ball deflection off the 2-pin, the LHB should use the Head-On 4-Pin Approach Position.

SPARE: 3-4-6-7-10   Key Pin: **3-Pin**   Spare Number: **594-S**

Opposite Spare: 559-S

LEFT HAND BOWLER: See Page 41
SPARE ZONE: Head-On 6-Pin Zone
CONTACT AREA: Far Right on 3-Pin
APPROACH POSITIONS AND TARGETS:
  3-6-9 System: Head-On 6-Pin Position—
                   Strike Target
  2-4-6 System: Strike Position—
                 Move Target 5 Boards RIGHT

RIGHT HAND BOWLER: See Page 34
SPARE ZONE: Head-On 6-Pin Zone
CONTACT AREA: Far Right on 3-Pin
APPROACH POSITIONS AND TARGETS:
  3-6-9 System: Head-On 6-Pin Position—
                  10-Pin Target
  2-4-6 System: Not Used on This Spare

Best Way to Convert: Keep Pin Count In Mind! Proper pin deflection and an accurate hit on the 3-pin are needed to convert this difficult split. It should be attempted almost like the 3-10 Baby Split, or the 3-4-6 Split. Hit the 3-pin on the far right as shown, sliding it across into the 4-pin. The ball should take out the 3-6 and 10-pins, and the 3 or 4-pin might take out the 7-pin. Ball deflection is needed to take out the 3-6-10-pins, so the RHB should use the Head-On 6-Pin Approach Position to increase ball deflection off the 3 and 6-pin. (Ball deflection works for the LHB on this split.) Make sure you hit the 3-pin on your conversion try to get maximum pin count if you miss the split.

SPARE: 3-5-6-7-9   Key Pin: **3-Pin**   Spare Number: **603-S**

Opposite Spare: 555-S

3
5
6
7
9

LEFT HAND BOWLER: See Page 41
SPARE ZONE: Head-On 3-Pin Zone
CONTACT AREA: Center on 3-Pin
APPROACH POSITIONS AND TARGETS:
3-6-9 System: Head-On 3-Pin Position—
        Strike Target
2-4-6 System: Strike Position—
        Move Target 3 Boards RIGHT

RIGHT HAND BOWLER: See Page 34
SPARE ZONE: Head-On 3-Pin Zone
CONTACT AREA: Right Center on 3-Pin
APPROACH POSITIONS AND TARGETS:
3-6-9 System: Head-On 3-Pin Position—
        10-Pin Target
2-4-6 System: Not Used on This Spare

Best Way to Convert: Keep Pin Count In Mind! Even getting four pins on this difficult split is going to take an accurate hit. The RHB should hit the 3-pin to the right of center to cover the 3-6 and 9-pins with the ball. The 3-pin should hit the 5-pin and send it (or the 3-pin) across the lane into the 7-pin. The LHB should hit just a little more towards the center of the 3-pin because the ball is coming from the left side, and cover the 3-6 and 9-pins with the ball too. Then, hopefully, the 5-pin (or 3-pin) will be deflected to the left into the 7-pin. Be sure you hit the 3-pin on your conversion attempt, to get maximum pin count if you should fail to make the spare.

5

SPARE: 3-5-6-9-10   Key Pin: **3-Pin**   Spare Number: **607**

Opposite Spare: 551

3
5
6
9
10

LEFT HAND BOWLER: See Page 41
SPARE ZONE: 3-Pin Zone
CONTACT AREA: Left on 3-Pin
APPROACH POSITIONS AND TARGETS:
3-6-9 System: 3-Pin Position—
        Strike Target
2-4-6 System: Strike Position—
        Move Target 2 Boards RIGHT

RIGHT HAND BOWLER: See Page 34
SPARE ZONE: Head-On 3-Pin Zone
CONTACT AREA: Right Center on 3-Pin
APPROACH POSITIONS AND TARGETS:
3-6-9 System: Head-On 3-Pin Position—
        10-Pin Target
2-4-6 System: Not Used on This Spare

Best Way to Convert: A precise hit that will carry the 9-pin is required to cover this difficult spare. The RHB should hit the 3-pin to the right center, enough for the ball to take out the 3-6 and 9-pins. The 3-pin should take out the 5-pin and the 6 take out the 10-pin. The LHB hits the 3-pin on the left to carry the 3-5 and 9-pins with the ball, as the 3-pin sends the 6-pin into the 10-pin. A full hit on the 3-pin could result in a chop for either the RHB or LHB. The LHB has a slight advantage in carrying the 9-pin on this spare since the Spare Leave is on the right side of the Pin Deck and the ball is coming at a greater angle from the left.

SPARE: 3-6-7-8-10　　Key Pin: **3-Pin**　　Spare Number: **613-S**

Opposite Spare: 565-S

3
6
7
8
10

LEFT HAND BOWLER: See Page 41
SPARE ZONE: Head-On 6-Pin Zone
CONTACT AREA: Far Right on 3-Pin
APPROACH POSITIONS AND TARGETS:
　3-6-9 System: Head-On 6-Pin Position—
　　　　　　　Strike Target
　2-4-6 System: Strike Position—
　　　　　　　Move Target 5 Boards RIGHT

RIGHT HAND BOWLER: See Page 34
SPARE ZONE: Head-On 6-Pin Zone
CONTACT AREA: Far Right on 3-Pin
APPROACH POSITIONS AND TARGETS:
　3-6-9 System: Head-On 6-Pin Position—
　　　　　　　10-Pin Target
　2-4-6 System: Not Used on This Spare

Best Way to Convert: Keep Pin Count In Mind! This unusual spare might more properly be in the Rares, but it does occur with some regularity. It is played exactly like the 3-8-10 or 3-7-8-10 Split. Hit the 3-pin on the far right to send it into the 8-pin. Either the 3-pin or the 8-pin might take out the 7-pin. The LHB should cover the 3-6-10-pins with the ball, although the 6-pin could take out the 10-pin. To increase ball deflection off the 3 and 6-pins, the RHB should use the Head-On 6-Pin Approach Position. Either the ball or the 6-pin should take out the 10-pin.

SPARE: 3-6-7-9-10　　Key Pin: **3-Pin**　　Spare Number: **614-S**

Opposite Spare: 564-S

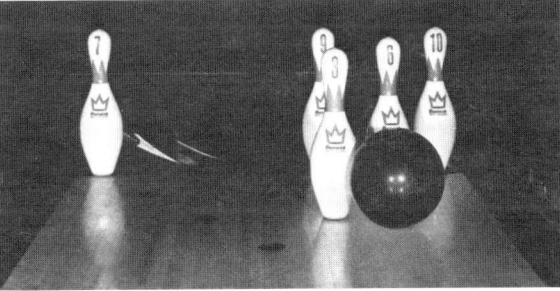

3
6
7
9
10

LEFT HAND BOWLER: See Page 41
SPARE ZONE: Head-On 6-Pin Zone
CONTACT AREA: Far Right on 3-Pin
APPROACH POSITIONS AND TARGETS:
　3-6-9 System: Head-On 6-Pin Position—
　　　　　　　Strike Target
　2-4-6 System: Strike Position—
　　　　　　　Move Target 5 Boards RIGHT

RIGHT HAND BOWLER: See Page 34
SPARE ZONE: Head-On 6-Pin Zone
CONTACT AREA: Far Right on 3-Pin
APPROACH POSITIONS AND TARGETS:
　3-6-9 System: Head-On 6-Pin Position—
　　　　　　　10-Pin Target
　2-4-6 System: Not Used on This Spare

Best Way to Convert: Keep Pin Count In Mind! Pin and ball deflection and an accurate hit are needed to make this very difficult split. The 9-pin presents the problem. Hit the 3-pin on the far right as shown, sending it into the 7-pin. The ball should cover the 3-6 and 10-pins, and either the ball or the 6-pin should take out the 8-pin—for the RHB. But the LHB will have to try to cover the 9-pin with the 6-pin since the LHB has ball deflection working against him or her. Using the Head-On 6-Pin Approach Position, the LHB should get favorable ball deflection to cover the 3-6 and 10-pins, and the 6-pin can take out the 9-pin.

SPARE: 4-6-7-8-10   Key Pin: **4-Pin**   Spare Number: **628-S**

Opposite Spare: 629-S

4
6
7
8
10

LEFT HAND BOWLER: *See Page 41*
SPARE ZONE: Head-On 7-Pin Zone
CONTACT AREA: Far Left on 4-Pin
APPROACH POSITIONS AND TARGETS:
3-6-9 System: Head-On 7-Pin Position—
7-Pin Target
2-4-6 System: Not Used on This Spare

RIGHT HAND BOWLER: *See Page 34*
SPARE ZONE: Head-On 7-Pin Zone
CONTACT AREA: Far Left on 4-Pin
APPROACH POSITIONS AND TARGETS:
3-6-9 System: Head-On 7-Pin Position—
Strike Target
2-4-6 System: Strike Position—
Move Target 7 Boards LEFT

Best Way to Convert: *(Big Five)(Greek Church)*
This is one of six spares requiring *forward* pin deflection. (See the list with the 4-6-7-9-10 Split.) All are very difficult to convert. Make a reasonable attempt on this one since your attempt should not cost any pin count. Hit the 4-pin on the far left as shown to cover the 4 and 7-pins with the ball. The 4-pin deflects off the 8-pin to try to take out the 6 and 10-pins. Either the 4 or 10-pin must deflect forward to take out the 6-pin. The Three Pin Cluster on the left could be driven into the pit and hope for a lucky bounce to take out the 6 and 10-pins. It is also possible to hit the 6-pin on the far right to slide it into the 4-7-8 for a spare.

5

SPARE: 4-6-7-9-10   Key Pin: **6-Pin**   Spare Number: **629-S**

Opposite Spare: 628-S

4
6
7
9
10

LEFT HAND BOWLER: *See Page 41*
SPARE ZONE: Head-On 10-Pin Zone
CONTACT AREA: Far Right on 6-Pin
APPROACH POSITIONS AND TARGETS:
3-6-9 System: Head-On 10-Pin Position—
Strike Target
2-4-6 System: Strike Position—
Move Target 7 Boards RIGHT

RIGHT HAND BOWLER: *See Page 34*
SPARE ZONE: Head-On 10-Pin Zone
CONTACT AREA: Far Right on 6-Pin
APPROACH POSITIONS AND TARGETS:
3-6-9 System: Head-On 10-Pin Position—
10-Pin Target
2-4-6 System: Not Used on This Spare

Best Way to Convert: *(Big Five)(Greek Church)*
This is one of the six difficult spares requiring *forward* pin deflection. A reasonable attempt should be made on this one since your attempt should not cost any pin count. Hit the 6-pin on the far right to cover the 6 and 10-pins with the ball. The 6-pin should hit the 9-pin and deflect to the left to take out the 7-pin and the 4-pin. Either the 6 or 7-pin must deflect forward to take out the 4-pin. The Three Pin Cluster on the right side could be driven into the pit and hope for a lucky bounce out of the pit. The 4-pin can also be deflected to the right to take out the 6-9-10. (See the 4-6-7-8-10; 4-6-8-10; 4-6-7-9; 4-6-9-10; and 4-6-7-8 Splits.)

SPARE: 1-2-3-4-5-7   Key Pin: **1-Pin**   Spare Number: **639**

Opposite Spare: 656

1
2
3
4 5
7

LEFT HAND BOWLER: See Page 41
SPARE ZONE: 1-Pin Zone
CONTACT AREA: Left on 1-Pin
APPROACH POSITIONS AND TARGETS:
3-6-9 System: Strike Position—
Strike Target
2-4-6 System: Strike Position—
Strike Target

RIGHT HAND BOWLER: See Page 34
SPARE ZONE: 1-Pin Zone
CONTACT AREA: Right on 1-Pin
APPROACH POSITIONS AND TARGETS:
3-6-9 System: Strike Position—
Strike Target
2-4-6 System: Strike Position—
Strike Target

Best Way to Convert: Both the RHB and LHB should use a normal strike ball, approach, release, and delivery to cover this difficult spare. The 5-pin is important, since the ball should cover it. The RHB hits the 1-3 pocket to cover the 1-3 and 5-pins with the ball. The 1-2-4-7 "Clothesline" should fall in domino fashion, as in a perfect strike hit. The LHB should hit the 1-2 pocket to cover the 1-2 and 5-pins with the ball. The 1-pin takes out the 3-pin, and the 2-pin sends the 4-pin into the 7-pin as in a perfect strike hit. (See "The Strike Ball" in Section I.)

6

SPARE: 1-2-3-4-5-9   Key Pin: **1-Pin**   Spare Number: **641**

Opposite Spare: 654

1
2
3
4
5
9

LEFT HAND BOWLER: See Page 41
SPARE ZONE: 1-Pin Zone
CONTACT AREA: Left on 1-Pin
APPROACH POSITIONS AND TARGETS:
3-6-9 System: Strike Position—
Strike Target
2-4-6 System: Strike Position—
Strike Target

RIGHT HAND BOWLER: See Page 34
SPARE ZONE: 1-Pin Zone
CONTACT AREA: Right on 1-Pin
APPROACH POSITIONS AND TARGETS:
3-6-9 System: Strike Position—
Strike Target
2-4-6 System: Strike Position—
Strike Target

Best Way to Convert: This spare requires a "Normal Strike Ball Hit" from both the LHB and RHB. The RHB hits the 1-3 pocket to cover the 1-3-5-9-pins with the ball, as the 1-pin sends the 2-pin into the 4-pin. The LHB hits the 1-2 pocket to cover the 1-2-5-pins with the ball. The 1-pin takes out the 3-pin; the 2-pin takes out the 4-pin; and the 5-pin takes out the 9-pin. For both the RHB and LHB, these are the normal pin deflections needed on a perfect strike hit.

SPARE: 1-2-3-4-7-9   Key Pin: **1-Pin**   Spare Number: **648**

Opposite Spare: 667

1
2
3
4
7
9

LEFT HAND BOWLER: See Page 41
SPARE ZONE: 3-Pin Zone
CONTACT AREA: Right on 1-Pin
APPROACH POSITIONS AND TARGETS:
3-6-9 System: 3-Pin Position—
         Strike Target
2-4-6 System: Strike Position—
         Move Target 2 Boards RIGHT

RIGHT HAND BOWLER: See Page 34
SPARE ZONE: 1-Pin Zone
CONTACT AREA: Right on 1-Pin
APPROACH POSITIONS AND TARGETS:
3-6-9 System: Strike Position—
         Strike Target
2-4-6 System: Strike Position—
         Strike Target

Best Way to Convert: A precise hit and good pin deflection are needed to make this difficult spare. The RHB should hit the 1-3 pocket as in a strike ball. The ball covers the 1-3-9-pins, and the 1-2-4-7 "Clothesline" should go down in "Domino Fashion" if pin deflection is successful. The LHB needs a 1-3 pocket hit and the same pin and ball deflection. Hitting the 1-pin too much towards the center, or on the extreme left or right side, would probably end in a miss. Several pins could be left standing.

6

SPARE: 1-2-3-5-6-8   Key Pin: **1-Pin**   Spare Number: **654**

Opposite Spare: 641

1
2
3
5
6
8

LEFT HAND BOWLER: See Page 41
SPARE ZONE: 1-Pin Zone
CONTACT AREA: Left on 1-Pin
APPROACH POSITIONS AND TARGETS:
3-6-9 System: Strike Position—
         Strike Target
2-4-6 System: Strike Position—
         Strike Target

RIGHT HAND BOWLER: See Page 34
SPARE ZONE: 1-Pin Zone
CONTACT AREA: Right on 1-Pin
APPROACH POSITIONS AND TARGETS:
3-6-9 System: Strike Position—
         Strike Target
2-4-6 System: Strike Position—
         Strike Target

Best Way to Convert: This spare requires a "Normal Strike Ball Hit" from both the LHB and RHB. The RHB hits the 1-3 pocket as shown, to cover the 1-3-5-pins with the ball. The 1-pin takes out the 2-pin; the 3-pin takes out the 6-pin; and the 5-pin takes out the 8-pin. The LHB hits the 1-2 pocket, to cover the 1-2-5-8-pins with the ball—the same pins covered by the ball in a perfect strike hit. The 1-pin sends the 3-pin into the 6-pin. For both the LHB and RHB these pin deflections are the same as those needed in a perfect strike hit.

SPARE: 1-2-3-5-6-10   Key Pin: **1-Pin**   Spare Number: **656**
Opposite Spare: 639

1
2
3
5
6
10

LEFT HAND BOWLER: See Page 41
SPARE ZONE: 1-Pin Zone
CONTACT AREA: Left on 1-Pin
APPROACH POSITIONS AND TARGETS:
3-6-9 System: Strike Position—
                            Strike Target
2-4-6 System: Strike Position—
                            Strike Target

RIGHT HAND BOWLER: See Page 34
SPARE ZONE: 1-Pin Zone
CONTACT AREA: Right on 1-Pin
APPROACH POSITIONS AND TARGETS:
3-6-9 System: Strike Position—
                            Strike Target
2-4-6 System: Strike Position—
                            Strike Target

Best Way to Convert: Both the RHB and LHB should use a "Normal Strike Ball Hit" to cover this difficult spare. The RHB hits the 1-3 pocket to cover the 1-3 and 5-pins with the ball. The 1-pin takes out the 2-pin; and the 3-pin sends the 6-pin into the 10-pin as in a perfect strike hit. The LHB hits the 1-2 pocket as illustrated, covering the 1-2 and 5-pins with the ball. The 1-3-6-10 "Right Side Clothesline" should fall in domino fashion, as in a perfect left handers strike hit. (See "The Strike Ball" in Section I.)

6

SPARE: 1-2-3-6-8-10   Key Pin: **1-Pin**   Spare Number: **667**
Opposite Spare: 648

1
2
3
6
8
10

LEFT HAND BOWLER: See Page 41
SPARE ZONE: 1-Pin Zone
CONTACT AREA: Left on 1-Pin
APPROACH POSITIONS AND TARGETS:
3-6-9 System: Strike Position—
                            Strike Target
2-4-6 System: Strike Position—
                            Strike Target

RIGHT HAND BOWLER: See Page 34
SPARE ZONE: 2-Pin Zone
CONTACT AREA: Left on 1-Pin
APPROACH POSITIONS AND TARGETS:
3-6-9 System: 2-Pin Position—
                            Strike Target
2-4-6 System: Strike Position—
                            Move Target 2 Boards LEFT

Best Way to Convert: A precise hit and good pin deflection are needed to make this difficult spare. The LHB and RHB should both hit the 1-pin on the left side as shown, covering the 1-2-8-pins with the ball. The 1-3-6-10 "Clothesline" should fall in "Domino Fashion" if pin deflection is successful. Hitting the 1-pin too much towards the center, or on the extreme left or right side could result in a miss. Several pins could be left standing.

SPARE: 1-2-4-5-7-8 Key Pin: **1-Pin** Spare Number: **677**

Opposite Spare: **733**

1
2
4
5
7
8

LEFT HAND BOWLER: *See Page 41*
SPARE ZONE: 1-Pin Zone
CONTACT AREA: Left on 1-Pin
APPROACH POSITIONS AND TARGETS:
3-6-9 System: Strike Position—
Strike Target
2-4-6 System: Strike Position—
Strike Target

RIGHT HAND BOWLER: *See Page 34*
SPARE ZONE: 1-Pin Zone
CONTACT AREA: Right on 1-Pin
APPROACH POSITIONS AND TARGETS:
3-6-9 System: Strike Position—
Strike Target
2-4-6 System: Strike Position—
Strike Target

Best Way to Convert: (*The Left Side*) A "Strike Hit" is needed by both the RHB and LHB to cover this spare. The LHB should hit the 1-2 pocket as shown, covering the 1-2-5 and 8-pins with the ball. The 2-pin should send the 4-pin into the 7-pin. The RHB should hit the 1-pin on the right, as in a strike pocket hit, covering the 1 and 5-pins with the ball. The 1-2-4-7 "Clothesline" should go down in "Domino Fashion," and the 5-pin should take out the 8-pin. Some RHB prefer a "high left center" hit on the 1-pin to get maximum pin count in case the spare is missed. We do not recommend that method.

6

SPARE: 1-3-5-6-9-10 Key Pin: **1-Pin** Spare Number: **733**

Opposite Spare: **677**

1
3
5
6
9
10

LEFT HAND BOWLER: *See Page 41*
SPARE ZONE: 1-Pin Zone
CONTACT AREA: Left on 1-Pin
APPROACH POSITIONS AND TARGETS:
3-6-9 System: Strike Position—
Strike Target
2-4-6 System: Strike Position—
Strike Target

RIGHT HAND BOWLER: *See Page 34*
SPARE ZONE: 1-Pin Zone
CONTACT AREA: Right on 1-Pin
APPROACH POSITIONS AND TARGETS:
3-6-9 System: Strike Position—
Strike Target
2-4-6 System: Strike Position—
Strike Target

Best Way to Convert: (*The Right Side*) A "Strike Hit" is needed by both the RHB and LHB to cover this difficult spare. The RHB should hit the 1-3 pocket to cover the 1-3-5 and 9-pins with the ball—as the 3-pin sends the 6-pin into the 10-pin. The LHB should hit the 1-pin on the left, as in a strike hit, covering only the 1 and 5-pins with the ball. The 1-3-6 and 10-pins should fall in "Domino Fashion," as the 5-pin takes out the 9-pin. Some LHB prefer a "high right center" hit on the 1-pin to get maximum pin count in case the spare is missed. We do not recommend that method.

SPARE: 1-2-3-4-5-7-8   Key Pin: **1-Pin**   Spare Number: **852**

Opposite Spare: 873

1
2
3
4
5
7
8

LEFT HAND BOWLER: See Page 41
SPARE ZONE: 1-Pin Zone
CONTACT AREA: Left on 1-Pin
APPROACH POSITIONS AND TARGETS:
3-6-9 System: Strike Position—
          Strike Target
2-4-6 System: Strike Position—
          Strike Target

RIGHT HAND BOWLER: See Page 34
SPARE ZONE: 1-Pin Zone
CONTACT AREA: Right on 1-Pin
APPROACH POSITIONS AND TARGETS:
3-6-9 System: Strike Position—
          Strike Target
2-4-6 System: Strike Position—
          Strike Target

Best Way to Convert: (*The Left Side Seven*) This spare requires a "Strike Hit" by both the RHB and LHB. The LHB hits the 1-2 pocket as indicated, to cover the 1-2-5 and 8-pins with the ball—as in a strike hit. Pin deflection takes out the other three pins. The RHB hits the 1-3 pocket to cover the 1-3 and 5-pins with the ball. Pin deflection takes out the other four pins, as in a perfect strike hit. (See "The Strike Ball" in Section I.)

7

SPARE: 1-2-3-4-5-7-9   Key Pin: **1-Pin**   Spare Number: **853**

Opposite Spare: 872

1
2
3
4
5
7
9

LEFT HAND BOWLER: See Page 41
SPARE ZONE: 1-Pin Zone
CONTACT AREA: Left on 1-Pin
APPROACH POSITIONS AND TARGETS:
3-6-9 System: Strike Position—
          Strike Target
2-4-6 System: Strike Position—
          Strike Target

RIGHT HAND BOWLER: See Page 34
SPARE ZONE: 1-Pin Zone
CONTACT AREA: Right on 1-Pin
APPROACH POSITIONS AND TARGETS:
3-6-9 System: Strike Position—
          Strike Target
2-4-6 System: Strike Position—
          Strike Target

Best Way to Convert: To cover this spare, both the RHB and LHB should use the same approach position, release, and delivery as if they were trying for a strike. A 1-3 pocket hit is needed by the RHB, and the 1-2 pocket for the LHB. The RHB covers the 1-3-5 and 9-pins with the ball—the same as in a perfect strike hit. The 1-2-4-7 "Left Clothesline" should fall in "Domino Fashion" as in a strike hit. The LHB should hit the 1-2 pocket to cover the 1-2 and 5-pins with the ball. The 1-pin takes out the 3-pin; the 5-pin takes out the 9-pin; and the 2-pin sends the 4-pin into the 7-pin; the same pin deflections as in a strike hit for the LHB. (See "The Strike Ball" in Section I.)

SPARE: 1-2-3-5-6-8-10   Key Pin: **1-Pin**   Spare Number: **872**

Opposite Spare: 853

1
2
3
5
6
8
10

LEFT HAND BOWLER: *See Page 41*
SPARE ZONE: 1-Pin Zone
CONTACT AREA: Left on 1-Pin
APPROACH POSITIONS AND TARGETS:
3-6-9 System: Strike Position—
                   Strike Target
2-4-6 System: Strike Position—
                   Strike Target

RIGHT HAND BOWLER: *See Page 34*
SPARE ZONE: 1-Pin Zone
CONTACT AREA: Right on 1-Pin
APPROACH POSITIONS AND TARGETS:
3-6-9 System: Strike Position—
                   Strike Target
2-4-6 System: Strike Position—
                   Strike Target

Best Way to Convert: To cover this spare both the RHB and LHB should bowl as if they were trying for a strike, since the same hit is needed. The RHB hits the 1-3 pocket to cover the 1-3 and 5-pins with the ball. The 1-pin takes out the 2-pin; the 5-pin takes out the 8-pin; and the 3-pin sends the 6-pin into the 10-pin. The LHB hits the 1-2 pocket to cover the 1-2-5-8-pins with the ball, as in a perfect strike hit. The 1-3-6-10 "Right Clothesline" should fall in domino fashion as in the perfect strike hit for the LHB. All pin deflections on this spare are the same as in a perfect strike hit for both the LHB and RHB. (See "The Strike Ball" in Section I.)

7

SPARE: 1-2-3-5-6-9-10   Key Pin: **1-Pin**   Spare Number: **873**

Opposite Spare: 852

1
2
3
5
6
9
10

LEFT HAND BOWLER: *See Page 41*
SPARE ZONE: 1-Pin Zone
CONTACT AREA: Left on 1-Pin
APPROACH POSITIONS AND TARGETS:
3-6-9 System: Strike Position—
                   Strike Target
2-4-6 System: Strike Position—
                   Strike Target

RIGHT HAND BOWLER: *See Page 34*
SPARE ZONE: 1-Pin Zone
CONTACT AREA: Right on 1-Pin
APPROACH POSITIONS AND TARGETS:
3-6-9 System: Strike Position—
                   Strike Target
2-4-6 System: Strike Position—
                   Strike Target

Best Way to Convert: *(The Right Side Seven)* This spare requires a "Strike Hit" by both the RHB and LHB. The RHB hits the 1-3 pocket as shown, to cover the 1-3-5 and 9-pins with the ball—as in a strike hit. Pin deflection takes out the other three pins. The LHB hits the 1-2 pocket, covering only the 1-2 and 5-pins with the ball. Pin deflection takes out the other four pins, as in a perfect strike hit. (See "The Strike Ball" in Section I.)

SPARE: 1-2-3-4-5-7-8-9   Key Pin: **1-Pin**   Spare Number: **974**

Opposite Spare: 986

1
2
3
4
5
7
8
9

LEFT HAND BOWLER: See Page 41
SPARE ZONE: 1-Pin Zone
CONTACT AREA: Left on 1-Pin
APPROACH POSITIONS AND TARGETS:
3-6-9 System: Strike Position—
            Strike Target
2-4-6 System: Strike Position—
            Strike Target

RIGHT HAND BOWLER: See Page 34
SPARE ZONE: 1-Pin Zone
CONTACT AREA: Right on 1-Pin
APPROACH POSITIONS AND TARGETS:
3-6-9 System: Strike Position—
            Strike Target
2-4-6 System: Strike Position—
            Strike Target

Best Way to Convert: To cover this spare both the RHB and LHB should bowl as if they were trying for a strike, since the same hit is needed. The RHB hits the 1-3 pocket to cover the 1-3-5 and 9-pins with the ball. Pin deflection takes out the other four pins as in a perfect strike hit. The LHB hits the 1-2 pocket to cover the 1-2-5 and 8-pins with the ball, and pin deflection takes out the other four pins as in a perfect strike hit. The LHB need not worry about leaving a "Solid 10" and the RHB can forget about a "10-Pin Tap," since the 10-pin is already down. (See "The Strike Ball" in Section I.)

8

SPARE: 1-2-3-5-6-8-9-10   Key Pin: **1-Pin**   Spare Number: **986**

Opposite Spare: 974

1
2
3
5
6
8
9
10

LEFT HAND BOWLER: See Page 41
SPARE ZONE: 1-Pin Zone
CONTACT AREA: Left on 1-Pin
APPROACH POSITIONS AND TARGETS:
3-6-9 System: Strike Position—
            Strike Target
2-4-6 System: Strike Position—
            Strike Target

RIGHT HAND BOWLER: See Page 34
SPARE ZONE: 1-Pin Zone
CONTACT AREA: Right on 1-Pin
APPROACH POSITIONS AND TARGETS:
3-6-9 System: Strike Position—
            Strike Target
2-4-6 System: Strike Position—
            Strike Target

Best Way to Convert: The RHB and LHB should bowl as if they were trying for a strike, since the same hit is needed to cover this difficult spare. The RHB hits the 1-3 pocket to cover the 1-3-5 and 9-pins with the ball. Pin deflection takes out the other four pins as in a perfect strike hit. The LHB hits the 1-2 pocket to cover the 1-2-5 and 8-pins with the ball. Pin deflection takes out the other four pins as in a perfect strike hit for the LHB. The RHB need not worry about the "Solid 7" Leave, and the LHB can forget about a "7-Pin Tap," since the 7-pin is already down. (See "The Strike Ball" in Section I.)

SPARE: 1-2-3-4-5-6-7-8-9   Key Pin: **1-Pin**

Spare Number: **1013**

Opposite Spare: 1016

1
2
3
4
5
6
7
8
9

LEFT HAND BOWLER: *See Page 41*
SPARE ZONE: 1-Pin Zone
CONTACT AREA: Left on 1-Pin
APPROACH POSITIONS AND TARGETS:
3-6-9 System: Strike Position—
  Strike Target
2-4-6 System: Strike Position—
  Strike Target

RIGHT HAND BOWLER: *See Page 34*
SPARE ZONE: 1-Pin Zone
CONTACT AREA: Right on 1-Pin
APPROACH POSITIONS AND TARGETS:
3-6-9 System: Strike Position—
  Strike Target
2-4-6 System: Strike Position—
  Strike Target

Best Way to Convert: The RHB can forget about a "10-Pin Tap," and the LHB need not worry about a "Solid 10-Pin" on this Leave, since the 10-pin is down. Both the LHB and RHB need a normal strike ball to cover this spare. The RHB hits the 1-3 pocket to cover the 1-3-5-9-pins with the ball, with pin deflection taking out the rest of the pin setup. The LHB hits the 1-2 pocket to cover the 1-2-5-8-pins with the ball, as pin deflection takes care of the rest. (See "The Strike Ball" in Section I.)

9

SPARE: 1-2-3-4-5-6-8-9-10   Key Pin: **1-Pin**

Spare Number: **1016**

Opposite Spare: 1013

1
2
3
4
5
6
8
9
10

LEFT HAND BOWLER: *See Page 41*
SPARE ZONE: 1-Pin Zone
CONTACT AREA: Left on 1-Pin
APPROACH POSITIONS AND TARGETS:
3-6-9 System: Strike Position—
  Strike Target
2-4-6 System: Strike Position—
  Strike Target

RIGHT HAND BOWLER: *See Page 34*
SPARE ZONE: 1-Pin Zone
CONTACT AREA: Right on 1-Pin
APPROACH POSITIONS AND TARGETS:
3-6-9 System: Strike Position—
  Strike Target
2-4-6 System: Strike Position—
  Strike Target

Best Way to Convert: The LHB does not have to worry about a "7-Pin Tap," and the RHB can forget about a "Solid 7-Pin Leave" on this spare, since the 7-pin is down. Both bowlers need a normal strike ball to cover this spare. The RHB hits the 1-3 pocket as shown, and the LHB hits the 1-2 pocket. For the RHB, the ball takes out the 1-3-5 and 9-pins, and pin deflection takes out the rest. The LHB covers the 1-2-5-8-pins with the ball, and pin deflection covers the rest. (See "The Strike Ball" in Section I.)

172

1
2
3
4
5
6
7
8
9
10

LEFT HAND BOWLER: See Page 41
SPARE ZONE: 1-Pin Zone
CONTACT AREA: Left on 1-Pin
APPROACH POSITIONS AND TARGETS:
3-6-9 System: Strike Position—
               Strike Target
2-4-6 System: Strike Position—
               Strike Target

RIGHT HAND BOWLER: See Page 34
SPARE ZONE: 1-Pin Zone
CONTACT AREA: Right on 1-Pin
APPROACH POSITIONS AND TARGETS:
3-6-9 System: Strike Position—
               Strike Target
2-4-6 System: Strike Position—
               Strike Target

Best Way to Convert: (*Full Rack*) This spare with all ten pins standing is included with the Probable Spares not only for completeness, but because it does occur after a gutter ball or foul on the first ball. (A *professional* bowler once rolled *two* gutter balls in the 10th frame on nationwide television and lost the match.) Also, a "Strike Ball" is used to cover about 20% of the Probable Spares! The RHB hits the 1-3 pocket as shown, so the ball takes out the 1-3-5 and 9-pins, and pin deflection takes the other six pins out. The LHB hits the 1-2 pocket as shown, so the ball takes out the 1-2-5 and 8-pins, and pin deflection takes out the other six pins as in a strike. (See "The Strike Ball" in Section I.)

10

SECTION III
PICTURES OF THE 774 RARE SPARES

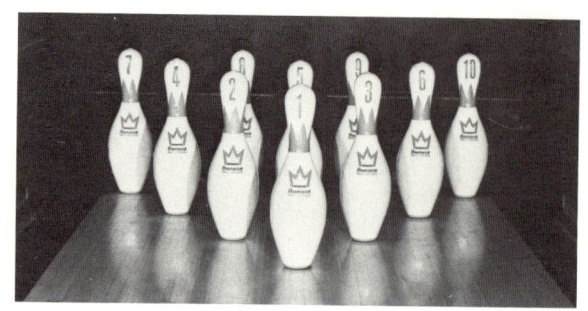

"No spare leave has been classified as impossible; only probable and rare. Any combination of pins might be left standing after the first ball is rolled."

A Rare Spare is one which may never occur, or at best so infrequently as to be considered unlikely to happen. This section contains a picture of the 774 spare leaves which have been classified as "rare." You will see very few of these spares in your entire bowling career. They are included here for two reasons:

1. These leaves are classified as "rare," not impossible. A logical explanation could describe how any of these spares might be left standing after the first ball is rolled. The material presented in Sections I and II should assist you in converting any of these rare spares, in the unlikely event that you leave any of them.

   Please see Exhibit 20. These are some of the most unusual spare leaves which have been left standing after the first ball was rolled. Notice that the 5-7-10 has been knocked down on the *first* ball, leaving the other seven pins untouched!

2. This book was designed to include every one of the 1,023 spare leaves that are possible with a ten pin setup. The 774 rare spares in this section, combined with the 249 probable spares in Section II, accomplishes this task. *No other combination of ten pins is possible.*

These 774 rare spares are grouped by the number of pins in each spare (spares with three pins, four pins, etc.). Within each group the spare leaves are in sequence by pin number, from the top of the page and from left to right. Thus, it is easy to locate any rare spare. *How many pins* in the leave will tell you which group it is in, and *the actual numbers* of the pins will allow you to locate the spare within the group. These rare spares are presented 18 to a page for convenience in reviewing them.

Under each picture is the Spare Number (remember that each one of the 1,023 possible spares has been assigned a number from 1 to 1,023). This is followed by the actual numbers of the pins in the spare. The letter "S" following the spare number identifies one of the 361 *rare splits.* The 98 *probable splits* are identified in the same way in Section II.

How many of these rare spares have you ever left? How many have you ever seen? We refer you to Appendix B, which gives many interesting facts about spares and splits. You should enjoy reading that material.

EXHIBIT 20
The Most Unusual Spare Leaves
That Have Ever Been Left Standing
After the First Ball Was Rolled.

Most of the 774 Rare Spares will never be left standing after the first ball is rolled. But the ones pictured here HAVE been left after the first ball. Can you determine what hit would leave each one?

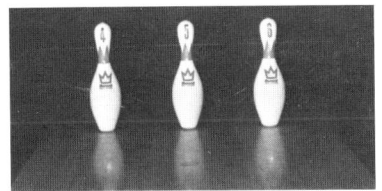

141-S   4-5-6

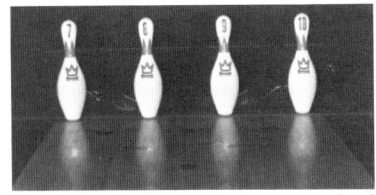

385-S   7-8-9-10

971   1-2-3-4-5-6-8-9

846-S   4-6-7-8-9-10

246   1-5-7-10

1014   1-2-3-4-5-6-7-8-10

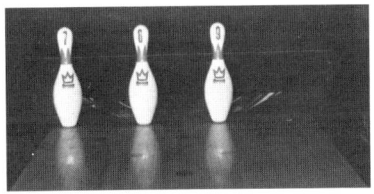

172-S   7-8-9

1009-S   2-3-4-6-7-8-9-10

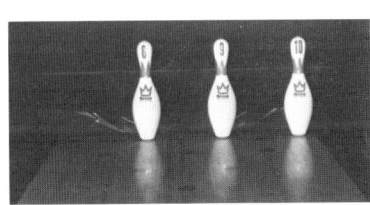

175-S   8-9-10

1022-S   2-3-4-5-6-7-8-9-10

861   1-2-3-4-6-8-9

969   1-2-3-4-5-6-7-9

Pictures of the 56 Rare Spares with Three Pins

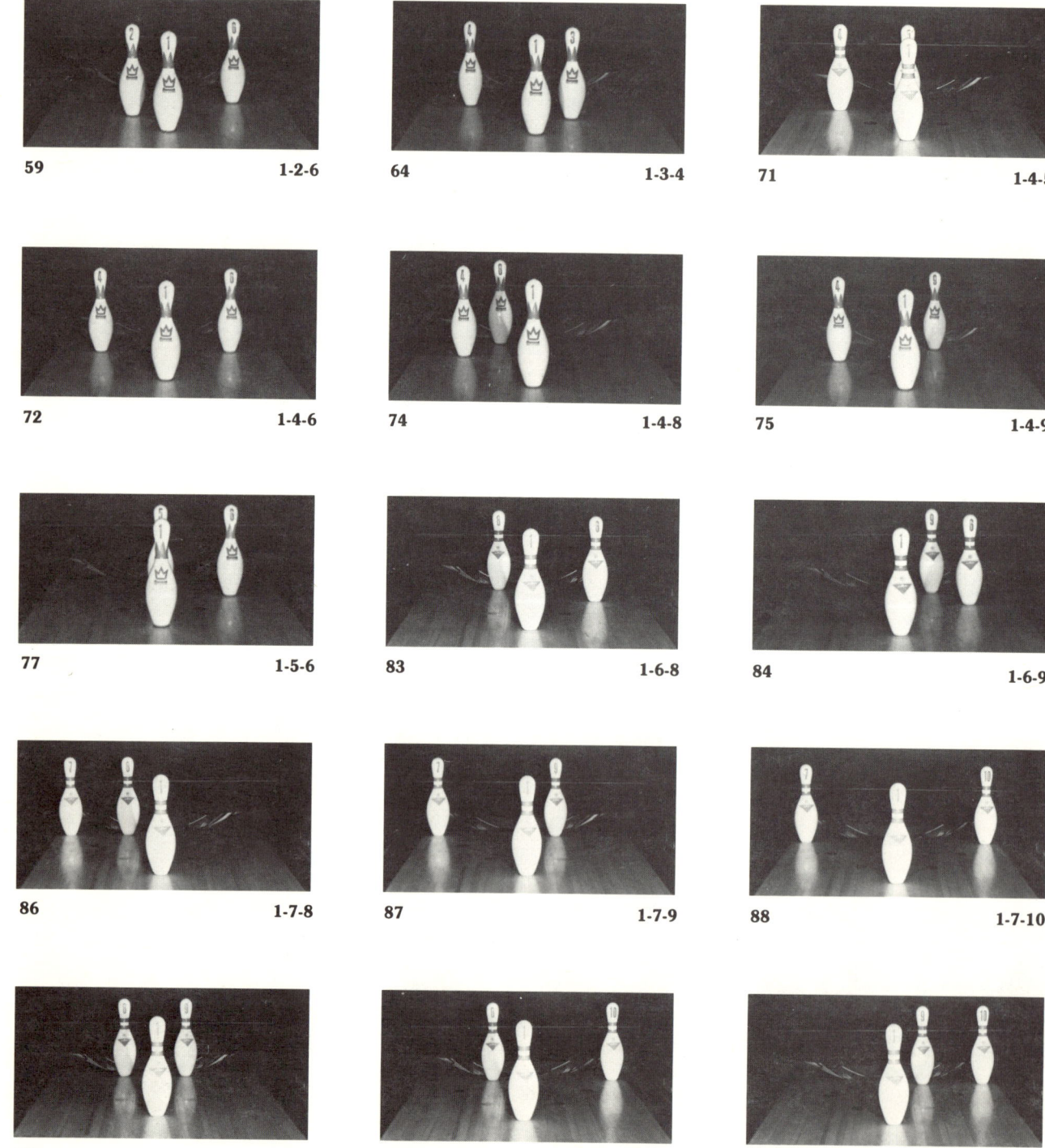

3

59 1-2-6	64 1-3-4	71 1-4-5
72 1-4-6	74 1-4-8	75 1-4-9
77 1-5-6	83 1-6-8	84 1-6-9
86 1-7-8	87 1-7-9	88 1-7-10
89 1-8-9	90 1-8-10	91 1-9-10

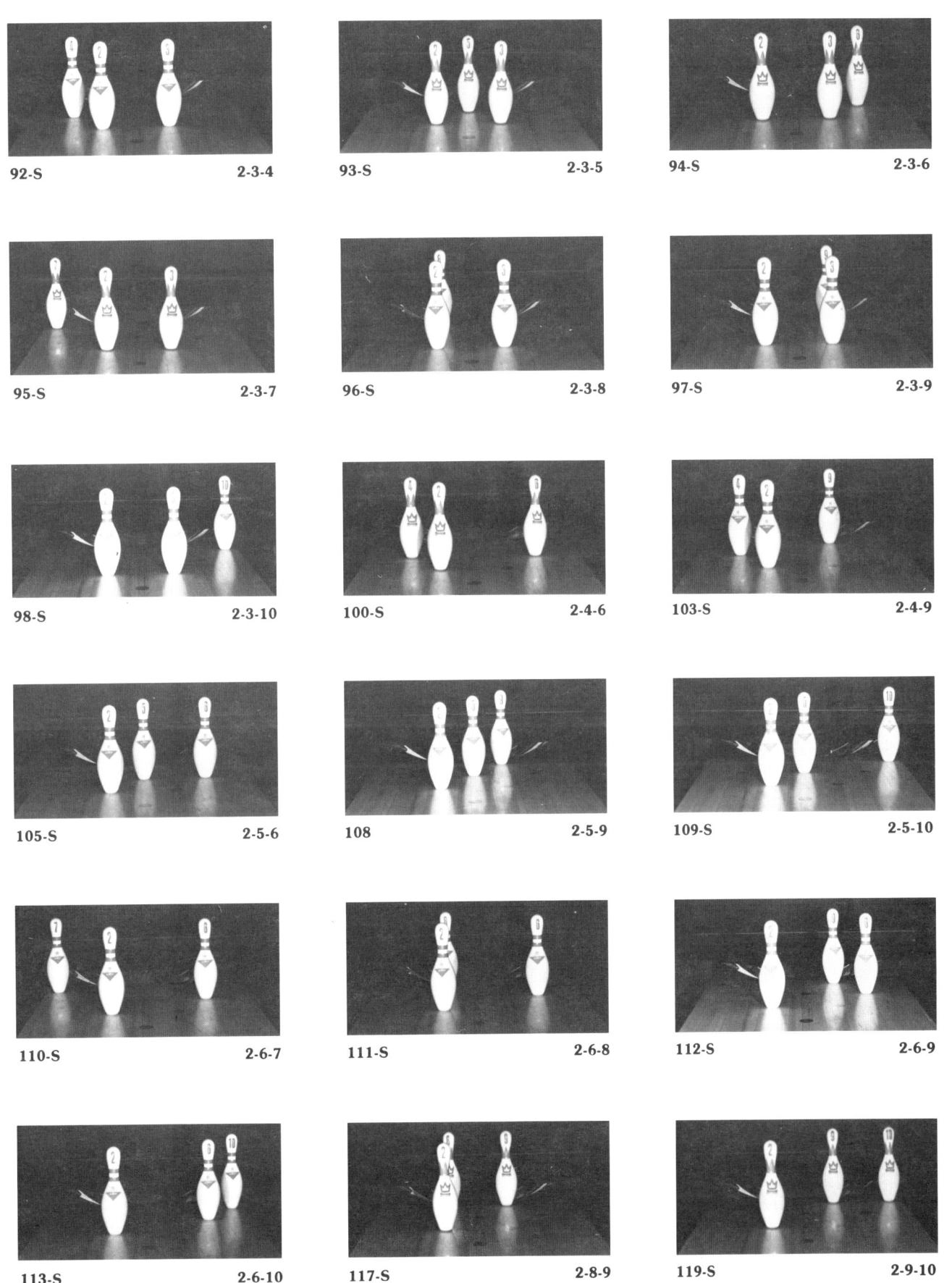

92-S   2-3-4

93-S   2-3-5

94-S   2-3-6

95-S   2-3-7

96-S   2-3-8

97-S   2-3-9

98-S   2-3-10

100-S   2-4-6

103-S   2-4-9

3

105-S   2-5-6

108   2-5-9

109-S   2-5-10

110-S   2-6-7

111-S   2-6-8

112-S   2-6-9

113-S   2-6-10

117-S   2-8-9

119-S   2-9-10

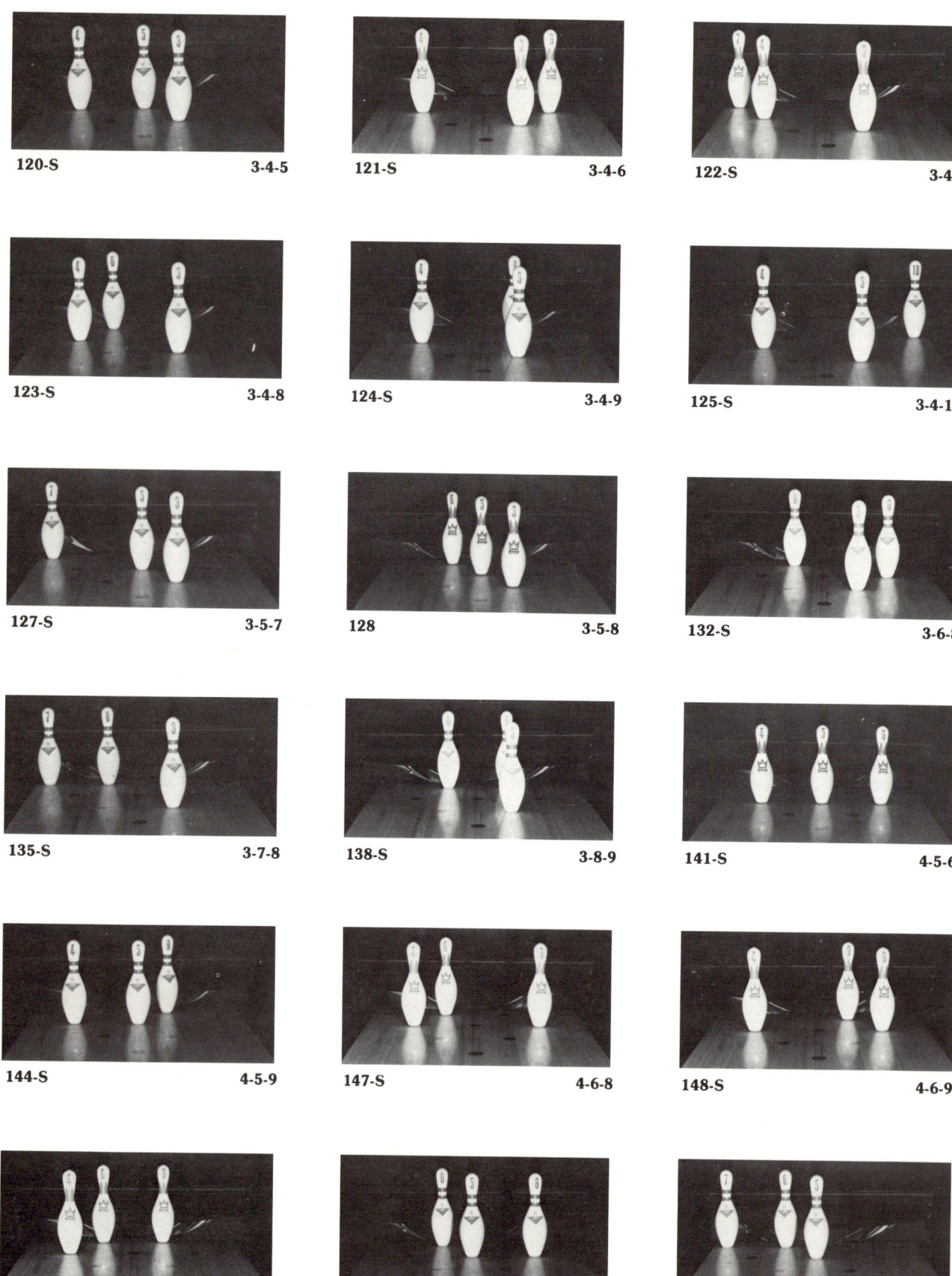

120-S   3-4-5

121-S   3-4-6

122-S   3-4-7

123-S   3-4-8

124-S   3-4-9

125-S   3-4-10

127-S   3-5-7

128   3-5-8

132-S   3-6-8

3

135-S   3-7-8

138-S   3-8-9

141-S   4-5-6

144-S   4-5-9

147-S   4-6-8

148-S   4-6-9

153-S   4-8-9

157-S   5-6-8

160-S   5-7-8

163   5-8-9

165-S   5-9-10

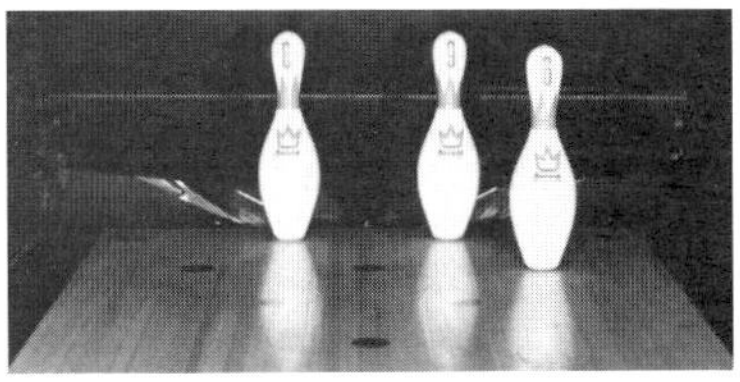

169-S   6-8-9

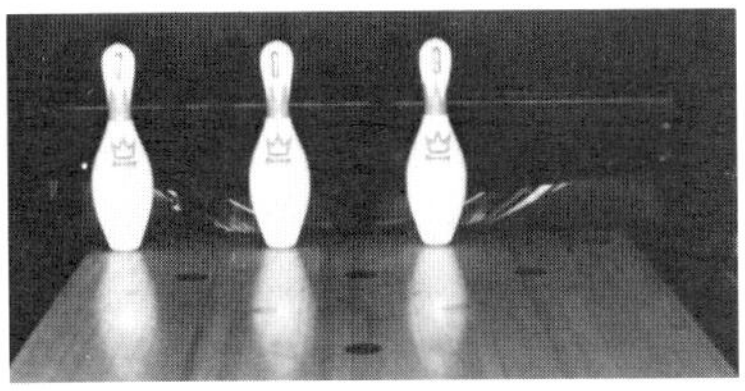

172-S   7-8-9

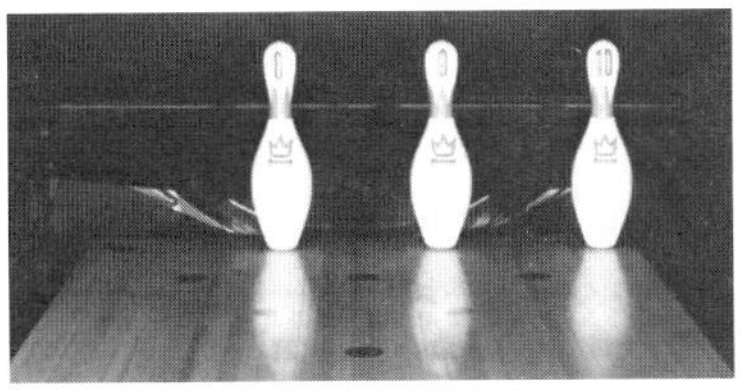

175-S   8-9-10

End of the 56 Rare Spares with Three Pins

3

Pictures of the 133 Rare Spares with Four Pins

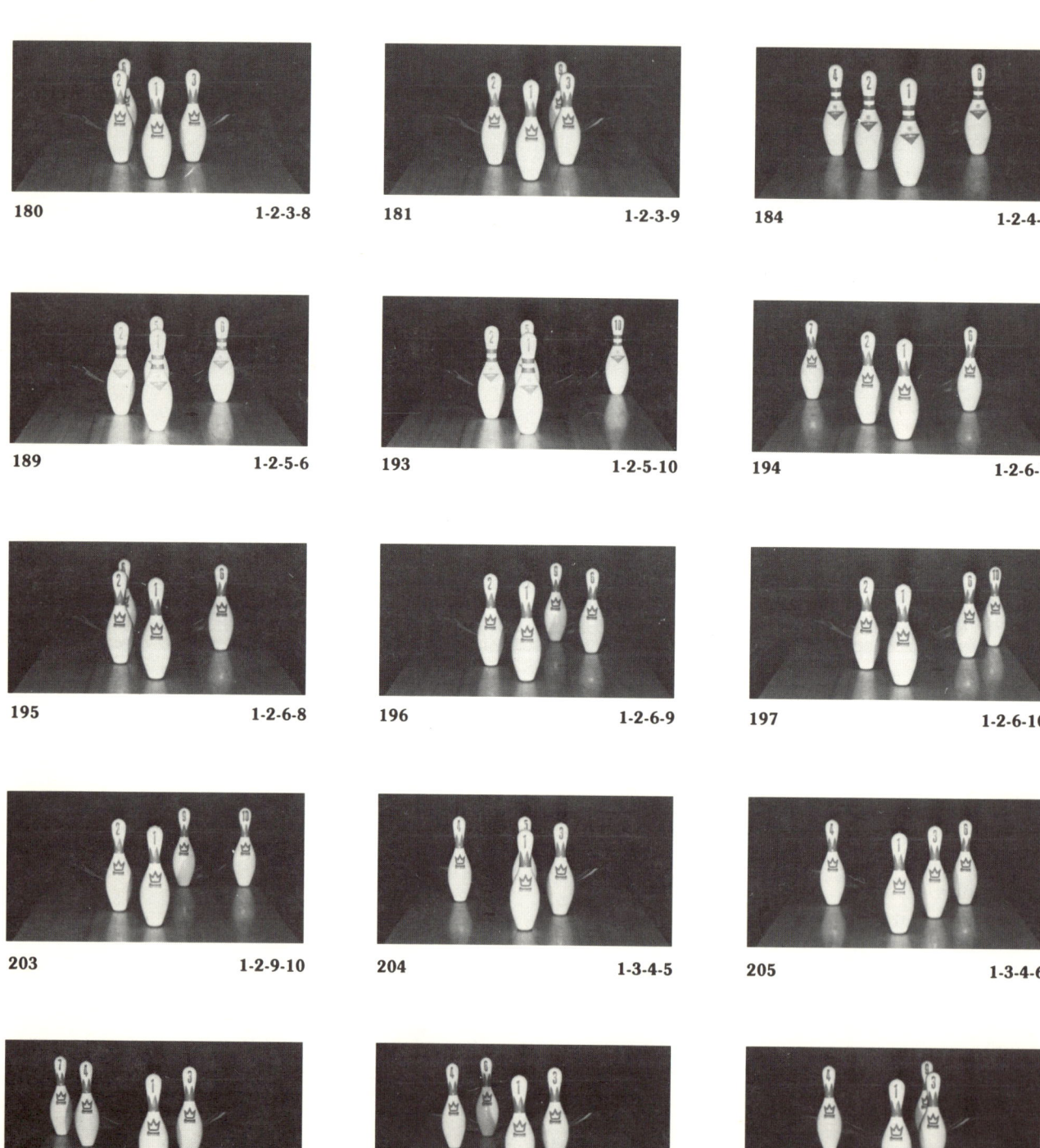

180   1-2-3-8

181   1-2-3-9

184   1-2-4-6

189   1-2-5-6

193   1-2-5-10

194   1-2-6-7

195   1-2-6-8

196   1-2-6-9

197   1-2-6-10

203   1-2-9-10

204   1-3-4-5

205   1-3-4-6

206   1-3-4-7

207   1-3-4-8

208   1-3-4-9

4

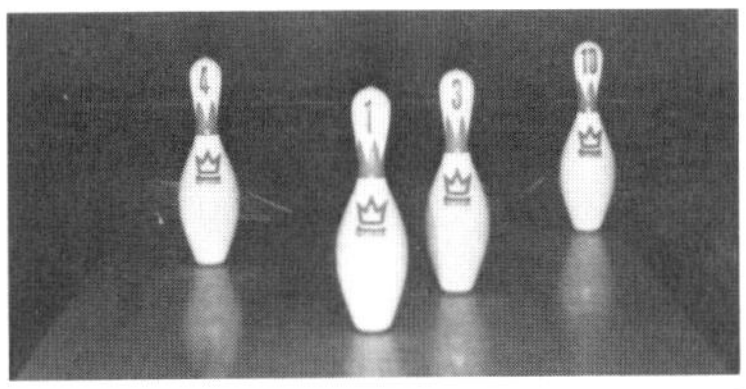

209 1-3-4-10	211 1-3-5-7	219 1-3-7-8
225 1-4-5-6	226 1-4-5-7	227 1-4-5-8
228 1-4-5-9	229 1-4-5-10	230 1-4-6-7
231 1-4-6-8	232 1-4-6-9	233 1-4-6-10
234 1-4-7-8	237 1-4-8-9	238 1-4-8-10
239 1-4-9-10	240 1-5-6-7	241 1-5-6-8

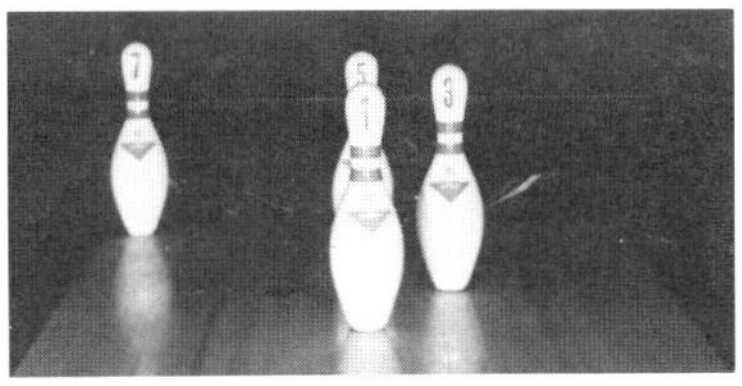

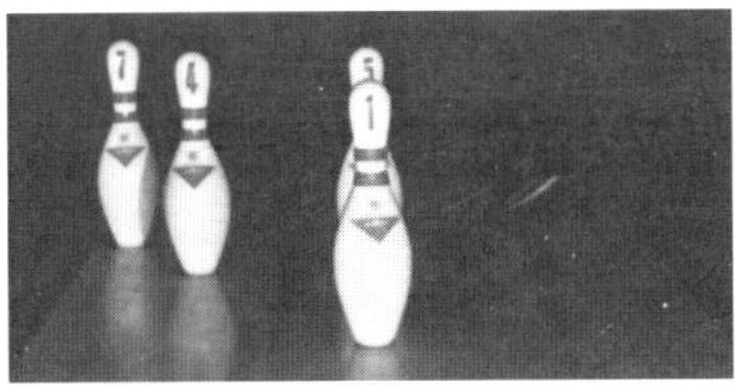

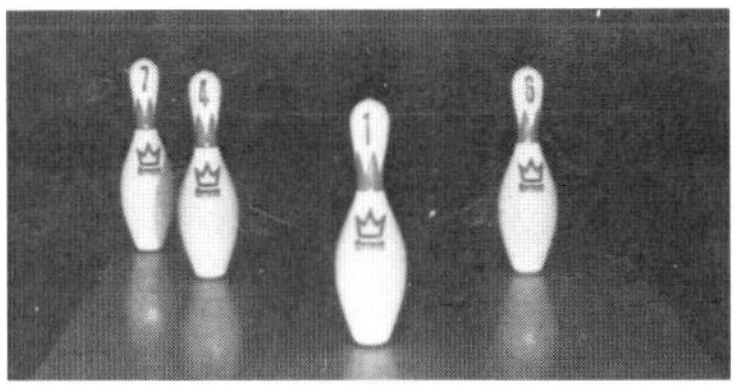

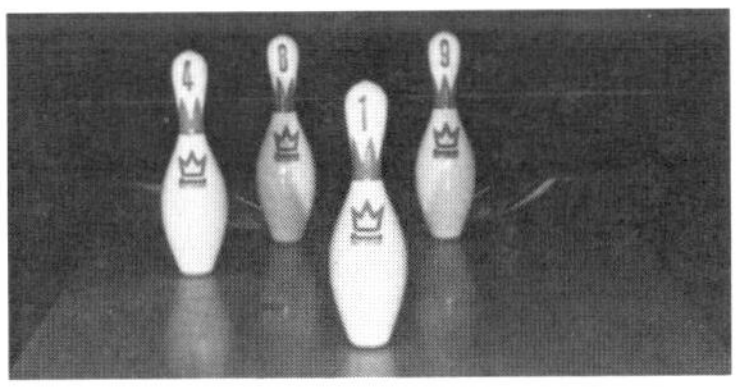

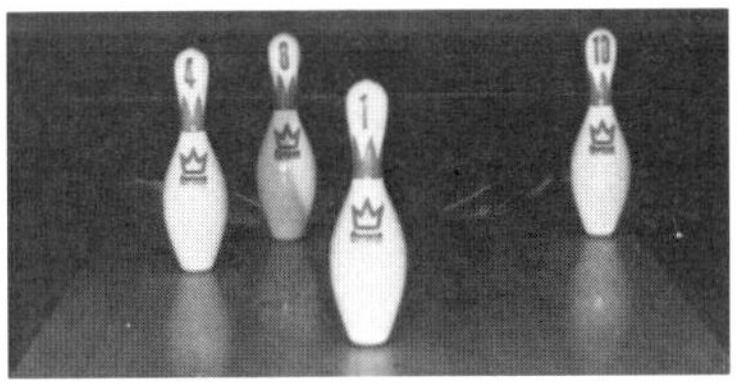

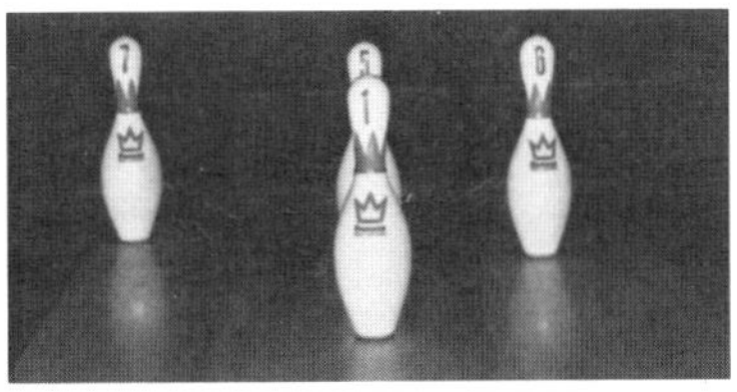

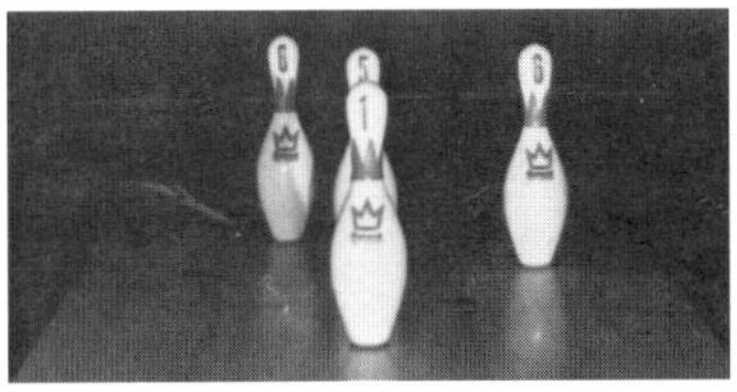

4

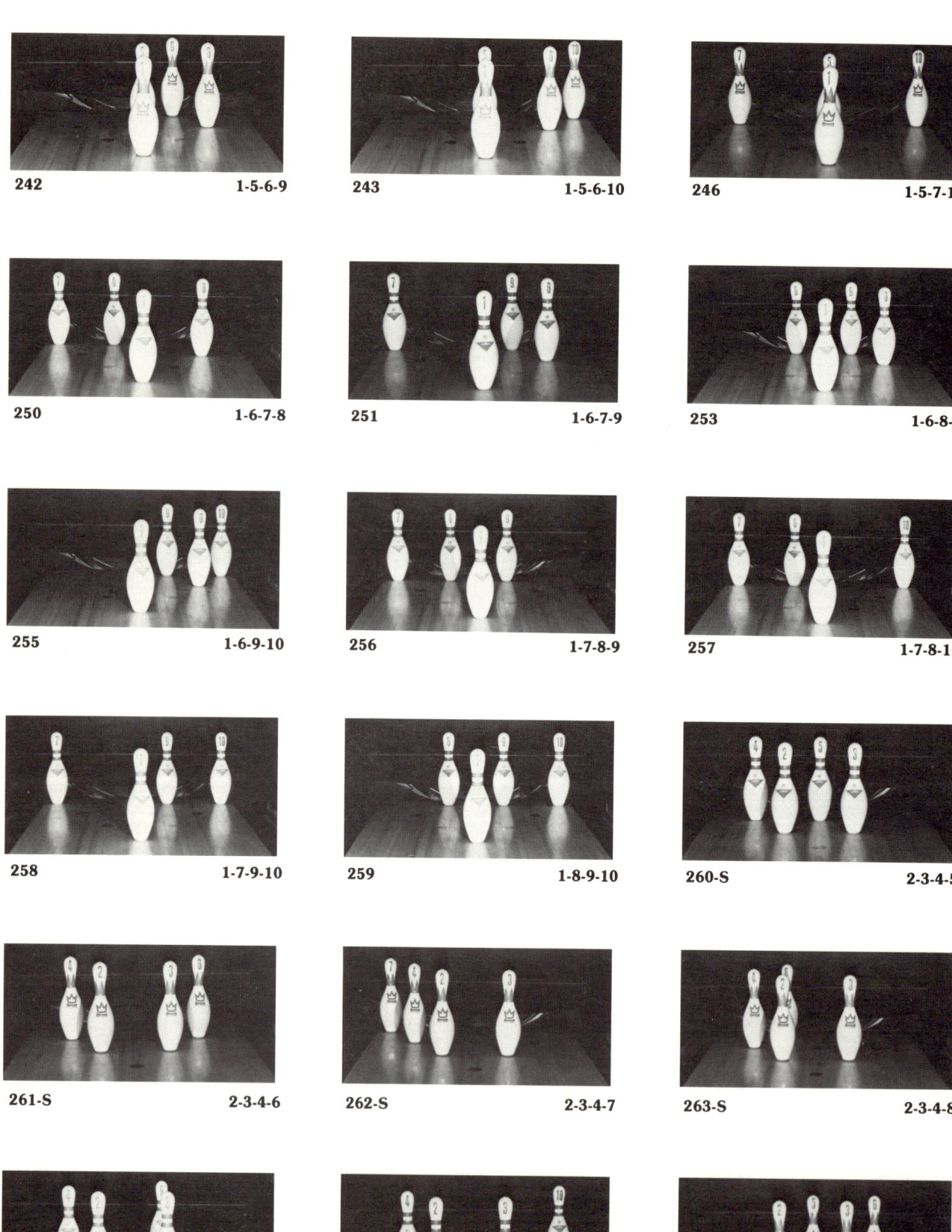

242   1-5-6-9

243   1-5-6-10

246   1-5-7-10

250   1-6-7-8

251   1-6-7-9

253   1-6-8-9

255   1-6-9-10

256   1-7-8-9

257   1-7-8-10

258   1-7-9-10

259   1-8-9-10

260-S   2-3-4-5

261-S   2-3-4-6

262-S   2-3-4-7

263-S   2-3-4-8

264-S   2-3-4-9

265-S   2-3-4-10

266-S   2-3-5-6

4

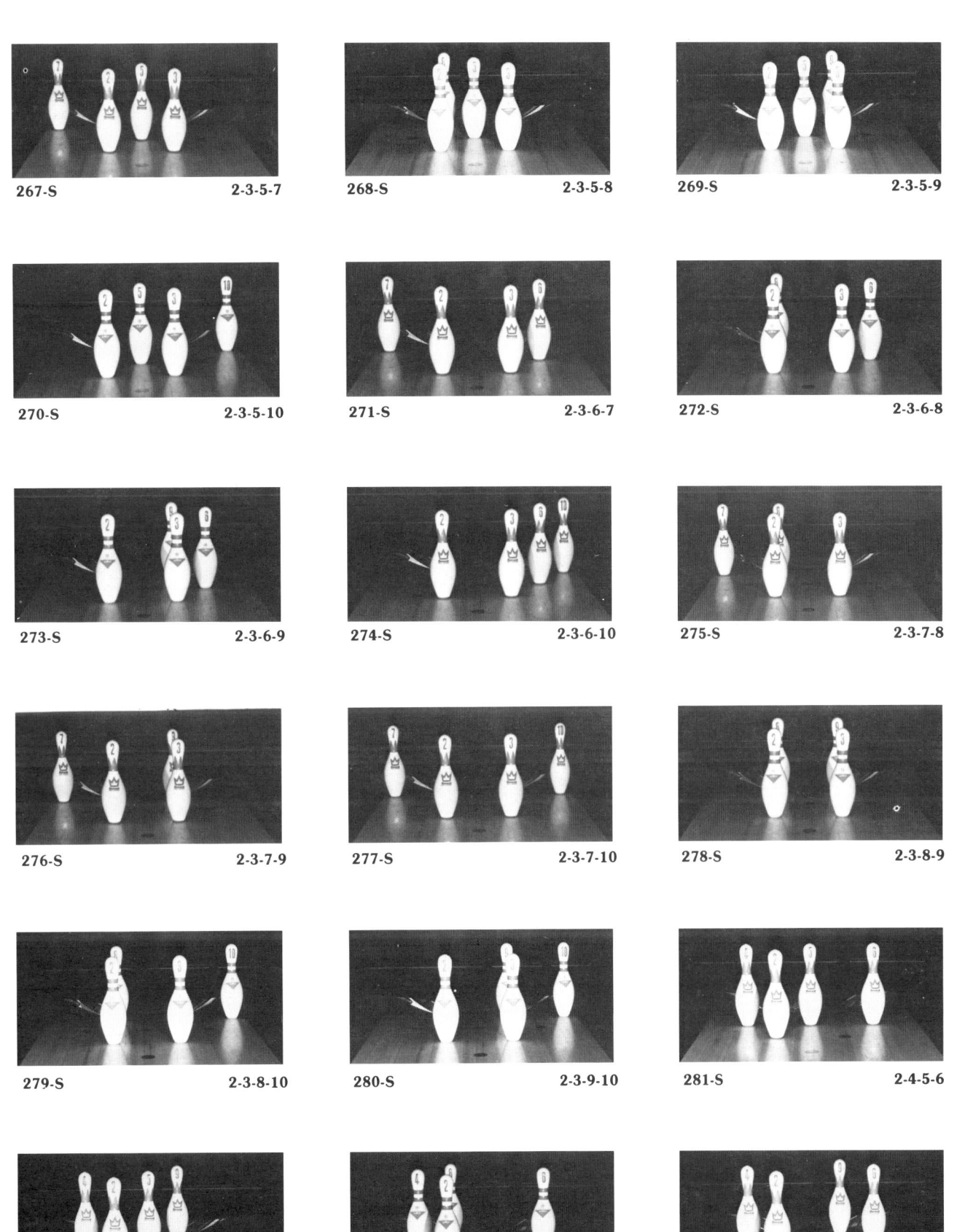

267-S   2-3-5-7   268-S   2-3-5-8   269-S   2-3-5-9

270-S   2-3-5-10   271-S   2-3-6-7   272-S   2-3-6-8

273-S   2-3-6-9   274-S   2-3-6-10   275-S   2-3-7-8

276-S   2-3-7-9   277-S   2-3-7-10   278-S   2-3-8-9

279-S   2-3-8-10   280-S   2-3-9-10   281-S   2-4-5-6

284   2-4-5-9   287-S   2-4-6-8   288-S   2-4-6-9

4

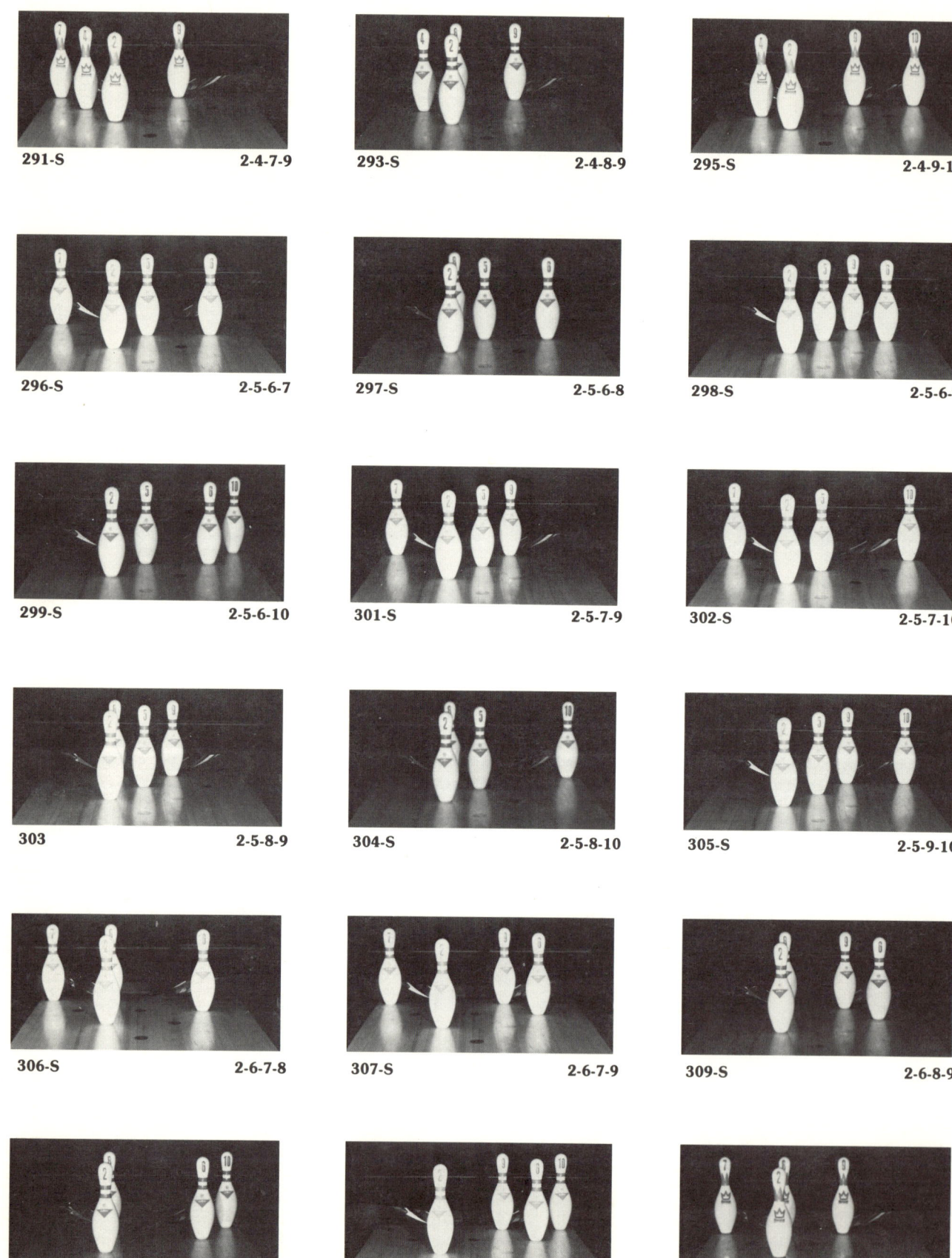

291-S   2-4-7-9

293-S   2-4-8-9

295-S   2-4-9-10

296-S   2-5-6-7

297-S   2-5-6-8

298-S   2-5-6-9

299-S   2-5-6-10

301-S   2-5-7-9

302-S   2-5-7-10

4

303   2-5-8-9

304-S   2-5-8-10

305-S   2-5-9-10

306-S   2-6-7-8

307-S   2-6-7-9

309-S   2-6-8-9

310-S   2-6-8-10

311-S   2-6-9-10

312-S   2-7-8-9

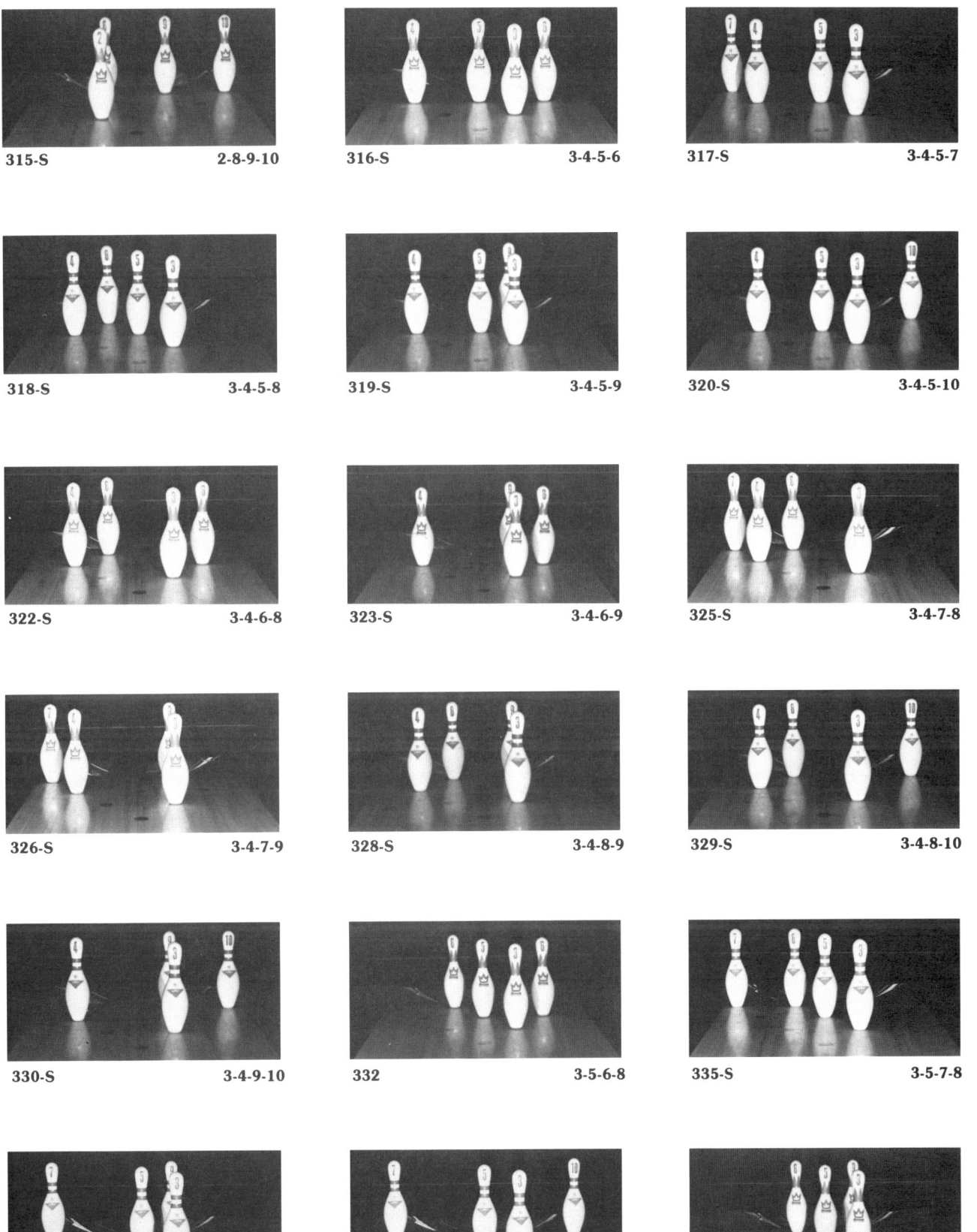

315-S   2-8-9-10

316-S   3-4-5-6

317-S   3-4-5-7

318-S   3-4-5-8

319-S   3-4-5-9

320-S   3-4-5-10

322-S   3-4-6-8

323-S   3-4-6-9

325-S   3-4-7-8

4

326-S   3-4-7-9

328-S   3-4-8-9

329-S   3-4-8-10

330-S   3-4-9-10

332   3-5-6-8

335-S   3-5-7-8

336-S   3-5-7-9

337-S   3-5-7-10

338   3-5-8-9

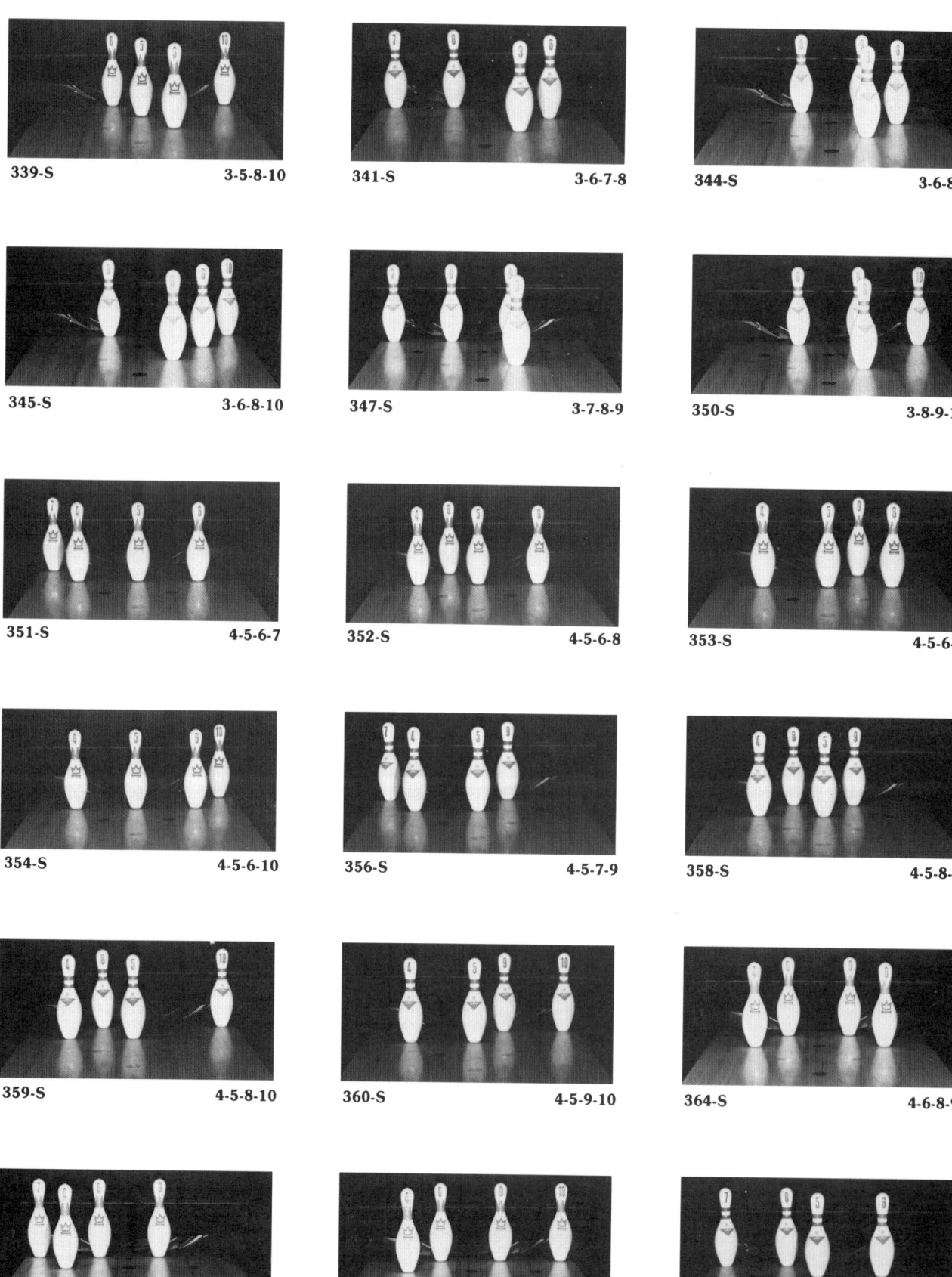

339-S 3-5-8-10

341-S 3-6-7-8

344-S 3-6-8-9

345-S 3-6-8-10

347-S 3-7-8-9

350-S 3-8-9-10

351-S 4-5-6-7

352-S 4-5-6-8

353-S 4-5-6-9

354-S 4-5-6-10

356-S 4-5-7-9

358-S 4-5-8-9

359-S 4-5-8-10

360-S 4-5-9-10

364-S 4-6-8-9

367-S 4-7-8-9

370-S 4-8-9-10

371-S 5-6-7-8

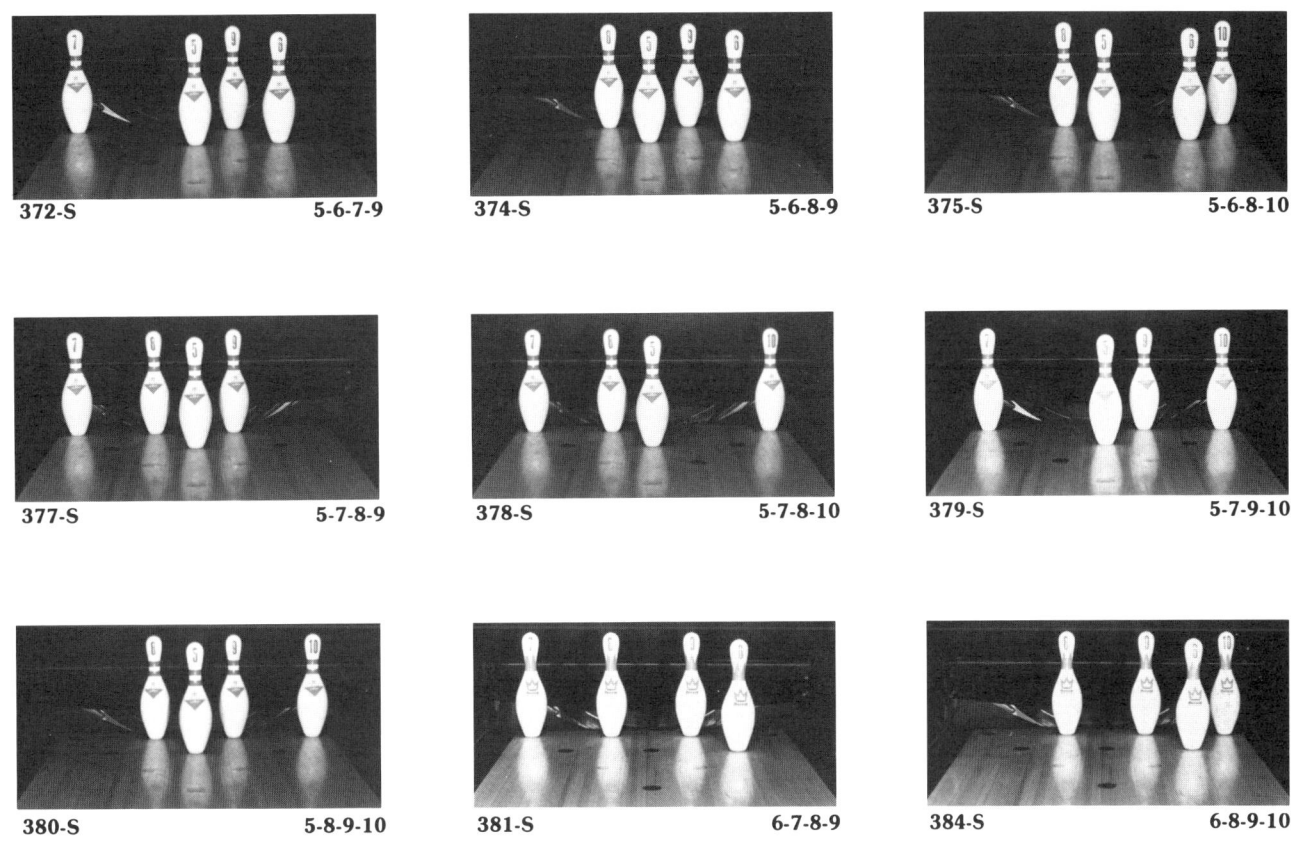

| 372-S | 5-6-7-9 | 374-S | 5-6-8-9 | 375-S | 5-6-8-10 |

| 377-S | 5-7-8-9 | 378-S | 5-7-8-10 | 379-S | 5-7-9-10 |

| 380-S | 5-8-9-10 | 381-S | 6-7-8-9 | 384-S | 6-8-9-10 |

4

385-S   7-8-9-10

End of the 133 Rare Spares with Four Pins.

Pictures of the 216 Rare Spares with Five Pins

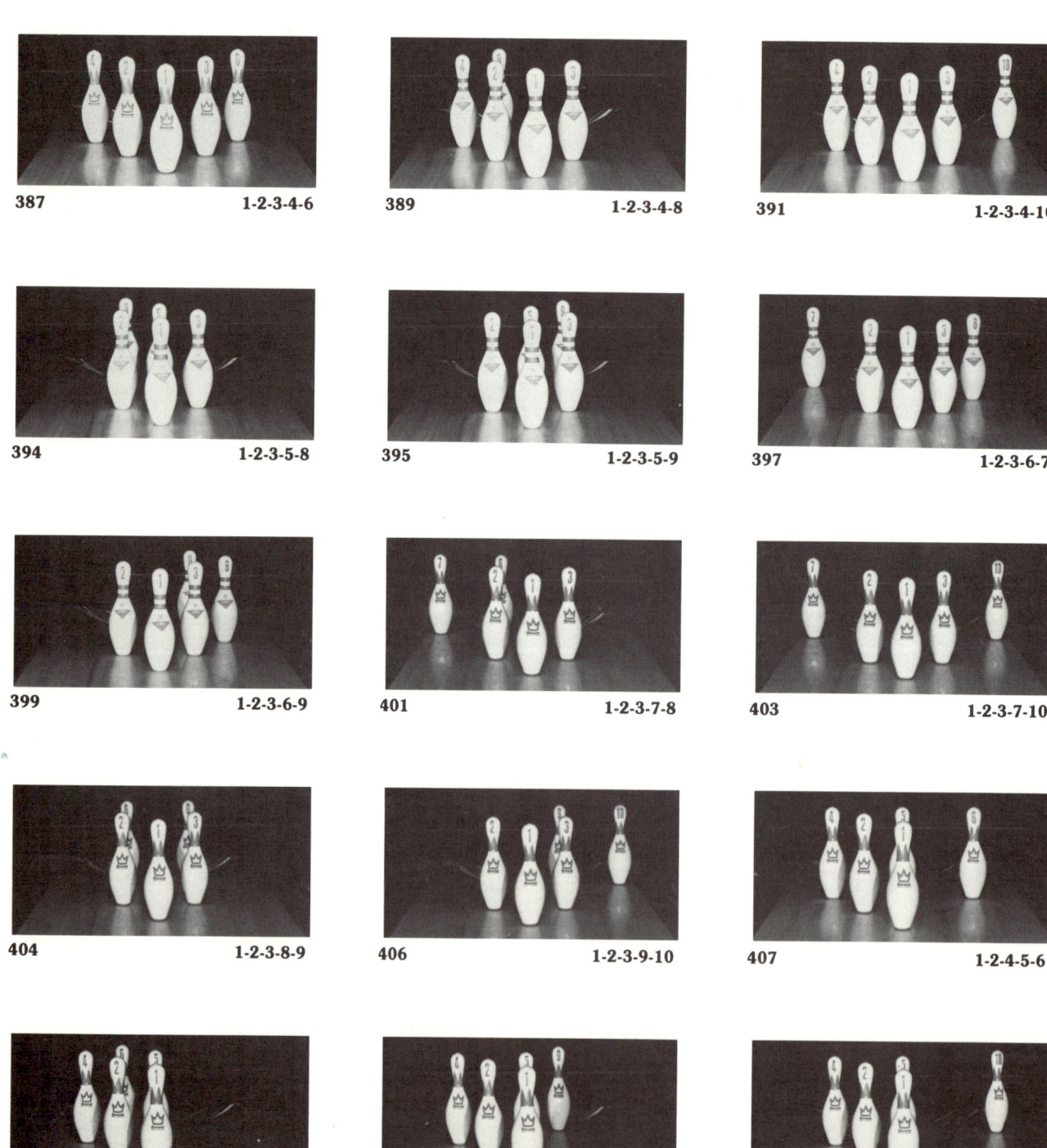

5

387 — 1-2-3-4-6	389 — 1-2-3-4-8	391 — 1-2-3-4-10
394 — 1-2-3-5-8	395 — 1-2-3-5-9	397 — 1-2-3-6-7
399 — 1-2-3-6-9	401 — 1-2-3-7-8	403 — 1-2-3-7-10
404 — 1-2-3-8-9	406 — 1-2-3-9-10	407 — 1-2-4-5-6
409 — 1-2-4-5-8	410 — 1-2-4-5-9	411 — 1-2-4-5-10

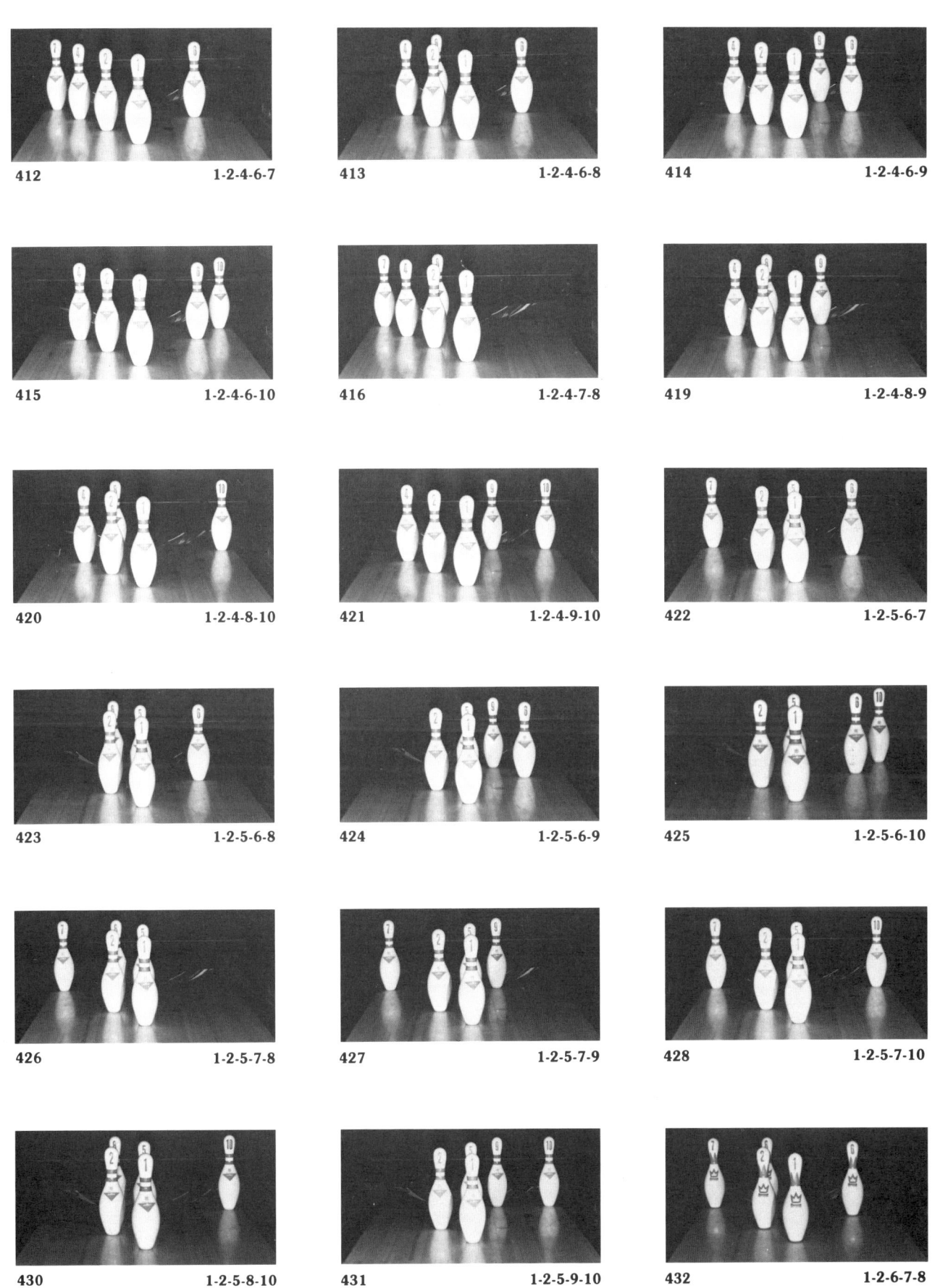

412   1-2-4-6-7

413   1-2-4-6-8

414   1-2-4-6-9

415   1-2-4-6-10

416   1-2-4-7-8

419   1-2-4-8-9

420   1-2-4-8-10

421   1-2-4-9-10

422   1-2-5-6-7

423   1-2-5-6-8

424   1-2-5-6-9

425   1-2-5-6-10

426   1-2-5-7-8

427   1-2-5-7-9

428   1-2-5-7-10

430   1-2-5-8-10

431   1-2-5-9-10

432   1-2-6-7-8

5

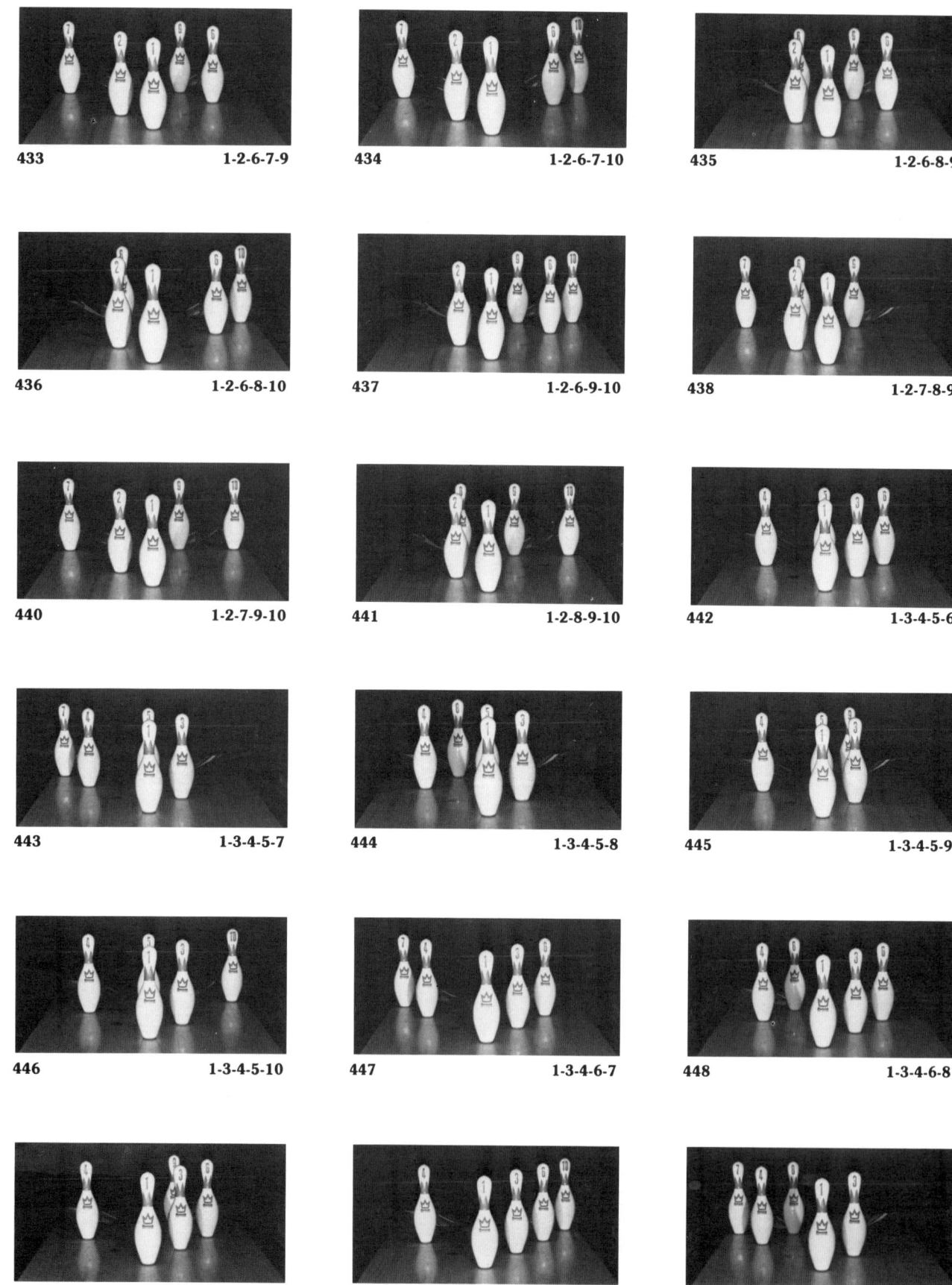

433 1-2-6-7-9

434 1-2-6-7-10

435 1-2-6-8-9

436 1-2-6-8-10

437 1-2-6-9-10

438 1-2-7-8-9

440 1-2-7-9-10

441 1-2-8-9-10

442 1-3-4-5-6

5

443 1-3-4-5-7

444 1-3-4-5-8

445 1-3-4-5-9

446 1-3-4-5-10

447 1-3-4-6-7

448 1-3-4-6-8

449 1-3-4-6-9

450 1-3-4-6-10

451 1-3-4-7-8

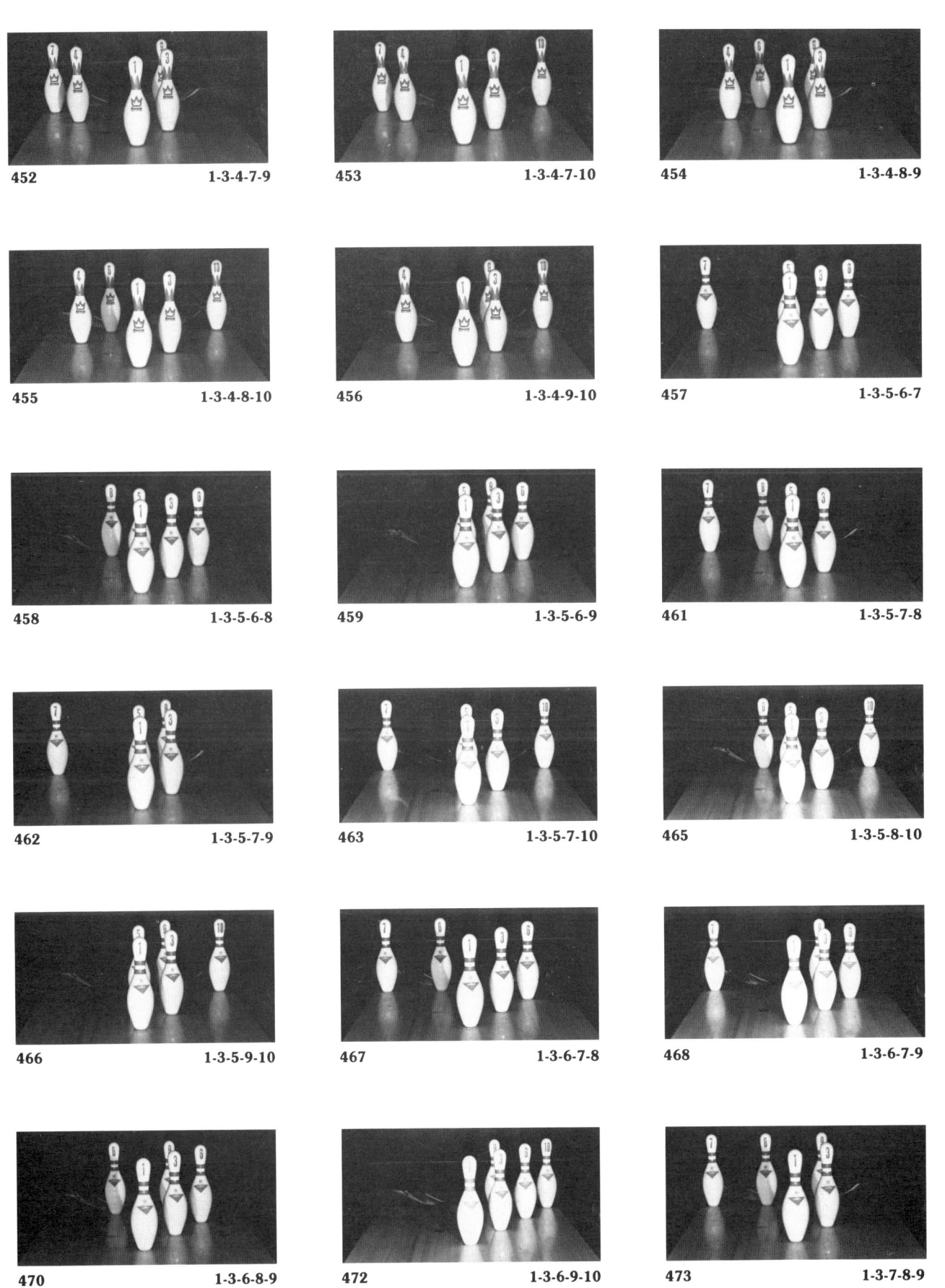

452   1-3-4-7-9

453   1-3-4-7-10

454   1-3-4-8-9

455   1-3-4-8-10

456   1-3-4-9-10

457   1-3-5-6-7

458   1-3-5-6-8

459   1-3-5-6-9

461   1-3-5-7-8

462   1-3-5-7-9

463   1-3-5-7-10

465   1-3-5-8-10

466   1-3-5-9-10

467   1-3-6-7-8

468   1-3-6-7-9

470   1-3-6-8-9

472   1-3-6-9-10

473   1-3-7-8-9

5

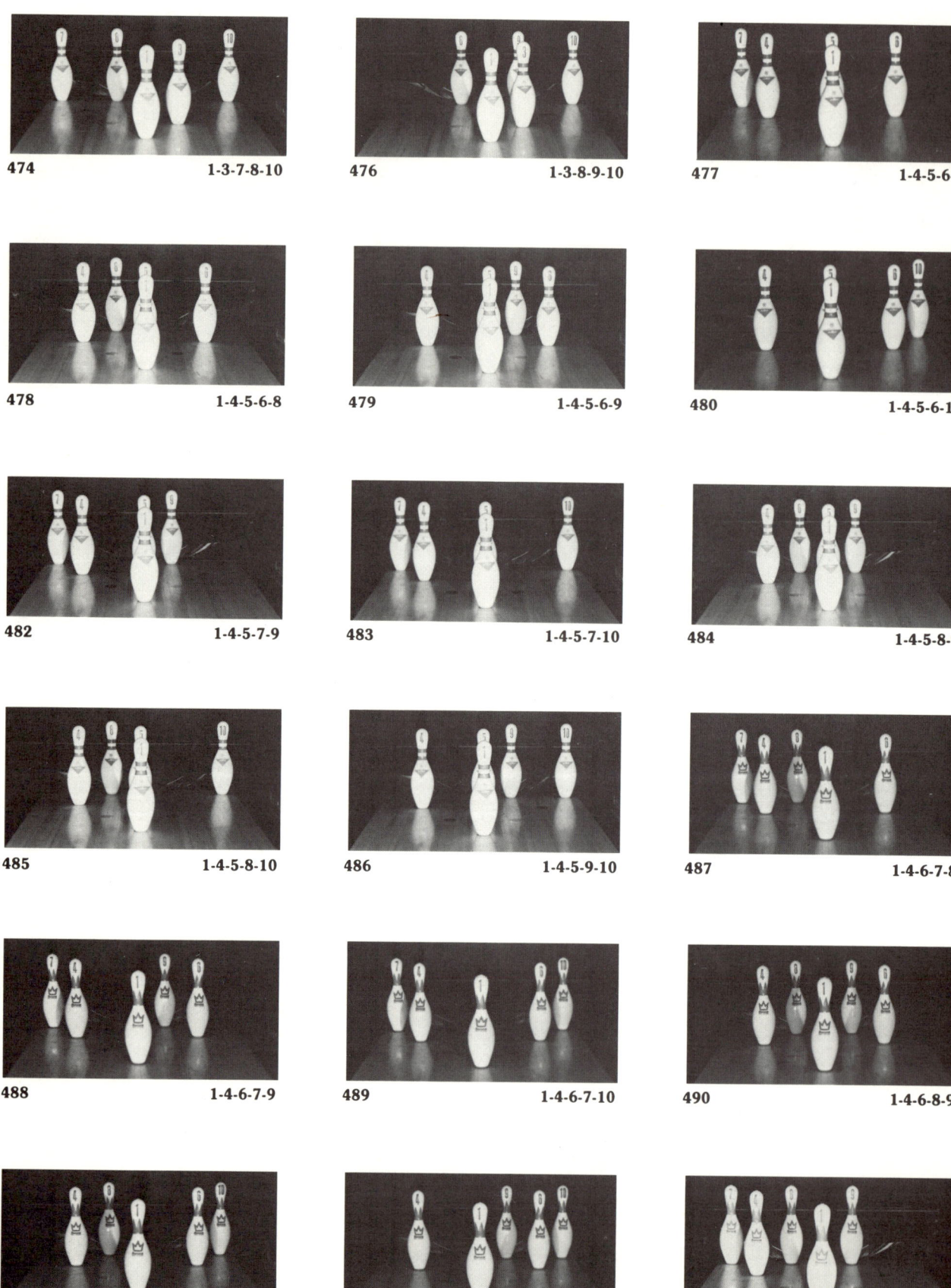

474   1-3-7-8-10

476   1-3-8-9-10

477   1-4-5-6-7

478   1-4-5-6-8

479   1-4-5-6-9

480   1-4-5-6-10

482   1-4-5-7-9

483   1-4-5-7-10

484   1-4-5-8-9

5

485   1-4-5-8-10

486   1-4-5-9-10

487   1-4-6-7-8

488   1-4-6-7-9

489   1-4-6-7-10

490   1-4-6-8-9

491   1-4-6-8-10

492   1-4-6-9-10

493   1-4-7-8-9

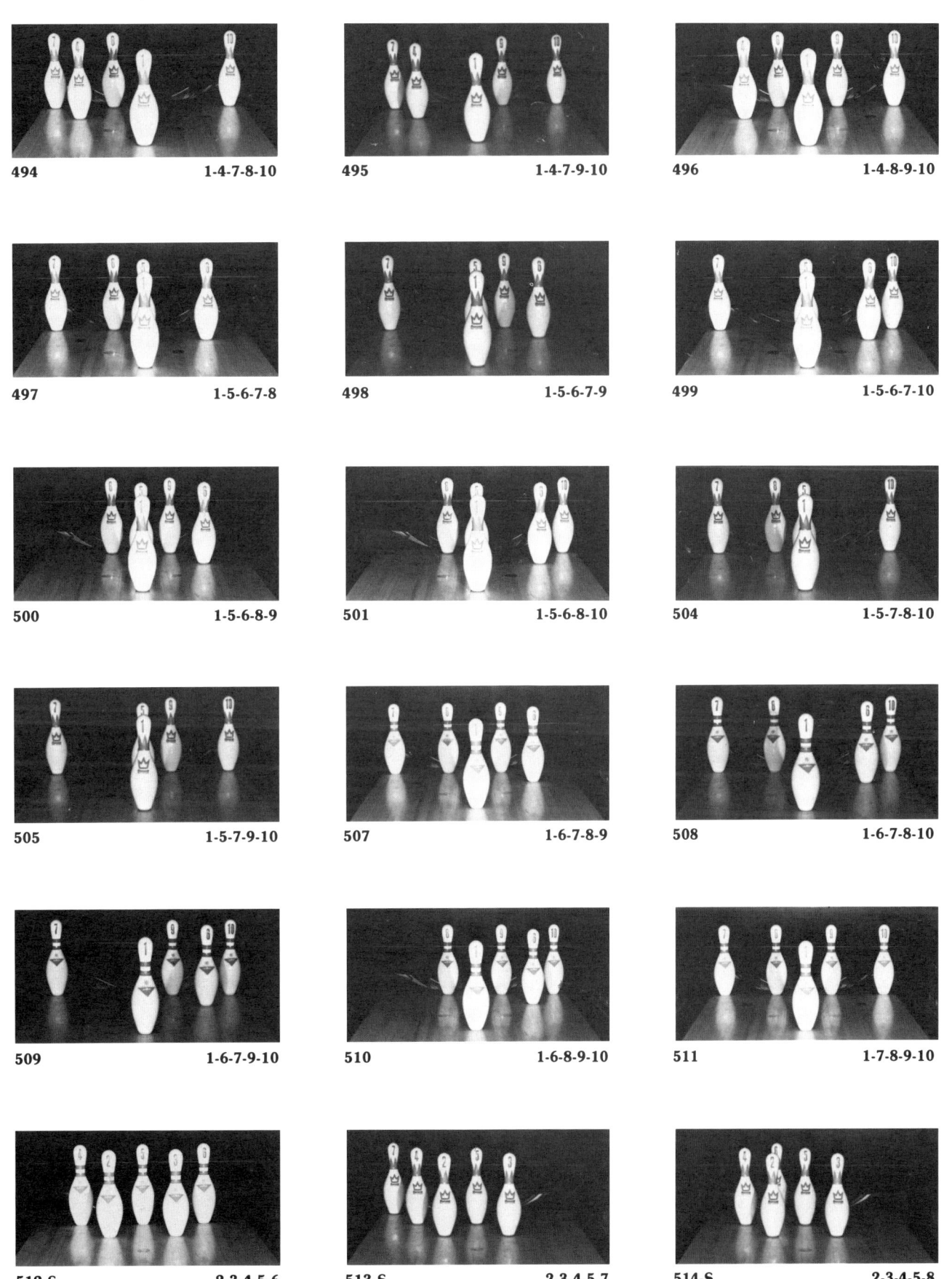

494   1-4-7-8-10

495   1-4-7-9-10

496   1-4-8-9-10

497   1-5-6-7-8

498   1-5-6-7-9

499   1-5-6-7-10

500   1-5-6-8-9

501   1-5-6-8-10

504   1-5-7-8-10

505   1-5-7-9-10

507   1-6-7-8-9

508   1-6-7-8-10

509   1-6-7-9-10

510   1-6-8-9-10

511   1-7-8-9-10

512-S   2-3-4-5-6

513-S   2-3-4-5-7

514-S   2-3-4-5-8

5

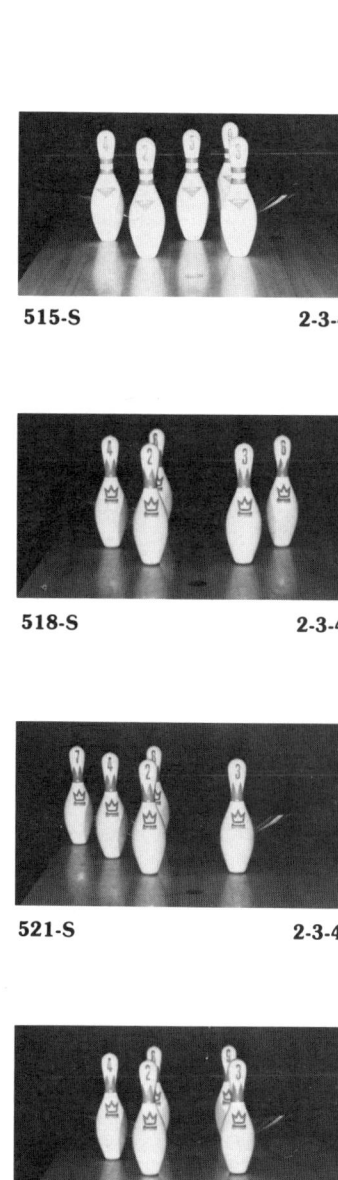

515-S 2-3-4-5-9

516-S 2-3-4-5-10

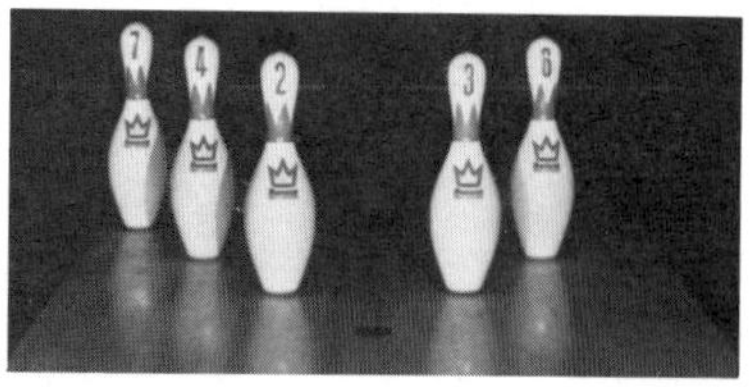

517-S 2-3-4-6-7

518-S 2-3-4-6-8

519-S 2-3-4-6-9

520-S 2-3-4-6-10

521-S 2-3-4-7-8

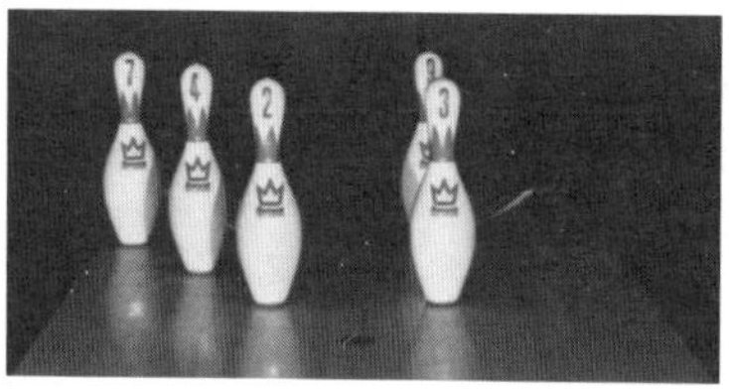

522-S 2-3-4-7-9

523-S 2-3-4-7-10

5

524-S 2-3-4-8-9

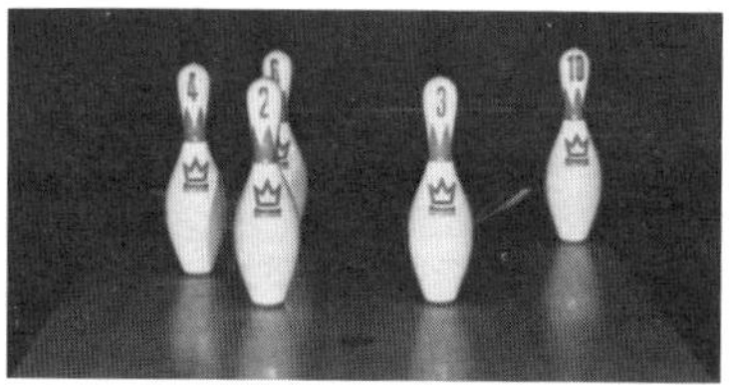

525-S 2-3-4-8-10

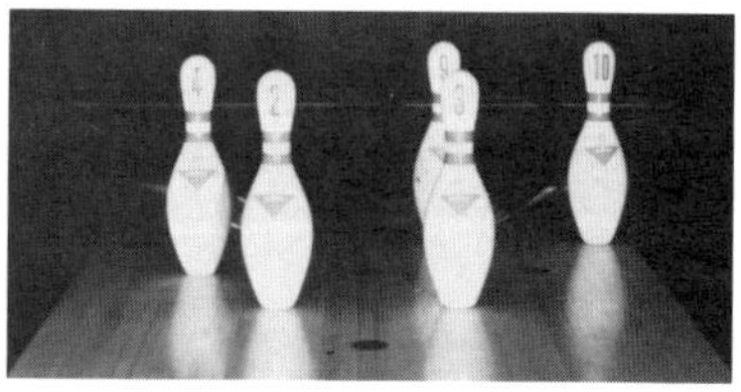

526-S 2-3-4-9-10

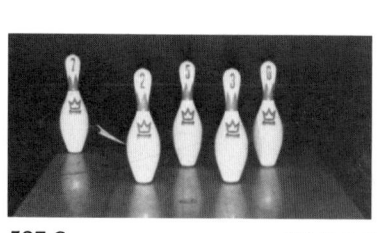

527-S 2-3-5-6-7

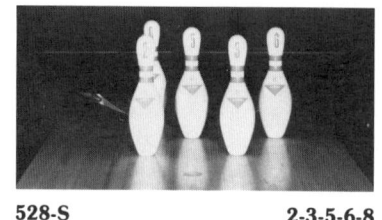

528-S 2-3-5-6-8

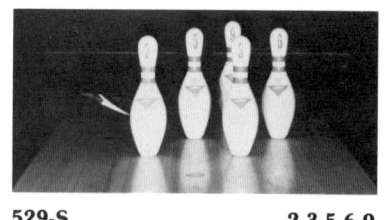

529-S 2-3-5-6-9

530-S 2-3-5-6-10

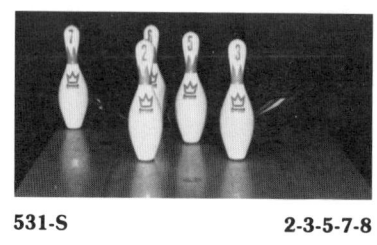

531-S 2-3-5-7-8

532-S 2-3-5-7-9

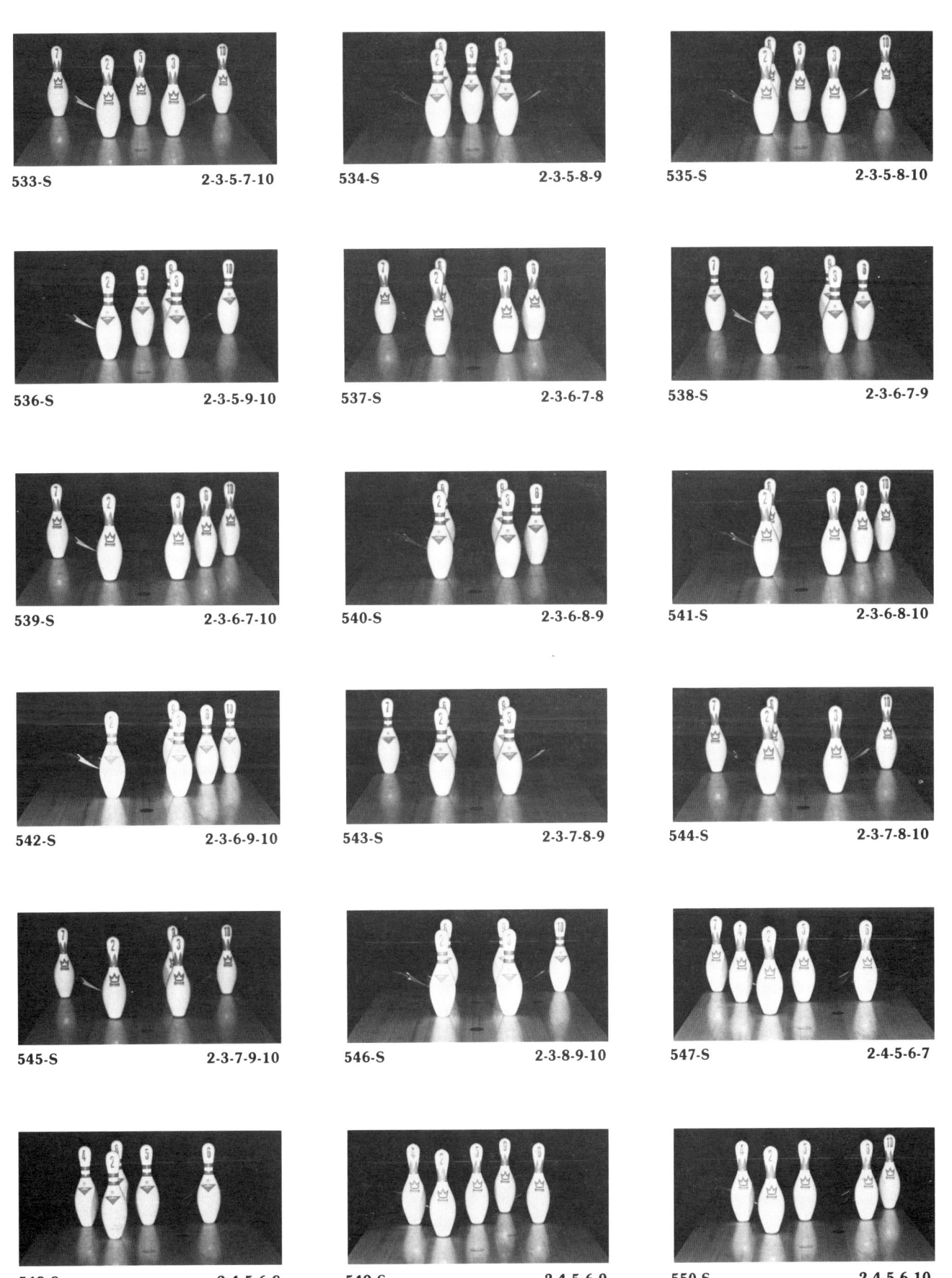

533-S   2-3-5-7-10

534-S   2-3-5-8-9

535-S   2-3-5-8-10

536-S   2-3-5-9-10

537-S   2-3-6-7-8

538-S   2-3-6-7-9

539-S   2-3-6-7-10

540-S   2-3-6-8-9

541-S   2-3-6-8-10

5

542-S   2-3-6-9-10

543-S   2-3-7-8-9

544-S   2-3-7-8-10

545-S   2-3-7-9-10

546-S   2-3-8-9-10

547-S   2-4-5-6-7

548-S   2-4-5-6-8

549-S   2-4-5-6-9

550-S   2-4-5-6-10

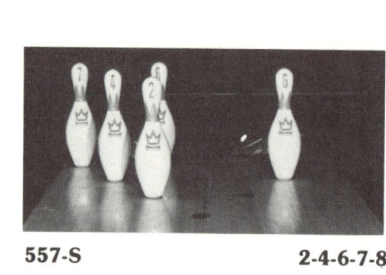

552   **2-4-5-7-9**

553-S   **2-4-5-7-10**

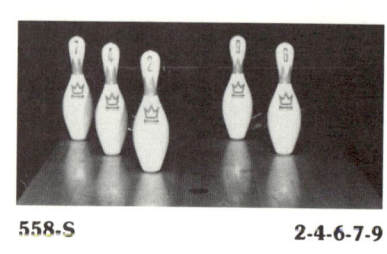

554   **2-4-5-8-9**

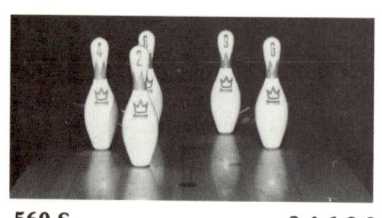

556-S   **2-4-5-9-10**

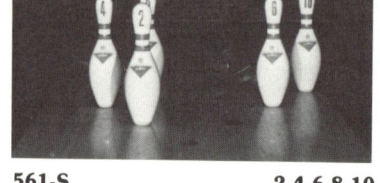

557-S   **2-4-6-7-8**

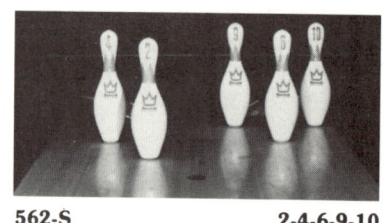

558-S   **2-4-6-7-9**

560-S   **2-4-6-8-9**

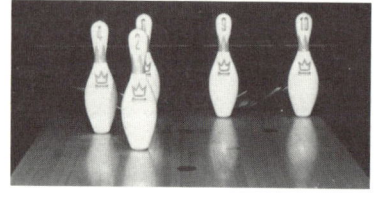

561-S   **2-4-6-8-10**

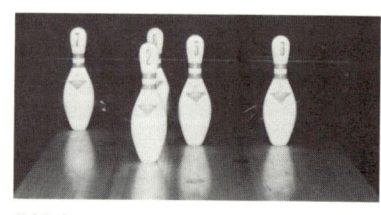

562-S   **2-4-6-9-10**

5

563-S   **2-4-7-8-9**

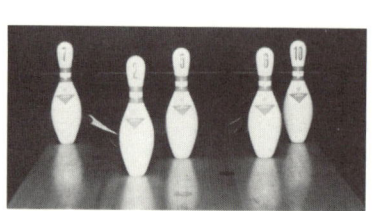

566-S   **2-4-8-9-10**

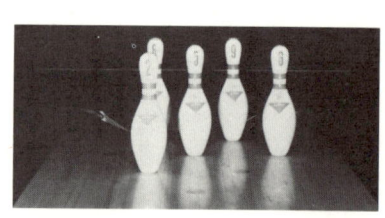

567-S   **2-5-6-7-8**

568-S   **2-5-6-7-9**

569-S   **2-5-6-7-10**

570-S   **2-5-6-8-9**

571-S   **2-5-6-8-10**

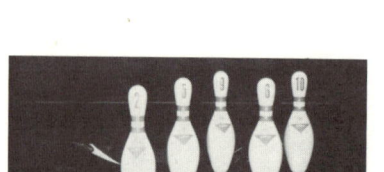

572-S   **2-5-6-9-10**

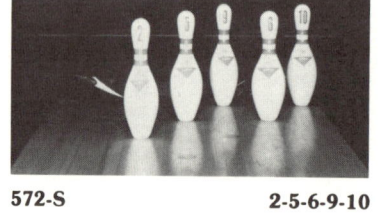

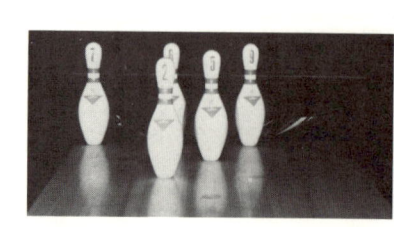

573-S   **2-5-7-8-9**

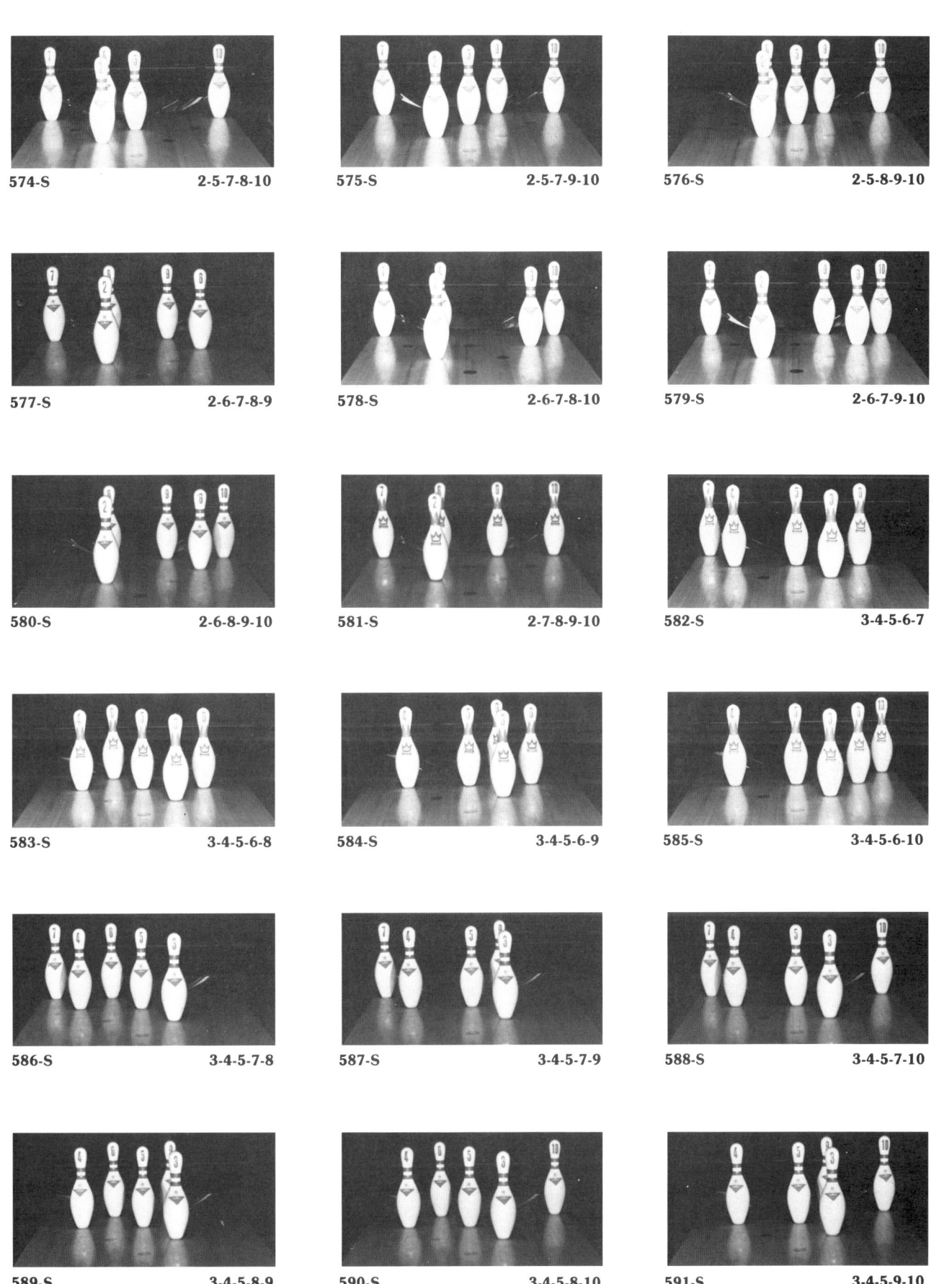

574-S   2-5-7-8-10

575-S   2-5-7-9-10

576-S   2-5-8-9-10

577-S   2-6-7-8-9

578-S   2-6-7-8-10

579-S   2-6-7-9-10

580-S   2-6-8-9-10

581-S   2-7-8-9-10

582-S   3-4-5-6-7

583-S   3-4-5-6-8

584-S   3-4-5-6-9

585-S   3-4-5-6-10

586-S   3-4-5-7-8

587-S   3-4-5-7-9

588-S   3-4-5-7-10

589-S   3-4-5-8-9

590-S   3-4-5-8-10

591-S   3-4-5-9-10

5

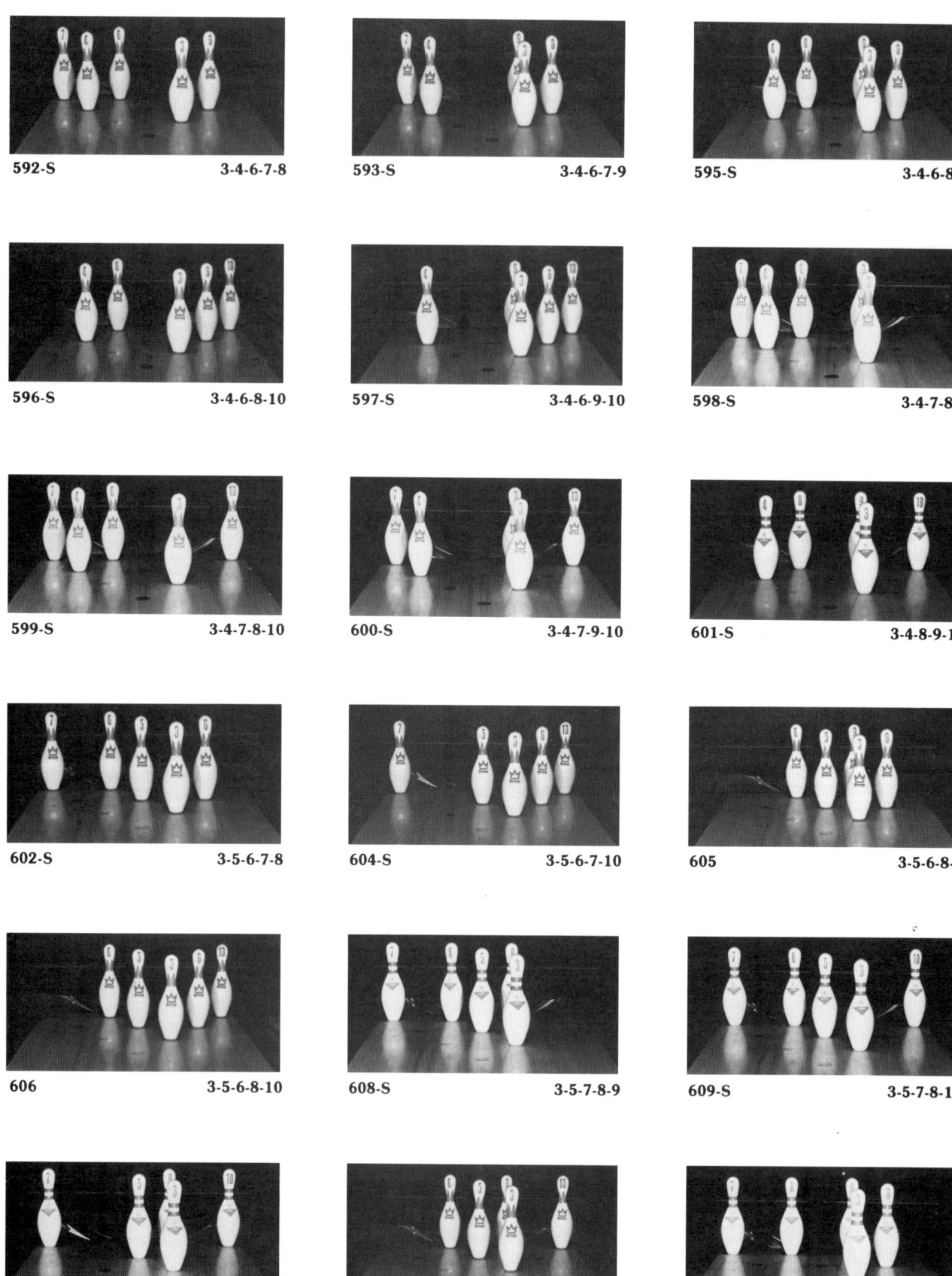

592-S   3-4-6-7-8

593-S   3-4-6-7-9

595-S   3-4-6-8-9

596-S   3-4-6-8-10

597-S   3-4-6-9-10

598-S   3-4-7-8-9

599-S   3-4-7-8-10

600-S   3-4-7-9-10

601-S   3-4-8-9-10

5

602-S   3-5-6-7-8

604-S   3-5-6-7-10

605   3-5-6-8-9

606   3-5-6-8-10

608-S   3-5-7-8-9

609-S   3-5-7-8-10

610-S   3-5-7-9-10

611-S   3-5-8-9-10

612-S   3-6-7-8-9

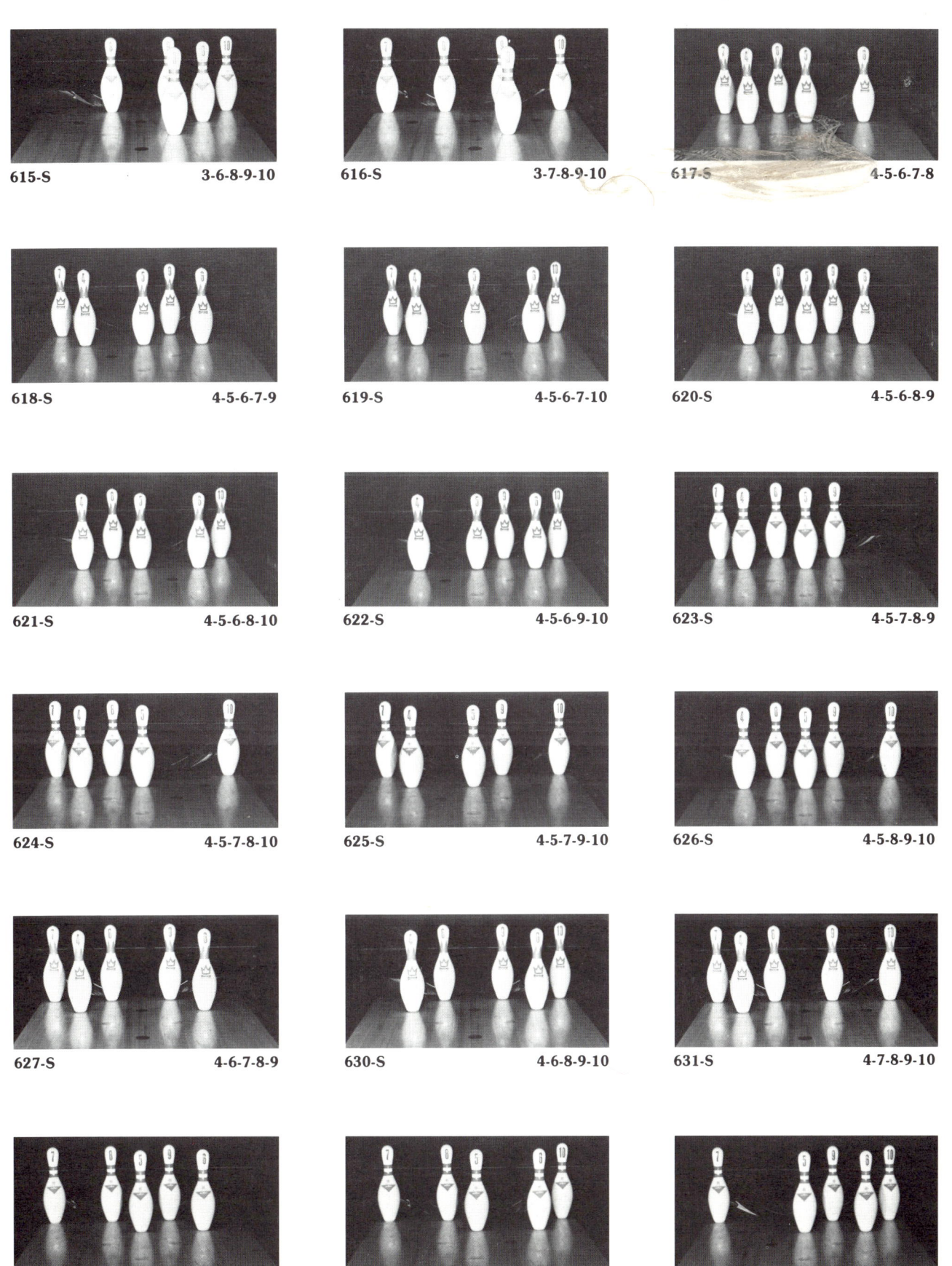

615-S   3-6-8-9-10

616-S   3-7-8-9-10

617-S   4-5-6-7-8

618-S   4-5-6-7-9

619-S   4-5-6-7-10

620-S   4-5-6-8-9

621-S   4-5-6-8-10

622-S   4-5-6-9-10

623-S   4-5-7-8-9

624-S   4-5-7-8-10

625-S   4-5-7-9-10

626-S   4-5-8-9-10

627-S   4-6-7-8-9

630-S   4-6-8-9-10

631-S   4-7-8-9-10

632-S   5-6-7-8-9

633-S   5-6-7-8-10

634-S   5-6-7-9-10

5

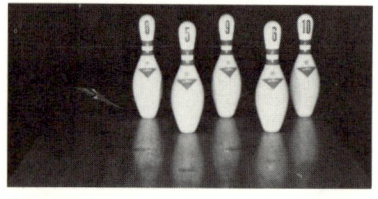

635-S   5-6-8-9-10

636-S   5-7-8-9-10

637-S   6-7-8-9-10

End of the 216 Rare Spares with Five Pins

5

Pictures of the 202 Rare Spares with Six Pins

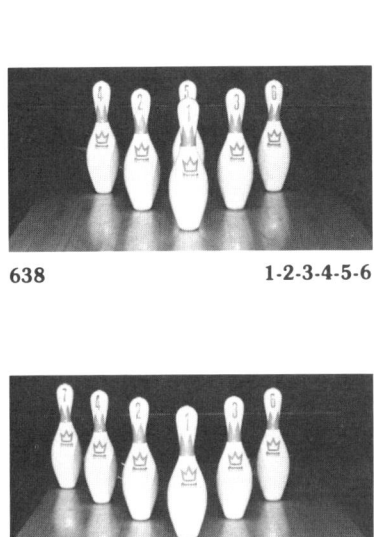

638   1-2-3-4-5-6

640   1-2-3-4-5-8

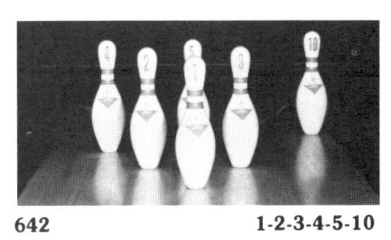

642   1-2-3-4-5-10

643   1-2-3-4-6-7

644   1-2-3-4-6-8

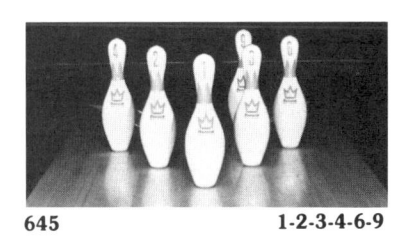

645   1-2-3-4-6-9

6

646   1-2-3-4-6-10

647   1-2-3-4-7-8

649   1-2-3-4-7-10

650   1-2-3-4-8-9

651   1-2-3-4-8-10

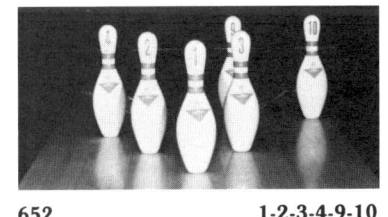

652   1-2-3-4-9-10

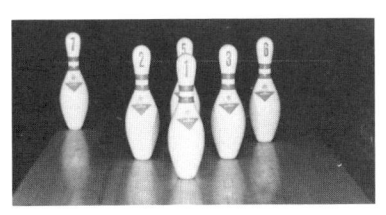

653   1-2-3-5-6-7

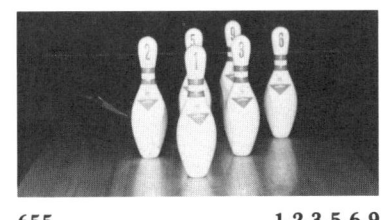

655   1-2-3-5-6-9

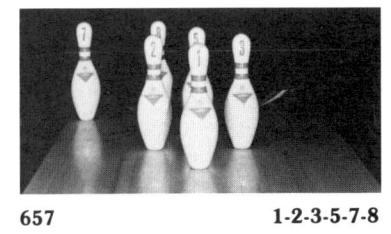

657   1-2-3-5-7-8

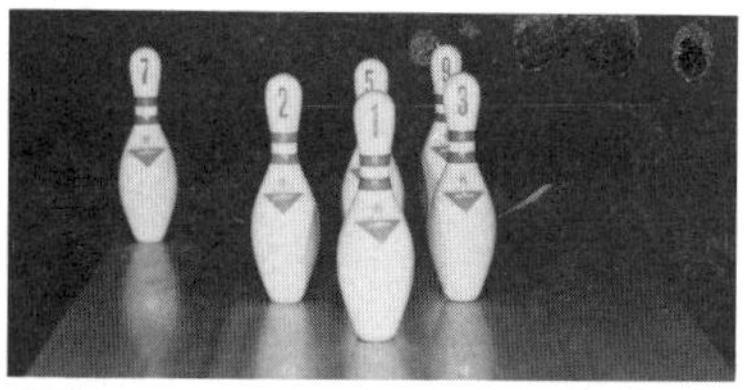

658   1-2-3-5-7-9

659   1-2-3-5-7-10

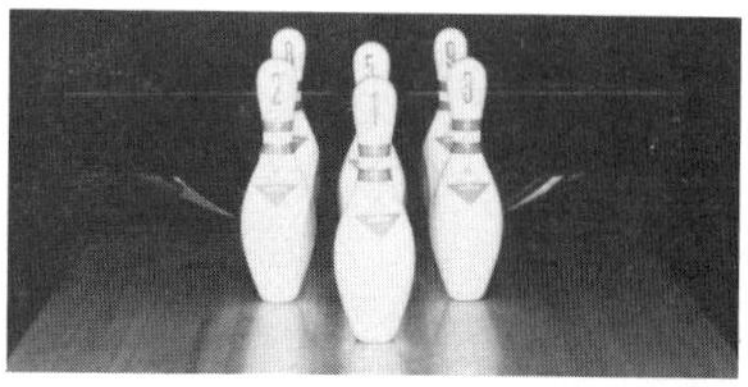

660   1-2-3-5-8-9

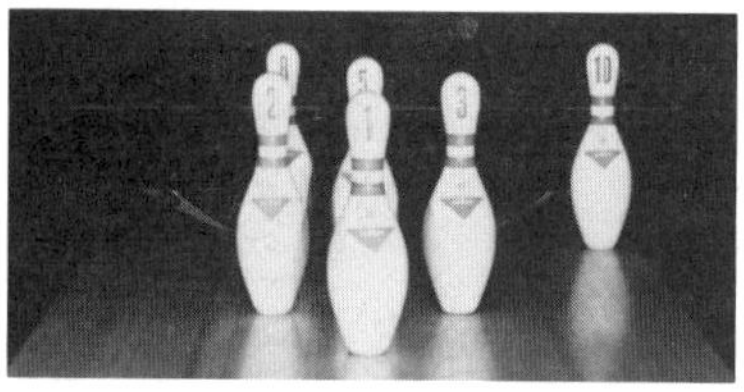

661   1-2-3-5-8-10

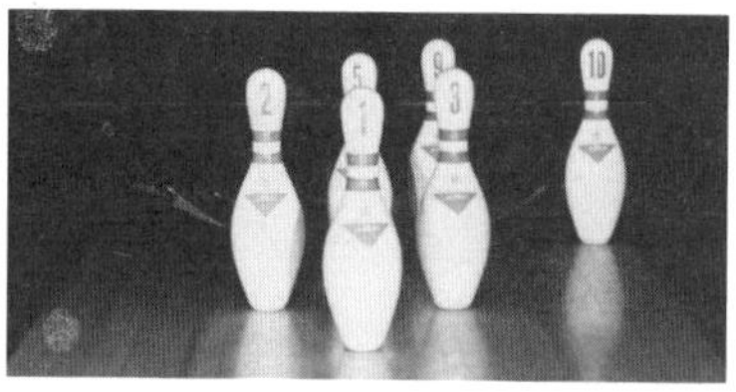

662   1-2-3-5-9-10

663   1-2-3-6-7-8

664   1-2-3-6-7-9

665   1-2-3-6-7-10

666   1-2-3-6-8-9

6

668   1-2-3-6-9-10

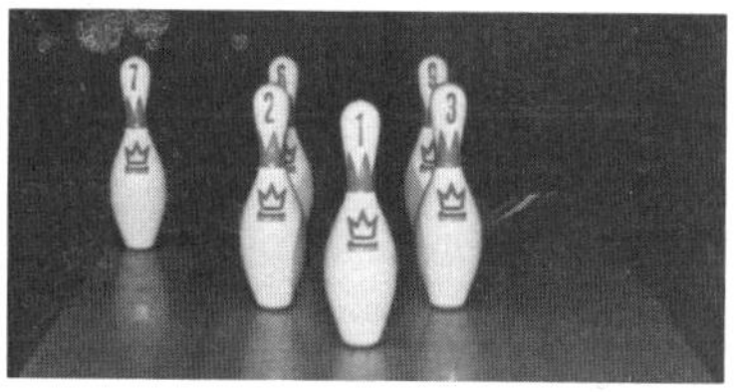

669   1-2-3-7-8-9

670   1-2-3-7-8-10

671   1-2-3-7-9-10

672   1-2-3-8-9-10

673   1-2-4-5-6-7

674   1-2-4-5-6-8

675   1-2-4-5-6-9

676   1-2-4-5-6-10

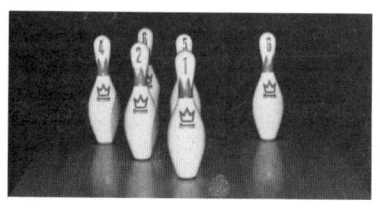

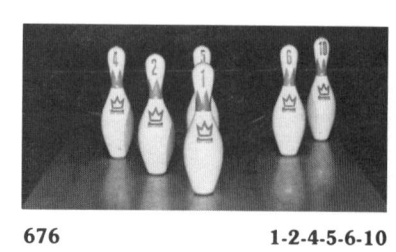

678   1-2-4-5-7-9

679   1-2-4-5-7-10

680   1-2-4-5-8-9

681   1-2-4-5-8-10

682   1-2-4-5-9-10

683   1-2-4-6-7-8

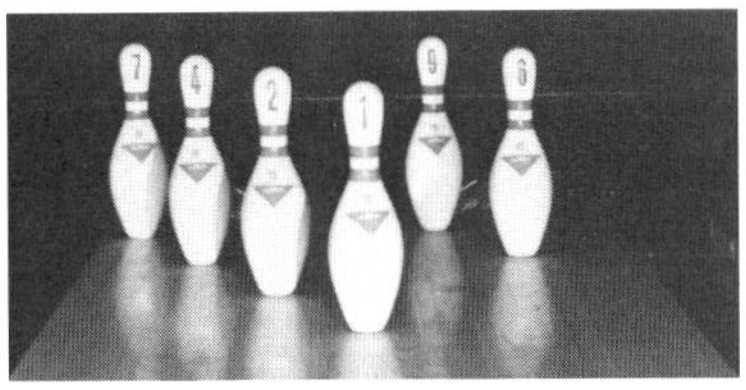

684   1-2-4-6-7-9

685   1-2-4-6-7-10

686   1-2-4-6-8-9

6

687   1-2-4-6-8-10

688   1-2-4-6-9-10

689   1-2-4-7-8-9

690   1-2-4-7-8-10

691   1-2-4-7-9-10

692   1-2-4-8-9-10

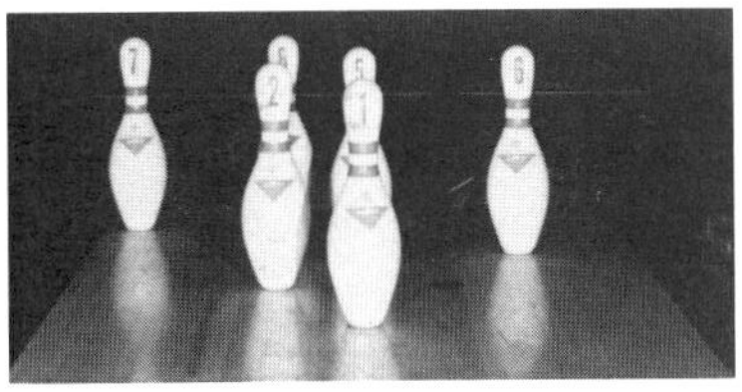

693   1-2-5-6-7-8

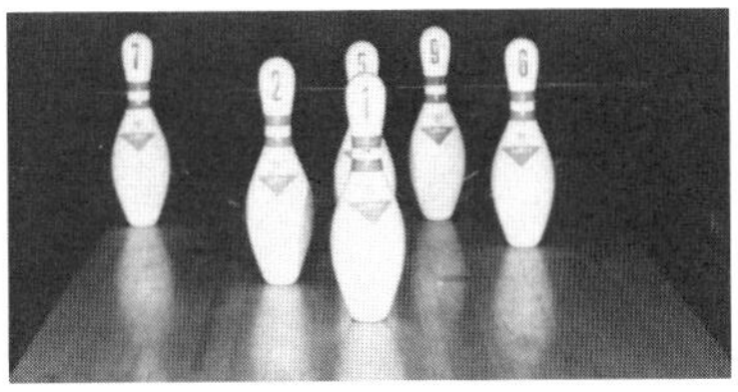

694   1-2-5-6-7-9

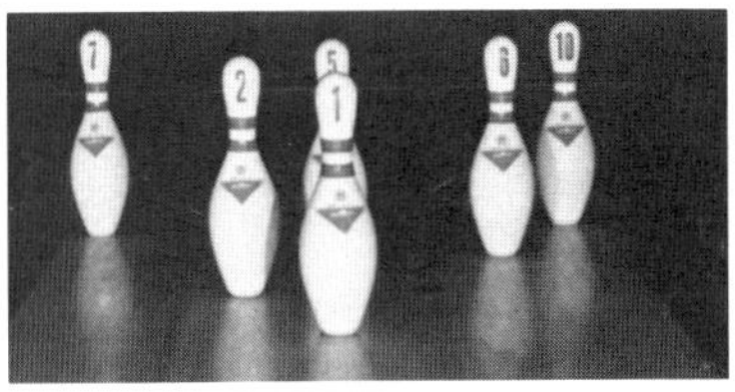

695   1-2-5-6-7-10

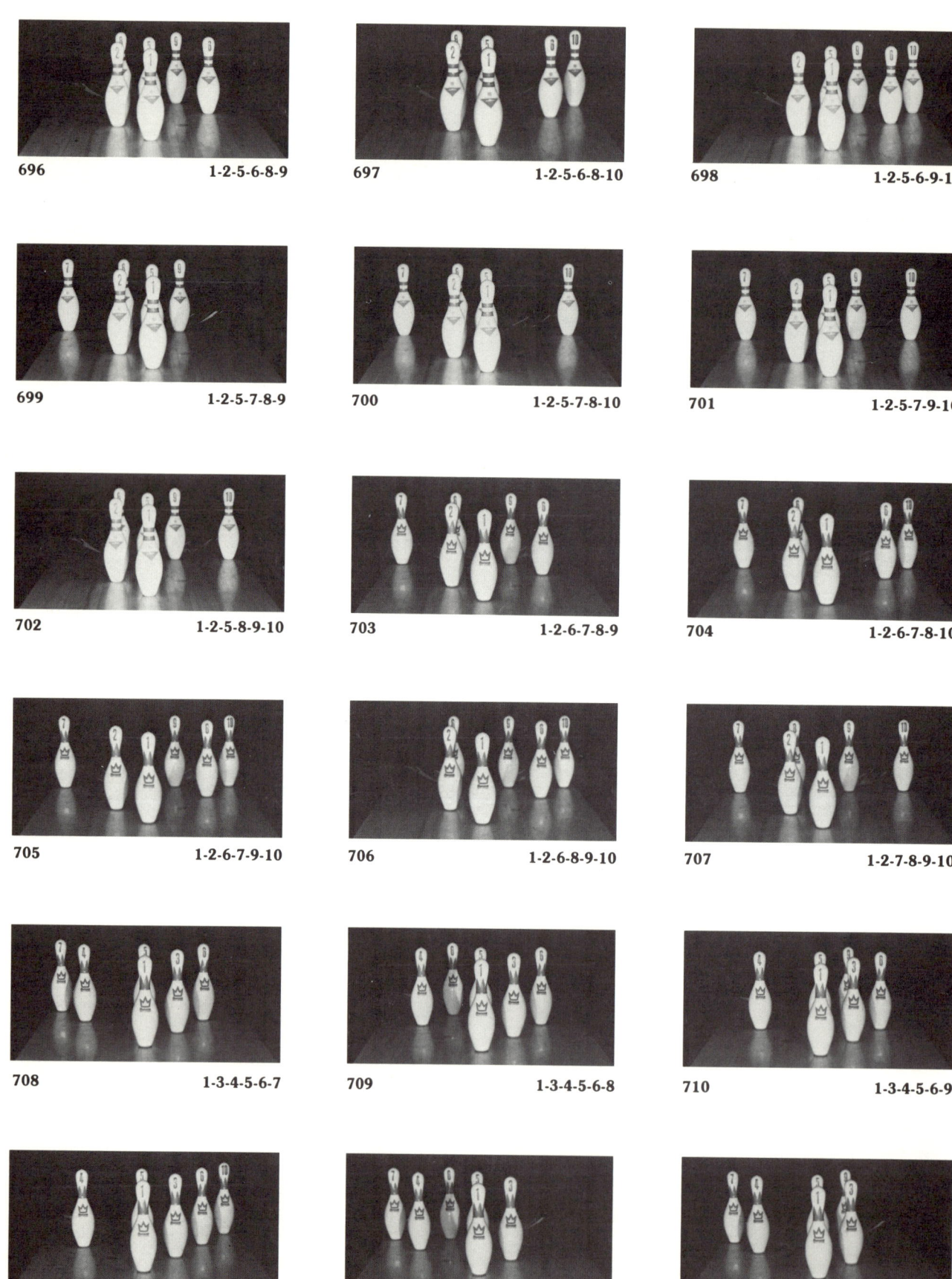

696   1-2-5-6-8-9

697   1-2-5-6-8-10

698   1-2-5-6-9-10

699   1-2-5-7-8-9

700   1-2-5-7-8-10

701   1-2-5-7-9-10

702   1-2-5-8-9-10

703   1-2-6-7-8-9

704   1-2-6-7-8-10

6

705   1-2-6-7-9-10

706   1-2-6-8-9-10

707   1-2-7-8-9-10

708   1-3-4-5-6-7

709   1-3-4-5-6-8

710   1-3-4-5-6-9

711   1-3-4-5-6-10

712   1-3-4-5-7-8

713   1-3-4-5-7-9

714   1-3-4-5-7-10

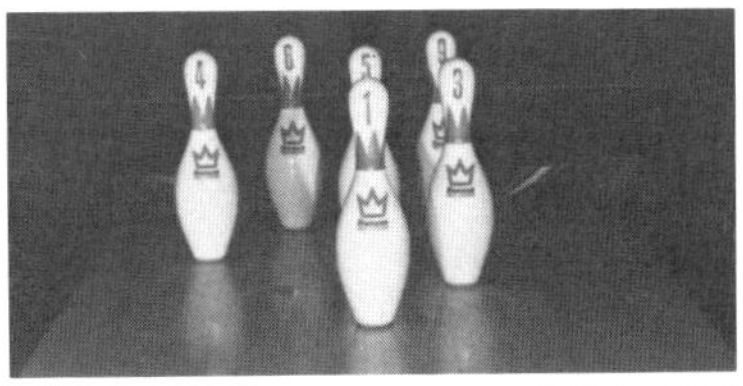

715   1-3-4-5-8-9

716   1-3-4-5-8-10

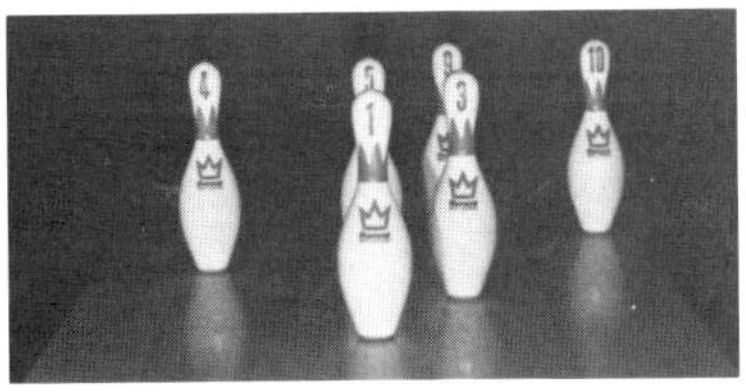

717   1-3-4-5-9-10

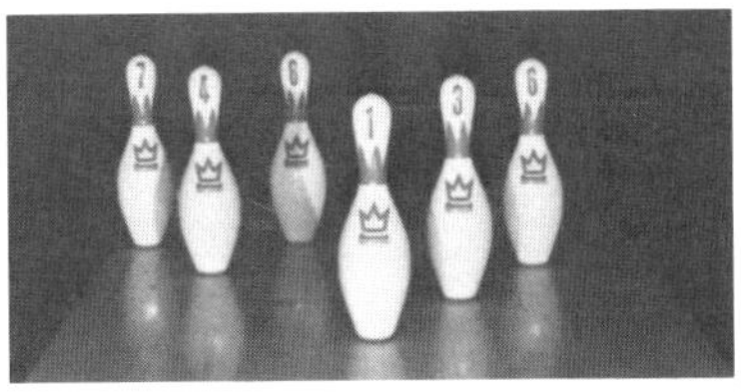

718   1-3-4-6-7-8

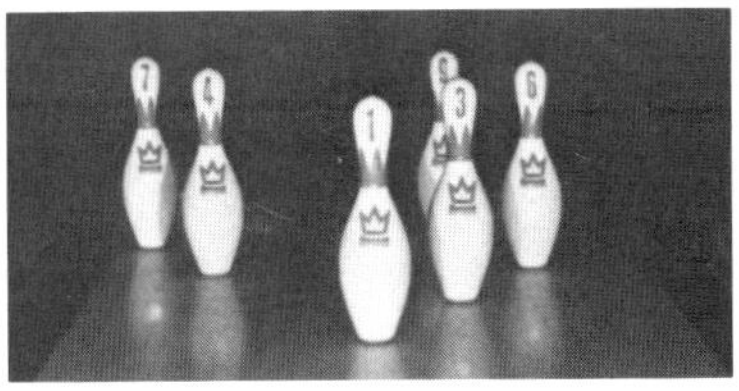

719   1-3-4-6-7-9

720   1-3-4-6-7-10

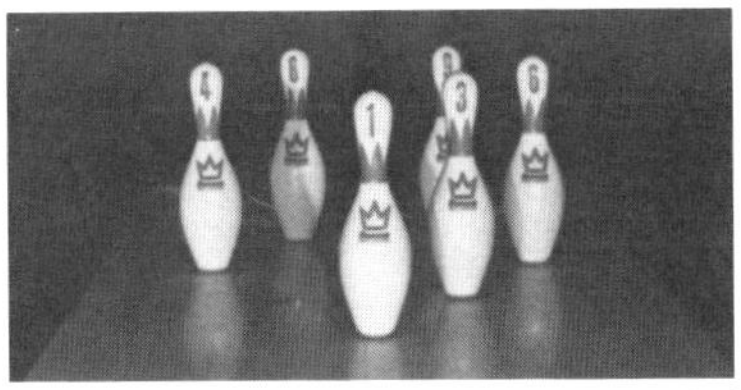

721   1-3-4-6-8-9

722   1-3-4-6-8-10

6

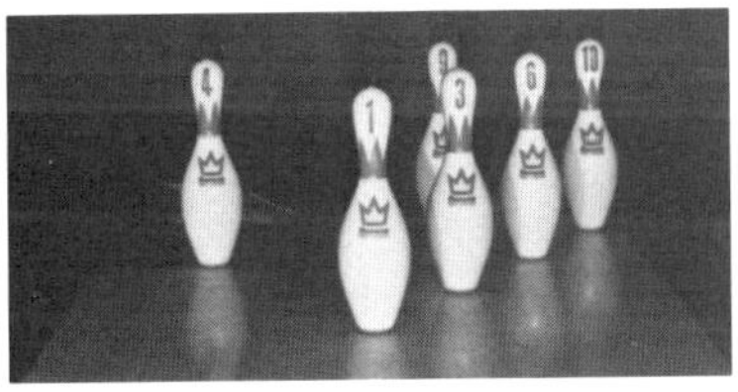

723   1-3-4-6-9-10

724   1-3-4-7-8-9

725   1-3-4-7-8-10

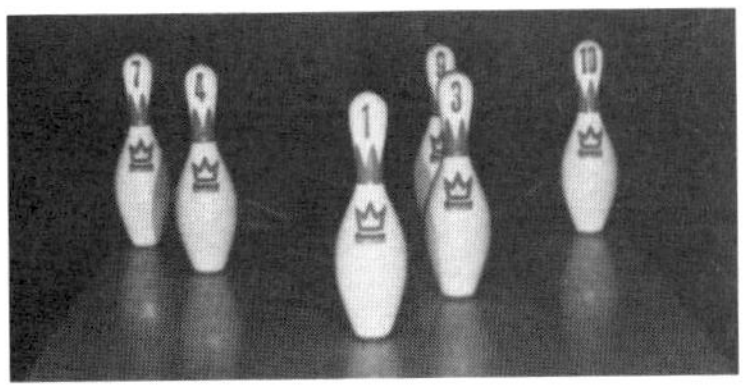

726   1-3-4-7-9-10

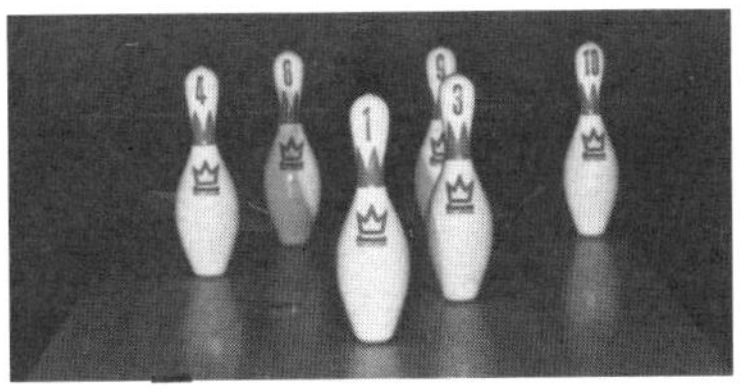

727   1-3-4-8-9-10

728   1-3-5-6-7-8

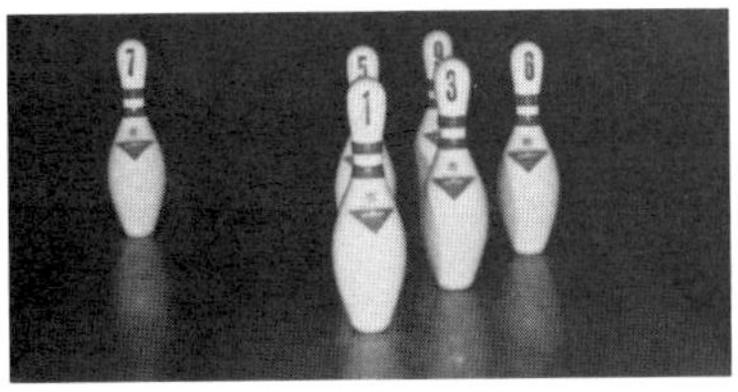

729   1-3-5-6-7-9

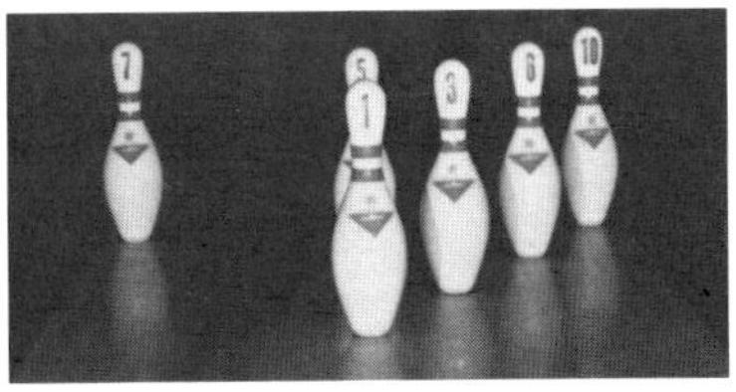

730   1-3-5-6-7-10

731   1-3-5-6-8-9

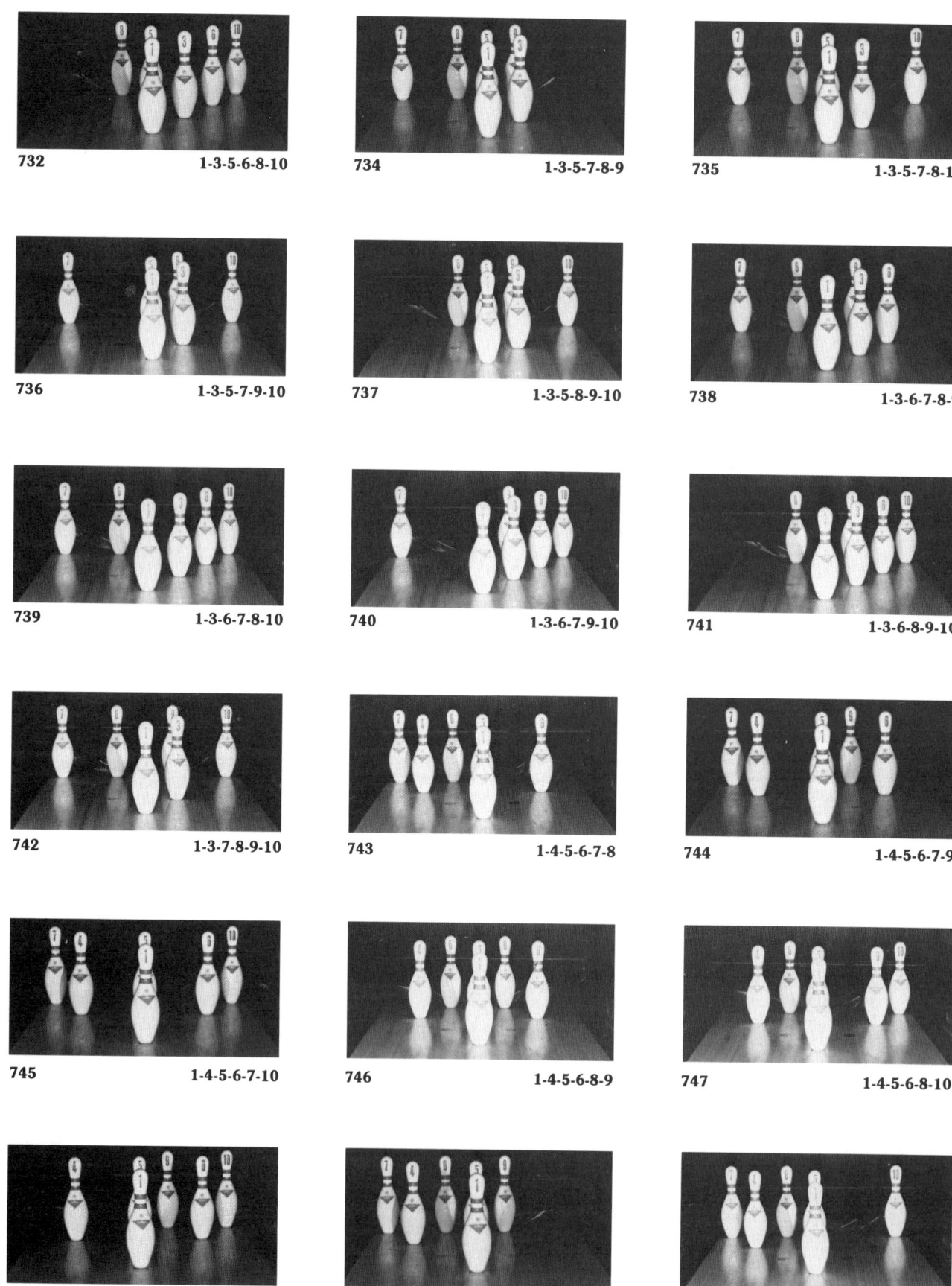

732 1-3-5-6-8-10

734 1-3-5-7-8-9

735 1-3-5-7-8-10

736 1-3-5-7-9-10

737 1-3-5-8-9-10

738 1-3-6-7-8-9

739 1-3-6-7-8-10

740 1-3-6-7-9-10

741 1-3-6-8-9-10

6

742 1-3-7-8-9-10

743 1-4-5-6-7-8

744 1-4-5-6-7-9

745 1-4-5-6-7-10

746 1-4-5-6-8-9

747 1-4-5-6-8-10

748 1-4-5-6-9-10

749 1-4-5-7-8-9

750 1-4-5-7-8-10

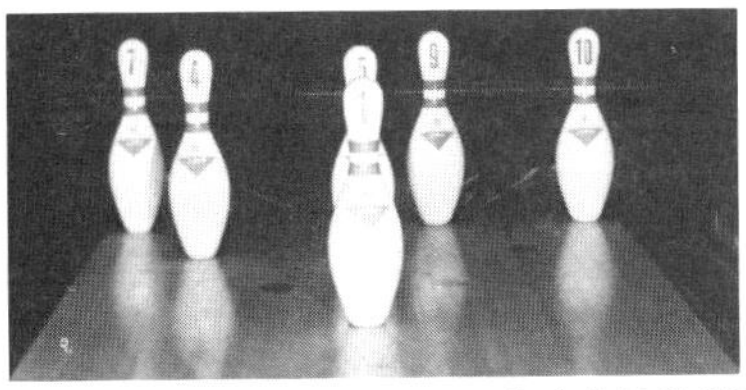

751	1-4-5-7-9-10
 752	1-4-5-8-9-10
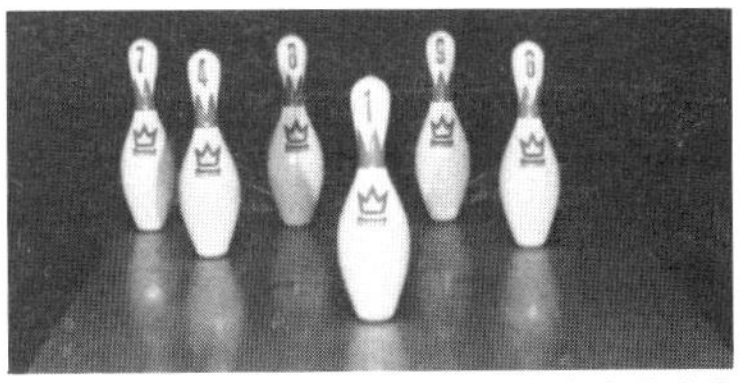 753	1-4-6-7-8-9
 754	1-4-6-7-8-10
 755	1-4-6-7-9-10
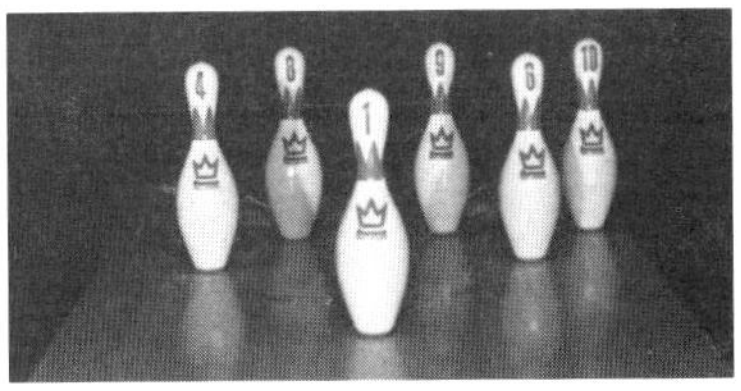 756	1-4-6-8-9-10
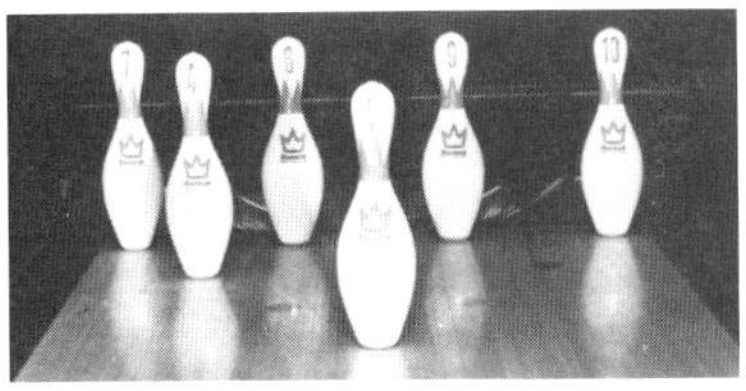 757	1-4-7-8-9-10
 758	1-5-6-7-8-9
 759	1-5-6-7-8-10
 760	1-5-6-7-9-10
 761	1-5-6-8-9-10
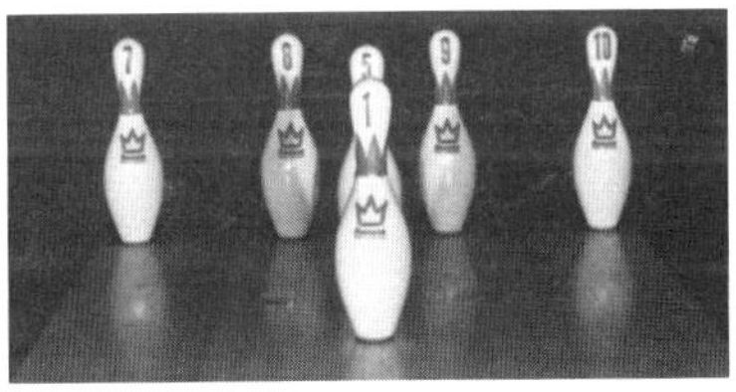 762	1-5-7-8-9-10
 763	1-6-7-8-9-10
 764-S	2-3-4-5-6-7
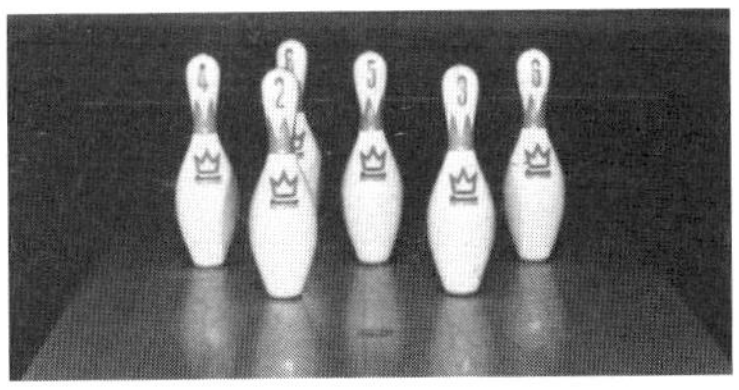 765-S	2-3-4-5-6-8
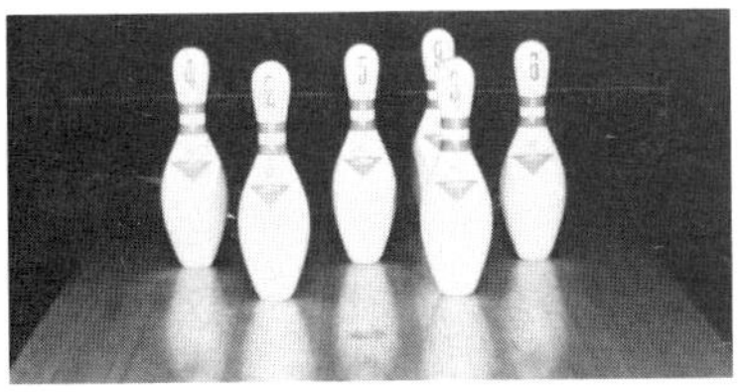 766-S	2-3-4-5-6-9
 767-S	2-3-4-5-6-10
 768-S	2-3-4-5-7-8

6

207

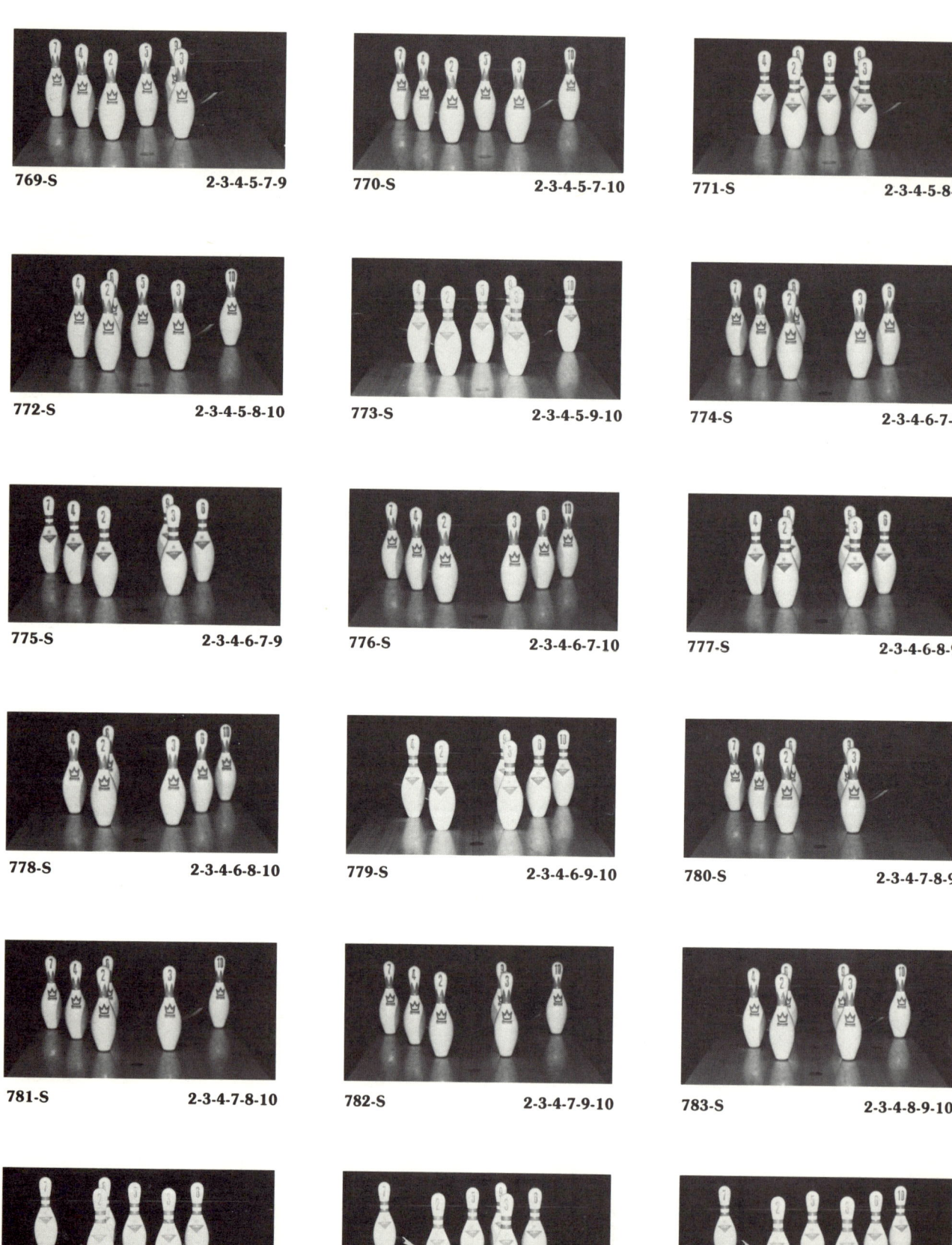

769-S　　　　2-3-4-5-7-9

770-S　　　　2-3-4-5-7-10

771-S　　　　2-3-4-5-8-9

772-S　　　　2-3-4-5-8-10

773-S　　　　2-3-4-5-9-10

774-S　　　　2-3-4-6-7-8

775-S　　　　2-3-4-6-7-9

776-S　　　　2-3-4-6-7-10

777-S　　　　2-3-4-6-8-9

6

778-S　　　　2-3-4-6-8-10

779-S　　　　2-3-4-6-9-10

780-S　　　　2-3-4-7-8-9

781-S　　　　2-3-4-7-8-10

782-S　　　　2-3-4-7-9-10

783-S　　　　2-3-4-8-9-10

784-S　　　　2-3-5-6-7-8

785-S　　　　2-3-5-6-7-9

786-S　　　　2-3-5-6-7-10

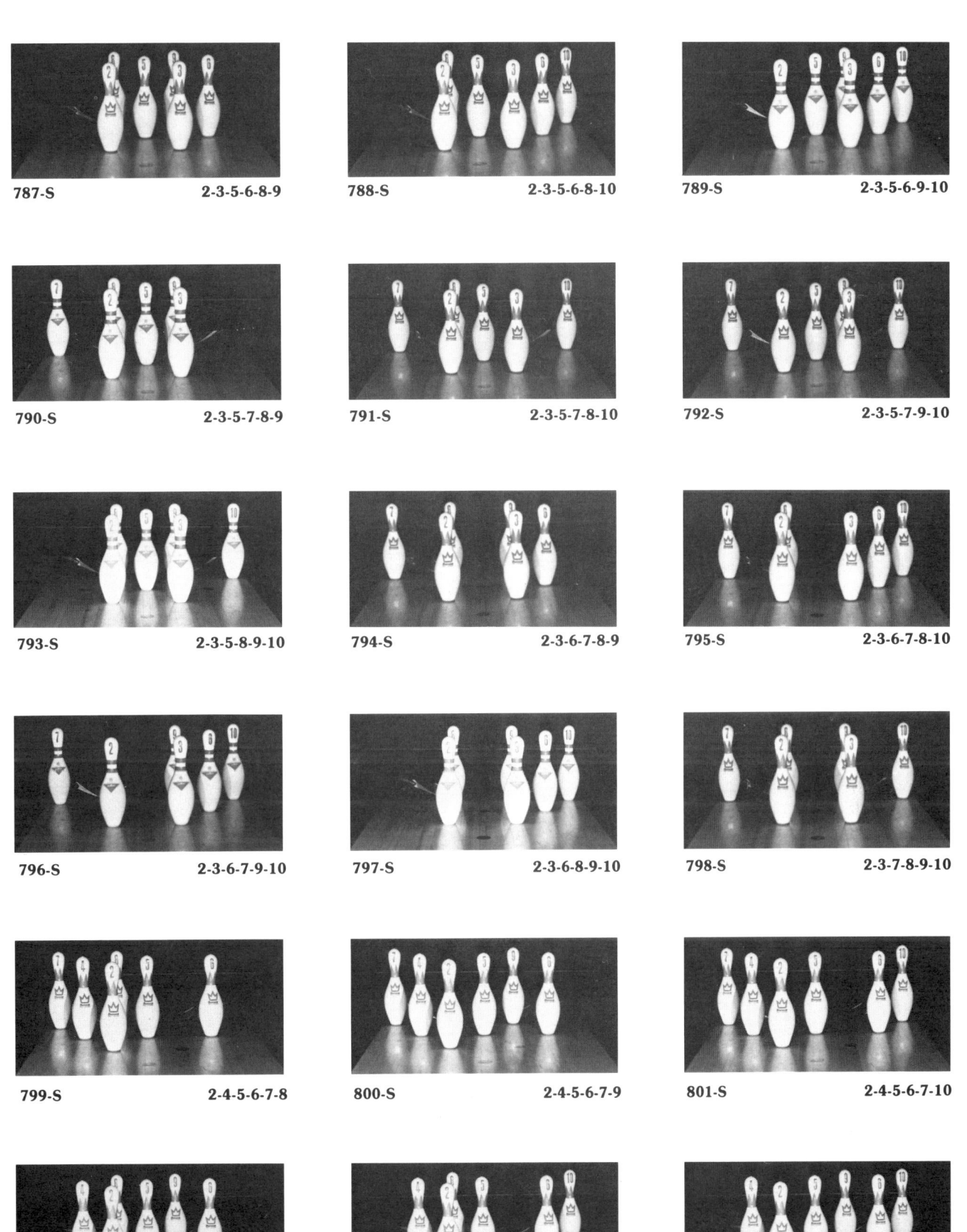

787-S   2-3-5-6-8-9

788-S   2-3-5-6-8-10

789-S   2-3-5-6-9-10

790-S   2-3-5-7-8-9

791-S   2-3-5-7-8-10

792-S   2-3-5-7-9-10

793-S   2-3-5-8-9-10

794-S   2-3-6-7-8-9

795-S   2-3-6-7-8-10

796-S   2-3-6-7-9-10

797-S   2-3-6-8-9-10

798-S   2-3-7-8-9-10

799-S   2-4-5-6-7-8

800-S   2-4-5-6-7-9

801-S   2-4-5-6-7-10

802-S   2-4-5-6-8-9

803-S   2-4-5-6-8-10

804-S   2-4-5-6-9-10

6

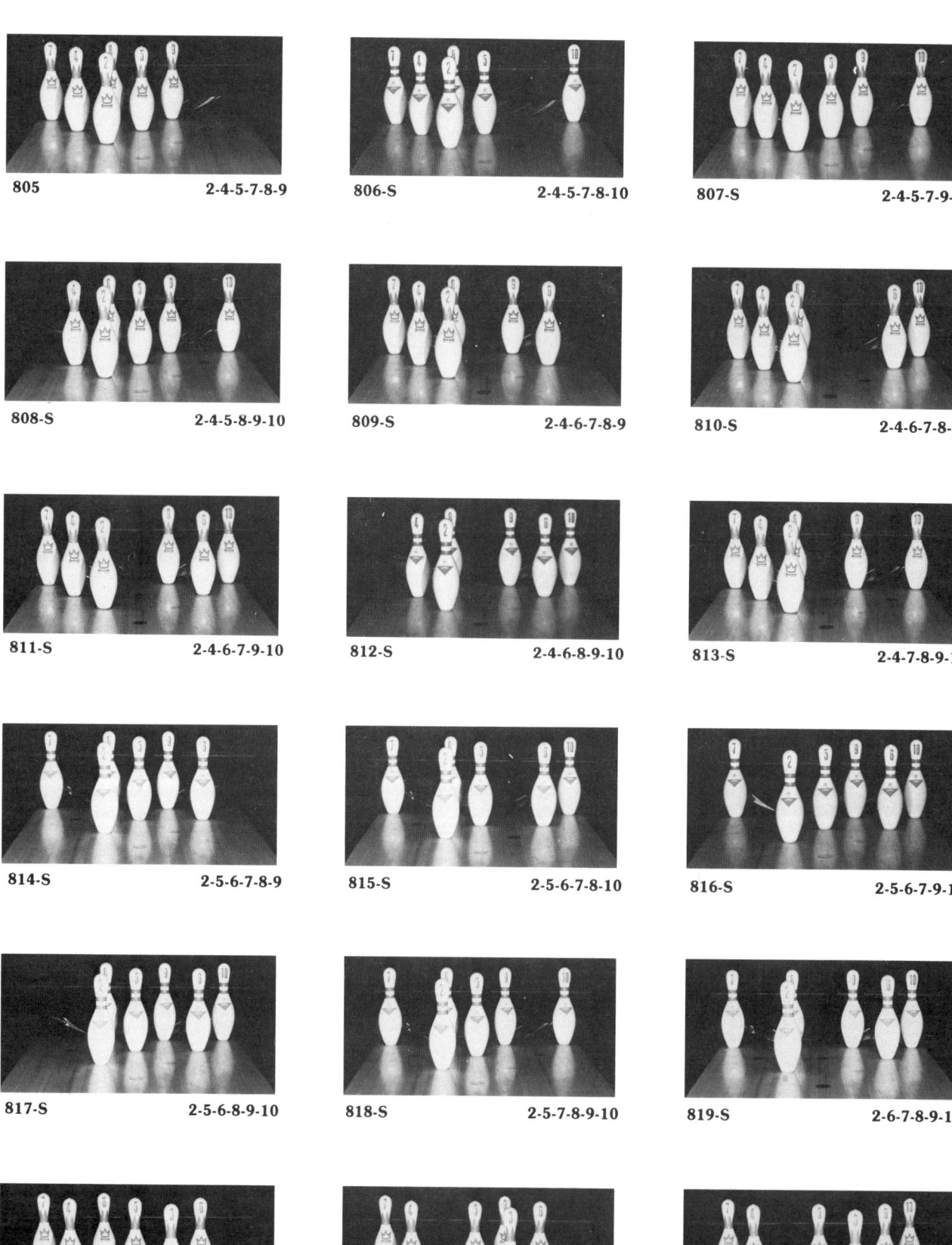

805   2-4-5-7-8-9

806-S   2-4-5-7-8-10

807-S   2-4-5-7-9-10

808-S   2-4-5-8-9-10

809-S   2-4-6-7-8-9

810-S   2-4-6-7-8-10

811-S   2-4-6-7-9-10

812-S   2-4-6-8-9-10

813-S   2-4-7-8-9-10

6

814-S   2-5-6-7-8-9

815-S   2-5-6-7-8-10

816-S   2-5-6-7-9-10

817-S   2-5-6-8-9-10

818-S   2-5-7-8-9-10

819-S   2-6-7-8-9-10

820-S   3-4-5-6-7-8

821-S   3-4-5-6-7-9

822-S   3-4-5-6-7-10

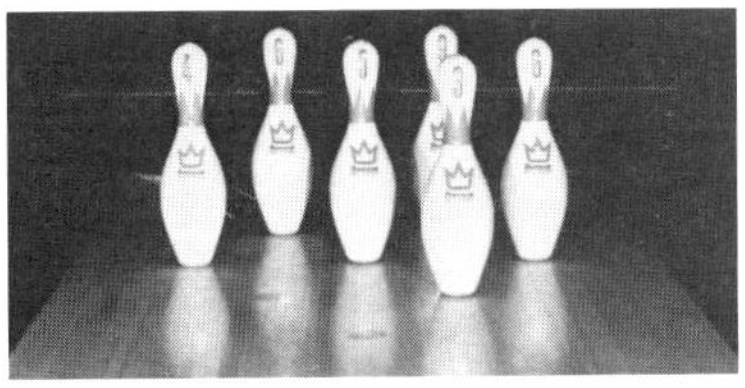

823-S 3-4-5-6-8-9

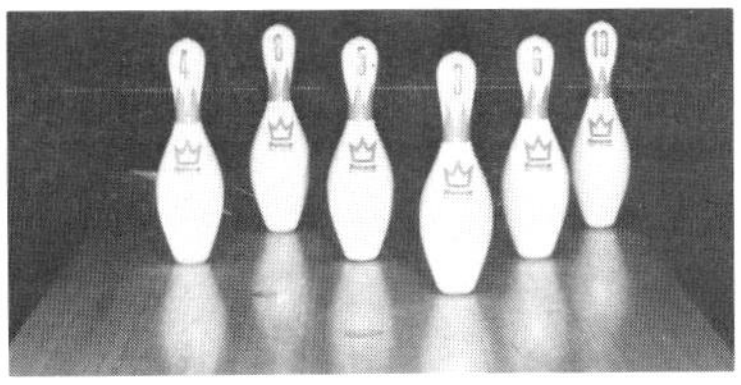

824-S 3-4-5-6-8-10

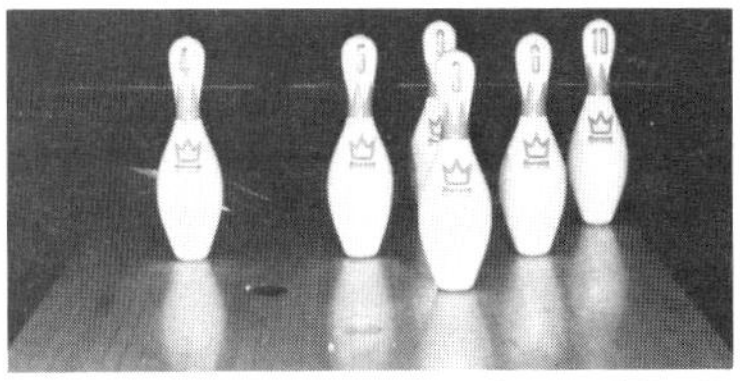

825-S 3-4-5-6-9-10

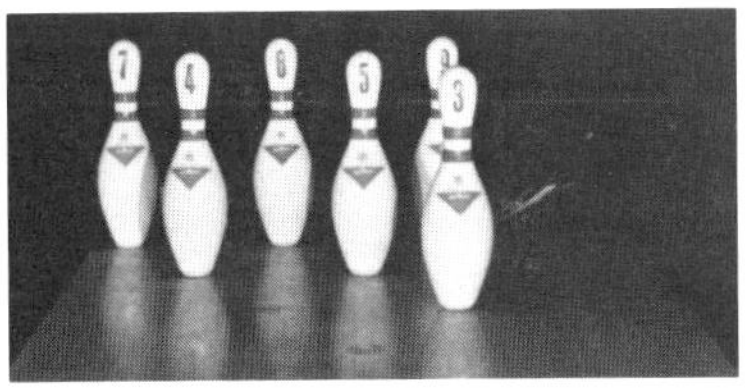

826-S 3-4-5-7-8-9

827-S 3-4-5-7-8-10

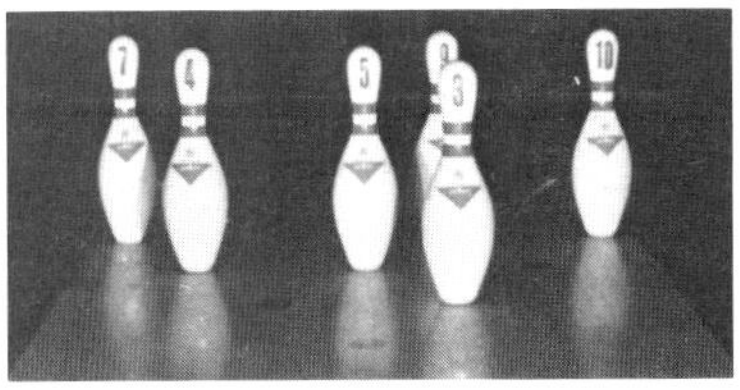

828-S 3-4-5-7-9-10

829-S 3-4-5-8-9-10

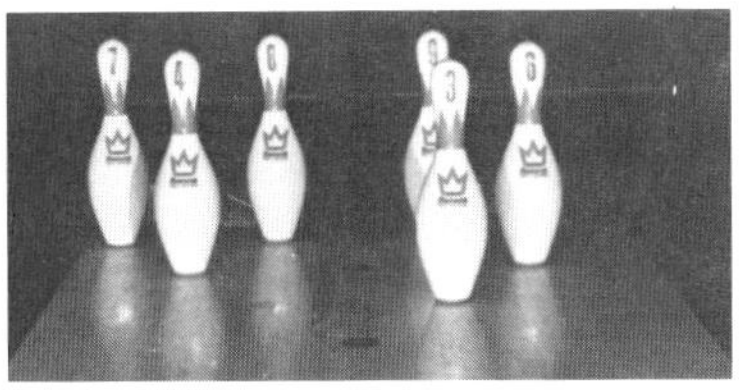

830-S 3-4-6-7-8-9

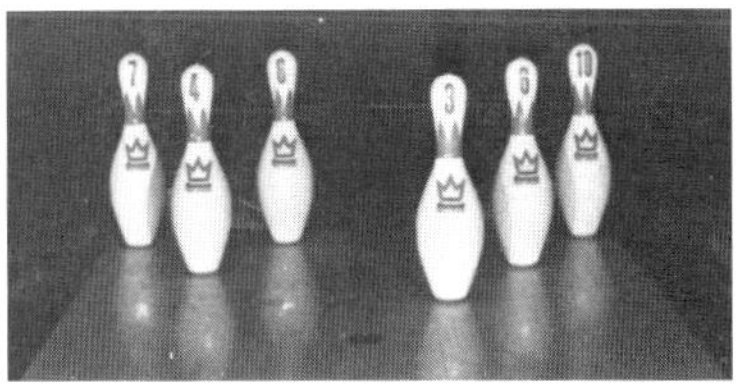

831-S 3-4-6-7-8-10

6

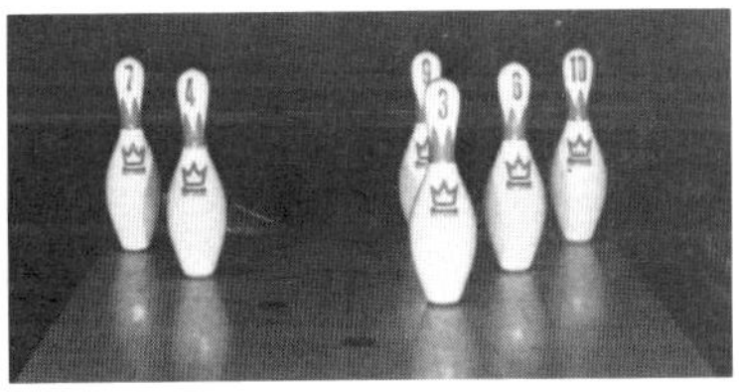

832-S 3-4-6-7-9-10

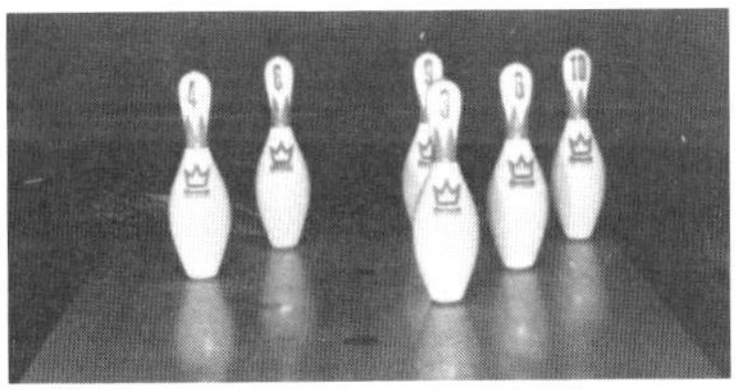

833-S 3-4-6-8-9-10

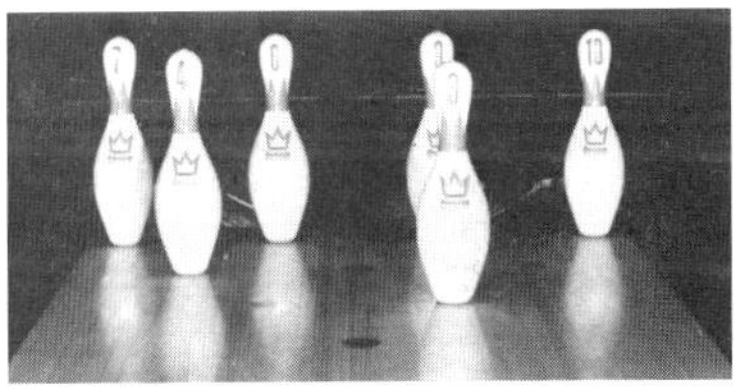

834-S 3-4-7-8-9-10

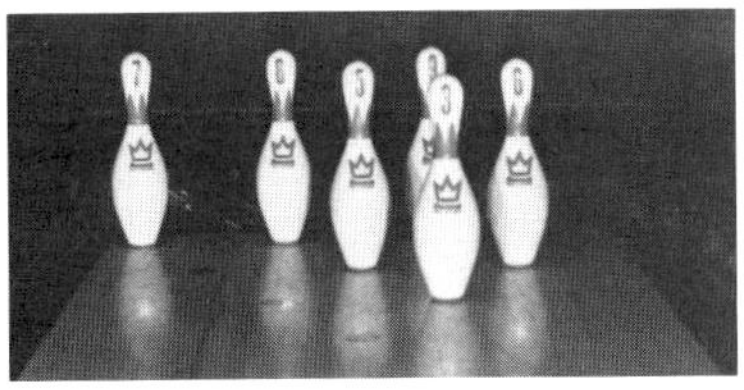

835-S 3-5-6-7-8-9

836-S 3-5-6-7-8-10

837-S 3-5-6-7-9-10

838 3-5-6-8-9-10

839-S 3-5-7-8-9-10

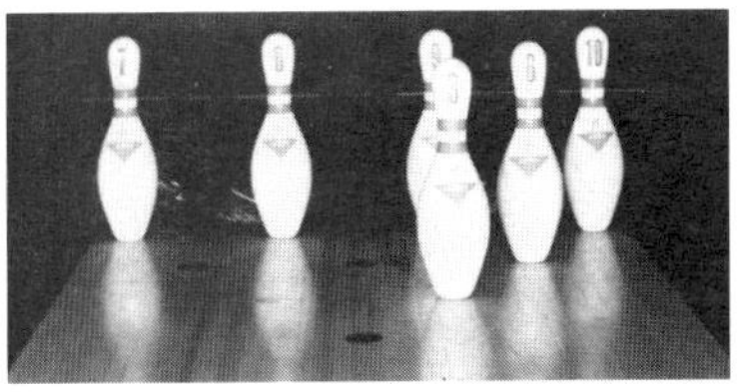

840-S 3-6-7-8-9-10

841-S   4-5-6-7-8-9

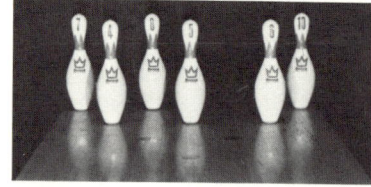

842-S   4-5-6-7-8-10

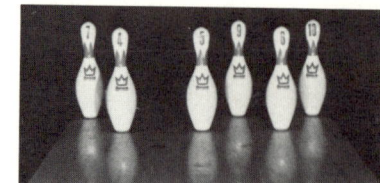

843-S   4-5-6-7-9-10

844-S   4-5-6-8-9-10

845-S   4-5-7-8-9-10

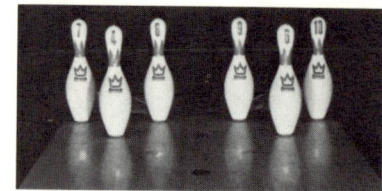

846-S   4-6-7-8-9-10

847-S   5-6-7-8-9-10

6

End of the 202 Rare Spares with Six Pins

Pictures of the 116 Rare Spares
with Seven Pins

848   1-2-3-4-5-6-7

849   1-2-3-4-5-6-8

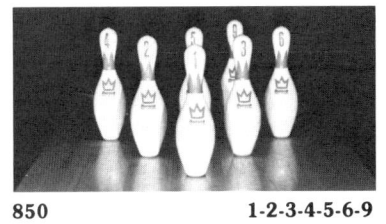

850   1-2-3-4-5-6-9

851   1-2-3-4-5-6-10

854   1-2-3-4-5-7-10

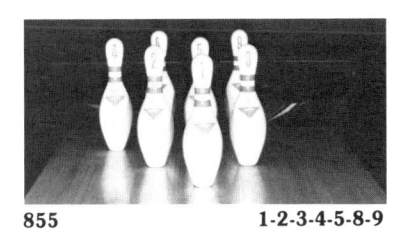

855   1-2-3-4-5-8-9

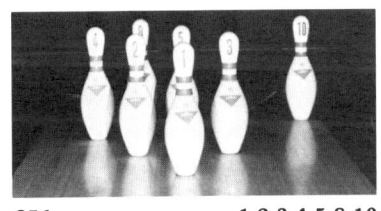

856   1-2-3-4-5-8-10

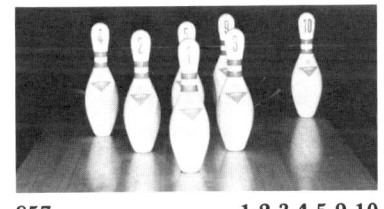

857   1-2-3-4-5-9-10

858   1-2-3-4-6-7-8

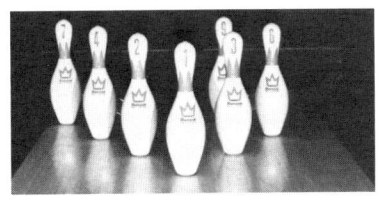

859   1-2-3-4-6-7-9

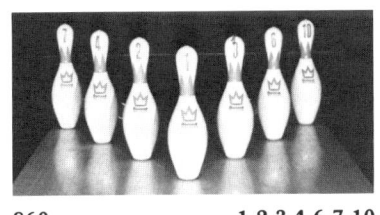

860   1-2-3-4-6-7-10

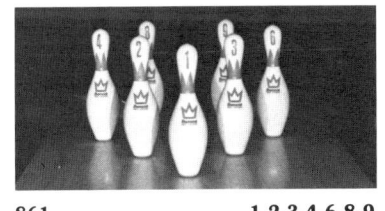

861   1-2-3-4-6-8-9

862   1-2-3-4-6-8-10

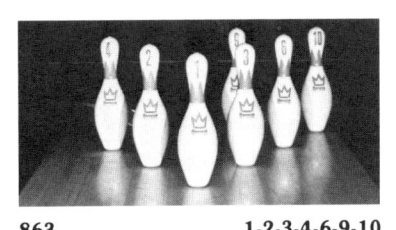

863   1-2-3-4-6-9-10

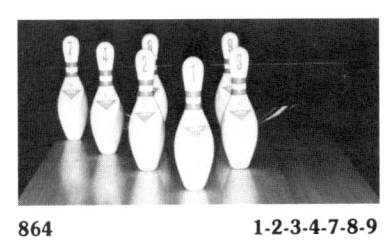

864   1-2-3-4-7-8-9

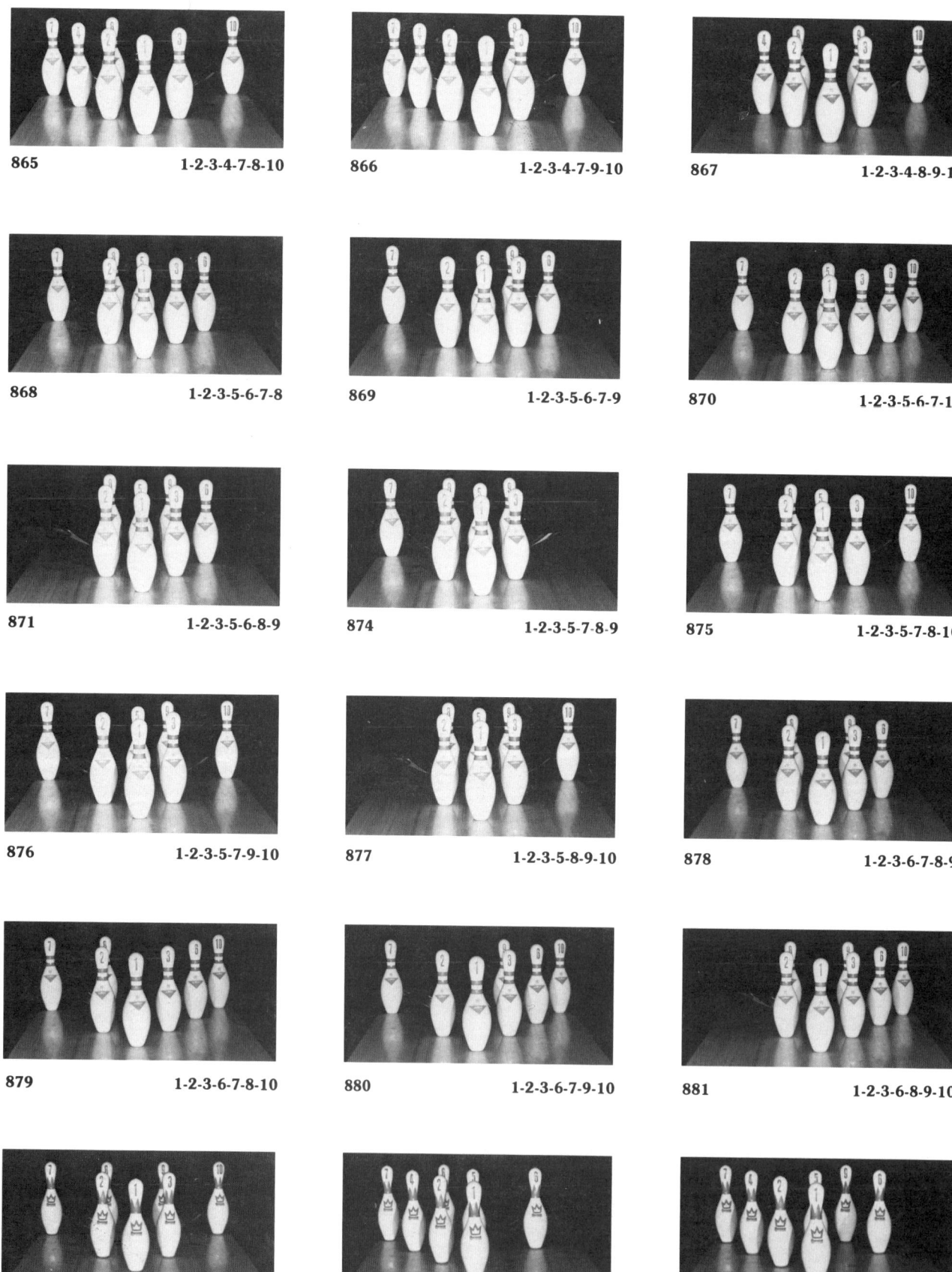

865   1-2-3-4-7-8-10

866   1-2-3-4-7-9-10

867   1-2-3-4-8-9-10

868   1-2-3-5-6-7-8

869   1-2-3-5-6-7-9

870   1-2-3-5-6-7-10

871   1-2-3-5-6-8-9

874   1-2-3-5-7-8-9

875   1-2-3-5-7-8-10

876   1-2-3-5-7-9-10

877   1-2-3-5-8-9-10

878   1-2-3-6-7-8-9

879   1-2-3-6-7-8-10

880   1-2-3-6-7-9-10

881   1-2-3-6-8-9-10

882   1-2-3-7-8-9-10

883   1-2-4-5-6-7-8

884   1-2-4-5-6-7-9

7

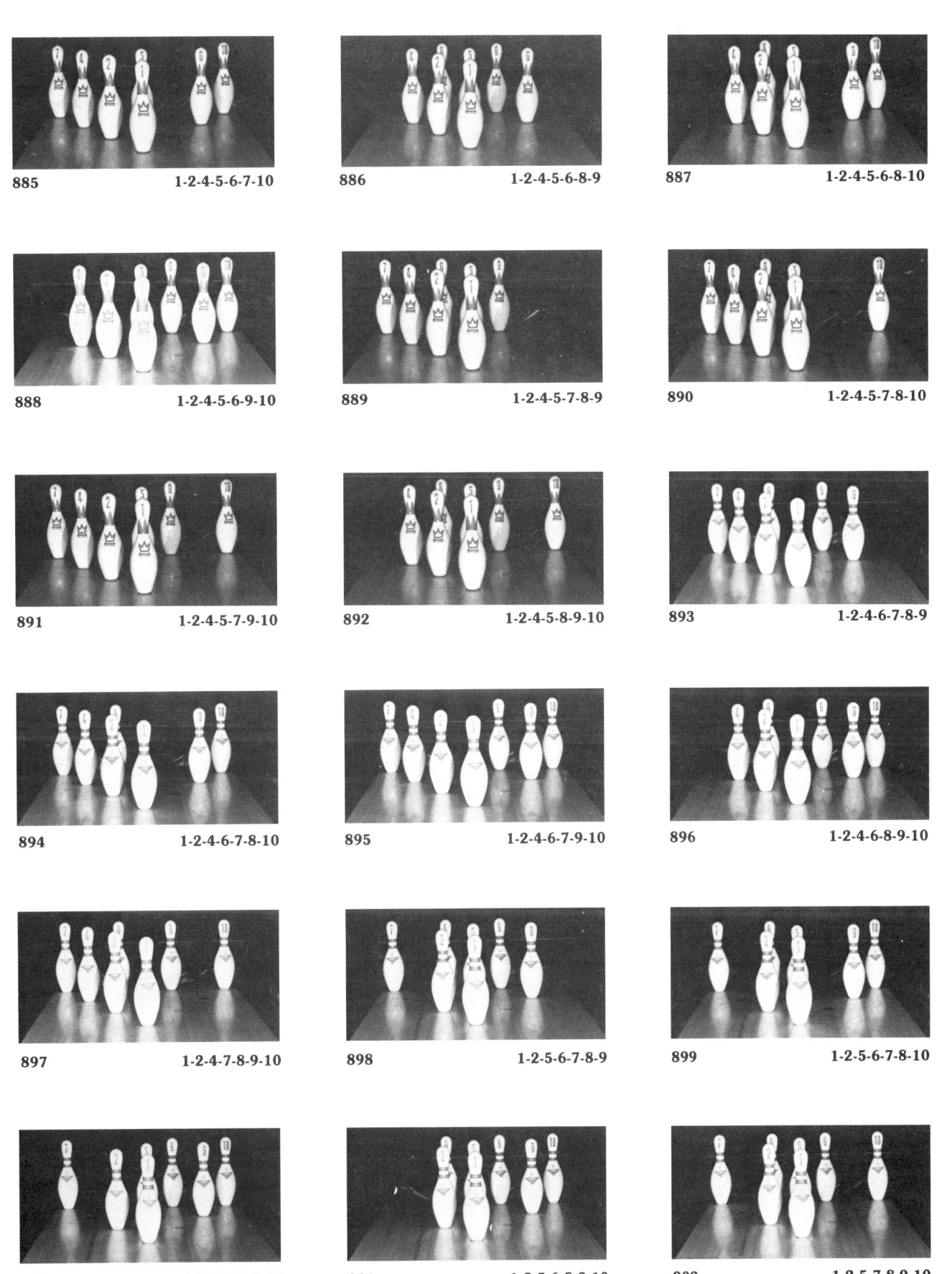

885 1-2-4-5-6-7-10

886 1-2-4-5-6-8-9

887 1-2-4-5-6-8-10

888 1-2-4-5-6-9-10

889 1-2-4-5-7-8-9

890 1-2-4-5-7-8-10

891 1-2-4-5-7-9-10

892 1-2-4-5-8-9-10

893 1-2-4-6-7-8-9

894 1-2-4-6-7-8-10

895 1-2-4-6-7-9-10

896 1-2-4-6-8-9-10

897 1-2-4-7-8-9-10

898 1-2-5-6-7-8-9

899 1-2-5-6-7-8-10

900 1-2-5-6-7-9-10

901 1-2-5-6-8-9-10

902 1-2-5-7-8-9-10

7

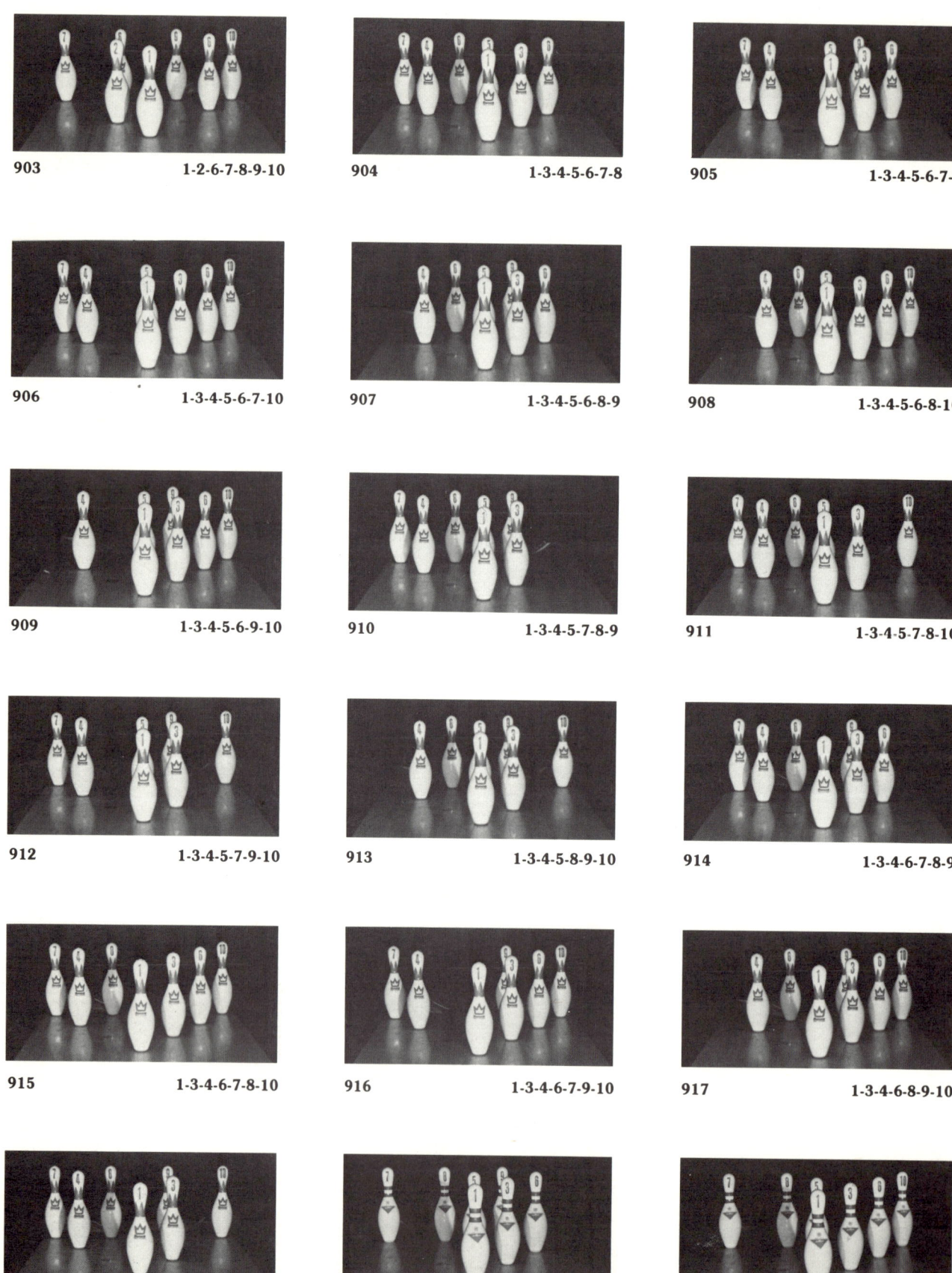

903   1-2-6-7-8-9-10

904   1-3-4-5-6-7-8

905   1-3-4-5-6-7-9

906   1-3-4-5-6-7-10

907   1-3-4-5-6-8-9

908   1-3-4-5-6-8-10

909   1-3-4-5-6-9-10

910   1-3-4-5-7-8-9

911   1-3-4-5-7-8-10

7

912   1-3-4-5-7-9-10

913   1-3-4-5-8-9-10

914   1-3-4-6-7-8-9

915   1-3-4-6-7-8-10

916   1-3-4-6-7-9-10

917   1-3-4-6-8-9-10

918   1-3-4-7-8-9-10

919   1-3-5-6-7-8-9

920   1-3-5-6-7-8-10

921   1-3-5-6-7-9-10

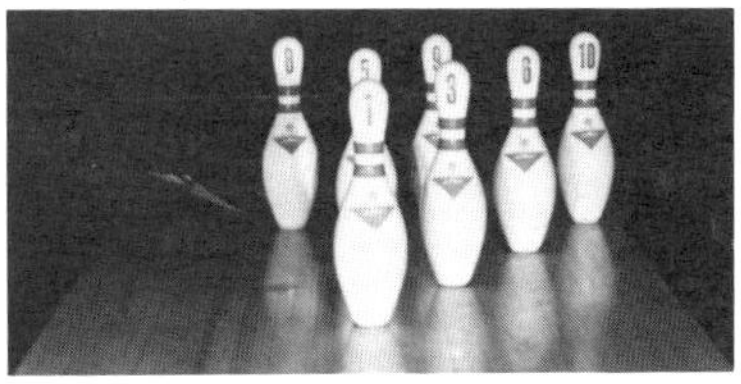

922   1-3-5-6-8-9-10

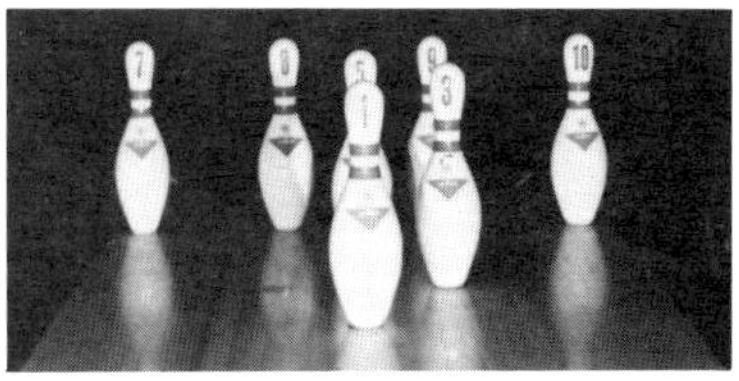

923   1-3-5-7-8-9-10

924   1-3-6-7-8-9-10

925   1-4-5-6-7-8-9

926   1-4-5-6-7-8-10

927   1-4-5-6-7-9-10

928   1-4-5-6-8-9-10

929   1-4-5-7-8-9-10

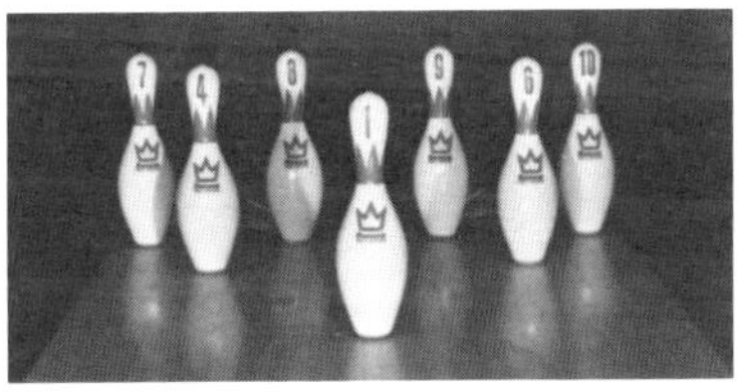

930   1-4-6-7-8-9-10

931   1-5-6-7-8-9-10

932-S   2-3-4-5-6-7-8

933-S   2-3-4-5-6-7-9

934-S   2-3-4-5-6-7-10

935-S   2-3-4-5-6-8-9

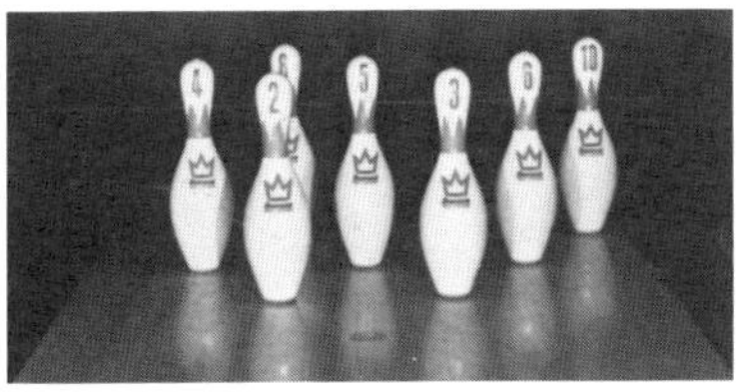

936-S   2-3-4-5-6-8-10

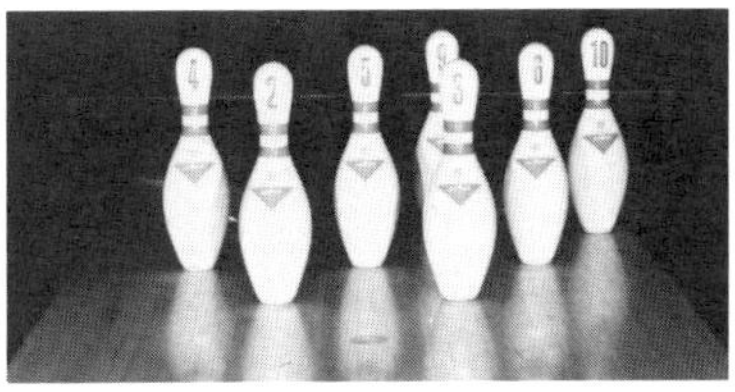

937-S   2-3-4-5-6-9-10

938-S   2-3-4-5-7-8-9

7

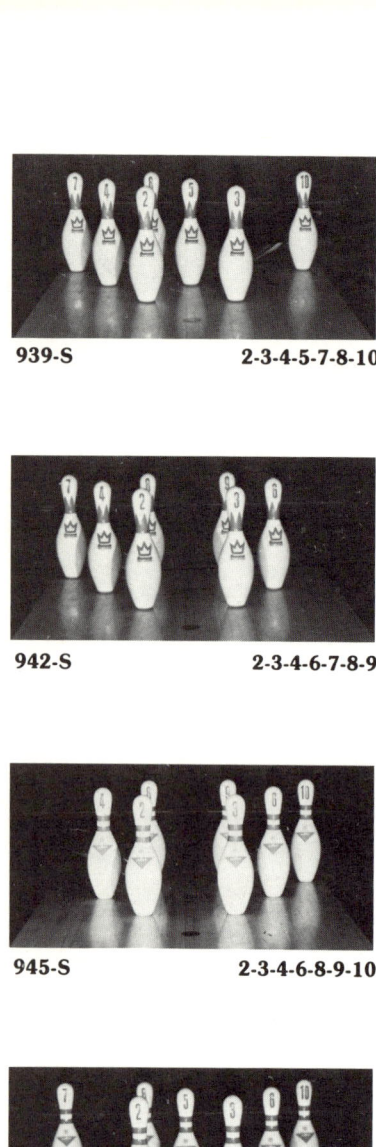

939-S   2-3-4-5-7-8-10

940-S   2-3-4-5-7-9-10

941-S   2-3-4-5-8-9-10

942-S   2-3-4-6-7-8-9

943-S   2-3-4-6-7-8-10

944-S   2-3-4-6-7-9-10

945-S   2-3-4-6-8-9-10

946-S   2-3-4-7-8-9-10

947-S   2-3-5-6-7-8-9

7

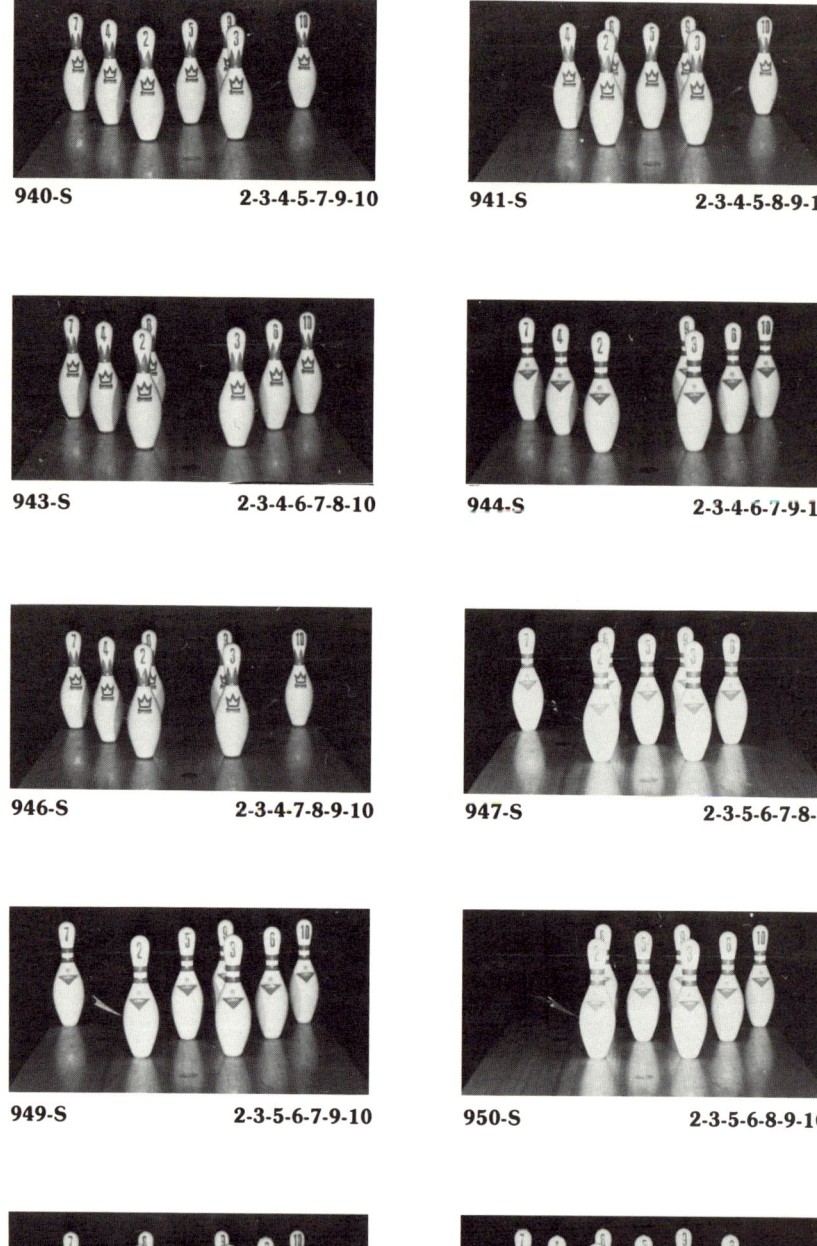

948-S   2-3-5-6-7-8-10

949-S   2-3-5-6-7-9-10

950-S   2-3-5-6-8-9-10

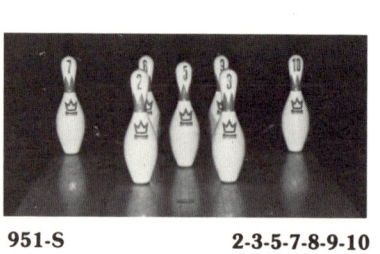
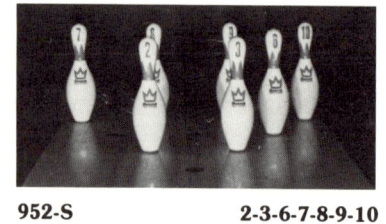
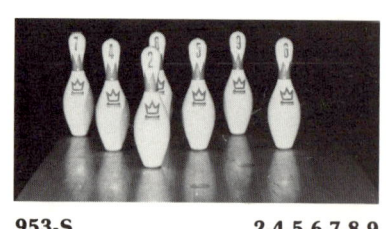

951-S   2-3-5-7-8-9-10

952-S   2-3-6-7-8-9-10

953-S   2-4-5-6-7-8-9

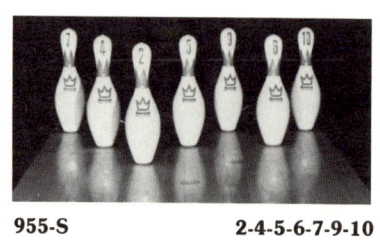
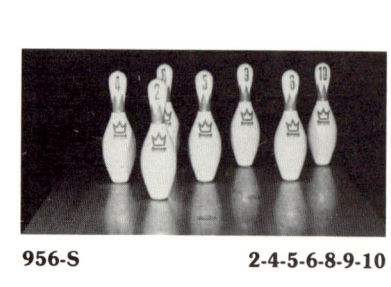

954-S   2-4-5-6-7-8-10

955-S   2-4-5-6-7-9-10

956-S   2-4-5-6-8-9-10

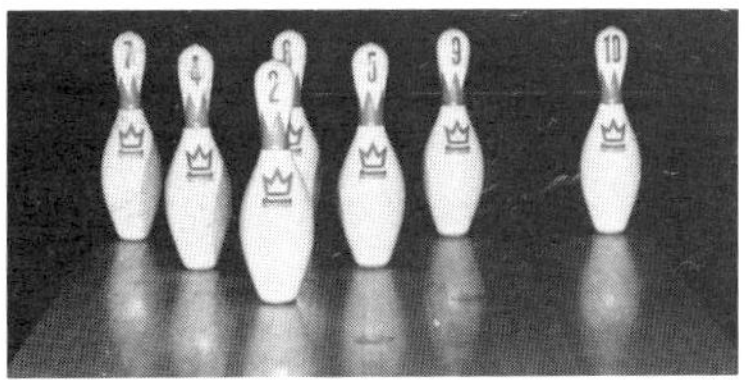

957-S 2-4-5-7-8-9-10	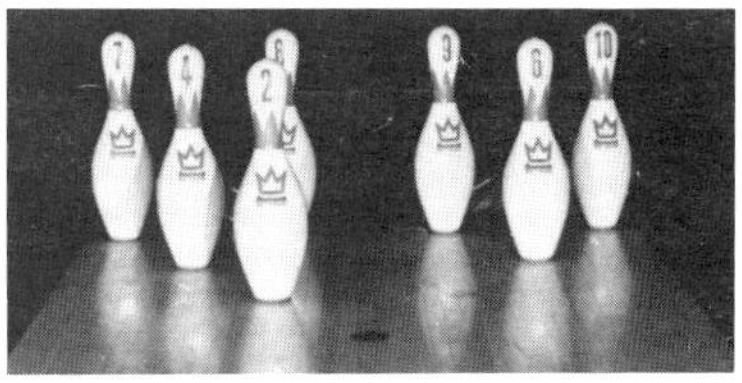 958-S 2-4-6-7-8-9-10	 959-S 2-5-6-7-8-9-10
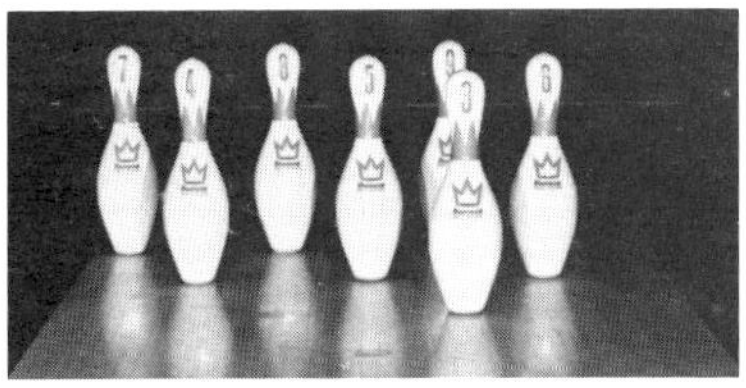 960-S 3-4-5-6-7-8-9	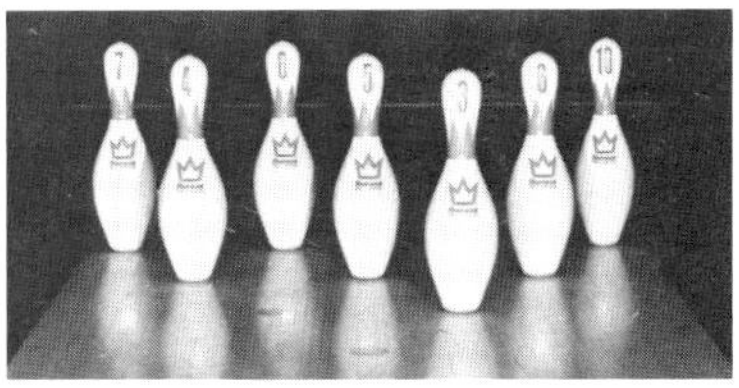 961-S 3-4-5-6-7-8-10	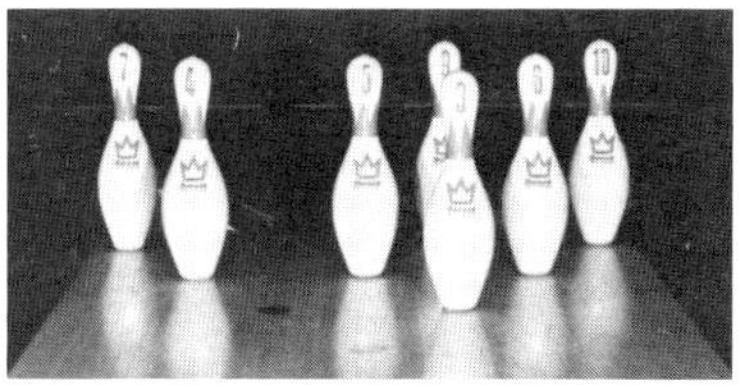 962-S 3-4-5-6-7-9-10
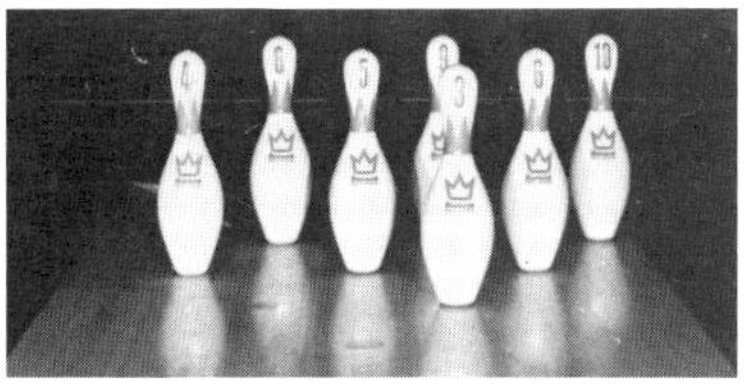 963-S 3-4-5-6-8-9-10	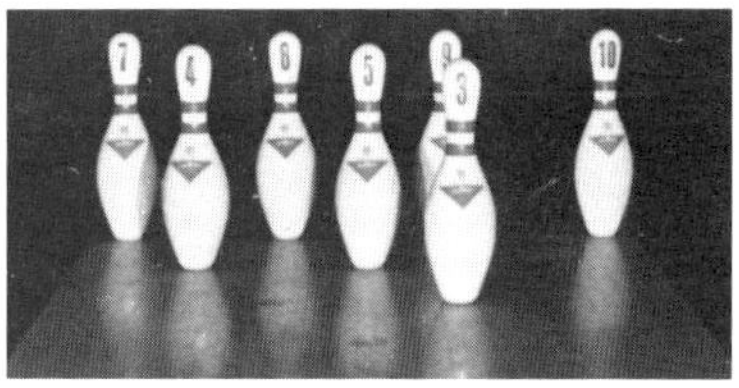 964-S 3-4-5-7-8-9-10	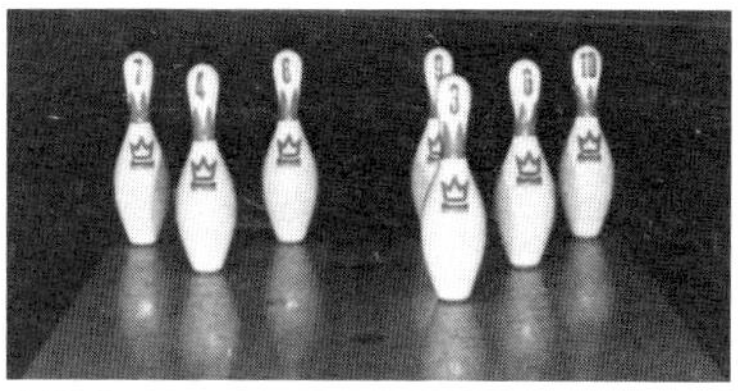 965-S 3-4-6-7-8-9-10
 966-S 3-5-6-7-8-9-10	 967-S 4-5-6-7-8-9-10	

End of the 116 Rare Spares with Seven Pins

Pictures of the 43 Rare Spares with Eight Pins

968 1-2-3-4-5-6-7-8

969 1-2-3-4-5-6-7-9

970 1-2-3-4-5-6-7-10

971 1-2-3-4-5-6-8-9

972 1-2-3-4-5-6-8-10

973 1-2-3-4-5-6-9-10

8

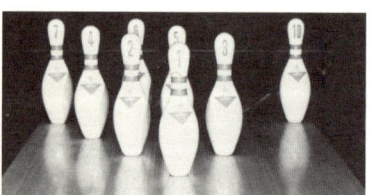

975 1-2-3-4-5-7-8-10

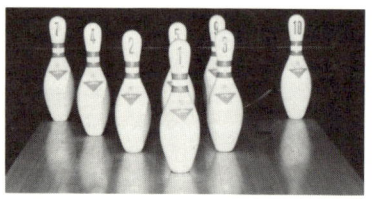

976 1-2-3-4-5-7-9-10

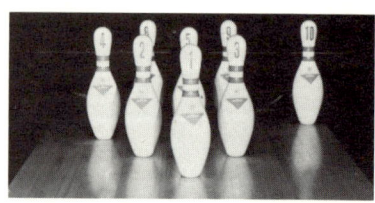

977 1-2-3-4-5-8-9-10

978 1-2-3-4-6-7-8-9

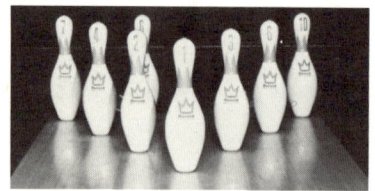

979 1-2-3-4-6-7-8-10

980 1-2-3-4-6-7-9-10

981 1-2-3-4-6-8-9-10

982 1-2-3-4-7-8-9-10

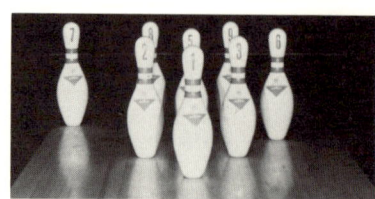

983 1-2-3-5-6-7-8-9

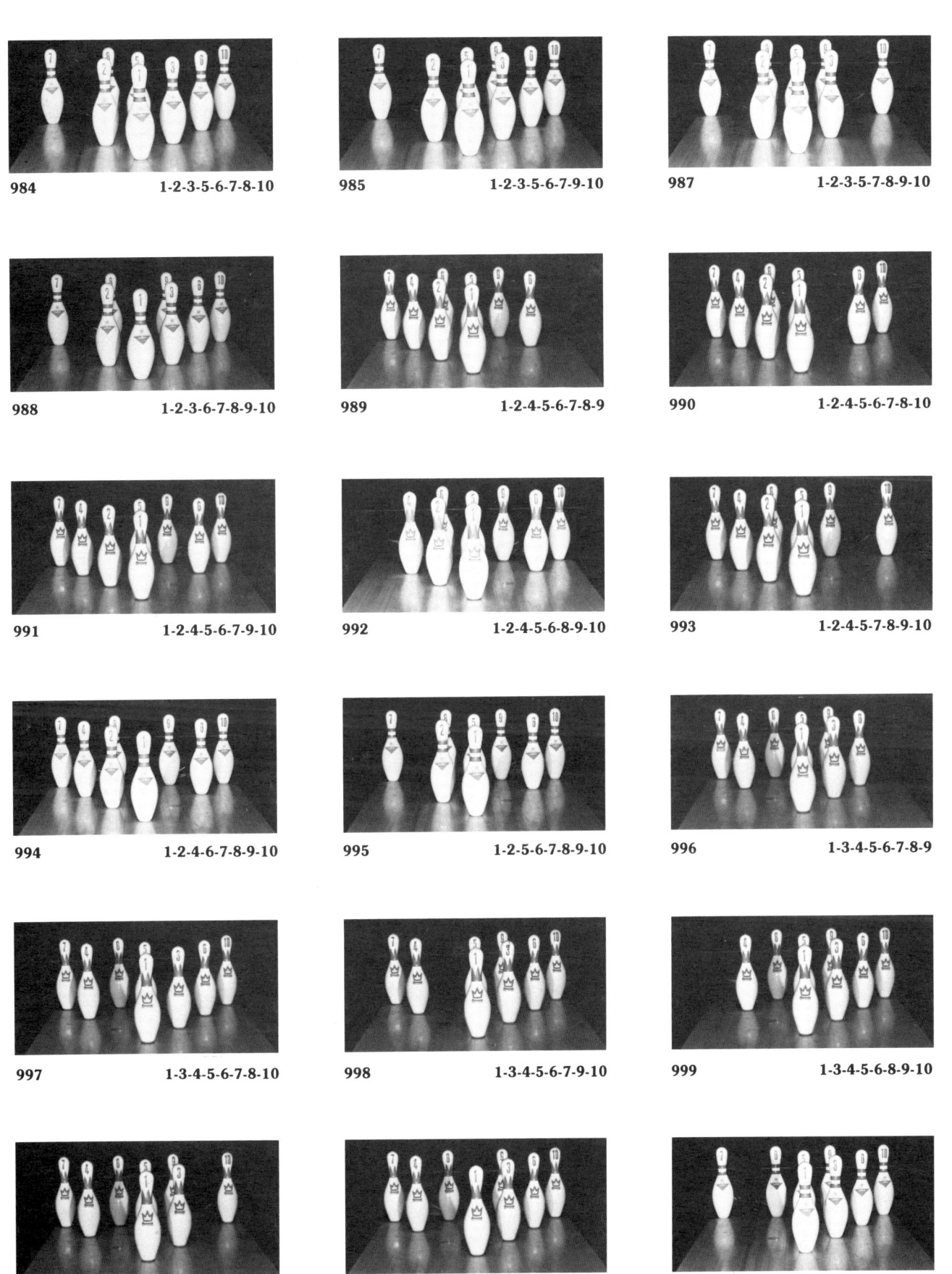

984   1-2-3-5-6-7-8-10

985   1-2-3-5-6-7-9-10

987   1-2-3-5-7-8-9-10

988   1-2-3-6-7-8-9-10

989   1-2-4-5-6-7-8-9

990   1-2-4-5-6-7-8-10

991   1-2-4-5-6-7-9-10

992   1-2-4-5-6-8-9-10

993   1-2-4-5-7-8-9-10

994   1-2-4-6-7-8-9-10

995   1-2-5-6-7-8-9-10

996   1-3-4-5-6-7-8-9

997   1-3-4-5-6-7-8-10

998   1-3-4-5-6-7-9-10

999   1-3-4-5-6-8-9-10

1000   1-3-4-5-7-8-9-10

1001   1-3-4-6-7-8-9-10

1002   1-3-5-6-7-8-9-10

8

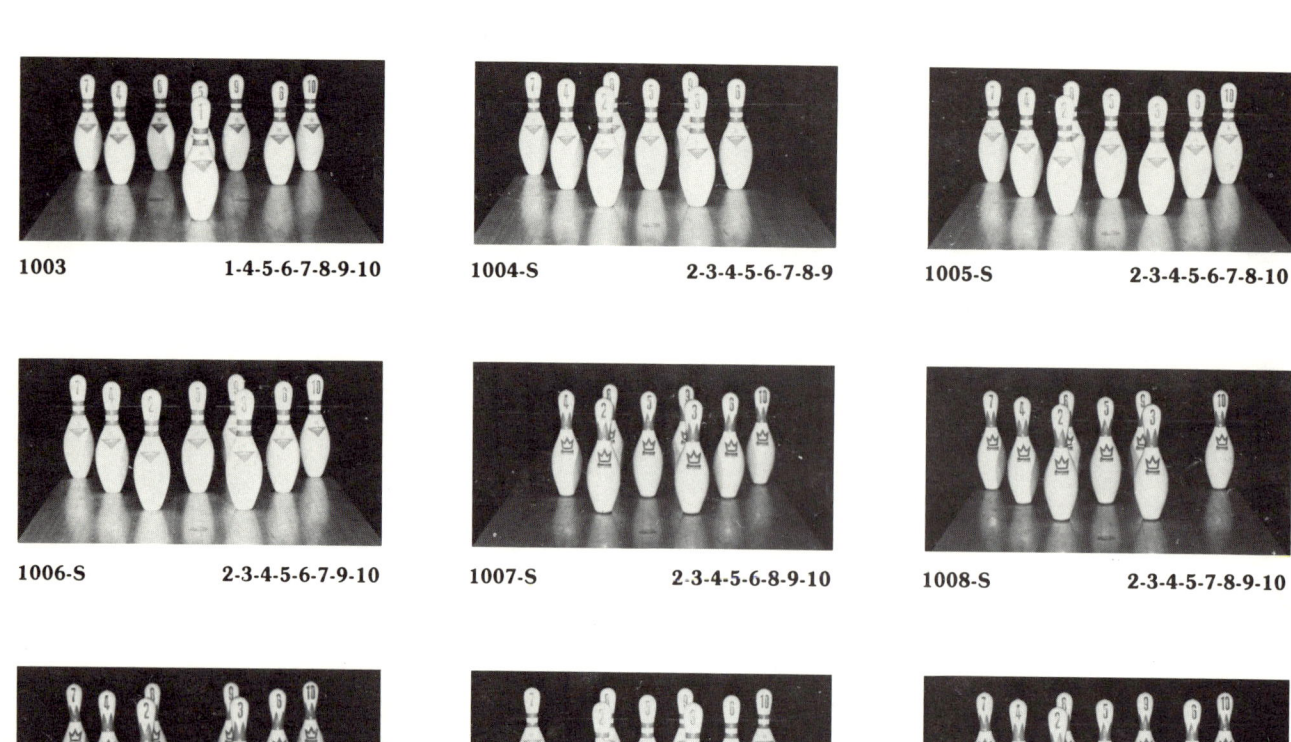

1003   1-4-5-6-7-8-9-10

1004-S   2-3-4-5-6-7-8-9

1005-S   2-3-4-5-6-7-8-10

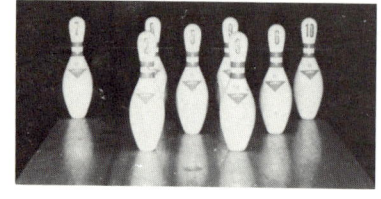
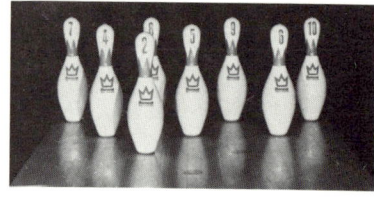

1006-S   2-3-4-5-6-7-9-10

1007-S   2-3-4-5-6-8-9-10

1008-S   2-3-4-5-7-8-9-10

1009-S   2-3-4-6-7-8-9-10

1010-S   2-3-5-6-7-8-9-10

1011-S   2-4-5-6-7-8-9-10

8

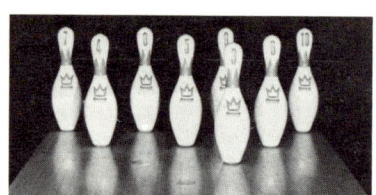

1012-S   3-4-5-6-7-8-9-10

End of the 43 Rare Spares with Eight Pins

Pictures of the 8 Rare Spares with Nine Pins

1014   1-2-3-4-5-6-7-8-10

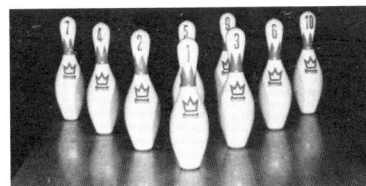

1015   1-2-3-4-5-6-7-9-10

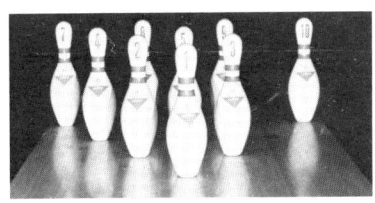

1017   1-2-3-4-5-7-8-9-10

1018   1-2-3-4-6-7-8-9-10

1019   1-2-3-5-6-7-8-9-10

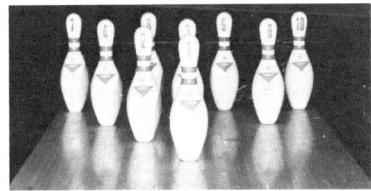

1020   1-2-4-5-6-7-8-9-10

9

1021   1-3-4-5-6-7-8-9-10

1022-S   2-3-4-5-6-7-8-9-10

End of the 8 Rare Spares with Nine Pins

APPENDIX A DICTIONARY OF BOWLING TERMS

Bowlers have a language all their own. The following list is the most complete and up-to-date dictionary of the words of bowling. Some of the terms are seldom used, but most are in general usage. A simple reading will immediately upgrade your knowledge of bowling, add to your understanding of instructional phrases and tune you in closer to the pro side of the game.

ABC: American Bowling Congress, world's largest sports participation organization, official rule-making body of tenpin bowling.

AJBC: American Junior Bowling Congress.

Alley: Playing surface, made of maple and pine boards.

All the way: Means finishing a game from any point with nothing but strikes.

Anchor: Last man to roll in team competition.

Apple: Bowling ball. Also applied to bowler who fails to come through in a clutch situation.

Approach: Same as "runway."

Arrows: Aiming points imbedded in the lane.

Baby the ball: Too delicate, not enough emphasis on delivering the ball with authority.

Baby split: The 2-7 or 3-10 split leave.

Baby split with company: The 2-7-8 or 3-9-10 split leave.

Backup: A ball that falls away to the right for right-handed bowlers, to the left for left-handed bowlers.

Backup alley: A lane that holds or tends to stop a ball from rolling to the right.

Balk: An incomplete approach in which the bowler does not deliver the ball. To interfere or cause another bowler to stop his approach or not complete it in his normal fashion.

Ball rack: Where the ball rests before it is rolled and after it returns from the pit. Also the structure used to store house balls.

Ball track: Area of lane where most balls are rolled.

Barmaid: A pin hidden behind another pin.

Bed: The alley bed, synonymous with a single lane.

Bedposts: The 7-10 split.

Beer frame: In team play, when all but one of the players scores a strike, the one who doesn't must treat. Also any designated frame in which the bowler who scores the least must pick up a refreshment tab, usually liquid.

Belly the ball: Increase the width of a hook from an inside starting angle.

Bench work, bench jockeying: Any type of conversation or other actions intended to upset an opponent.

Bicycle: Hidden pin, same as "barmaid."

Big ball: A working hook that enables a bowler to carry strikes on something less than perfect pocket hits.

Big ears: The 4-6-7-10.

Big fill: Nine or 10 pins on a spare or on a double strike.

Big five: Spare leave of three on one side and two on the other.

Big four: The 4-6-7-10, same as "big ears."

Blind: Score allowed for absent member, usually low, as a penalty.

Blocked: A lane maintenance condition in which oil or some sort of lane finish is used to create a track.

Blow: A missed spare.

Blow a rack: A solid strike hit.

Blowout: Downing all the pins but one.

Board: A lane consists of individual strips of lumber called boards. Pros call them by number, fifth board, fifteenth board, etc., for targeting purposes.

Body english: Contortion of the arms, legs and trunk in an attempt to steer the ball after it has left the hand.

Bolsa: Same as "thin hit."

Bonus: In match play bowling, pins awarded for winning game, usually 30 or 50.

Box: Frame.

BPAA: Bowling Proprietors Association of America. Trade organization of the people who own bowling centers.

Break: A lucky shot. Also a stopper after a number of consecutive strikes.

Bridge: Distance separating finger holes.

Brooklyn: Left of headpin for a right-handed bowler. Right of headpin for a left-handed bowler.

Broom ball: A ball that hits the pocket in such a way that the pins scatter as though they were swept with a broom.

Bucket: The 2-4-5-8 spare leave for righty; 3-5-6-9 for lefty.

CC: Double century or a 200 game.

Channel: Depression to right and left of lane to guide ball to pit should it leave the playing surface on the way down.

Charge: Term used by pros to describe a sensational spurt of high scoring.

Cheese cakes: Lanes on which strikes come easy.

Cherry: Knocking down the front pin of a spare leave while a pin behind and/or to the left or right remains standing.

Choke: Fail to accomplish objective because of nervousness or fright. Same as "apple." Also cutting arm swing short.

Chop: Same as "cherry."

Christmas tree: The 3-7-10 leave for a righty or 2-7-10 for a lefty.

Cincinnati: The 8-10 split.

Classified: Leagues or tournaments with average limitations.

Clean game: Strike or spare in each of the ten frames.

Clothes line: The 1-2-4-7 or 1-3-6-10 spare leave.

Clutch: Pressure situation.

Count: Number of pins knocked down on first ball of each frame.

Cranker: Bowler who uses cranking motion to roll wide hook ball.

Creeper: Slow ball.

Crooked arm: Hook ball bowler who bends his elbow.

Cross: Going to the left side for a righty. Same as "Brooklyn." Going to the right side for a lefty.

Crow hopper: Loose, clawlike grip on ball at release point.

Curtain: Anchor man missing in final frame when a spare would have won for his team.

Curve: Ball that breaks from right to left (for righty) in a huge arc. (Left to right for a LHB.)

Cushion: Padding at rear of pit to absorb shock of ball and pins.

Cutter: Sharp-breaking hook which seems to slice the pins down.

Dead apple, dead ball: Ineffective ball, usually fades or deflects badly when it hits the pins.

Dead wood: Pins knocked down but remaining on the lane or in the gutter. Must be removed before continuing play.

Deflection: The movement of the ball or pins when both come into contact with each other.

Dime store: The 5-10 split.

Dinner bucket, dinner pail: Same as "bucket."

Dive: The action of a ball that hooks greatly at the last split second.

Division boards: Where the pine and maple meet on a lane.

Dodo: A bowling ball over the legal weight or out of proper balance.

Double: Two strikes in a row.

Double pinochle: The 4-6-7-10 split, same as "big ears," "big four."

Double wood: Any two pins, when one is directly behind the other, the 1-5, 2-8 and 3-9.

Dovetails: Area of lane where maple and pine boards join. Also called "splice."

Drive: Another name for alley or lane. Also the revolving action of a ball as it contacts the pins.

Dummy: Same as "blind."

Dutch 200: A 200 game scored by alternating strikes and spares.

Emblem: The logo on a bowling ball, usually signifying the heaviest part of the ball.

Error: A miss. Same as "blow."

Faith, Hope, Charity: The 2-7-10 or 3-7-10 split, same as Christmas tree.

Fast: In different sections of the country the meaning is exactly the opposite. In one area it means a lane that allows a ball to hook easily, while in another area it means a lane that holds down the hook.

Fence posts: The 7-10 split.

Field goal: Ball rolled between two pins of a wide split.

Fill: Pins knocked down following a spare.

Fit split: Any split when it's possible for the ball to hit both pins (for example, the 4-5 split).

Flat alley: A lane that despite perfect levelness doesn't run or hold with respect to the action of the ball.

Flat arc: The curved path of a ball in process of delivery when it is too low to the approach or off to either side and so not part of a perfect circle.

Flat ball: Ineffective ball, few revolutions, little action.

Floater: A ball that goes where the lane lets it. A ball released badly with no particular lift or turn.

Foul: Touching or going beyond the foul line at delivery.

Foul line: The marking that determines the beginning of the lane.

Foundation: A strike in the ninth frame.

Foundation, early: A strike in the eighth frame.

Frame: A tenth part of a game of bowling.

Frozen rope: A ball rolled with excessive speed almost straight into the pocket.

Fudge: Decrease revolutions on ball.

Full hit: A ball striking near the center of the

headpin on a strike attempt or the middle of any pin you may be aiming at.

Full roller: A ball that rolls over its full circumference.

Getting the wood: A better than average score. Also making sure you take one pin down on an almost impossible split.

Goal posts: The 7-10 split. Same as "bedposts," "fence posts."

Golden gate: The 4-6-7-10 split. Same as "double pinochle," "big ears," "big four."

Grab: Means the friction between the lane and the ball is good, causing a sudden hook.

Grasshopper: An effective ball, particularly on light pocket hits.

Graveyards: Low-scoring lanes. In a high-scoring center applied to the lowest scoring pair of lanes.

Groove: Ball track or indentation in lane. Also applied to bowler who is performing well and has his approach and arm swing almost mechanically perfect.

Gutter: Same as "channel."

Gutter ball: A ball that goes into the gutter.

Half hit: Midway between a full hit and a light hit.

Handicap: Pins awarded to individuals or teams in an attempt to equalize competition.

Hard way: Rolling 200 by alternating strikes and spares. Same as "Dutch 200."

High board: Due to atmospheric conditions a board in a lane may expand or contract a tiny bit, but enough to change the course of a bowling ball should the ball roll in that area. Most boards contract leaving a low area or a low board, but it is still mistermed as a high board.

High hit: Ball contacting a pin near its center.

Higher: More to the left (RHB) or right (LHB).

Hold, holding alley: A lane that resists hook action of a ball.

Hole: The 1-3 pocket, 1-2 for lefties. Also another name for "split."

Home alley: Favorite lane or pair of lanes for individuals or teams.

Honey: A good ball.

Hook: A ball that breaks to the left (RHB) or to the right (LHB).

Hook alley: A lane on which the ball will hook easily.

Hot: When a bowler or team starts lining up strikes.

House ball: Bowling ball provided by center.

Inside: A starting point near the center of the lane as opposed to the outside, near the edge of the lane.

In there: A good pocket hit.

Jack Manders: Rolling through the middle of a 7-10 or any wide split. Same as "field goal."

Jam: Force the ball high into the pocket.

Jersey side: To the left of the headpin.

Kickback: Vertical division boards between lanes at the pit end. On many hits the pins bounce from the kickback knocking additional pins down.

Kick off: Smooth, effective ball delivery.

Kindling wood: Light pins.

Kingpin: The headpin or the number 5 pin, varying with local usage.

Kitty: Money collected from team members for misses, low games, and other set fines. Used to defray expenses in tournaments or divided equally at end of season.

Kresge: Whereas the 5-10 split is called the Woolworth, the 5-7 is often called the Kresge.

Lane: Playing surface. Same as "alley."

Late 10: When the 10 pin hesitates, and is the last to go down on a strike.

Leadoff: First man in a team lineup.

LHB: Left handed bowler.

Lift: Means giving the ball upward motion with the fingers at the point of release.

Light: Not full on the target pin, too much to the right or left.

Lily: The 5-7-10 split.

Line: The path a bowling ball takes. Also one game of bowling.

Loafing: Not lifting or turning the ball properly, with the result that the ball lags and doesn't reach the target.

Lofting: Throwing the ball well out on the lane rather than rolling it.

Looper: An extra-wide hook ball, usually slow.

Loose hit: A light pocket hit which gives good pin action off the kickback.

Low: Light or thin hit on the headpin, as opposed to a high hit.

Maples: Pins.

Mark: A strike or spare.

Match play: Portion of tournament in which bowlers are pitted individually against each other.

Medal play: Strictly total pin scores.

Miss: An error or blow.

Mixer: Ball with action causing the pins to bounce around.

Mother-in-law: The 7 pin.

Move in: To start from or near center of approach.

Move out: To start from or near corner position on approach.

Mule ears: The 7-10 split.

Murphy: Baby split.

Nose hit: A first ball full on the headpin.
Nothing ball: Ineffective ball.
NBC: National Bowling Council.

One in the dark: Rear pin in the 1-5, 2-8 or 3-9 spare.
Open: A frame that doesn't produce a strike or spare.
Open bowling: Nonleague or nontournament play, for fun or practice.
Out and in: A wide hook rolled from the center of the lane toward the gutter; the ball hooks back to the pocket—going out, then in.
Outside: Corner or near corner position of playing lanes.
Over: In professional bowling scoring a 200 average is used as par. The number of pins above the 200 average is the number of pins over or in the black.
Over turn: To apply too much spin to the ball and not enough finger lift.

Pack: A full count of ten.
Part of the building: Expression referring to 7, 8, 9 or 10 pin when it stands after what seems to be a perfect hit.
PBA: Professional Bowlers Association.
Pick: To knock down only the front pin from a spare leave. Same as "cherry" or "chop."
Pie alley: A lane that is easy to score on.
Pinching the ball: Gripping the ball too hard.
Pine: Softer wood used beyond division boards, takes over where maple ends.
Pit: Space at end of lane where ball and pins wind up.
Pitch: Angle at which holes in bowling ball are drilled.
Pocket: The 1-3 for righties, 1-2 for lefties.
Point: To aim more directly at the pocket, high and tight.
Poison ivy: The 3-6-10.
Poodle: To roll a gutter ball.
Position rounds: Designated parts of a league or tournament schedule which call for teams or players to meet each other based on their standings. First place meets second, third meets fourth, fifth meets sixth, etc.
Pot game: Competition in which two or more bowlers post some sort of stake and high man takes it all.
Powder puff, puff ball: Slow ball that fails to carry the pins.
Powerhouse: A hard, strong ball for a strike, carrying all ten pins into the pit.
Puddle: A gutter ball.
Pumpkin: Bowling ball that hits soft.
Punch out: Strike out.

Quick eight: A good pocket hit which leaves the 4-7 for righties, 6-10 for lefties.

Railroad: Better known as "split."
Rap: When a single pin remains standing on a good hit.
Rat club: A team shooting horribly low scores for one game.
Reading the lanes: Discovering whether a lane hooks or holds, and where the best place is to roll the ball to score high.
Return: The track on which balls roll from pit to ball rack.
Reverse: A backup ball.
Revolutions: The turns a ball takes to go from the foul line to the pins.
RHB: Right handed bowler.
Run, running lane: A lane on which the ball hooks easily.
Runway: Starting area. Also known as platform, approach. Ends at the foul line, where the lane starts.

Sandbagger: Bowler who keeps his average low purposely in order to receive a higher handicap than he deserves.
Sandwich game: Same as "Dutch 200."
Scenic route: Path taken by big curve ball.
Schleifer: Thin-hit strike where pins seem to fall one by one.
Scratch: Rolling without benefit of handicap. Actual score.
Set: Ball holding in the pocket.
Short pin: A pin rolling on the alley bed which just fails to reach and hit a standing pin.
Shotgun shot: Rolling the ball from the hip.

Sidearming: Allowing the arm to draw away from its proper position during back and forward swing.
Sleeper: A pin hidden behind another pin.
Slick: Lane condition highly polished, tends to hold back hook.
Slot alley: Lane on which strikes come easy.
Small ball: Type of ball that doesn't mix the pins, must hit pocket perfectly for strikes.
Snake eyes: The 7-10 split.
Snow plow: A ball that clears all the pins for a strike.
Soft alley: A lane on which strikes come easy.
Sour apple: Weak ball, one that leaves the 5-7, 5-10 or 5-7-10 split.
Span: Distance between thumb and finger holes.
Spare: All pins down with two balls.
Spare leave: Refers to pins standing after first ball is rolled.

Spiller: A light-hit strike in which the pins seem to melt away, taking a longer time than other type strikes.

Splasher: A strike where the pins are downed quickly.

Splice: Where maple and pine boards join on the lane.

Split: A spare leave in which the headpin is down and the remaining combination of pins have an intermediate pin down immediately ahead of or between them. There are 459 possible splits in ten pins.

Spot: Target on lane at which the bowler aims, could be a dot, a dark board or an arrow.

Steal: Get more pins than you deserve on a strike hit.

Stiff alley: A lane with a tendency to hold a hook ball back.

Strap the ball: Get maximum lift.

Strike: All ten pins down on the first ball.

Strike out: Finish the game with strikes.

Strike split: The 8-10. Ball looks like a good strike ball, but leaves the split. The 7-9 for left handed bowlers.

String: A number of continuous strikes. Also, in some areas, one game of bowling.

Sweeper: A wide-breaking hook which carries a strike as though the pins were pushed with a broom.

Sweepstakes: Bowling tournament.

Tandem: Two pins, one behind the other.

Tap: When a pin stands on an apparently perfect hit.

Telephone poles: Heavy pins.

Thin hit: A pocket hit when the ball barely touches the headpin.

Throwing rocks: Piling up strikes with a speed ball.

Topping the ball: At ball release when fingers are on top of the ball instead of behind or to the side. Causes a bad ball with little action.

Touch: Pin standing on a good hit.

Tripped 4: When the 2 pin takes out the 4 pin by bouncing off the kickback.

Turkey: Three strikes in a row.

Turn: Motion of hand toward pocket area at point of ball release.

Umbrella ball: A high hit on the nose resulting in a strike.

Under: In professional bowling scoring, a 200 average is used as par. The number of pins below the 200 average is the number of pins the bowler is under or in the red.

Up the hill: Refers to coaxing a ball over a high board into the pocket.

Venting: Drilling a small hole (not a finger hole) to relieve suction in the thumb hole.

Washout: The 1-2-10 or 1-2-4-10 leave. Also, 1-3-7 and 1-3-6-7 leaves, and similar leaves.

Water in the ball: A weak ball, one that leaves an 8-10, 5-7 or 5-10.

WIBC: Women's International Bowling Congress.

Winding them in: Refers to big-hook-ball bowlers who get their hooks around the pocket consistently.

Wood: (a) In handicapping, the number of pins given. ("How much wood will you give me?") (b) In scoring, number of pins knocked down. ("He didn't get all the wood.")

Wooden bottles: Pins.

Woolworth: The 5-10 split.

Working ball: A ball with enough action to mix the pins on an offpocket hit and have them scramble each other for a strike. The same ball will break up splits when it hits the nose.

X: Symbol for strike.

Yank the shot: When a bowler hangs on to the ball too long and pulls it across his body.

Zero in: Find the right strike spot on a lane.

General Facts:

Perhaps no more than 300 different spare leaves have ever been left standing after the first ball was rolled. This figure includes the 249 Probable Spares in Section II, and about 50 or less of the Rare Spares in Section III (including the ones pictured in Exhibit 20). To our knowledge, no record exists of the exact number of spare leaves that have been left standing.

Of the 1,023 possible spare leaves, 459 are splits and 564 are non-splits.

There are really 1,024 possible "leaves" after the first ball is thrown. We just call the leave in which *no pins* are standing a Strike!

There are 512 possible spare leaves in which the 5-pin is standing. There are 512 possible spare leaves in which the 1-pin is standing. This is true for any pin! (The 1-pin is in 112 of the 249 Probable Spares.)

Of the 249 Probable Spares, 139 call for the same hit from either a RHB or LHB. The other 110 call for different hits. Of course, it is possible to convert any given spare in a number of ways.

For any spare in which pins ARE standing, there is a "mirror image" spare leave in which only those pins are NOT standing. For example, for the spare with all ten pins standing, there is the "leave" with all pins down. For the spare with the 1-pin standing, there is the leave in which only the 1-pin is down. For the leave in which the 5-7-10 are standing, there is the leave in which only these three pins are down. Etc.

Only ONE spare leave is shaped like the symbol for a Strike, an (X). It is the 2-3-5-8-9. (There is only ONE way to strike—knock all ten pins down!)

Only one spare leave is shaped like the square box in which the score is marked. We call it the Square Spare; the 2-3-8-9.

Several leaves are shaped like the symbol for a Spare, a (/). The longest is the 1-3-6-10.

Several leaves are shaped like the symbol for a miss, a (-). The longest is the back row, the 7-8-9-10.

The 1-pin is *not* always the Key Pin when it is part of a spare leave. (See the 1-6-10; the 1-4-7; etc.)

There are 512 possible spare leaves in which the 1-pin is NOT standing, and 459 of these leaves are splits! Thus, 90% of the time that the 1-pin is down, a split is standing. (However, only 40% of the probable spare leaves are splits.)

Some of the records for spares CONVERTED are: 30 consecutive by one bowler; 38 in a single game by a team; 101 in a three game series by one team.

A "perfect spare game" is all nine-pin counts and spares in each frame. This has been achieved many times. The score is 190. (A strike on the last ball makes a 191 game, and this also has been achieved.)

The *candidate* for the most unusual spare leave to every occur, in the opinion of the authors, is the one in which ONLY the 9-pin was knocked down! The 10-pin was hit on the extreme right side; spun like a top over towards the 9-pin to topple it; and spun back to stand on its original spot! (Knocking down *only* the 5-7-10 on the *first* ball might be another candidate for most unusual spare leave.) See Exhibit 20 for both of these unusual leaves.

There was a two pin spare leave in which the 6-pin had a sleeper. The 10-pin slid sideways and stood up directly behind the 6-pin.

The 5-pin has been left standing on a head-on 1-pin hit, *at least two times!* Once the ball stopped after toppling the 1-pin, leaving all other nine pins standing. This resulted in a leave of the only split with nine pins in it, the maximum possible. The other time the 5-pin stood on a head-on 1-pin hit was when the 4-5-6 split was left! The 5-pin was tossed up against the rack and circled back down to settle on its original spot!

A RHB, rolling a hook, once sent his ball between the 3 and 8-pins. He left the 3-6-8-10 split.

AND NOW LET'S TALK A LITTLE ABOUT UNUSUAL EVENTS WITH SPLITS!

Of the 459 Possible Splits, 98 are classified as Probable. These splits are listed in Exhibit 4, Section I, under SPLITS AND SPARES. The 361 Rare Splits are in Section III, all indicated by the letter "S" after the Spare Number.

The 459 Possible Splits are divided as follows: 0

with one pin; 24 with two pins; 71 with three pins; 116 with four pins; 120 with five pins; 82 with six pins; 36 with seven pins; 9 with eight pins; and only 1 with nine pins. Notice that a split must contain at least two pins and no more than nine. Both extremes have been left for conversion.

Rarely does any split that has been left for conversion contain more than five pins. However, the 4-6-7-8-9-10 split has been left standing after the first ball was rolled!

One split has been left for conversion that contained all 459 possible split leaves. It is Spare Number 1,022-S, in which only the 1-pin is down. This was left by a very young bowler who rolled such a slow ball that it stopped when it hit the 1-pin, toppling it straight backward and leaving a nine pin split!

Several individual bowlers have left 10 splits in a single game, and at least one individual left 11 splits in a game.

One team left 37 splits in a single game, and 49 in the three game series. Two teams left a total of 75 splits in one match.

On more than one occasion the entire team has *left and converted* a split in the same frame. One bowler *converted* 9 splits in one game.

AND NOW, A LITTLE ABOUT SPECIFIC SPLITS!

The 8-10 split: Has been left 5 consecutive times by a bowler; 6 times in a single game, and 12 times in a three game series. It has been *converted* twice in the same game by several people.

The 7-10 split: Is *converted* almost 3,000 times each season, or about 300 times per month during the bowling season; Has been *converted* twice in the same game by several bowlers; Has been left 6 consecutive times by one person, and left 6 times in one game; Has been left 12 times in one three game series; Has been knocked down on the FIRST BALL on several occasions. This does not count as a conversion. (A professional Bowler once "achieved" this feat.)

The 4-6-7-10 split: Is also *converted* almost 3,000 times each season, or about 300 times per

month during the bowling season; Has been left 4 consecutive times by one individual; 5 times in a single game; and has been *converted* TWICE in a single game by several people.

The 3-10 split: Has been *converted* 8 consecutive times by one person, and 7 consecutive times by another. Has been converted by hitting only the 10-pin, which then came out of the pit to take out the 3-pin. The ball has gone between both pins without touching either one on several occasions. This has happened with Right Handed Bowlers only, so far as we know.

The 5-7-10 split: Is the single split that is rarely ever converted. To our knowledge only one conversion has been authenticated, although, it probably has been converted on other occasions. It has been left standing 3 times in a single game. It also has been knocked down on the FIRST BALL. The 10-pin went into the pit, came back to knock the 7-pin into the 5-pin, and left the other seven pins standing.

The 4-6 split: Has been *converted* twice in the same game by several people, and on one occasion, by teammates. It was converted on nationwide television in the FIRST frame, of the FIRST game of the FIRST time that this Left Handed Bowler had appeared on the television finals of a PBA Tournament. He slid the 4-pin directly across into the 6-pin.

The 5-7 split: Has been converted 5 consecutive times by one bowler.

The 6-7-10 split: Has been converted 3 consecutive times by one bowler.

The 7-9 split: Has been converted in two consecutive frames by one bowler.

NOTE: For more interesting and unusual facts about the game of bowling, including statistics on spares, strikes, splits, triplicates, etc., see BOWLING, The Official Publication of the American Bowling Congress, in Greendale, Wisconsin. This monthly magazine reports unusual happenings On The League Front, and includes an annual summary of significant records in the bowling world.

APPENDIX C
BOOKS FOR ADDITIONAL READING

Anthony, Earl (with Dawson Taylor)
"Winning Bowling," 1977, Contemporary Books, Inc., Chicago, Illinois.

Chapter 10, The Spares and How to Make Them, contains many pictures and descriptions of spare leaves. The authors have divided all spares into four groups, and present samples of each group. In Chapter 11, The Splits and How to Make Them, they discuss the strategy for split attempts, and when not to seriously try for a split conversion. Several good pictures are presented in these two chapters.

Johnson, Don, "Inside Bowling,"
Henry Regnery Company (now Contemporary Books, Inc.), 1973, Chicago, Illinois.

Chapter 4, Shooting Spares, presents a strong argument for the importance of spares to the professional bowler. Johnson states that "picking up spares is the key to winning consistently," and that the pros must make 95% of their spares in order to survive tour competition. He discusses the 3-6-9 and 2-4-6 Spare Systems, and illustrates several groups of spares leaves. Page 48 illustrates the seven targeting Arrows imbedded in the lanes about 15 feet out from the foul line. Page 26 gives a view of the lane, indicating the dimensions of the lane, the Dots on the approach which are used for determining the proper approach position, and the targeting Arrows on the lanes which are used to select the proper target for all strikes and spares. Many other useful tips on bowling can be found throughout the book.

Kouros, Thomas C., "Par Bowling,"
(Progressive Method of Bowling Instruction), Progressive Bowling Development, P.O. Box 181, Palatine, Illinois, 1976.

This book offers a great deal to any bowler, although he does not devote sufficient space to spare shooting. He does, however, recognize the importance of spares, and makes a strong case for knowing how to shoot for them. Kouros feels that ". . . spare bowling is one of the foundations of a high average bowler." "If you are going to become a high average bowler you must be an excellent spare bowler," he continues. Pages 122–134 would be useful reading about spares, and other parts of the book elaborate on material we have presented in Sections I and II of this book. If you are a serious bowler, you would be well advised to look into Kouros's book.

Pezzano, Chuck, "Professional Bowlers Association Guide to Better Bowling," Simon and Schuster, Inc., 1974, New York, New York.

Many of the top bowling professionals have contributed to this very useful addition to the literature of bowling. The book contains tips from a wide range of successful tour bowlers. This provides a perspective on what works for different kinds of bowlers. A chapter discusses various approaches to spare shooting, as well as coverage of the funamentals of strike shooting.

Ritger, Dick and Judy Soutar, BOWLERS GUIDE, American Bowling Congress and Women's International Bowling Congress, 1976 Revised Edition, Greendale, Wisconsin.

This popular publication was prepared and produced by the Public Relations Departments of the ABC and WIBC. It contains many sections directly related to spare shooting, such as: Spot, Line, Area, and Pin Bowling; the 3-6-9 Spare Systems; Adjustments; Making a Spare; etc. It also includes special sections for Senior Bowlers, Junior Bowlers, and a section devoted exclusively for the Left Handed Bowler. The co-authors use a very modern approach to teaching the fundamentals of bowling.

Weiskopf, Herman, "The Perfect Game,"
Prentice-Hall, Inc., 1978, Englewood Cliffs, New Jersey.

This large and extensive book contains two sections which are directly related to our comprehensive discussion of spare making. Chapter 6, "The Perfect Strike" gives some of the best color photographs of the ball and pin deflection needed for a perfect strike that you will ever see. Since 20% of all spares are made by a "strike hit," this chapter will make interesting reading. Page 198 also gives a series of photographs to illustrate an "imperfect hit," the 10-pin tap. Pages 248–251 contain the second related section. These pages, called "The Sparemaker" give diagrams of 20 spare leaves, showing the path of the ball from the foul line to contact on the key pin. Many other instructional photographs are included in the book.